The Information Specialist's Guide
to Searching and Researching
on the Internet and the
World Wide Web

Ernest Ackermann
Mary Washington College

Karen Hartman
Mary Washington College

ABF Content
8536 SW St. Helens Drive, Suite D
Wilsonville, OR 97070
503/682-7668

President and Publisher	Jim Leisy (jimleisy@fbeedle.com)
Manuscript Editor	Eve Kushner
Production	Tom Sumner
	Stephanie Welch
	Susan Skarzynski
Development Editor	Sue Page
Marketing Group	Cary Crossland
	Carrie Widman
	Jason Smith
	Marc Chambers
Order Processing	Chris Alarid
	Lois Allison

Printed in the U.S.A.

Names of all products herein are used for identification purposes only and are trademarks and/or registered trademarks of their respective owners. Franklin, Beedle & Associates, Inc., makes no claim of ownership or corporate association with the products or companies that own them.

Rights and Permissions
Franklin, Beedle & Associates, Incorporated
8536 SW St. Helens Drive, Suite D
Wilsonville, Oregon 97070

Library of Congress Cataloging-in-Publication Data

Ackermann, Ernest C.
   The information specialist's guide to searching and researching on the Internet and the World Wide Web / Ernest Ackermann, Karen Hartman.
      p.   cm.
   Rev. ed. of: Searching and researching on the Internet and the World Wide Web. 1997.
   Includes index.
   ISBN 1–887902–31–7
   1. Computer network resources. 2. World Wide Web (Information retrieval system). I. Hartman, Karen. II. Ackermann, Ernest C. Searching and researching on the Internet and the World Wide Web. III. Title.
   ZA4201.A25   1998
   025.04—dc21   98–37563
                                                                        CIP

ABF Content is an imprint of Franklin, Beedle & Associates, Incorporated.

To my family—Lynn, Karl, and Oliver—and to the memory of my parents

Henry Ackermann (1904 – 1977)
Marie Ackermann (1914 – 1997)
always encouraging, always loving.
—E. A.

———————————

To Jack, Tracy, and Hilary

—K. H.

Contents

Preface xiv

Chapter 1

Introduction to the World Wide Web
page 1

About This Book 2
    Click and Double-Click 2
The World Wide Web as an Information Resource 2
Hypertext and Hypermedia 5
Activity 1.1   First Look at Using a Web Browser
                   to Find Information on the Web 6
Key Terms and Concepts 11
    Client/Server 11
    HTTP (Hypertext Transfer Protocol) 11
    HTML (Hypertext Markup Language) 11
    URL (Uniform Resource Locator) 12
    Error Messages 13
    Bookmarks 14
    Common Types of Files on the Internet and the Web 14
    Sharing and Copying Information Found
    on the Internet and the World Wide Web 16
    Selected Web-based Guides to the Internet
    and the World Wide Web 17
Information Sources Available on the Web 18
    Directories or Subject Catalogs 18
    Search Engines 18
    Meta-search Tools 18
    Virtual Libraries 19
    Specialized Databases 19
    Library Catalogs Accessible on the World Wide Web 19
    FTP Archives 19
    Email Discussion Groups 19
    Usenet Newsgroups 20
Summary 20
    Selected Terms Introduced in This Chapter 22

Chapter 2

Browser and Bookmark Essentials
page 23

Surveying a Browser's Features 24
Starting and Stopping the Web Browser 25
    Starting the Web Browser 25
    Ending a Session on the WWW; Stopping the Browser 26
Exploring the Web Browser's Window 26
    Toolbars 30
Using the Right Mouse Button 34
Getting Around a Page and the World Wide Web 35
    Moving Through a Page 36
    Moving Between Pages 36
Getting Help 39
    Online Help 40
    Frequently Asked Questions (FAQ) 40
    Usenet Newsgroups 40
Activity 2.1   Using a Search Engine 41
Saving, Printing, and Mailing Items from the WWW 49
    Saving Web Pages in a File 49
    Saving Items on a Web Page into a File 50
    Printing a Web Page 51
    Mailing a Web Page 51
    Using a Web Browser with Local Files 51
Using Bookmarks to Keep Track of Resources 53
    Add a Bookmark 53
    Display the Bookmark List 53
    Jump to an Item in the Bookmark List 54
    Delete an Item from the Bookmark List 54
    Search the Bookmark List 54
Activity 2.2   Working with the Bookmark List 54
Summary 58
    Selected Terms Introduced in This Chapter 60

Chapter 3

Using the World Wide Web for Research
page 61

Browsing the World Wide Web: Using Directories 62
Activity 3.1   Using a Directory
                to Browse for Information 64
    Browsing Versus Searching a Directory 68

Finding Information Gems in Virtual Libraries 69
    Subject Guides 69
    Reference Works 70
    Specialized Databases 71
Activity 3.2   Finding Resources in a Virtual Library 71
Searching the World Wide Web: Using Search Engines 77
    Search Engine Similarities 78
    Search Engine Differences 80
Activity 3.3   Using Boolean Search Operators 80
Activity 3.4   Using Phrase Searching
                to Find Information 84
Using Several Search Engines Simultaneously:
Meta-search Tools 89
Activity 3.5   Using a Meta-search Tool
                to Find Information 91
Summary 95
    Selected Terms Introduced in This Chapter 95

Chapter 4

Directories and Virtual Libraries
page 97

    Major Directories on the World Wide Web 98
Characteristics of Directories 98
    Strengths 99
    Weaknesses 100
Browsing and Searching Directories 101
    Browsing 101
    Searching 103
Two Major Directories and How to Use Them 104
Activity 4.1   Yahoo! 104
Activity 4.2   LookSmart 111
Virtual Libraries: Directories with a Difference 115
    The Major Virtual Libraries 115
Activity 4.3   The Argus Clearinghouse 116
Activity 4.4   The Librarians' Index to the Internet 120
Summary 123
    Selected Terms Introduced in This Chapter 123

Chapter 5

Search Strategies for Search Engines
page 124

The Major Search Engine Databases
on the World Wide Web 125
Search Engine Databases 125
    Indexing 125
    When to Use Search Engine Databases 126
Search Features Common to Most Search Engines 126
    Boolean Operators 127
    Implied Boolean Operators 128
    Phrase Searching 129
    Proximity Searching 129
    Truncation 129
    Wildcards 129
    Field Searching 130
    Case Sensitivity 130
    Concept Searching 130
    Limiting by Date 130
Output Features Common to Most Search Engines 131
    Relevancy Ranking 131
    Annotations or Summaries 131
    Results Per Page 131
    Sorting Results 131
    Duplicate Detection 131
    Modification of Search Results 132
    Meta-tag Support 132
A Basic Search Strategy: The 10 Steps 132
    Search Tips 134

Activity 5.1   Search Strategies in AltaVista
               and Northern Light 134
               Performing a Search in AltaVista 134
               Performing the Same Search in Northern Light ... 140

Activity 5.2   Search Strategies in Infoseek 144

Activity 5.3   Search Strategies in MetaCrawler 148

Summary 153
    Selected Terms Introduced in This Chapter 153

Chapter 6
Using Search Engines
page 154

Activity 6.1   Search Strategies in HotBot 155

Activity 6.2   Search Strategies in
                AltaVista's Simple Search Mode 162

Using Search Engines for Specific Information 168

Activity 6.3   Finding Specific Information in Excite 168

Summary 174

Chapter 7
Specialized Databases
page 175

Overview of Specialized Databases 176
    Bibliographic and Full-text Databases 176
    Proprietary and Free Databases 176
    Accessing Fee-based Databases 177
How to Find Free Specialized Databases 177
Using Specialized Databases 178
    Searching for Medical Information 179
Activity 7.1   Searching MEDLINE 179
    Searching for Company and Industry Information 186
Activity 7.2   Finding Company Information 187
    Searching for Legal Information 195
Activity 7.3   Searching for United States
                Supreme Court Opinions 195
Summary 199
    Selected Terms Introduced in This Chapter 200

Chapter 8
Searching Library Catalogs
page 201

Overview of the Development of Online Catalogs 202
    Why Search a Remote Library Catalog? 202
Characteristics of Online Library Catalogs 203
Ways to Find Library Catalogs 204
    Libweb at Berkeley http://sunsite.berkeley.edu/libweb 204
    LIBCAT http://www.metronet.lib.mn.us/lc/lc1.html 204
    webCATS http://www.lights.com/webcats 204
Activity 8.1   Using Libweb to Find a National Catalog 205

Activity 8.2   Using LIBCAT to Find Special Collections 210

Activity 8.3   Using webCATS to Find Special Libraries 216

Summary 223

Selected Terms Introduced in This Chapter 223

Chapter 9

FTP: Searching Archives, Downloading Files
page 224

Understanding the URL Format for FTP 225

Downloading a File by Anonymous FTP 226

Method 1: View the File First, and Then
Save It Using the File Menu 227

Method 2: Save the Hyperlink in a File Without Viewing
It by Using the Right Mouse Button or Shift and Click 227

Activity 9.1   Retrieving a File by Anonymous FTP 228

Locating FTP Archives and Other Sites for Finding Software 231

Downloading and Working with Files from Software Archives ... 232

Shareware Often Comes in Packages 232

Downloading and Installing Software 233

Obtaining a Copy of PKZIP or WinZip 234

Acquiring Antivirus Software 234

Using Software Archives and FTP Search Services 235

Activity 9.2   Downloading and Installing Software
from a Software Archive 237

Using an FTP Client Program 243

Summary 246

Selected Terms Introduced in This Chapter 247

Chapter 10

Finding Email Addresses, Phone Numbers, and Maps
page 248

Advantages and Disadvantages of Using These Services.......... 249

Activity 10.1 Finding an Individual's Email Address,
Phone Number, and Mailing Address 251

Privacy and Ethics Issues 255

Activity 10.2 Search for a Business Address, a Phone Number,
a Map, and Driving Directions.......................... 256

Keeping Current: White Pages and Map Web Services 261

Lists of White Pages Web Services 261

Map Services 261
Summary 261
    Selected Terms Introduced in This Chapter 262

Chapter 11

Searching Email Discussion Group Archives and Usenet Newsgroup Archives
page 263

Email Discussion Groups 264
    Essential Information About Discussion Groups............... 264
    Ways to Join, Contribute to, and Leave a List 266
    Ways to Find and Retrieve a Group's Archives 268
    Ways to Locate Discussion Groups About Specific Topics ... 269
Activity 11.1   Finding a Discussion Group 270
    Sources of Information About
    Discussion Groups on the Internet............................. 273
Usenet Newsgroups 274
    Essential Information About Usenet News 275
    Organization of Usenet Articles 276
    FAQs 278
    Ways to Locate Newsgroups About Specific Topics 278
    Sources of Information About Usenet News on the Web 279
    Ways to Search Usenet Archives 280
Activity 11.2   Searching Usenet News Using Deja News 281
Etiquette in a Discussion Group or a Usenet Newsgroup 285
Summary 287
    Selected Terms Introduced in This Chapter 289

Chapter 12

Evaluating Information Found on the WWW
page 290

Reasons to Evaluate 291
Guidelines for Evaluation 292
    Guidelines 292
    Discussion and Tips... 293
Activity 12.1   Using a URL and Search Engines
               to Investigate a Resource 295
Activity 12.2   Applying Guidelines
               to Evaluate a Resource................................. 304

Information on the World Wide Web
About Evaluating Resources................................... 309
    Guides to Evaluating Library Resources 309
    Brief Guides to Evaluating Web Resources 309
    Extensive Guides to Evaluating Resources
    on the World Wide Web 310
    Bibliographies for Evaluating Web Resources 310
Summary 310

Chapter 13

Citing Web and
Internet Resources
page 312

URL Formats 313
Styles for Citing Web Resources 315
    Web Pages... 318
    FTP Resources.. 320
    Gopher Resources.. 321
    Email Resources 321
    Usenet Articles 323
    Electronic Journals 323
Information on the Web About Citing Electronic Resources 324
Summary 325

Chapter 14

Putting It All Together:
Two Sample Research Projects
page 326

Project 1—Finding Resources for a Research Paper 327

Activity 1-A   Search a Directory to Find Resources 327

Activity 1-B   Find and Search a Specialized Database........... 332

Activity 1-C   Formulate and Submit a Search Query
               to a Search Engine 336

Activity 1-D   Locate and Search a Library Catalog................ 340

Activity 1-E   Search a Usenet Archive............................. 344

Activity 1-F   Evaluate the Resources Found 346

Activity 1-G   Cite the Sources in a Bibliography 349

Project 2—Using the Internet for Market Research 351

Activity 2-A   Search a Virtual Library 352

Activity 2-B   Search a Specialized Database 357

Activity 2-C   Perform a Search in a Search Engine 363

Activity 2-D   Evaluate the Resources Found 369

Activity 2-E   Cite the Resources Found 371

Summary 373

Chapter 15

Social Issues, Legal Issues, and Security

page 374

Brief History of the Internet 375

Privacy and Civil Liberties 376

    What's Reasonable to Expect in Terms of Privacy and
Civil Liberties as They Relate to Use of the Internet? 376

    Email Privacy 377

    Privacy on the Web 380

    Unwarranted Search and Seizure 382

    Offensive Material and Libel 383

Intellectual Property and Copyright..................................... 386

Internet Security 388

    Giving Out Information About Yourself and Your Family 390

Summary 392

    Selected Terms Used in This Chapter 393

Appendix A   Annotated List of Selected Search Tools   395

Appendix B   Selected Directories   409

Appendix C   Virtual Libraries   418

Appendix D   Ways to Stay Current   423

Glossary   427

Index   437

Preface

This book gives a straightforward and accessible approach to using the World Wide Web and the Internet for finding information. It is for information specialists—researchers, librarians, and others whose work (and passion, we hope) involves working with information. It's also very useful for almost anyone interested in tapping the Web and the Internet for information. People with experience working with the Web and those who are first learning will find it beneficial. It concentrates on an interesting and important topic, finding information, and deals with readily available tools and resources and techniques for effective use. It also serves as a guide to the appropriate methods to acquire, evaluate, and cite resources.

The material in this book derives directly from our experiences. We are continuously involved in teaching others about using the Web as a resource for research. We lead workshops for librarians, teachers, and other groups of professionals interested in using the resources on the Internet in our work; and we give presentations about finding and evaluating resources on the Web. As a reference librarian and a professor of computer science, we work as researchers ourselves.

In the course of this book, you'll see how to find answers to research and reference questions, as well as how to find email addresses, street addresses, maps, and shareware programs. We discuss several different types of information resources—subject guides, search engines, and specialized databases. We also discuss research skills and strategies to help you find whatever interests you. Not all the work involved in searching is done online. Before going online you need to know how to formulate search strategies. Reading the text and working through the activities and projects, you'll come to understand that for every research question you ask, you will need to go through a process to create the most appropriate search strategy. You also need to decide whether to use a subject guide, search engine, or other type of resource. You'll see that this search formation process or methodology guarantees a more precise result and is applicable to any search engine or database.

We give details for several step-by-step activities using most of the major search engines, directories, virtual libraries, and other information resources on the Web and the Internet. The demonstrations in the text were developed using Netscape Navigator version 4 on a personal computer using Windows 95. You'll find, however, that the essential search skills, the ways to determine which type of resource to use, and

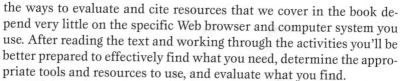

the ways to evaluate and cite resources that we cover in the book depend very little on the specific Web browser and computer system you use. After reading the text and working through the activities you'll be better prepared to effectively find what you need, determine the appropriate tools and resources to use, and evaluate what you find.

The Internet and the World Wide Web have had a profound effect on the way we find information and do research. Part of this is due to the astounding increase in the amount of information resources available and the tools we have at our disposal for finding information. Soon after an initial exposure to using a Web browser we start discovering the wide range of sources of information and the ways we can access them. Instead of spending hours combing through books, library catalogs, and indexes, making endless telephone calls, or traveling to far-off places, with a few clicks of a mouse, we can find an enormous amount of information on virtually any subject.

This explosion in information resources raises a number of important issues. We really do need to know how to search the WWW *effectively*. Sometimes we may get frustrated with the Internet or the Web because there appears to be too much extraneous information, yet we are anxious to get as much good information as we can. We need to know how the different search engines are constructed so that as new search engines appear we will have developed skills that enable us to search any database. We also need to know when a search engine isn't the most appropriate resource to use. In some cases we'll want to use a virtual library or a Web directory. With all the information making up the Web, we also need to know how to evaluate sources we find.

Organization

Throughout the book we put the emphasis on effectively using the resources and tools on the Internet and the Web for searching and researching. We discuss some technical details of how the resources are organized and how the tools do their work, but within the context of getting more precise results. We also emphasize formulating search strategies, understanding how to form search expressions, critically evaluating information, and citing resources. We carry these themes throughout the book. The 10-step search strategy developed in Chapter 5, for example, is applied in many of the following chapters. This emphasis combined with the numerous step-by-step activities throughout the book give what we feel is a good blend of techniques and concepts that are useful and beneficial to both the learner and the practitioner.

The arrangement of the chapters lays out a specific path through the material. We start with an introduction to the Internet and the Web, cover using a browser, bookmarks, and some other technical details, and then move to using the Web for research. There we introduce a number of fundamental concepts and tactics for finding information on the Web. From there we move to the resources we can browse: directories and virtual libraries. Next we cover developing a search strategy, constructing search expressions, and using the common features of various search engines and other searchable indexes. This is followed by numerous examples of using search engines and discussions of using specialized databases and library catalogs. There are other resources to use to find information: FTP, email, maps, discussion groups, and Usenet newsgroups; we take them up in the next three chapters. Evaluating resources and citing resources are considered next. Chapter 14 demonstrates, within the context of doing a research project, many of the concepts and techniques introduced and discussed in earlier chapters. The last chapter addresses some of the legal and ethical issues related to using the Internet and the WWW.

There are other paths through this material; however, we feel you should go through Chapter 3 before moving on to other chapters in the book. You may skip or select certain topics from the first two chapters if you feel a complete introduction to the Internet and the Web and using a Web browser isn't necessary. Chapter 5 is essential to the discussions about searching in the remainder of the text. If using library catalogs doesn't fit into your plans then you may skip Chapter 8. If you're pressed for time and need to concentrate on research skills then you can skip Chapters 9 and 10 and may want to skip Chapter 11. Evaluating resources can be considered any time after you have become experienced with the nature of information on the Internet. The research projects in Chapter 14 deal with many of the tools and resources discussed in earlier chapters, but the projects are constructed in such a way that you could focus on individual portions of each.

Each of the chapters contains one or more step-by-step activities to demonstrate fundamental skills and concepts. Some of the text depends on the reader becoming a participant in the activities or having other experiences using the Internet and the World Wide Web. By following the activities and trying them out, the reader/participant can gain some first-hand, guided experience. Including these activities is a bit of a risk because of the dynamic nature of the Internet and the World Wide Web. Nothing is frozen in place and it may be that when you work with these you'll see differences in the way information is displayed. Don't let that deter you. Using the World Wide Web and the Internet means adapting to changes. Be persistent and use your skills to make accommodations to a changing, but important, environment. One of the things that makes the Web exciting and vigorous is the way things are changing to become more useful.

Supplemental Materials

The book has an accompanying Web site "Searching and Researching on the Internet and the WWW" with the URL **http://www.mwc.edu/ ernie/search-web.html**. Hyperlinks on that page will take you to individual Web pages for each chapter and appendix. These contain up-to-

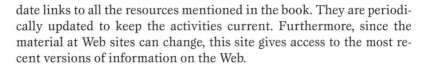
date links to all the resources mentioned in the book. They are periodically updated to keep the activities current. Furthermore, since the material at Web sites can change, this site gives access to the most recent versions of information on the Web.

Acknowledgments

There are many people to thank for the encouragement, friendship, support, and help that carried us through the many months of work on this project. We owe our greatest thanks, as always, to our immediate and extended families. They, more than anyone else, have made it possible for us to complete this work. Ernie wishes to thank his wife Lynn for all her help, love, and support—reading drafts and making improvements, being encouraging and supportive always, and (as she says) keeping herself amused. He also wants to thank his children, Karl and Oliver, for their special encouragement, interest, and advice, and for giving him the most important reasons for writing. Karen wishes to especially thank her husband, Jack, and their daughters Tracy and Hilary for their patience and support throughout the many months while she's worked on this book. They never complained that she was unavailable for conversation and help on most weekends and evenings.

We want to thank all the people who fall into the categories of friends, colleagues, and students in Fredericksburg, Virginia, and Mary Washington College who've given us their support, encouragement, help, and understanding. We also want to thank all the people involved with developing, producing, and improving the ways we can use the Web and the Internet for research and finding information.

Franklin, Beedle, & Associates has been a very supportive and cooperative publisher and has helped us greatly throughout this project. The folks we've worked with most directly include Jim, Stephanie, Tom, Susan, Cary, Carrie, Jason, Marc, Sue, Chris, and Lois.

This book has been through several reviews and we want to thank our reviewers—Mimi Will, Kris Chandler, Bill O'Connor, Lois Davis, Kathy Finney, and Dave Bullock—for their helpful, insightful, and frank comments and suggestions.

We hope you like this book and find it useful. Please feel free to send us email letting us know your opinions, suggestions, or comments about our work. When you have the time, visit our home pages on the Web.

Ernest Ackermann
Department of Computer Science
Mary Washington College
ernie@mwc.edu
http://www.mwc.edu/ernie

Karen Hartman
Simpson Library
Mary Washington College
khartman@mwc.edu
**http://www.library.mwc.
edu/ ~ khartman**

1
Chapter

Introduction to the World Wide Web

Every day millions of people around the world use their computers to access the information on the Internet that makes up the World Wide Web. They search for and retrieve information on all sorts of topics in a wide variety of areas. The information can appear in a variety of digital formats, such as text, images, audio, or video. Individuals, companies, research labs, libraries, news organizations, television networks, governments, and other organizations all make resources available. People communicate with each other using electronic mail; they share information and make commercial and business transactions. All this activity is possible because tens of thousands of networks are connected to the Internet and exchange information in the same basic ways. The World Wide Web (WWW) is part of the Internet, but it's not a collection of networks. Rather, it's the information that is connected or linked in a sort of web. Never before has so much information from such a wide variety of sources and in so many formats been available to the public.

Using a Web browser—the computer program or software that lets you access the World Wide Web—you can find information on almost any topic with just a few clicks of your mouse button. Some of the resources on the Web have been classified into directories that you can easily browse by going from one category to another. Several search tools (programs that search the Web for resources) are readily available. When you type a keyword or phrase into a form and click on a button or icon on the screen, a list of items appears in the browser's window. You simply click on the ones you want to retrieve. The amount and variety of information available are astounding, but it's sometimes difficult to find appropriate material.

This chapter covers some of the basic information and concepts you need to begin finding information on the World Wide Web. The sections in this chapter are as follows:
  * The World Wide Web as an Information Resource
  * Hypertext and Hypermedia
  * Key Terms and Concepts
  * Information Sources Available on the Web

About This Book

This book is designed to help anyone who uses the World Wide Web to find information or research a topic. We'll cover the tools and methods with which you search for resources on the WWW, and we will explain how to access and use those tools. We'll go over the methods and techniques to use so you can be effective and efficient in your searching and researching. We'll also talk about how to evaluate and cite resources within the context of a research project. The text and activities are designed to give you the experience you need to tap the cornucopia of information on the WWW, find the resources you want, and—just as important—evaluate the material you've found.

Each of the chapters contains at least one detailed activity in which you work with a Web browser to access information on the World Wide Web. These activities demonstrate concepts and techniques. As you read the activities and follow along, you'll receive step-by-step instructions for working with the World Wide Web. Remember, though, that these activities reflect the WWW at the time of writing. Because some things change frequently, they may not appear to you on your screen as they do in this book. The World Wide Web and the Internet are constantly changing, but don't let that hold you back. Be persistent and use your skills to work in this important environment. Change is one of the things that make the Internet and the World Wide Web exciting, vigorous, and useful.

At the end of each chapter, we provide a chapter summary and a list of terms. The terms are defined in the chapter and also appear in the glossary at the back of the book.

Click and Double-Click

We'll be using the term *click on* regularly. To click on something, you use a mouse to point to it and then press the mouse button. If your mouse has two buttons, press on the left button. To double-click, press the (left) button twice in rapid succession without moving the mouse.

This book assumes you have Microsoft Windows. If you're in another windowed environment, on a workstation that uses X Windows, or on a Macintosh, you'll find that most of the instructions are the same.

The World Wide Web as an Information Resource

You can think of the **World Wide Web (WWW)** as a large collection of information that's accessible through the Internet. The **Internet** is a collection of tens of thousands of computer networks that exchange information according to some agreed-upon, uniform rules or protocols. Because of this uniformity, a computer connected to one of the Internet's networks can transport text and images and display them on a computer connected to another part of the Internet.

Whether you've worked on the WWW before or not, you'll be pleased with how easy it is to use. It's also enticing. The World Wide

Web gives a uniform means of accessing all the different types of information on the Internet. Since you only need to know one way to get information, you can concentrate on what you want, not on how to obtain it. The Internet is commonly used throughout the world, so there is easy and relatively quick access to information on a global scale. That alone is remarkable, but it gets better. The information on the Web is often in a multimedia format called a *Web page,* which may combine text, images, audio, or video. This format lets us take advantage of modern computers' multimedia capabilities. A Web page can also contain links to other resources or information on the World Wide Web. This is why it's called a web: one page contains links to another, and that one contains links to another, and so on. Since the information can be anywhere in the world, the term World Wide Web is most appropriate.

Tim Berners-Lee, credited with the concept of the WWW, made the following statement in the document "About The World Wide Web": "The World Wide Web (known as 'WWW', 'Web' or 'W3') is the universe of network-accessible information, the embodiment of human knowledge." (By the way, you can find that document on the WWW by using the URL **http://www.w3.org/www**. We'll say more a little later about how to use URLs.) Berners-Lee has made a strong statement, but it's certainly true. There's a wide range of materials available on such subjects as art, science, humanities, politics, law, business, education, and government information. In each of these areas you can find scientific and technical papers, financial data, stock market reports, government reports, advertisements, and publicity and news about movies and other forms of entertainment. Through the WWW you can find information about many types of products, information about health and environmental issues, government documents, and tips and advice on recreational activities such as camping, cooking, gardening, and travel. You can tour museums, plan a trip, make reservations, visit gardens throughout the world, and so on. Just a little bit of exploring will show you the wide range and types of information available.

To access the Web, you start a program on your computer called a *Web browser*. The browser makes the connections to a specific WWW site, retrieves information from the site, and displays it in a window on your screen. The information in the window is often in multimedia format; it may have text, images, video, or audio. From there, you can go to other locations on the Internet to search for, browse, and retrieve information. You use a mouse to move a hand or pointer to an icon, menu item, region of a map or image, button, or underlined portion of the window, and click the mouse button (the left one if your mouse has more than one button). These items are called **hyperlinks**, or *links* for short. If you've clicked on a link in the document, the browser follows that link; the current document is replaced or another window pops up. Some Web pages, including those you'll use for searching and researching, have a place for you to type in a word or phrase, fill out a form, or check off options.

Items that are accessible through the WWW give hypertext access to the Internet. In order for this to work, there are standard ways of specifying the links and creating documents that can be displayed as part of the WWW. Information is exchanged according to a specific set of rules, or *Hypertext Transfer Protocol (HTTP)*; each link has a particular format, or a *Uniform Resource Locator (URL)*; and Web pages are written using a language called *Hypertext Markup Language (HTML)*, which the browser can interpret.

The browser window also has text and icons in the borders, outside the portion of the window containing the Web page. Clicking on text or icons in the upper border of a window pops up a menu or a dialog box from which you can choose an action. Figure 1.1 shows these and other portions of a browser window.

Throughout this book, we'll use version 4 of Netscape Navigator as the browser. If you're using a different browser—such as an earlier version of Netscape Navigator, Microsoft Internet Explorer, or the AOL browser—you'll see lots of similarities. While your view might be slightly different, we've tried not to rely on any special features of Netscape Navigator 4. That way, the explanations and activities will be meaningful regardless of the browser you're using.

Figure 1.1 shows the home page for the Library of Congress. When a site has several Web pages available, as the Library of Congress's Web site does, the one that acts as the first or introductory page is called the *home page*. The term home page is used in other ways as well. Lots of people have Web pages that tell something about themselves; a page like that is called a personal home page. The first page you see when you start your browser is called the home page for the browser.

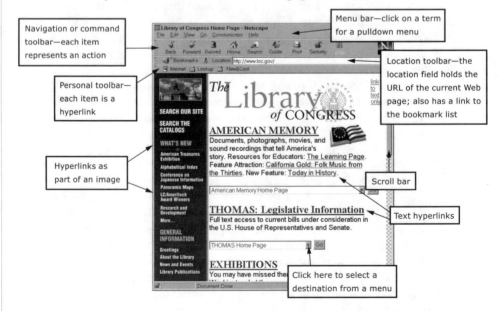

Figure 1.1—Home Page for the Library of Congress

Hypertext and Hypermedia

When you use the WWW, you work in a hypertext or *hypermedia* environment. That means you move from item to item and back again without having to follow a predefined path. You follow hyperlinks according to your needs. Sometimes the items you select are part of other sentences or paragraphs; the links to other Internet resources are presented in context. The links can also be represented by icons or images, or they may be regions in a map or display. Working with hyperlinks is fundamental to using the World Wide Web effectively, so we'll go into a little bit of detail on this topic.

The term *hypertext* is used to describe text that contains links to other text. When the hypertext and links are from a variety of media (text, video, sound), as is the case in the WWW, we use the term hypermedia. On a screen or page, certain items will be boldfaced, underlined, or colored differently. Each one represents a link to another part of the current document, screen, page, file, image, or other Internet resource. Selecting one of these links allows you to follow or jump to the information the link represents. You can also return to a previous link. There's a definite starting point, but the path you take after that is your choice. You are not constrained by having to go in some sort of straight line; you can think of being able to move up, down, right, or left from any link.

As an example, we'll look at an excerpt from a hypertext glossary. The definitions and explanations in the glossary are connected through hypertext. The excerpt here comes from a glossary of Internet terms that accompanies the book *Learning to Use the World Wide Web*, by Ernest Ackermann. This glossary is available on the WWW in hypertext form. To see it, use the URL **http://www.mwc.edu/ernie/ lrn-web-glossary.html**. Here's the excerpt:

> **Web Page**   The information available and displayed by a **Web browser** as the result of opening a local file or opening a location (**URL**). The contents and format of the Web page are specified using **HTML**.

If you used your mouse to select one of the underlined words or phrases and if you clicked on it, you'd be taken to another part of the glossary. For example, choosing (**URL**) takes you to a definition of URL (Uniform Resource Locator). From there you could browse the glossary by following other links, or you could return to the entry for Web Page. You could always follow the links back to the place you started. The information in the glossary wouldn't change, but the way you accessed it and the order in which you did so would change.

Before we discuss other concepts related to the World Wide Web, let's do an activity that shows what we might see when we start a Web browser and search for some information. We'll use Netscape Navigator, a popular browser, for all the activities in the book. Except for some of the details we give in Chapter 2, we won't focus on the features of the Web browser you use. We hope that the explanations and activities will be meaningful to you regardless of your browser.

 Tip

This is the first of many activities in this book. Each activity is divided into two parts: "Overview" and "Details." In the first part, "Overview," we discuss what we'll be doing and enumerate the steps we'll follow. The section "Details" goes through the steps, shows the results we got when we tried the activity, and provides some discussion. Your results might be different from what's shown here, but that's part of the dynamic nature of the Web; things are always changing. Don't let those changes confuse you. Follow the steps, use what's here as a guide, and pay attention to what you see. As you work through this and other activities, *Do It!* indicates something for you to do. These activities demonstrate fundamental skills that don't change, even though the number of results obtained or the actual screens may look very different.

Activity 1.1 First Look at Using a Web Browser to Find Information on the Web

Overview

Here we're assuming the program is properly set up on your computer and that you have a way of connecting to the Internet.

In going through the steps of this activity, we'll start the browser, explain some of the items you'll see on your screen, and then look at a subject directory that gives you access to lots of information. Finally, we'll exit the Web browser. We'll follow these steps:

1. Start the Web browser.
2. Go to the Yahoo! directory.
3. Explore the WWW.
4. Exit the Web browser.

These steps will allow us to look at using a Web browser and Netscape Navigator and will set a context for some of the concepts and terms in this book. Now for the details.

Details

1 Start the Web browser.

You start the Web browser Netscape Navigator either by clicking on an icon labeled **Netscape** or choosing **Netscape** from a menu. In some cases you may have to select a program group from the list of programs you can run, or you may have a shortcut to Netscape on your desktop. If you're using a different browser, you'll probably start it in the same way but by clicking on another icon.

Suppose the Netscape icon is on your desktop.

❋*Do It!* Double-click on the Netscape icon. Locate an icon that looks like one of the following:

Netscape
Communicator

Netscape
Communicator

Clicking this icon starts Netscape Navigator. A window similar to the one in Figure 1.1 will appear on your screen, although the contents will be different.

In some cases, clicking the icon will cause your computer to go through the steps necessary to connect to the Internet. If you use a modem to connect to the Internet, the program to use the modem will start, and the modem will dial a number to connect to the Internet.

If you're familiar with a windowed environment, you should feel very comfortable using a Web browser. You work with many of the items in this window in the same way as with any other window. You can resize the window or switch between the window and an icon that represents the window. The menu commands are listed across the top row. They include:

File Edit View Go Communicator Help

The menu bar contains items (such as **File**, **Edit**, and **Help**) that are common to several windowed applications. Each command has a pulldown menu; click on the command and a menu will appear.

The browser's window also has several icons in the command toolbar, as we've pointed out in Figure 1.1. You can use them to go from one Web page to another, print a Web page, stop the current page that is loading, and so forth. For example, you click on the icon labeled **Back** to go to the previous Web page. Some of the icons take you to other Web pages or services. Click on the button labeled **Search** to get a Web page with hyperlinks to several search engines.

It's important for you to know how to get online help. As you may have guessed, one way is to use the pulldown menu item **Help**, which has a link to online help.

2   Go to the Yahoo! directory.

There's lots of information on the WWW, and it's just about impossible to keep track of it all. To assist you, some hyperlinks are arranged by category to create directories. One popular, large, and well-designed directory is named Yahoo! (You can get to that directory and some others by clicking on the button labeled **Search**.) Here we'll go directly to the home page for Yahoo! by typing its URL in the location field (also called the location box) of the browser window and then pressing the **Enter** key. The location field is shown in Figure 1.1. It should hold the URL of the current Web page. The field is labeled either **Location:** or **NetSite:**.

❋*Do It!* Use the mouse to point to the location field and click the (left) mouse button.

When you click on the location field, it changes color. By typing, you can replace the current URL.

❋*Do It!* Type **http://www.yahoo.com** in the location field and press **Enter**.

This URL brings you to the beginning of the Yahoo! directory—its home page. After you type new text into the location field, its label will change to **Go to:** as shown in Figure 1.2.

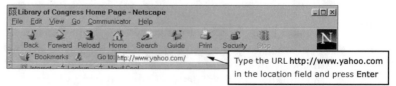

*Figure 1.2—Location Field with the URL **http://www.yahoo.com***

When you press **Enter**, your Web browser sends a request to the Yahoo! Web server, the computer that makes Yahoo! Web pages available. The server then sends the Web page with the address (or URL) **http://www. yahoo.com**—the Yahoo! home page—to your computer. The Web page is sent across the Internet. If there aren't any problems and your Internet connection isn't too slow, you ought to have the Yahoo! home page on your screen in a few seconds. (Pretty neat, huh?) The home page for Yahoo! appears in Figure 1.3.

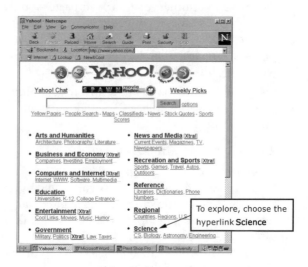

Figure 1.3—Home Page for Yahoo!

You don't have to type the complete URL in the location field when you're using Netscape Navigator version 2 or later. Omitting the leading **http://www.**, you can just type **yahoo.com** in the location field. The browser will retrieve the page whose full URL is **http://www. yahoo.com**.

3   Explore the WWW.

An easy way to explore the WWW is to follow hyperlinks. When you start with a directory such as Yahoo!, you can do plenty of exploring. Clicking on the link **Science** as indicated in Figure 1.3 will take you to a window such as the one shown in Figure 1.4.

✿*Do It!* Use the mouse to point to the hyperlink **Science** and click on the (left) mouse button.

In Figure 1.4, we've pointed out an advertisement near the top of the window. You may come across these sorts of ads on lots of Web pages. If you click on the ad, the browser will bring up another Web page that's designed to inform you about or sell you a product or a service. Feel free to look, but remember that the advertisement is likely to be marketing something and will definitely take you away from the task at hand.

In the next step we're going to click on the hyperlink **Astronomy**. If that one isn't in your window, use the scroll bar to go down the page, as indicated in Figure 1.4.

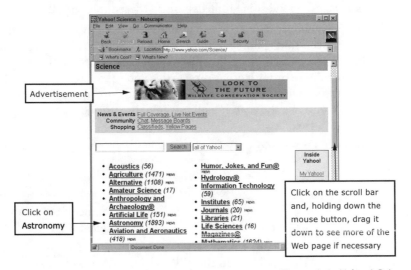

Figure 1.4—Yahoo! Science

You can see that there are still many topics to explore. We will choose one.

✿*Do It!* Use the mouse to point to the hyperlink **Astronomy** and click once with the (left) mouse button.

Figure 1.5 shows a portion of the Web page under the heading "Astronomy."

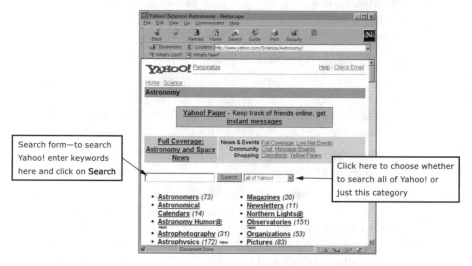

Figure 1.5—Yahoo! Science: Astronomy

There are lots of links to follow here, and you can follow these to explore the WWW. You'll find you can move from page to page easily with a little practice. Press the **Back** toolbar button to go back through previous pages. Spend some time exploring these topics or others.

All pages from Yahoo! contain a search form that you can use to search for information. There are times you'll want to do a search rather than browse the directory, and we discuss that in Chapter 3. Before you start a search here or with other directories and search tools, be sure to read whatever online material is available about help, tips, or options. Learning how to use the search facilities of a directory or search engine will save you time later.

When you're ready, go on to the next step.

4   Exit the Web browser.

Of course, you can exit Netscape Navigator in the same way you exit most other windowed applications. You can do one of the following:

- Click on **File** in the menu bar and select **Exit**.
- Press ⟨**Alt**⟩ + **F** and then **X**.
- Double-click on the button in the upper-left corner of the window.

The window will close, and you will have ended this session with Netscape Navigator. If you're paying by the minute or hour for the connection and you want to stop working with the Internet for the time being, be sure your connection is terminated.

End of Activity 1.1

In Activity 1.1 we looked at starting the Web browser, browsing the Web directory Yahoo!, and ending a browser session.

Now we'll go over some key terms and concepts related to the Web and the way information is presented on it.

Key Terms and Concepts

In this section we'll discuss some of the terms and concepts that are important to know about as you're working with the Internet and the Web. The topics we'll cover include:

- Client/Server
- HTTP (Hypertext Transfer Protocol)
- HTML (Hypertext Markup Language)
- URL (Uniform Resource Locator)
- Error Messages
- Bookmarks
- Common Types of Files on the Internet and the Web
- Sharing and Copying Information Found on the Internet and the World Wide Web
- Selected Web-based Guides to the Internet and the World Wide Web

Client/Server

When you start a WWW browser or follow a hyperlink, the browser sends a request to a site on the Internet. That site returns a file that the browser then has to display. This sort of interaction in which one system requests information and another provides it is called a *client/server* relationship. The browser is the client, and a computer at the site that provides the information is the server.

HTTP (Hypertext Transfer Protocol)

The documents or screens are passed from a server to a client according to specific rules for exchanging information. These rules are called *protocols*. The protocol used on the WWW is named HTTP, which stands for Hypertext Transfer Protocol, because the documents, pages, or other items passed from one computer to another are in hypertext or hypermedia form.

HTML (Hypertext Markup Language)

The rules for creating or writing a Web page are all specified as HTML— Hypertext Markup Language. This language provides the formal rules for marking text. The rules govern how text is displayed as part of a Web page. HTML would be used, for example, to mark text so that it appears in boldface or italics. In order for text or an icon to represent a hyperlink, it has to be marked as a link in HTML, and the URL has to be included. The URL doesn't appear, however, unless someone looks at the page with a browser. Web pages are usually stored in files with names that end in **.html** or **.htm**.

In order for you to see or hear what's in the file, the browser has to be able to interpret the file's contents. Depending on the type of file, the browser may display text, graphics, or images. If the file is written using HTML, the browser interprets the file so that graphics and images are displayed along with the text. Depending on the HTML code in the file, the text is displayed in different sizes and styles, and hyperlinks are represented on the page.

URL (Uniform Resource Locator)

The hyperlinks are represented in a specific format called a URL, or Uniform Resource Locator. The portion of the Netscape window labeled **Location:** holds the document's URL. Each Web page has a URL as its address. For example, the URL for the Library of Congress's home page is **http://www.loc.gov**.

The URLs that point to Web pages or home pages all start with **http://**, because they are all transmitted according to HTTP. You'll see something different for URLs that access information through other Internet services or protocols. *FTP*, or *File Transfer Protocol*, was one of the first protocols used on the Internet to exchange files. It's still in common use. For example, the URL for the NASA collection of space images is **ftp://ftp.jpl.nasa.gov/pub/images**.

You'll find it helpful to think of a URL as having the form:

```
how-to-get-there://where-to-go/what-to-get
```

You'll see in later chapters that URLs are used in the following ways:

- All hyperlinks on Web pages are represented as URLs.
- The entries in the bookmark and history file are stored as URLs.
- You type in a URL when you want to "open a location" (direct your browser to retrieve or go to a specific Web page).

When you cite a resource on the World Wide Web, you include the URL for it. You'll also want to include the URL when you're telling someone else about a resource, such as in an email message. It's much more effective to include URLs. Here's an example:

A good resource for information about African studies is the "African Studies" page **http://www.vibe.com/ history/africanstudies/africanwww.html** of the *World Wide Web Virtual Library* at **http://vlib.stanford.edu/ Overview.html**

People reading this message can use their browsers to go directly to the items you mention.

We will now show you the different parts of a URL so that you have a better idea about the information a URL conveys:

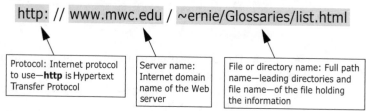

| Protocol: Internet protocol to use—**http** is Hypertext Transfer Protocol | Server name: Internet domain name of the Web server | File or directory name: Full path name—leading directories and file name—of the file holding the information |

Most URLs have this format. By indicating which Internet protocol to use, they tell you how to retrieve the information. By naming both the Web server and the file or directory holding the information, they tell you where the site is located. If only a server name is present and not a file name, as in **http://www.loc.gov**, you still retrieve a file; by default, the server passes along a certain file, usually named **index.html**. Sometimes you'll see URLs written without **http://** in front. You can safely omit **http://** when you open a Web page or location by typing the URL into the browser's location field.

Error Messages

As amazing as some computer systems are, they generally need very precise instructions. So you have to be careful about spacing (generally there aren't blank spaces in a URL), the symbols used (a slash and a period are not interchangeable), and the case of the letters. Here's an example:

The URL for the frequently asked questions (FAQ) for finding email addresses is **http://www.qucis.queensu.ca/FAQs/email/finding.html**. Replacing email with EMAIL, as in the URL **http://www.qucis.queensu.ca/FAQs/EMAIL/finding.html**, will cause the server to report an error back to the browser. The following will be displayed:

```
404 Not Found
The requested URL /FAQs/EMAIL/finding.html was not
found on this server.
```

The error message tells us that part of the URL was correct—the name of the Web server, **www.qucis.queensu.ca**—but that the Web server could not find the file on the server because there was something wrong with the rest of the URL.

A message such as this is called a *404 Error*. You may see this message if the URL is incorrect, if a Web page has been removed from a Web server, or if it is no longer available. If you click on a hyperlink and get a 404 message, you may have come upon what is sometimes called a *dead link*.

Here's another message you may see:

```
403 Forbidden
Your client does not have permission to get URL
/ernie/abc.html from this server.
```

That means the URL was correct and the file is on the server, but the file isn't available to the public.

If the URL contains the name of a Web server that your browser can't find, you'll see an error message such as this:

```
Host Name Lookup Problem
Check the spelling and try again.
```

Bookmarks

When you find a site on the Web that you'd like to visit again, you can save it for future reference with what Netscape calls a ***bookmark*** to the site. A bookmark is a link to a Web page, and the collection of the bookmarks you've saved is called the ***bookmark list***. You'll find using bookmarks very useful. We show how you can manage the bookmark list in the next chapter.

To save a Web page as a bookmark, click on **Bookmarks** in the menu bar and then click on **Add Bookmark**. That puts the bookmark in the bookmark list. To visit a site you've saved as a bookmark, click on **Bookmarks** in the menu bar and then either click on a bookmark that's in the list or click on **Go to Bookmarks** to select one. Selecting **Go to Bookmarks** also lets you manage the bookmark list.

Common Types of Files on the Internet and the Web

Web pages can contain text, images, video, audio, and other types of information. Either these will be part of the Web page or there will be hyperlinks to information in a variety of formats. Although information can appear as text, it is sometimes stored in a compressed format (to save space) or in some other form. In many cases, the Web browser can display the information in the file if it's an image or a video, or it can convert the file's contents to sound if it's an audio file (and if your computer is equipped with a sound card and speakers or earphones). In other cases, you need to get the appropriate software so that your computer can deal with the files.

Sometimes you can tell the file type by its name. The letters at the end of a file name following a dot (.) are called the file extension portion of the file name. Files whose names end with **.txt** or **.text**, for example, usually contain only plain, printable characters.

We won't go into all the details here, but we will list some of the more common file formats. For more information about using different file formats, check the online help that comes with your browser—click on **Help** in the menu bar of Netscape Navigator—or use your browser to access the following two excellent resources (we list titles, authors, and URLs):

- *Common Internet File Formats*, Eric Perlman and Ian Kallen, **http://www.matisse.net/files/formats.html**
- *Multimedia File Formats on the Internet*, Allison Zhang, **http://www.lib.rochester.edu/multimed/contents.htm**

Text Files

Plain text files contain plain printable characters, like the ones you see on this page, but without special fonts or typefaces, such as italic or bold. They're also called ASCII (rhymes with "pass key") files. ASCII stands for American Standard Code for Information Interchange, and it is the standard code used to represent characters in digital format in a computer. All browsers can display these files, and they often appear as if they were typed on a typewriter or computer terminal. Files of this type usually have names that end with **.txt** or **.asc**.

PostScript file format was invented by Adobe Systems. The files contain text but usually not in a readable format. The files also contain commands that a printer or display device interprets; the commands pertain to formatting, different fonts, font sizes, and images in the file. Files of this type usually have names that end with **.ps**.

Adobe Systems also invented PDF (Portable Document Format). These files contain instructions so that they can be displayed with different fonts and typefaces, different colors, and images. You can view these files on your computer if you have Adobe Acrobat software, which is free from the *Adobe Acrobat* Web site, **http://www.adobe.com/prodindex/acrobat**.

Compressed Files

Files are compressed to save space on a server and to transfer a file over the Internet more quickly. There are many types of compressed files, but the most common are those ending with **.zip**. If you retrieve a file in compressed format, you'll need software to uncompress the file. Two popular shareware programs work with these types of files:

- PKZIP **http://www.pkware.com**
- WinZip **http://www.winzip.com**

The frequently asked questions (FAQ) for the Usenet newsgroup comp.compression, **http://www.cis.ohio-state.edu/hypertext/faq/usenet/compression-faq/top.html**, contains lots of detailed questions and answers about compressed files.

Image Files

Graphic images are stored in files in a variety of formats. As a part of a Web page or on their own, most browsers can display images stored in GIF (Graphics Interchange Format) or JPEG (Joint Photographic Expert Group) format. Files with images in these formats have names ending with **.gif**, **.jpg**, or **.jpeg**. Another format, TIFF (Tagged Image File Format), can store high-quality images. Files with images in TIFF have names ending in **.tif** or **.tiff**. If your browser cannot display files in TIFF, you'll have to get some other software to display them. Two shareware programs can display images in various formats and can convert from one format to another:

- LView Pro

  http://www.lview.com
- Paint Shop Pro

  http://www.jasc.com/psp.html

Audio Files

These files contain information that's in an audio or sound format. With a sound card and speakers, you can play such files on your computer. Audio files often have one of the following three formats:

- Next/Sun format (file names end with **.au**)
- Waveform audio format (WAV), a standard format for computers using Microsoft Windows (file names end with **.wav**)
- RealAudio format (file names end with **.ra**)

If you're using Netscape Navigator version 3 or later, the browser contains the software to deal with all three types. Next/Sun and WAV files tend to be very large and thus may take a long time to retrieve. The RealAudio format uses a different technology called *streaming* in which sound becomes available as it's transferred to your computer through the Internet. A free player for RealAudio files is available from the URL **http://www.real.com/products/player/index.html**.

Multimedia Files

With these types of files, you can view video and hear accompanying sound. It's similar to viewing a movie or television. Two popular formats are MPEG (Moving Picture Expert Group) and QuickTime (created by Apple Computer). Netscape Navigator version 3 or later can display files in MPEG format. File names in this format end with **.mpg** or **.mpeg**. QuickTime file names end with **.mov** or .qt. A QuickTime player is available at no cost at **http://www.apple.com/quicktime**.

Sharing and Copying Information Found on the Internet and the World Wide Web

Much of what you find on the WWW can be saved in a file on your computer, which makes it easy to share and distribute information on the Web. Exchanging information was one of the main reasons the WWW project (and the Internet) began. There's also a drawback to this. Free access to information makes it difficult to control unauthorized distribution of anything that's available through the WWW. Anyone with a

Web browser can make an exact digital copy of information. This may be illegal. In many cases, documents on the Web come with statements explaining the rules for personal use. For example, here's a quote from **http://sunsite.unc.edu/expo/vatican.exhibit/exhibit/About.html** describing limitations to use of the materials in the exhibit "Rome Reborn" offered by the Library of Congress:

> The text and images in the Online Exhibit ROME RE-BORN: THE VATICAN LIBRARY AND RENAISSANCE CULTURE are for the personal use of students, scholars, and the public. Any commercial use or publication of them is strictly prohibited.

Remember that anything available in electronic form on the Internet or World Wide Web is a copyrighted work, and you need to treat it in the same way as a book, magazine, piece of art, play, or piece of recorded music. Just because something is available on the WWW doesn't mean that you may copy it. You are allowed to copy the material for personal use, but in almost every case, you cannot use it for commercial purposes without written permission from the copyright holder. *The Copyright Website*, **http://www.benedict.com**, by Benedict O'Mahoney, is a good resource for information about copyright issues.

Selected Web-based Guides to the Internet and the World Wide Web

Taking advantage of the resources on the World Wide Web, using a Web browser, and knowing about the Internet aren't difficult, but they require a lot of knowledge. If you're not familiar with the Web or the Internet, you may want to look at some Web-based guides. We will now present a list of some of the good ones available on the Web, giving you the name of the resource and its URL. To access any of these guides, double-click on the location field (it should turn blue), type the URL, and press **Enter**.

- *The HelpWeb: A Guide To Getting Started on the Internet*
  http://www.imagescape.com/helpweb/welcome.html

- *Internet Web Text,* John December
  http://www.december.com/web/text

- *Library of Congress Brief Guides to the Internet*
  http://lcweb.loc.gov/loc/guides/aboutinet.html

- *Newbies Anonymous: A Newcomer's Guide to the Internet*
  http://www.geocities.com/thetropics/1945/index1.htm

- *UCSD Science & Engineering Library—About the Net*
  http://scilib.ucsd.edu/aboutnet/aboutnet.html

There's a Web site to accompany the book you're reading, as well as some of our other books about using the Internet and the Web. Here's a list:

- *Learning to Use the Internet*
  http://www.mwc.edu/ernie/lrn-net.html
- *Learning to Use the World Wide Web*
  http://www.mwc.edu/ernie/Lrn-web.html
- *Searching and Researching on the Internet and the World Wide Web*
  http://www.mwc.edu/ernie/search-web.html

Information Sources Available on the Web

Because there's so much information available on the Web, it has to be organized so that you can find what you need. There must also be tools or programs to help you locate information. Throughout this book, we'll be discussing the major information sources on the Web.

Directories or Subject Catalogs

There are directories, arranged by subject, of a general collection of Internet and WWW resources. Several of the directories contain reviews or descriptions of the entries. We discuss them in detail in Chapter 4.

One way to access several of these is to go to the Web page with the URL **http://home.netscape.com/escapes/search** or to click on the button called **Search** in the command toolbar of Netscape Navigator 4. Another way is to go to the section "Searching the Internet" of the *Internet Scout Toolkit* at **http://scout.cs.wisc.edu/scout/toolkit/searching/index.html** and to click on "Subject Catalogs" or "Annotated Directories."

Search Engines

Search engines provide keyword searching capability. These are covered in Chapters 5 and 6.

One way to access several of these is to go to the Web page with the URL **http://home.netscape.com/escapes/search** or to click on the button **Search** in the command toolbar of Netscape Navigator 4. Another way is to go to the Web page for *Library of Congress Brief Guides to the Internet,* "Locating Information on the Internet," **http://lcweb.loc.gov/loc/guides/locate.html**.

Meta-search Tools

Meta-search tools allow you to use several search engines. A meta-search tool usually allows you to search several search engines or directories simultaneously. Many meta-search tools take your query, search several databases or search engines simultaneously, and then integrate the results. Some meta-search tools are good places to find lists of specialized databases.

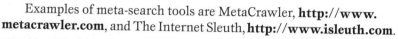
Examples of meta-search tools are MetaCrawler, **http://www. metacrawler.com**, and The Internet Sleuth, **http://www.isleuth.com**.

Virtual Libraries

Virtual libraries are directories or subject catalogs consisting of Web resources that librarians or other information specialists have selected and evaluated. Arranged by subject, these are directories of a general collection of Internet and WWW resources. Several of the directories contain reviews or descriptions of the entries. We discuss them in detail in Chapters 4 and 7.

Two excellent examples are *The Internet Public Library*, **http://www.ipl.org**, and *Librarians' Index to the Internet*, **http://sunsite.berkeley.edu/internetindex**.

Specialized Databases

Specialized databases can be comprehensive collections of hyperlinks in a particular subject area or self-contained indexes that are searchable and available on the Web. We discuss specialized databases in Chapter 7.

The Internet Sleuth, **http://www.isleuth.com**, accesses more than 1,500 specialized databases and directories.

Library Catalogs Accessible on the World Wide Web

Libraries have often been at the forefront of making resources available through the Internet, and thousands of libraries allow Internet and Web access to their catalogs of holdings. We discuss searching library catalogs in Chapter 8.

Some resources for library catalogs accessible on the World Wide Web are *webCATS*, **http://library.usask.ca/hywebcat**, and *Libweb*, **http://sunsite.berkeley.edu/libweb**.

FTP Archives

FTP stands for File Transfer Protocol. Dating back to the early 1970s, it's the original protocol used to share files among computers with access to the Internet. Before the appearance of the World Wide Web, FTP was the most popular and effective way of sharing information and resources. Naturally, people started collecting files and saving them in archives available to anyone with a connection to the Internet. There are thousands of FTP archives containing information in various formats, such as text, data, programs, images, and audio. We discuss using FTP and FTP archives in Chapter 9.

Several Web sites allow you to search FTP archives and make it relatively easy to retrieve files through FTP. One is *Filez*, **http://www.filez.com**.

Email Discussion Groups

Email discussion groups are sometimes called *interest groups*, *listservs*, or *mailing lists*. Internet users join, contribute to, and read messages to the entire group through email. Several thousand different groups exist.

Individual groups may keep archives of the postings to the group, but most archives are arranged by date. In many cases, it's more appropriate to think of the group's members rather than the group's archives as a good resource for information. We discuss email discussion groups and archives in more detail in Chapter 11.

Several services let you search for discussion groups. One is Liszt, **http://www.liszt.com**.

Usenet Newsgroups

Usenet newsgroups are collections of group discussions, questions, answers, and other information shared through the Internet. The messages are called articles and are grouped into categories called newsgroups. The newsgroups number in the thousands, with tens of thousands of articles posted daily. We discuss Usenet and searching archives of Usenet articles in more detail in Chapter 11.

Many search engines include the option of searching archives of Usenet articles, and some services—such as Deja News, **http://www. dejanews.com**—keep large archives of Usenet articles.

Summary

Millions of people around the world use the Internet for communication, research, business, a source of information, and recreation. One of the most popular and effective ways to tap into its resources is through the World Wide Web (WWW). The WWW is a vast collection of information that's connected like a web. There is no beginning or end; the information is accessible in a nonlinear fashion through connections called hyperlinks. You view the resources on the WWW by using a program called a Web browser. This book concentrates on the Netscape Navigator browser. You navigate through the WWW by pointing to hyperlinks (underlined or boldfaced words or phrases, icons, or images) and clicking once with the mouse. To use the WWW and the Internet effectively, you need to know how to find and use the services, tools, and programs that give you access to their resources, as well as the sources of information.

It's possible to link information in almost any digital form on the World Wide Web. Text files, programs, charts, images, graphics files, digitized video, and sound files are all available. Not only can you find things from a variety of media, but you also get a great deal of information in many categories or topics.

When using the WWW, you work in a hypertext or hypermedia environment. Items, services, and resources are specified by a Uniform Resource Locator, or URL. Web browsers use these URLs to specify the type of Internet service or protocol needed and the location of the item. For example, the URL for the Web page "Explore the Internet" (the Library of Congress) is **http://lcweb.loc.gov/global/explore.html**. The protocol or service in this case is HTTP, or Hypertext Transfer Protocol, and a Web browser using that URL would contact the Internet site **lcweb.loc.gov** and access the file **explore.html** in the directory named **global**.

The documents on the WWW are called Web pages. These are written and constructed using a language called Hypertext Markup Language (HTML).

A Web browser is used to access the information and resources on the World Wide Web. Whenever you start the browser or access a hyperlink, the browser—which is a computer program—sends a request to have a file transferred to it. The browser then interprets the information in the file so that it can be viewed in the browser's window, or in some cases viewed through another program. For example, if a hyperlink points to a text file, the file is then displayed in the window as ordinary text. If the hyperlink points to a document written in Hypertext Markup Language (HTML), then it's displayed by the browser. If the file is a sound file or an animation, then a program different from the browser may be started so the file can be heard or seen. Most of the facilities and capabilities are built into the browser, but in some cases your computer needs to be equipped with special equipment or programs. For instance, if a hyperlink points to a sound file, your computer needs to have a sound card, speakers, and the software to play the sounds.

Starting a Web browser usually means first activating your connection to the Internet and then clicking on an icon or command to start Netscape Navigator. If the cost of using the Internet depends on how much time you spend on the Net, then be sure to terminate the Internet connection when the Web session is over.

A number of different types of information sources are available on the World Wide Web. Those include:

❋ Directories of a general collection of Internet and WWW resources, arranged by subject.

❋ Search engines, which are tools that provide keyword searching capability.

❋ Meta-search tools, which allow you to access databases from one place.

❋ Virtual libraries, which are directories or subject catalogs consisting of selected Web resources.

❋ Specialized databases, which contain comprehensive collections of hyperlinks in a particular subject area, or which are self-contained, searchable indexes made available on the Web.

❋ Library catalogs accessible on the World Wide Web.

❋ FTP archives, which are collections of files in various formats available on the Internet.

- Email discussion groups, of which several thousand groups exist to share opinions and experiences, ask and answer questions, or post information about a specific topic.

- Usenet newsgroups, which are collections of group discussions, questions, answers, and other information that have been shared through the Internet.

Selected Terms Introduced in This Chapter

bookmark

bookmark list

client/server

File Transfer Protocol (FTP)

home page

hyperlink

hypermedia

hypertext

Hypertext Markup Language (HTML)

Hypertext Transfer Protocol (HTTP)

Internet

Uniform Resource Locator (URL)

Web browser

World Wide Web (WWW)

2
Chapter

Browser and
Bookmark Essentials

A Web browser helps you access the World Wide Web, the information on the Internet. In Chapter 1, we mentioned some details about using a browser. Chapter 2 will address the practical issues that arise when using a Web browser. This chapter will also explore the commands and tools that allow you to use the information and resources on the Web most effectively. We will focus on using Netscape Navigator version 4, but we'll do that in such a way that you'll be able to learn about other popular browsers, such as Netscape Navigator 3 or Microsoft Internet Explorer. There are lots of similarities between all these browsers.

We'll also cover the bookmark features of Netscape Navigator and discuss ways to manage bookmarks. You use bookmarks to save the locations, URLs, and names of useful and interesting Web pages or Web sites. With bookmarks, these sites will be easy to access whenever you're using a browser—they'll just be a click or two away.

The sections in this chapter are as follows:
* Surveying a Browser's Features
* Starting and Stopping the Web Browser
* Exploring the Web Browser's Window
* Using the Right Mouse Button
* Getting Around a Page and the World Wide Web
* Getting Help
* Saving, Printing, and Mailing Items from the WWW
* Using Bookmarks to Keep Track of Resources

Surveying a Browser's Features

Before we begin, let's discuss what you can expect from a Web browser. Of course, a Web browser will allow you to look at Web pages throughout the WWW or to connect to various sites to access information and explore resources. The Web browser will enable you to follow the hyperlinks on a Web page and to type in a URL for it to follow. The browser will have a number of other commands readily available through menus, icons, and buttons. And what about the times you need help? Your browser includes an easy way to find online help, as well as built-in links to other resources on the Web that can give you help or answers.

You'll definitely want a way to save links to sites you've visited on the WWW so you can return to them during other sessions. Web browsers meet this need in two ways—with a *history list*, which keeps a record of the Web pages you've come across in recent sessions, and with a *bookmark list*, which you use to note the WWW pages you want to access in the future. Some browsers call these bookmarked sites *favorites*. The name of the site and its URL are kept in these lists. The browser contains tools to manage and arrange the bookmark list. For example, you'll be able to sort bookmarks and organize them into folders.

Web browsers include the means for you to search for information on a current Web page. You'll be able to save a Web page on your computer, print the page, and email its contents to others.

Some Web pages are designed using *frames*. This design allows for several independent Web pages—with their own scroll bars and URLs—to be displayed in one window. When a page is in a frame, the browser allows you to save, print, or email a particular frame. Take a look at *Search Techniques Quiz - WebNet 97,* **http://www.mwc.edu/ernie/searchtechquiz.html**, as an example of a site that uses frames.

When you use the Web for searching and researching, you may need to fill out a form or transmit some information in a secure manner. Your browser can correctly display and handle this sort of Web page.

World Wide Web pages can contain text and images, as well as hyperlinks to digital audio, digital video, or other types of information. Your Web browser is probably equipped to handle many of these types. But whether you can access something also depends on the software and hardware on your computer. If you don't have the programs and the hardware (a sound card and speakers) to play a sound file, then your Web browser will be unable to handle sound files.

Web browsers do let you add to the list of software they use to display or play different media, however. If you come across a file or hyperlink to something the Web browser isn't configured to handle, you can add *helper applications* or *plug-ins*. These programs allow you to work with certain types of files. You do this by setting preferences for your browser. In setting preferences, you can choose the font and colors used for displaying text, set your email address, and select other items.

We'll go over setting preferences and working with helpers when appropriate in this chapter.

Here's a list of sources for more complete and detailed information:

For Netscape Navigator version 4:

❋ The section "The Preference Panels" of online help. (Press **1**, click on **About Navigator**, and then click on **The Preference Panels**.)

For Netscape Navigator version 3:

❋ *Learning to Use the World Wide Web: Academic Edition* by Ernest Ackermann.

❋ *Netscape Navigator Handbook*, available online with URL **http://home.netscape.com/eng/mozilla/3.0/handbook**.

Starting and Stopping the Web Browser

A Web browser is a computer program, or software, which is run on your computer. Just like other programs, it has to be started before you use it. When you're finished browsing the Web, you'll want to end the Web session by stopping the browser or exiting the program.

Starting the Web Browser

Before you can start the browser, you need access to the Internet. If your computer is directly connected to a network, you have access to the Internet. If you gain access to the Internet by using a modem, you likely have SLIP or PPP access to the Internet. *SLIP (Serial Line Internet Protocol)* and *PPP (Point-to-Point Protocol)* are standards for transmitting information on the Internet over serial lines. A *modem* is a serial device, meaning that information is transmitted one bit at a time. To activate your connection, it may be enough to start Netscape Communicator or Navigator. This will start a program that dials the correct number and then prompts you for a login name and password. If you have a network card in your computer and you connect to your local network or the Internet through a cable, then different protocols are used. There are other variations, so it's a good idea to check with the folks who provide your Internet connection for the exact details.

If you're using Communicator, you may have to set up or select a user profile before you access Navigator. The first time you set up a user profile, you'll need to supply your name and email address, so be sure you know an email address to use before you start. You'll also be asked for the Internet address of the SMTP gateway (the computer that sends your email out) and the Internet address of your POP or IMAP server (the computer that receives and sends email to your computer). SMTP? POP server? This may seem confusing, but don't worry! Just be sure to get that information from your Internet service provider (ISP) or the people who support your computer system.

To start a Netscape session, double-click on the Netscape icon. Look for an icon that looks like one of the following:

Netscape
Communicator

Netscape
Communicator

Ending a Session on the WWW; Stopping the Browser

Ending a session on the WWW means stopping or leaving the browser program. You stop the Web browser program in the same way that you end almost any other Windows program or application. Here are some ways to do that:

* Double-click on the upper-left corner.
* Click on the **X** in the upper-right corner.
* Click on **File** in the menu bar, and then click on **Exit**.
* Press **Alt** + **F**, and then press **X**.

If you use a modem to connect to the Internet, then you may want to end the modem session when you're done using the browser. Think of it as hanging up a phone after a conversation. Here are some ways to do that, in case that doesn't happen automatically when Netscape closes:

* Click on the button **Disconnect** in the dialog box or window that represents your dialup networking connection.
* Select a command from a pulldown menu that hangs up the phone (modem).
* Choose an item from a menu that starts a logout or bye program.

If there is more than one open window with a connection to the Internet, such as another browser window or an email window, then you can close the current window without disconnecting from the Web or Internet. Follow any of the first three steps above for stopping a Web browser program, or press **Alt** + **F**, and then press **Q**.

Exploring the Web Browser's Window

When you start a WWW browser, a window opens on your screen. It's the Web browser's job to retrieve and display a file inside the window. What is in the window will change as you go from site to site, but each window has the same format. The items that help you work with the Web document in the window include the scroll bar, the menu bar, and the toolbar, which are the same every time you use the browser. The major components of a Web page are labeled in Figure 2.1. They include the following:

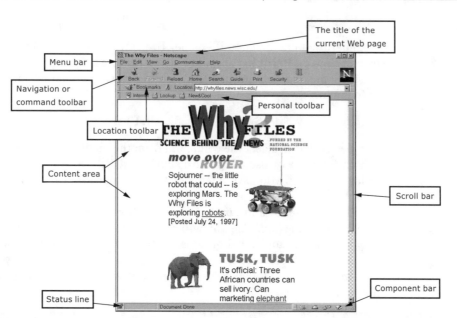

Figure 2.1—Navigator Window with Major Components Labeled

Title

The title of the Web page is created when the page is written. A page's title is not the same as its URL, just as a book's title is different from its library call number.

Menu Bar

The *menu bar* near the top of the window includes:

File **Edit** **View** **Go** **Communicator** **Help**

You choose any of these by moving the mouse pointer to the word and clicking on it. You can also activate one of these choices by using the **Alt** key along with the underlined letter. For example, to display the menu associated with **File**, use **Alt** + **F**.

Selecting an item from the menu bar brings forth a pulldown menu with several options. For example, if you click on **File**, you see the menu shown to the right.

Select any item in that menu either by clicking on it with the mouse or by pressing the underlined character in its name. To print the current Web page, you can click on **Print** in this menu or you can press **P** (upper- or lowercase). Some items on the menu are followed by **Ctrl +** a letter, such as the following:

<u>S</u>ave As...   **Ctrl + S**

This means that to select the command from the menu, you can either click on **Save As** or use a keyboard shortcut, Ctrl + **S**. With this particular command, you save a copy of the Web page in a file on your computer.

When you select an item that's followed by ..., as in **Save As...**, it brings up a dialog box. The box will request more information or will ask you to select additional options. If, for example, you select **Save As...**, you will then need to type in or select a file name. When you select an item that's followed by an arrow, as with **New**, it brings up another menu.

Tip

Giving commands using the keyboard—keyboard shortcuts.

You can access all the commands for using a Web browser by pointing and clicking on a word, icon, or portion of the window, but sometimes you may want to give a command using the keyboard. To do this, use the keys labeled Ctrl or Alt, along with another key. For example, to mail a document to an Internet address, you can select **Mail** from a menu or use Ctrl+M. Using Ctrl+M means holding down the key labeled Ctrl, pressing the key labeled M, and then releasing them both. As another example, giving the command Alt+H will display a menu of items to select for helpful hints. You hold down the key labeled Alt, press H, and then release them both.

Here are some details about each of the pulldown menus:

File
Using the commands in the **File** menu, you can open a new browser window, send an email message, or open a page in the Web editor (Composer) that's part of Netscape Communicator. You can also use this menu to open a page in the browser—either a Web page (which you would open by giving its URL) or a file on your computer. You can go in "offline" mode, which means working with files or messages on your computer without being connected to the Internet. The menu options also allow you to print, mail, or save the current document into a file. One item related to printing lets you select a printer, and another lets you preview a document before it's printed. This menu has items that permit you to close the window, end the WWW session, or both. There are also menu items that let you work with frames if they're present.

Edit

Use the **Edit** menu to copy items from the current document to other applications, such as a word processor. You can also use **Copy** and **Paste** to copy URLs or email addresses from one window into the location field or address field of a message. In addition, the menu contains the item **Find**, which presents a dialog box that lets you search the current document for a word or phrase. The items **Search Internet** and **Search Directory** are used to search for items on the Internet or to search for email addresses or phone book information. **Preferences** brings up a screen through which you set preferences; these determine how the Web browser operates, what items appear in the window, and how a document looks. For example, you can set the programs that will be run to view images and play sound or video as part of a Web page. You can control what's shown on the screen and how Netscape works with your network and computer system. There's a separate item for the preferences that you must set to use email and Usenet news. These include the domain names or IP (Internet Protocol) addresses of the mail and news servers.

View

The items on the **View** menu change what you see and how you view those items. You can use this menu to hide any of the toolbars (or to show them if they're not in view) or to change the font size (the size of the letters in the Web page). You also use the **View** menu to reload a copy of the current document; this is useful if there have been some changes to the source page since it was originally loaded or if the images in a document were not loaded automatically. The menu has items to stop the current page from loading or to stop animations. The item **Page Source** lets you view the source version of the current page so you can see which HTML commands were used to create it. Selecting **Page Info** shows information about the current document, such as when it was last modified and whether it's a secure document (used for commercial or private transactions).

Go

Items in the **Go** menu take you to different documents or pages that you have viewed during the current Netscape session. Netscape keeps a list of the pages (the history list) you've traveled through to reach the current document. You can choose **Back** to return to the previous page or **Forward** to move to a page from which you've just come back. You can also go to the home page for that session or to any of the recent pages on the history list.

Communicator

An important use of the **Communicator** menu is to access the bookmark list. With that list, you can look up names of URLs that you've put in the list, add new items, and otherwise manage the bookmark list.

The complete history list is available from this menu. You can also use this menu to reach the other components of Netscape Communicator, including the email system (Messenger Mailbox), Usenet newsreader (Collabra Discussion Groups), the Web page editor (Composer), Address Book, and others. Selecting **Security Info** gives information about the current Web page, including whether it was sent in a secure (encrypted) mode and the name of the Web server from which it was sent.

Help

Choose the **Help** menu to obtain information about using the Web browser. This menu includes a link to online help, product information and support (which itself has links to lots of helpful information), and information about netiquette, plug-ins or helpers, and other items.

Toolbars

Web browsers, like other Windows software, have one or more rows of icons called *toolbars* just below the menu bar. Each icon works like a button. When you press it with the mouse, some operation or action takes place. In some cases, a dialog box pops up. For example, if you click on the icon to print the current document, you can select a printer and specify whether you want to print the whole document or just a part of it. The icons give you a visual clue to the operation or action they represent. The commands they represent are all available through the items on the menu bar, but the icons give a direct path—a shortcut—to the commands. There are three toolbars in Netscape Navigator version 4: the navigation toolbar (also called the command toolbar), the location toolbar, and the personal toolbar. You can hide each toolbar by clicking on its left edge, making it disappear from the browser window. Click on the edge again to make it reappear.

Navigation Toolbar

Table 2.1 explains all the items in the navigation toolbar—also called the command toolbar.

Name	Explanation
Back, Forward	These two buttons with directional arrows move between documents or Web pages that you've already seen. **Back** takes you to the previous page, and **Forward** can only be used if you've previously used **Back**. To obtain a list of sites to go back to or forward to, put the mouse pointer on either of these icons and click the *right* mouse button.
Reload	This button reloads the current Web page from the source. If the page didn't load completely, if the loading process was disturbed in some way,

or if the source has changed since you last accessed it, you may want to reload the Web page.

Home
: This button takes you to your home page, the one you first saw when you started Netscape.

Search
: This button takes you to a Web page where you select a service to search the WWW. This is a good guide to different search services. For some items, you type in one or more keywords and wait for results. You'll get a Web page with hyperlinks to resources that match the keyword(s) you typed. This takes you to the same Web page as clicking on the directory button **Net Search** in previous versions of Netscape.

Images
: This button appears only if Netscape Navigator has been set so that it will *not* automatically display images while loading a Web page. With that setting, Web pages load more quickly. To load the images, click on this button. To set a preference for automatically or not automatically loading images, select **Preferences** from **Edit** in the menu bar, then select **Advanced**, and finally click on the box next to **Automatically load images**.

Guide
: This item represents a menu of several guides to Web or Internet resources and a hyperlink to the Netscape Web guide to sites, news, and events on the Internet. Click with the right mouse button to bring up the menu. The entries are as follows: **The Internet**, a guide to sites, news, and events on the Internet; **People**, a guide to white pages services for finding email and street addresses; **Yellow Pages**, a guide to businesses on the Web; and **What's New & What's Cool**, a guide to new and noteworthy Web sites. Click with the left mouse button to go to Netscape's guide to the Internet.

Print
: This button allows you to print the current document. You can specify whether you want to print all or some of the pages, as well as other options about the printing.

Security
: This button displays the page dealing with security information. It brings up the same page you would see if you selected **Security Info** from the

Communicator menu in the menu bar. You can use this option to check security, obtain encryption information about the current Web page, set a Netscape password for yourself, and perform other security-related tasks.

Stop

This button stops a current Web page from loading. This is useful if it's taking a long time to contact a site or load a page.

Table 2.1—Items in the Navigation Toolbar

Location Toolbar

The location toolbar includes the Bookmark Quickfile icon, which serves as a link to the bookmark list; the Page Proxy icon, which lets you add sites to the bookmark list, personal toolbar, or the desktop; and the location field, which holds the URL for the current Web page. We'll discuss the essential features of each.

The Bookmark Quickfile icon labeled **Bookmarks** is used to bring up a menu of items:

- The first item, **Add Bookmark**, lets you add the URL and title of the current Web page to the bookmark list. The title is what you see when you look through the list. Once something is in the bookmark list, you can access the Web page in one or two clicks. The bookmark list is therefore very useful when you're doing research.

- The last item, **Edit Bookmarks**, lets you arrange bookmarks into folders, rename items, delete items, and otherwise manage the list.

- The second item, **File Bookmark**, is used to highlight a folder in the list. It's used with the Page Proxy icon to the right of the Bookmark Quickfile icon.

You use the Page Proxy icon, or Page icon for short, to copy the URL of the current Web page. Move the mouse pointer over the icon and hold down the left mouse button. Then drag it to the desktop to make a shortcut to the Web page. Click on the shortcut and you'll go directly to the Web page. Alternately, drag it to the personal toolbar where it is added as an icon. As a third option, drag it to the Bookmarks icon and add it to the bookmark list, or click on **File Bookmark** and select the folder to which it will be added.

The location field holds the URL of the current Web page. In Activity 1.1, we showed how you can go directly to a Web page by clicking on the location field, typing in the URL, and pressing Enter. Clicking on the arrow displays a list of URLs for Web pages you've visited recently. Click on any one to go directly to it.

Personal Toolbar

The personal toolbar contains icons that represent Web pages. Clicking on an item takes you directly to that Web page. What you see the first time you use Netscape varies depending on what version you're using or whether someone else has used the browser. Figure 2.1 shows three icons in the personal toolbar. The one titled **Internet** is a hyperlink to the Netscape Internet guide. The others, titled **Lookup** and **New&Cool**, represent folders that contain several hyperlinks to Web sites.

There are two ways to put items in the personal toolbar. One way is to use the Page icon to place (drag and drop) an icon for the current Web page into the personal toolbar. In this way, the personal toolbar consists of hyperlinks to Web sites. Another way is to select a folder (a collection of bookmarks) in the bookmark list as the one that will be used for the personal toolbar entries. Check the online help for a way to do that. Personal toolbar entries give you quick access to a collection of bookmarks that might be useful when you're researching a topic.

Content Area or Document View

The *content area* is the portion of the window that holds the document, page, or other resource as your browser presents it. It can contain text or images. Sometimes the content area is divided into or consists of several independent portions called *frames*. Each frame has its own scroll bar, and you can move through one frame while staying in the same place in others.

The content area holds the Web page you're viewing, which likely contains hyperlinks in text or graphic format. Clicking on a hyperlink with the *left* mouse button allows you to follow the link. Clicking with the *right* mouse button (or holding down the mouse button without clicking if your mouse has only one button) brings up a menu that gives you options for working with a hyperlink. We discuss using the right mouse button in a later section.

Scroll Bar

Netscape has horizontal and vertical *scroll bars*. The horizontal one is at the bottom of the window, and the vertical one is at the right of the window. These scroll bars and their associated arrows help you move through the document. The scroll bars work the same way as those in common Microsoft Windows applications.

Status Line

When you are retrieving a document, opening a location, or following a hyperlink, the bar along the bottom of the window (the *status line*) holds the URL that's being used. It also lets you know whether a site is being contacted, if it's responding, and how the transmission is pro-

Chapter 2

gressing. The bar on the left, called the *progress bar*, gives a graphical view of how much of the complete page has been received.

The icon on the left that looks like a lock is the Security icon. Clicking on it brings up the same window as clicking on the Security icon in the navigation toolbar. If it looks like the lock is open, then the document you're viewing has not passed through secure channels. If the lock is closed, then some security has been put in place during the transmission of the Web page or document.

Information available through the World Wide Web passes across the Internet. That means that any site on the path of the transmission can intercept the packets that make up the document or Web page. Thus, it's difficult to guarantee the security or privacy of information (such as a credit card number) exchanged on the WWW. We all face that same problem whenever we use a portable wireless telephone.

Netscape Communications Corporation and others provide the means to guarantee secure transmissions. If the document you're working with is secure, the lock will be closed. It's not a good idea to send sensitive or valuable information through the WWW if the lock isn't closed, but that's always up to you.

Component Bar

Netscape Communicator consists of several software tools for working on the Web and the Internet. The *component bar* gives quick access to some of these: Navigator for browsing the Web, Mailbox for working with email, discussion groups for working with Usenet news, and Composer for writing Web pages. Clicking on any of these takes you to them. If mail arrives while you're using Netscape, a green arrow appears as part of the mail icon.

Using the Right Mouse Button

Most of what we've said about using the mouse relates to using the *left* mouse button, but Netscape Navigator 4 takes advantage of the *right* mouse button as well. Some of these features are also available with Netscape Navigator 3. If your mouse has only one button, then holding it down is usually equivalent to pressing the right button on a mouse with two or more buttons.

Here are some of the ways to use the right mouse button:

- If the mouse pointer is on the **Back** or **Forward** icons, clicking the right mouse button brings up a list of sites; you can go backward or forward to these. Select one from the list and click on it.

- You can use the right mouse button to copy and paste information from a Web page, email, or other windowed source. Say that you're working with Netscape email or are in the content area of a Web page and are *not on a hyperlink*. Using the mouse, move the cursor or pointer to the beginning of the text you want to copy. Hold down the left mouse button, use the mouse to highlight the text, then click the right mouse button and select **Copy**. Now move the mouse pointer to where you want to paste the text—maybe you've copied a URL and want to put it in the location field. Press the right mouse button and select **Paste**. If you are pasting a URL into the location field or some other field in a form, be sure to click on the location field with the left mouse button first to highlight the text you want to replace.

✳ If the mouse pointer is in the content area but *not on a hyperlink*, clicking the right mouse button brings up a menu with several useful items, many of which appear as part of other menus or toolbars. These include items to go **Back** or **Forward** to a Web page and to **Reload** or **Stop** loading the current Web page. You can set the background image as wallpaper for your desktop, save the image in a file, add the current page to the bookmark list, create a desktop shortcut to the page, or send the Web page via email.

✳ If the mouse pointer is *on an image*, then you have the same choices as when it's in the content area and not on a hyperlink. In addition, you can view the image in a separate window, save the image in a file, or copy the URL for the image (in case you want to include it in a Web page you're constructing).

✳ If the mouse pointer is *on a hyperlink* (remember, when it's over a hyperlink, the pointer changes to a hand) and you click the right mouse button, then a menu appears with all the same items as when the pointer isn't on a hyperlink. In addition, the menu includes items to open the link in a new, separate window or to open it in Netscape Composer. You can also save the Web page represented by the link to a file, or you can copy the link, which means copying the URL for later use with the paste operation.

Getting Around a Page and the World Wide Web

You've probably spent some time browsing the World Wide Web and some of the resources and information it has to offer. In this section, we'll go over how to move around within a page and how to go from one page or location to another. Knowing this, you'll be able to get around the WWW effectively.

Chapter 2

Moving Through a Page

When you start a WWW browser, you see a portion of a page or document in the window. As you may remember, the starting page is called the *home page*. Many of these pages contain more information than is immediately displayed, so you need to know how to move through a document. You can do this by using the scroll bars, using the keyboard, or searching for a specific word or phrase.

Using the Scroll Bars

You can move around or through a document by using the vertical and horizontal scroll bars on the right and bottom of the window. The scroll bars on a Netscape Navigator window are used the same way as on any other window.

Using the Keyboard

Pressing the up or down arrow will move you up or down one line. Pressing the **PgUp** key moves up one window length, and pressing **PgDn** moves down one window length. Pressing **Ctrl** + **Home** takes you to the beginning of the document, and pressing **Ctrl** + **End** takes you to its end.

Finding Text or Searching a Page

You can search a document for a word, portion of a word, phrase, or any string of characters. To find a string, you first have to bring up the dialog box labeled **Find**, as shown in Figure 2.2. There are two ways to do this—either select **Edit** from the menu bar and choose **Find in Page...**, or press **Ctrl** + **F** on the keyboard.

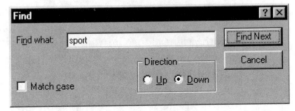

Figure 2.2—Find Box

Once the Find dialog box is up, type in a string (words or characters) and press **Enter** or click on the **Find Next** button. You can cancel a search by clicking on the **Cancel** button. You can search in one of two directions. **Down** searches from your current position to the end of the document. **Up** searches from the current position to the beginning of the document. Mark the **Match case** box if you want to match the capitalization in the string exactly.

Moving Between Pages

As you work with and browse the World Wide Web, you'll often go from one page to another. Much of the time, you do this by clicking on hyperlinks, but you can also go directly to a Web page, document, or location by typing its URL and then letting the browser retrieve it for you. To move between pages you've already visited during a session, you can use the **Back** or **Forward** arrow icons on the toolbar. Web browsers also let you save URLs or titles of the pages you've visited in one session so that you can access them easily during that or any other session. This information is saved in the *history list* (a list of all sites visited during recent sessions) and in the *bookmark list* (a list of hyperlinks to sites you have explicitly saved from one session to the next).

 Tip

When you can't wait—breaking a connection or stopping a page.

Press the key labeled [Esc] or click on the **Stop** icon to stop a page from being loaded into your browser or to stop Netscape from trying to connect to a site. When you want to follow a link or go after a document, click on hypertext or an icon. Watch the status bar to see if the remote site holding the information has been contacted and if it's responding. Your Web browser will try for a certain amount of time (a minute or so) to contact the remote site. If you don't want to wait that long or you don't want to wait for the browser to display a complete page, press [Esc] or the **Stop** icon. This doesn't close the browser; it just interrupts the transmission or attempted connection.

Going Directly to a Web Page

We'll describe two ways to go directly to a Web page, document, or location. In both cases, you type the URL and press [Enter]. The browser attempts to make the connection, and if it can retrieve the page, it will bring the page up on the window.

If the browser can't retrieve the page, check your typing to make sure you have the URL right. There could be other problems as well. If the page is not available to the public, you'll see the message "403 Forbidden" in the window. If the page doesn't exist, you'll get the message "404 Not Found." It could also be that the site is out of service or too busy to handle your request.

One way to go directly to a Web page is to click on the location field. After the pane changes color, type the URL and press [Enter]. We did that in Activity 1.1.

Another way to go directly to a Web page is to click on **File** in the menu bar and then to select **Open Page** (the keyboard shortcut is [Ctrl] + **O**). A dialog box labeled **Open Page** pops up on the screen, as shown in Figure 2.3. Type the URL of the site you want to go to, be sure you've selected Navigator as the way you want the page opened, and click on the button labeled **Open**. (Figure 2.3 shows the dialog box filled in with the URL for the *World Wide Web Virtual Library*, **http://**

vlib.stanford.edu/Overview.html. Why not try it and browse the library?) The Web browser then attempts to make the connection, and the page you've requested replaces the current one in the window. You can also use this method to view a local file—one that's on a disk drive on your computer or local network.

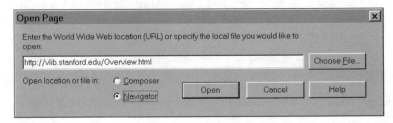

Figure 2.3—Dialog Box to Open a Page

Using Back and Forward

You can move to a previous Web page by clicking on either of the icons **Back** or **Forward**. You can also go back or forward by selecting either option from the **Go** menu in the menu bar. The keyboard shortcuts are **Alt** + **←** to move backward and **Alt** + **→** to go forward. You can also move in these directions by pressing the right mouse button (while the pointer is on a Web page) and then selecting **Back** or **Forward** from the menu that pops up on the screen.

Keeping Track—The History List

The Web browser keeps a record of the path you've taken to get to the current location. To see the path and select a site from it, click on **Go** in the menu bar. The browser keeps track of all the Web pages visited recently in the history list. The number of days an item may be kept on the list is set in the Preferences panel category titled Navigator. To get to the spot where you can set it, click on **Edit** in the menu bar, select **Preferences**, and then click on **Navigator**. You can use this list to go directly to a Web page without having to go through all the pages in between.

To bring up the history list, press **Ctrl** + **H** from the keyboard, or click on **Communicator** from the menu bar and select **History** from that menu.

Figure 2.4 illustrates a portion of a sample history list. You can select and highlight any item by using the up or down arrow on the keyboard or by using the mouse. Once you've highlighted the location you want, double-click on the highlighted item. If you click on the right mouse button, a menu pops up that allows you to go directly to the Web page or to add the name and URL of the highlighted item to the bookmark list. You will want to add the name of a Web page (and its URL) to the bookmark list when you want to be able to return to it in another session on the WWW. Figure 2.4 shows some of the information in the history list about the sites visited through Navigator.

Figure 2.4—History List

Keeping Track—The Bookmark List

The bookmark list is a collection of hyperlinks to Web pages that you want to save from session to session. They could be your favorite sites, ones you find useful, or ones you've looked at briefly but want to return to in the future (particularly good when you're starting to research a topic). Each item on the bookmark list is a Web page title, and each entry is a hyperlink. The browser includes a program to let you manage and arrange the list.

To use the bookmark list to go from the current Web page to another, first view the list onscreen by clicking on the Bookmarks icon in the location toolbar and move the mouse over the entries. When you've highlighted the one you want, click with the left mouse button.

Another way to bring up the list is to select **Bookmarks** from the **Communicator** menu in the menu bar. Pressing Ctrl + **B** from the keyboard produces the list in editing mode. In that mode, you can not only highlight and select an item but also manipulate the entries on the list. Figure 2.5 shows a portion of a bookmark list with folders.

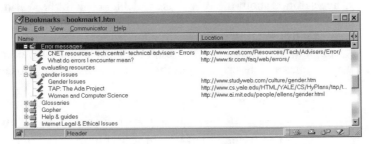

Figure 2.5—Portion of a Bookmark List

Getting Help

There are several ways to get help with using Netscape Navigator. Online help is available while you're using Netscape. There is a list of frequently asked questions (FAQ) with answers about using Netscape. Several Usenet newsgroups are dedicated to discussions about using a WWW browser.

Online Help

To receive online help while using Netscape Navigator, click on **Help** on the menu bar. This pulls down a menu from which you can select one of several types of information, including **Help Contents**. You can also activate this option by pressing the function key [F1]. Online help starts in a separate window. It contains information that you may need while using Navigator or other parts of Communicator. Another useful item is **Product Information and Support**. Clicking on that takes you to a Web page supported by Netscape Communications. That Web page has many useful links for getting answers to your questions about using Netscape products.

Frequently Asked Questions (FAQ)

Frequently asked questions or *FAQ* is a traditional way to collect common questions and provide answers on the Internet. As you browse the Internet, you'll see FAQs on all sorts of topics. Netscape maintains several FAQs about its products. You can access them by choosing **Help** in the menu bar and **Product Information and Support** from the pulldown menu or by explicitly opening a location using the URL.

You'll find the "World Wide Web FAQ" very useful. It's available in English and other languages at several sites on the WWW. You should pick the one closest to you. The primary site is *Boutell.Com, Inc.*, **http://www.boutell.com/faq/**.

Usenet Newsgroups

There are several (at least 15) Usenet newsgroups that host discussions about the WWW, and each maintains its own FAQ. A list of Usenet newsgroups about the WWW is available through the World Wide Web FAQ mentioned above.

One direct link to the list of newsgroups is **http://www.boutell. com/faq/ngroups.htm**. You ought to check this URL because it has the names and descriptions of the groups, and it's likely to contain new ones as they're created.

You may want to read the following Usenet newsgroups:

- **comp.infosystems.www.browsers.ms-windows**

  For discussion of Web browsers used with Microsoft Windows and NT operating systems.

- **comp.infosystems.www.announce**

  Used to announce new Web pages.

Now we'll take a break from our detailed description of how to use a Web browser, and we'll go through an activity. The activity provides practice with using commands to browse a section of the WWW.

Tip

Remember that the Web is always changing and that your results may differ from those shown here. Don't let this confuse you. The activities demonstrate fundamental skills. These skills don't change, even though the number of results obtained or the actual screens may look very different.

Activity 2.1   Using a Search Engine

Overview

In this activity, we'll search for information on the World Wide Web. We'll start by using a ***search engine***, a program or service designed to search for information available through the WWW, to help us find resources about a specific topic. A search engine is a collection of software programs that collect information from the Web, index it, and put it in a database so it can be searched. A search engine also contains tools for searching the database; that's the part we'll use most of the time.

We type keywords or a phrase into a search form on a Web page, possibly set some options, and then click on a search button on the Web page. In what is usually a short time, we will see matching entries from the database—usually 10 per page. Each of the results contains a hyperlink to the entry, as well as a brief excerpt from the resource. All the results are ranked according to relevance or how closely they match the query.

Most of the search engines have indexed millions of Web pages, so it's likely that you'll get more results than you can check. The key to successful searching is to make your search phrase or keywords as precise as possible. We'll discuss ways of doing that in much more detail in Chapters 5 and 6.

Clicking on the icon **Search** in the command toolbar brings up a list of several search engines. Those and others are listed in Appendix B and throughout this text.

The topic for the search is Chinese art, specifically painting. Why that topic? Well, it's always nice to look at, try to understand, and learn about art, and we'll be able to use the topic to demonstrate some ways to use a search engine and move around the Web from page to page ("surfing"). We'll also go over using the online help from the search engine to make our search more precise.

When you try this activity, you're likely to see some differences in the results, because new resources are always being added to the search engine's database. Concentrate on the steps to take. You'll use the same techniques for other topics.

The search engine we'll use for this activity is AltaVista. It's very popular, has a large database of Web pages (more than 30 million), and gets high ratings in the popular and computer press. We'll use the keywords *Chinese art painting* to start, since that phrase describes the topic both generally (Chinese art) and specifically (painting). We'll go directly to the Web page for AltaVista by typing in its URL and typing the keywords for the search. After we see the first list of results, we'll look at the online help available through AltaVista to make the search more precise. Then we'll look at some of the results by following some of the hyperlinks.

Here are the steps we'll follow:

1. Start the browser.
2. Go to the home page for AltaVista.
3. Type in the keywords and start the search.
4. Read the online help.
5. Modify the search phrase to get more precise results.
6. Follow some of the hyperlinks returned by AltaVista.
7. End the session.

While you're going through the steps in this activity, practice using the **Back** and **Forward** icons. If you click on **Forward** as many times as you click on **Back**, you won't lose your place.

Details

1   Start the browser.

❋*Do It!* Double-click on the Netscape icon. Look for an icon that looks like one of the following:

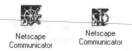

Netscape Communicator   Netscape Communicator

2   Go to the home page for AltaVista.

❋*Do It!* Click on the location field, type **http://www.altavista.digital.com**, and press ⎡Enter⎤.

When you start your Web browser, your home page will appear on the screen. We're going to access AltaVista by typing its URL in the location field, as shown in Figure 2.6.

Figure 2.6—Going to AltaVista by Typing Its URL

Soon after you press ⎡Enter⎤, the search page for AltaVista ought to appear in the browser window, as shown in Figure 2.7.

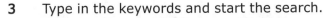

3   Type in the keywords and start the search.

✿*Do It!* Type **Chinese art painting** in the search field and click on
Search as shown in Figure 2.7.

To start a search, you type a word or phrase in the search field, then
click on the button labeled **Search**. Figure 2.7 shows the keywords typed
into the box. In Chapters 5 and 6, we'll explain several of the features in
such search engines as AltaVista, but it's worth noting that there are
hyperlinks on this page to get help, go to a page where you can use
advanced techniques, or refine your search keywords. We'll stick with a
simple search for this activity.

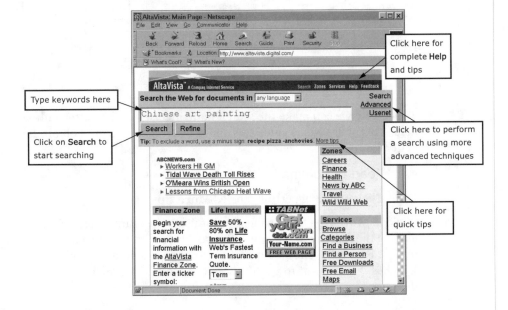

Figure 2.7—Search Page for AltaVista with Keywords Typed In

After you click on **Search**, the search engine returns a list of hyperlinks
to resources that contain information containing one or more of the
words in the search phrase. A portion of that page is shown in Figure 2.8.
You see that the search engine found nearly half a million items! They
are arranged in order so that those which may be most relevant are
listed first. There are 10 on this page. We don't show it here, but if you
move to the end of the page (use the down arrow keys, press **PgDn**, or
use the vertical scroll bar), there's a link you can select to go to the next
10 items.

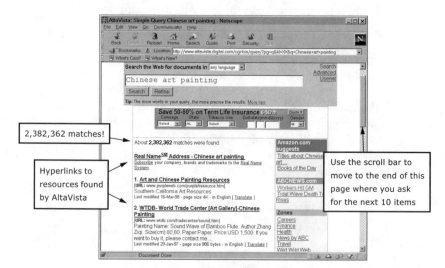

2,382,362 matches!

Hyperlinks to
resources found
by AltaVista

Use the scroll bar to
move to the end of this
page where you ask
for the next 10 items

Figure 2.8—Portion of First Page of Search Results

To see how we can make the search more precise, we'll read the online help. That will give us some tips about using AltaVista and obtaining better results.

4   Read the online help.

❀*Do It!* Click on the hyperlink labeled **More tips**.

Click on **More tips** to get some tips for using the search engine and for making the search more precise. The goal is to obtain more appropriate results. Figure 2.9 shows a portion of AltaVista's help page for simple searches. You'll want to use the scroll bar to read through the tips on the page.

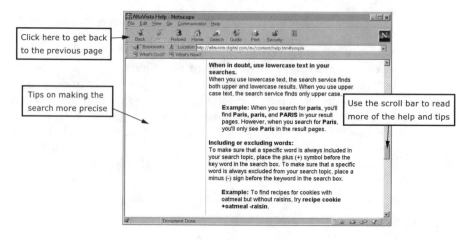

Click here to get back
to the previous page

Tips on making the
search more precise

Use the scroll bar to read
more of the help and tips

Figure 2.9—AltaVista's Help for Simple Searches

Reading the text, we find several useful pieces of information:

* We can require a match for phrases, not just individual words, by including a phrase in quotes.

* The search is case sensitive (*Chinese* gives different results from *chinese*).

* We may require certain words or phrases by putting a **+** in front of them. We can prohibit certain words by putting a **–** in front.

We're interested in Chinese art, specifically painting, so we'll modify the search by using the phrase *Chinese art* and by requiring the term *painting*. Looking through our initial results, we see that some are from sites that give us the opportunity to buy some of the art. This time we're just looking, so we'll exclude the term *buy*. With more searching experience, we'd learn that colleges and universities commonly put course listings or course descriptions on the Web. To bypass those for now, we'll exclude the term *courses*. We'll use the following:

"Chinese art" + painting -buy -courses

The AltaVista search page includes a hyperlink labeled **refine** that we could also use to modify the search phrase. When we click on **refine**, we find terms that AltaVista supplies. These words are synonyms and antonyms of those in the search phrase. Which to use? You can see that sometimes it's better to use **refine** if we need help coming up with terms. If those terms don't apply to our needs or if we think of our own terms, then we don't need to use **refine**.

5   Modify the search phrase to get more precise results.

We'll go back to the previous page so that we can enter our new search terms and get more precise results.

❋*Do It!* Click on the **Back** button in the toolbar.

❋*Do It!* Click on the search field, modify the search terms to **"Chinese art" + painting -buy -courses** and then click on the **Search** button.

To replace the search terms, you can click on the field pane to the right of the last word, backspace over the terms, and type new terms. You can also use the left and right arrow keys to add characters or to delete them from the search terms.

Figure 2.10 shows a portion of the previous page with the new search terms typed in.

Figure 2.10—AltaVista Search Form with Modified Search Phrase

6   Follow some of the hyperlinks returned by AltaVista.

Figure 2.11 shows the first few results of the search. We reduced the number from nearly half a million to about 6,600. That's still lots to consider, but the first few have a good chance of being ones we'd like to see. You can access the items listed by clicking on the hyperlinks. For each item, there's a brief description that you can use as a guide to help you decide whether to follow the link. For now we'll follow the hyperlink for **China the Beautiful**, as it looks the most promising. (If that one isn't listed, pick another that you think is appropriate.)

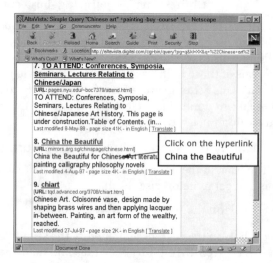

Figure 2.11—First Few Results of Modified AltaVista Search

✿*Do It!* Click on the hyperlink **China the Beautiful**.

Figure 2.12 shows the Web page "China the Beautiful." It has links to lots of topics related to Chinese art and Chinese literature. We see that there are links called **Paintings Gallery** and **Links to Museums and Art Galleries**. Further down the page there's a link called **Paintings**. We'll follow this one first; you're free to follow any you'd like. Before we follow any links, why don't we set a bookmark for this Web page?

Click on **Bookmarks** to save the link to this page in the Bookmark List

The hyperlink **Paintings** is further down this Web page

Hyperlink **Paintings Gallery**

Hyperlink to other links for museums and galleries

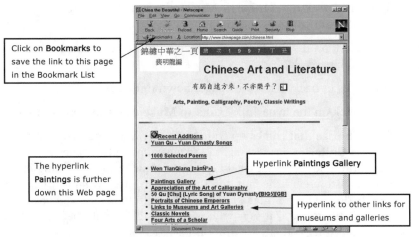

Figure 2.12—"China the Beautiful" Web Page

✤*Do It!* Click on **Bookmarks** on the location toolbar and then select **Add Bookmark**.

An alternate way to add this page to the bookmark list is to use the keyboard shortcut ⌈**Ctrl**⌋ + **D**. With this added to the bookmark list we'll be able to come back to this site any time we'd like without having to go through the search. Now on to explore the other hyperlinks.

✤*Do It!* Use the scroll bar to move to the portion of the page that includes the link **Paintings**. Click on the hyperlink **Paintings**.

Clicking on the hyperlink **Paintings** brings up a list of links, as shown in Figure 2.13. Feel free to follow any of them to see images and, in some cases, to learn about the painters. You can use the **Back** button in the toolbar to return to this list.

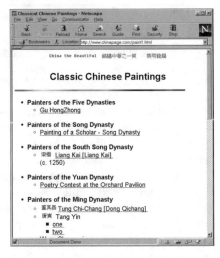

Figure 2.13—"Classic Chinese Paintings" Web Page

Now let's check out **Links to Museums and Art Galleries** on the Web page "China the Beautiful."

✹*Do It!* Click on the **Back** icon to return to the "China the Beautiful" Web page.

This takes us back to the Web page shown in Figure 2.12.

✹*Do It!* Click on the hyperlink **Links to Museums and Art Galleries**.

The Web page that comes up from the hyperlink **Links to Museums and Art Galleries** has several links to museums and art galleries around the world, and we could easily spend an hour or more looking at the exhibits. Browse a little, but don't get lost or forget whatever else you need to do today. We'll take a look at the bottom of the Web page (see Figure 2.14) to see if it says who is responsible for all these fine Web pages and to see if there are other links to follow.

✹*Do It!* Use the scroll bar or the **PgDn** key to get to the bottom of the Web page.

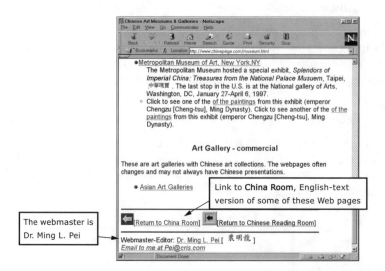

Figure 2.14—Bottom of "Chinese Art Museums & Galleries" Web Page

The information at the bottom of the page says that Dr. Ming L. Pei is the site's webmaster. That means he's responsible for maintaining the pages at this Web site. If we click on his name, we can read more about him and see that he also created this Web site. You may have noticed that the Web pages we looked at contained some Chinese characters. Some browsers are not able to display those characters. An all-English-language version of these pages is available if you click on the hyperlink **China Room**. We'll leave that for you to explore.

There are still lots of links we may want to follow, and we can do that by using the **Back** button in the command toolbar to return to the

AltaVista page with the search results. We've also added one item to the bookmark list, and we can go directly to that page by clicking on **Bookmarks** in the location toolbar and selecting it from the list of bookmarks. There are still lots of items you may want to explore. Feel free to do so. Just remember, there may be other things going on in your life or work right now that need attention!

7   End the session.

You knew when we started that this had to end sometime. Now's the time. (You can, however, keep the Web browser open so that you're ready for the next activity.)

❋*Do It!* Click on **File** on the menu bar and select **Exit** from the menu.

That's it!

End of Activity 2.1

In this activity, we used a search engine to find hyperlinks to Web pages about Chinese art, specifically painting. After using the online help, we used search terms to make the search more precise. When you look at some of these Web pages, you may want to make the search even more specific. Perhaps you're interested in looking at the work and finding information about a specific painter, style of painting, or location. You can do that by modifying the search phrase or coming up with a new one.

Saving, Printing, and Mailing Items from the WWW

Suppose you're working on the WWW and you come across a document, data, program, picture, sound or video clip, or anything you'd like to save. Or maybe you want to email one of those items to someone else or get a printed copy of it. A Web browser comes with tools and commands to let you do these things. Commands are available through the pulldown menu under **File** in the menu bar, through some of the icons in the command toolbar, and through keyboard shortcuts.

Remember, just because something is available on the WWW doesn't necessarily mean you may make a copy of it. In many cases, the material—text, images, sound—can't be used for commercial purposes without written permission.

Saving Web Pages in a File

You can save any Web page in a file on your computer. When a page is saved, you get the text portion along with the HTML code for the page. Images, audio, and other types of elements in the page are not included because these things exist in files other than the one that holds the text you see on the screen. You may want to save a Web page in a file on your computer so you can access it in the future without connecting to the Internet. If the Web page has frames, click on the frame you want to save before following these steps.

To save a page, click on **File** in the menu bar and select **Save As** from the menu. The keyboard shortcut is $\boxed{\text{Ctrl}}$ + **S**. A dialog box opens in which you confirm or give the name of the file to hold the page.

By default, a page is saved in source format, which means that it includes the text along with the HTML commands or tags used to create the page. It's really useful to see how others have used HTML to create and make Web pages when you're thinking about translating your designs for Web pages into HTML. To save only the text without HTML, you need to be sure the file name ends with **.txt** and that the file type selected is Plain Text. Figure 2.15 shows this.

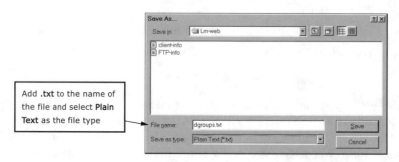

Add **.txt** to the name of the file and select **Plain Text** as the file type

Figure 2.15—Dialog Box with Options Set to Save Text Only

Saving Items on a Web Page into a File

Almost anything that has a hyperlink to it can be saved in a file. You can save items after you receive them—like saving a Web page to a file once the page is on the screen—or you can save them beforehand. All the items are saved as files. Often, you're able to tell the type of information in a file by looking at the extension of the file name, such as **.doc** for a Microsoft Word file, **.gif** for an image, or **.wav** for an audio file. Saving a file from the Internet is called ***downloading*** the file.

To save whatever is on the other end of a hyperlink without viewing it first, move the mouse pointer to the hyperlink and click the *right* mouse button. When a menu pops up, select **Save Link As**. Another way to do this is to move the mouse pointer over the hyperlink, hold down the $\boxed{\text{Shift}}$ key, and click the (left) mouse button.

The link can point to anything on the WWW—another Web page, a document in a special format (such as a document prepared with a word processor or spreadsheet), an image, a compressed archive of files, a video file, an audio file, or even other possibilities. (Who knows what you'll find on the WWW?)

You can save an image in the browser window to a file by moving the mouse pointer over the image, clicking the *right* mouse button, and selecting **Save Image As** from the menu.

Whenever you save a file from the Internet, either directly or through a hyperlink, there's a possibility that the file will contain a computer virus or other software that may damage or erase your files. After you save a file, check it with antivirus software, which is a program that checks a file for a virus. A good source for information about computer viruses is *virus - PC Webopaedia Definition and Links*, **http://www.pcwebopedia.com/virus.htm**.

Printing a Web Page

You can print whatever you see in your browser window with a printer that's connected to your computer. When a Web page is printed, everything you see in the window—text, graphics, images—is passed on to the printer.

Giving the command to print brings up a dialog box in which you can select the printer, determine the number of copies, and indicate which pages of the Web page you want to print. The phrase *pages of the Web page* may seem strange, but remember that a Web page isn't a physical page. A Web page may contain only text, but it may also be in multimedia form. The Web page, in fact, exists only in electronic form. You can preview the printing by picking the preview option. This will give you an idea of the printed Web page's physical layout.

Mailing a Web Page

The text on a Web page can be mailed to any Internet address. Mailing a page means sending only the text on the page or sending the source. The *source* is the text, as well as all the HTML statements that specify hyperlinks, control the page format, and identify the source of the images and graphics on the page. In this sense, mailing a Web page is similar to saving a Web page in a file.

To mail a Web page, click on **File** in the menu bar and select **Mail Document**. A window pops up in which you indicate where you want to send the email, the subject, and anything else you'd like to write or include. The URL for the current Web page is automatically included in the message. You can send the page (either text or source) as an ***attachment*** to the email, or you can send it quoted (as text) in the body of the message. If you find something on a page that you want to share with others, it might be appropriate to mail them the URL. If they don't have access to a WWW browser, then it would be better to attach or quote the Web page. If you "quote" or copy the Web page text in the body of your message, you can edit the text and send only a portion of the page.

Using a Web Browser with Local Files

You can use a Web browser to view files on a disk on your computer. You don't need the Internet to access these files, called *local files*. It's really convenient to use your Web browser to look at local files—sometimes easier than opening another application or program to view a file. Once you view a file with the Web browser, you can work with it just like any Web page, including printing it or sending it by email. This is also a convenient way to check Web pages while they're being developed.

The local file has to be one with which your browser can work. You can't expect it to display a spreadsheet file without a program that lets you work with spreadsheets. On the other hand, you can expect it to work well with a text file or HTML file. The browser will let you view graphics or images if they're stored in GIF (file names end with **.gif**) or JPEG format (file names end with **.jpg**).

These types of files work well, because your browser is already configured to work with such file types. For other types of files, you may have to set some *helper applications* in the preferences section of your browser. When you want to view a file, the browser starts a program called a *viewer* that lets you look at the file's contents. For example, if it's a text file, it's displayed in the window just as it appears. If it's a GIF, then the browser starts a viewer that lets you look at images. If it's an HTML file, the browser displays it by following all the HTML commands. If there is no viewer for your file, Netscape lets you know and gives you a chance to name a viewer for the file. A viewer is more than a program that lets you look at a file. It can also be a program that lets you hear the sound encoded in an audio file.

To view a local file, choose **File** from the menu bar and then select **Open Page**. This will bring up a dialog box, as shown in Figure 2.3. When that happens, you can type in the file name. Alternately, you can browse through your files. Click on **Choose File** until you find the one you'd like to view. That opens another dialog box titled **Open**. You can look for files of a specific type or all files by making a choice in the item labeled **Files of type...**.

If the browser can work either directly or through a helper application, it will. If not, a dialog box will appear that lets you associate a helper application with files of that type. If you know the helper application you want to use, fill it in. If not, you may have to ask someone else for assistance.

Here are some places to check on the WWW for helper applications:

- "Windows Helper Applications," Netscape Communications Corporation, Inc., Mountain View, CA, **http:// home.netscape.com/assist/helper_apps/ windows_helpers.html**

- "Learning to Use—Helper Applications," TeamWeb, University of Texas, Austin, TX, **http:// wwwhost.cc.utexas.edu/learn/use/helper.html**

- "WWW Browsers, MIME and Helper Applications," Doug Tower,University of California, San Diego, CA, **http:// ssdc.ucsd.edu/dt/helpers.html**

Using Bookmarks to Keep Track of Resources

You can save links to interesting and useful Web pages by adding hyperlinks to your bookmark list. The bookmark list is the name Netscape gives to the collection of hyperlinks you've saved; each one is like a bookmark into the World Wide Web. Whenever you're using the browser, you can call up your bookmarks and follow any of the links. You'll want to keep adding bookmarks to Web pages as you collect sources for research. Netscape and other Web browsers give you the tools to add, delete, annotate, and rename the bookmarks. You can also arrange them into folders, list them various ways, keep different files of bookmarks, and otherwise manage the collection. We will now go over some of the essential bookmark operations, and you'll see that sometimes there is more than one way to perform each one.

Add a Bookmark

Adding a bookmark means placing a Web page on the bookmark list. The phrase *bookmark a Web page* also means the same thing. Here are various ways to add a bookmark:

- Use the keyboard shortcut $\boxed{\text{Ctrl}}$ + **D**.

- Click the *right* mouse button when the mouse pointer is on the Web page, frame, or hyperlink, and select **Add Bookmark**.

- Click on the Bookmarks icon in the location toolbar and select **Add Bookmark** from the menu.

- Drag and drop: Move the mouse pointer to the Page Proxy icon in the location bar and hold down the left mouse button. Without letting go of the mouse button, drag the icon to the Bookmarks icon. A menu appears. Drag the Page Proxy icon to **Add Bookmark** on the menu and let go of the mouse button. The Web page is added to whatever folder is set to hold new bookmarks. To add a bookmark to any folder, drag the Page Proxy icon to the Bookmarks icon as before and choose **File Bookmarks** from the menu. That brings up a list of the folders in the bookmark list. After you drag the icon to a folder, "drop" it.

Display the Bookmark List

To display the bookmark list in a separate window, do one of the following:

- Use the keyboard shortcut $\boxed{\text{Ctrl}}$ + **B**.

- Click on the Bookmarks icon in the location bar and select **Edit Bookmarks** from the menu. This displays the bookmark list as a menu. You can use the mouse to display a folder or select an item in the list.

Jump to an Item in the Bookmark List

Jumping to an item means going directly to the Web page that the item represents. First display the bookmark list, then move the mouse to the bookmark you want to use and click on it. If the bookmarks are arranged in folders or categories, select a category and then a bookmark.

Delete an Item from the Bookmark List

To remove an entry from the bookmark list, display the bookmark list in a separate window, and click on the item to delete. Once you select an item in this way, you can delete it by pressing the **Delete** key.

Search the Bookmark List

If there are many entries in the bookmark list, you may want to search the list for an entry. First, open the bookmark list in a separate window. Click on **Edit** and then select **Find**. (You can also use the keyboard shortcut **Ctrl** + **F**.) When a dialog box appears, type the word or phrase and click on the button labeled **OK**.

The bookmark list has many features. You'll learn how to take advantage of them after gaining experience and feeling comfortable with the bookmark list. We'll go over a few features in the next activity.

Activity 2.2   Working with the Bookmark List

Overview

In this activity, we'll add items to the bookmark list. Then, we'll create a folder or category and add some items to it. When the bookmark list is displayed in its own window (see Figure 2.5), the commands for working with the list are all available through the window's menu bar. Here are a few things you can do from the pulldown menus:

- Insert a new bookmark, new folder, or new separator.
- Import a bookmark file.
- Save the current bookmark list to a file from the **File** menu.
- Cut, copy, paste, delete, or find items in the list.
- Access **Properties** from the **Edit** menu.
- Sort the bookmarks.
- Set the selected folder as the personal toolbar.
- Set the selected folder that will be used to hold new bookmarks.
- Select **Update Bookmarks** from the **View** menu to have Netscape see whether any of the bookmarks have changed since they were last visited.

In this activity, you'll see several different windows without a clear connection of how you get from one to another. That's intentional. We want to concentrate on setting and using bookmarks. The windows that appear here could have come from one session or several sessions.

Details

Suppose you've started your Web browser in the same way as in previous activities and you're browsing the home page for the World Wide Web Virtual Library. A URL for that site is **http://vlib.stanford.edu/Overview.html**. You'll want to add this page to your bookmark list so you can return to it in the future without having to type in the URL or remember the path you took to get there.

❋Do It! Press **Ctrl** + **D** to add the current Web page to the bookmark list.

Suppose that while you're browsing the Virtual Library, you select the category "Archaeology," and then you come upon the Web page "ArchNet: Museums and Research Facilities," **http://archnet.uconn.edu/museums**, shown in Figure 2.16.

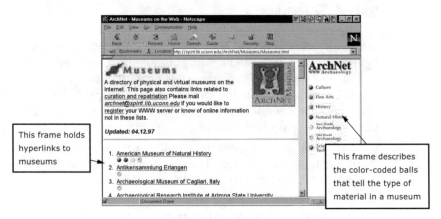

Figure 2.16—ArchNet: Museums and Research Facilities

From here, you visit several museums on the list and add some to the bookmark list. If the bookmark list was empty when we started or had no folders, then the bookmarks are added one after the other. If folders already exist, the new bookmarks are added to the folder that's labeled with a graphic image indicating it is the "new bookmarks" folder. For now, we'll assume that there weren't any folders in the bookmark list.

❋Do It! To view the bookmark list, use the keyboard shortcut **Ctrl** + **B**.

We discussed other ways of viewing the bookmark list in the section before this activity. You may want to try one of those instead.

Figure 2.17 shows the current bookmark list.

Chapter 2

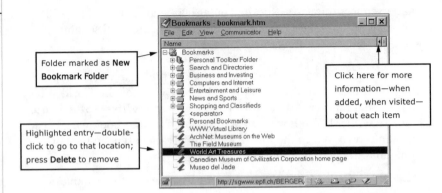

Folder marked as **New Bookmark Folder**

Click here for more information—when added, when visited— about each item

Highlighted entry—double-click to go to that location; press **Delete** to remove

Figure 2.17—Bookmark List

Clicking once on an entry highlights it. To jump to the location specified by the item, double-click on it.

To delete or remove an entry from the bookmark list, highlight it and press the **Delete** key.

To change the name or other information about a bookmark item, select **Properties** from the pulldown menu under **View**. Select or highlight several entries by highlighting one and holding down the **Ctrl** key as you click on others. You can delete a group in the same way as you delete one item. To sort the entries in alphabetical order, highlight a group and choose one of the sort options—**By Name**, **By Location**, **By Created On**, or **By last visited**—from the menu under **View**.

Close the bookmark window by pressing **Ctrl** + **W** or clicking on the **X** in the upper-right corner. The window can stay open while you're doing other things on your computer or on the Internet.

You can add more items any other time you're browsing or working with information on the World Wide Web. At some point, you may want to arrange your bookmarks into categories. Starting with the bookmark list shown in Figure 2.17, we'll add one folder titled Museums and put all the museum sites in that folder. Once the bookmark window is open, do the following steps to create a folder:

❋*Do It!* Click on **File** in the menu bar and select **New Folder**.

Clicking on **New Folder** brings up the window shown in Figure 2.18, except that the first pane shows **New Folder** and the second larger one is empty.

❋*Do It!* Click on the top frame and type **Museums**. Click on the bottom frame and type **Interesting Museums on the World Wide Web**. Click **OK** when you're finished.

Figure 2.18 shows the new folder window with all the information entered. Netscape automatically fills in the date on which this new piece of data was added.

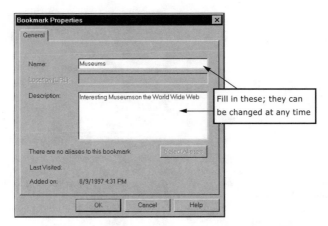

Fill in these; they can be changed at any time

Figure 2.18—Bookmark Properties Window for a Folder

After you click **OK**, the folder is added to the bookmark list as shown in Figure 2.19.

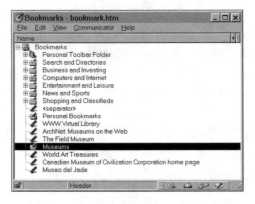

Figure 2.19—Bookmark List with Newly Added Folder "Museums"

You can insert each of the hyperlinks or entries that represent a museum into the new folder by using the "drag and drop" technique we mentioned earlier. Here are the instructions to move the item "The Field Museum" into the folder.

❀*Do It!* Click on **The Field Museum** and hold down the (left) mouse
button. Drag the highlighted entry to the folder called **Museums** and release the button.

Another way to move an item to a folder is to highlight the item, select **Cut** from the **Edit** menu, highlight the folder, and select **Paste** from the **Edit** menu.

After all the entries for museums are placed in the folder, the bookmark list will look as shown in Figure 2.20.

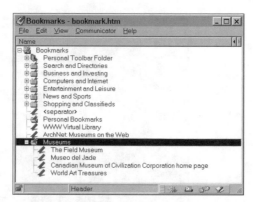

Figure 2.20—Bookmark List Showing Entries in the Folder "Museums"

As we said earlier, there are other things you can do with the bookmark list. Here are some things you may want to try:

- Double-click on the open folder to close it so that only the folder name appears in the list.
- Double-click again to open the folder.
- Move items that aren't in the folder to the bottom of the list in the same way that you added items to the folder.
- Sort the items in the list by highlighting more than one and choosing one of the sort or list options from the **View** menu.

End of Activity 2.2

Activity 2.2 showed how to arrange bookmarks into a folder. Once you start collecting bookmarks, it's a good idea to think about organizing them. You'll also want to think about deleting or discarding bookmarks when you don't need them anymore.

Summary

A Web browser is used to access the information and resources on the World Wide Web. Whenever you start the browser or access a hyperlink, the browser—which is a computer program—sends a request to have a file transferred to it. The browser then interprets the information in the file so that it can be viewed in the browser's window, or in some cases, viewed through another program. For example, if a hyperlink points to a text file, then the file is displayed in the window as ordinary text. If the hyperlink points to a document written in Hypertext Markup Language (HTML), then it's displayed by the browser. If the file is a sound file or an animation, then a program different from the browser is started so the file can be heard or seen. Most of the facilities and capabilities are built into the browser, but in some cases, your computer needs to be equipped with special equipment or programs. A good example of this is when a hyperlink points to a sound file. Your computer needs to have a sound card, speakers, and the software to play the sounds.

Starting a Web browser usually means first activating your connection to the Internet and then clicking on an icon or command to start Netscape Navigator. If the cost of using the Internet depends on how much time is spent being connected, then be sure to terminate the Internet connection when the Web session is over.

The commands you use to work with the Web browser are available through the menu bar, the toolbars (command toolbar, location toolbar, personal toolbar), and the keyboard. These features, along with the scroll bars, stay the same, regardless of what you're viewing or working with on the World Wide Web. The menu bar is a collection of pulldown menus that you can use for almost every operation or command. The **Help** menu lets you select one of several ways to teach yourself about Netscape, including an online manual. The command toolbar has a number of icons that give quick access to some of the commands in the pulldown menu. The **Search** icon displays a list of search services. Several commands are also available as keyboard shortcuts, meaning that you can type them directly on the keyboard instead of using a mouse. The location toolbar gives quick access to URLs and Web sites saved in the bookmark list or in the location field.

The browser lets you access, retrieve, work with, and enjoy the information and resources that make up the World Wide Web. To coin a phrase, the browser is your window to the Web.

Once a page is in the browser's window, you can move around the page using the keyboard, scroll bars, or mouse. You can search for words in the page. Move the mouse to a hyperlink (the pointer turns to a hand) and click on it to follow it. A URL can be typed in the location bar, or you can select a command or icon to open a location. In any of these cases, the browser will follow the URL you've typed or the hyperlink you've clicked on to view another Web page.

The browser keeps track of the sites you've visited during recent sessions. It does this so that you can backtrack and return to sites during a session. The history list holds records of and links to all the sites that you have visited recently. You can collect a set of hyperlinks in a list called the bookmark list. These will be available from one session to the next. The browser contains commands to let you maintain and manage your bookmark list.

Provided you're not breaking copyright laws or conventions, you can save information found on the World Wide Web into a file, print it, or mail it to an Internet address. You can also use the browser to view local files. When you're developing your own Web pages, you may want to use this method to test them before making them available to anyone on the Internet.

Chapter 2

Selected Terms Introduced in This Chapter

attachment	menu bar
bookmark list	plug-in
content area	Point-to-Point-Protocol (PPP)
downloading	scroll bar
frames	search engine
frequently asked questions (FAQ)	Serial Line Internet Protocol (SLIP)
helper application	status line
history list	toolbar

3
Chapter

Using the
World Wide Web
for Research

The World Wide Web has revolutionized the way we do research. Instead of spending hours combing library indexes and catalogs, making endless telephone calls, or traveling to far-off places, with a few clicks of the mouse you can find an enormous amount of information on virtually any subject. The World Wide Web can answer quick reference questions such as "What are the symptoms of decompression sickness?" or "What is the population of Egypt?" It can also help you research deeper subjects such as recycling or congressional campaign contributions in the last election.

In the course of this chapter, you'll see how to find answers to these research and reference questions. We'll provide you with an introduction to research skills on the World Wide Web so that you can begin to go out and find whatever interests you. In later chapters, we will cover research skills in more detail.

The sections in this chapter are as follows:
  * Browsing the World Wide Web: Using Directories
  * Finding Information Gems in Virtual Libraries
  * Searching the World Wide Web: Using Search Engines
  * Using Several Search Engines Simultaneously: Meta-search Tools

You will learn the difference between **browsing** and **keyword searching** the WWW, and you will see examples that focus on each method. You'll discover when it is better to use a **directory** or **subject catalog** (topical lists of selected WWW resources, hierarchically arranged) and when it makes sense to start with a **search engine** (a tool that provides keyword searching ability of all known WWW resources). We will also cover the advantage of using virtual libraries, directories that contain only selected WWW resources. We will discuss employing several search engines simultaneously by using **meta-search tools**. We'll introduce you to a couple of different search engines and take you through the steps of using them.

If you know different tactics for finding information on the WWW, your searches will be more successful. We'll provide activities in this chapter that will give you practice in browsing and keyword searching. Once you learn how to use the WWW to its fullest potential, you will be amazed at what you can locate in a short period of time.

Let's start researching!

Browsing the World Wide Web: Using Directories

There are two basic ways to find information on the World Wide Web: you can browse directories by subject, or you can search by keyword in search engines. In this section, we'll focus on browsing directories; we'll cover keyword searching in search engines later in the chapter. While search engine databases are created by computer programs, directories are created and maintained by people. Directories don't cover the entire Web. In fact, directories are very small collections of resources, compared with the huge databases that search engines employ.

Browsing directories can be a very effective way to find the resources you need, especially if you need general information on a subject, such as recycling. If you are at the beginning of your research, or if you are searching for an overview of the topic at hand, it may also be helpful to use a directory. Many of the major search tools contain a directory and a search engine. Using these you can try both methods in one service. The directory part of the search engine is usually a subset of the entire database, and the sites listed in a directory are often evaluated, summarized, and given ratings. Some directories provide rudimentary search interfaces as well. Here are the most well-known directories on the World Wide Web:

- Galaxy
  http://galaxy.einet.net
- Infoseek
  http://www.infoseek.com
- LookSmart
  http://www.looksmart.com

❅ Lycos TOP 5 %
http://point.lycos.com/categories

❅ Magellan Web Reviews
http://www.mckinley.com

❅ NetGuide
http://www.netguide.com

❅ WebCrawler Channels
http://www.webcrawler.com

❅ Yahoo!
http://www.yahoo.com

Directories, or subject catalogs, are topical lists of selected Web resources that are arranged in a hierarchical way. By *hierarchical*, we mean that the ***subject categories*** are arranged from broadest to most specific. For example, the following is a ***hierarchy***:

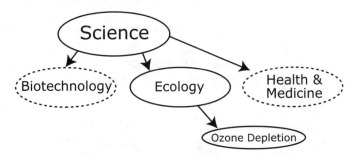

In this example, *Ecology* is a subcategory of *Science*, and *Ozone Depletion* is a subcategory of *Ecology*.

In a hypertext environment, such as the World Wide Web, browsing from one subject to a more detailed part of that subject is quite simple. We click on **Science**, which is the ***top-level category*** or heading, and the computer screen fills with a list of subject categories that are narrower than *Science*. This might include, for example, *Biotechnology*, or *Health & Medicine*, or, in our case, *Ecology*.

When we click on **Ecology**, the screen fills with even more subject categories, and we choose the subject we want, which is *Ozone Depletion*. In this case, the hierarchy ends here. After we choose **Ozone Depletion**, the screen fills in with a list of Web pages that we can now choose by clicking on their titles. This process is referred to as a ***structured browse***.

Some hierarchies have several levels, whereas others have only two. It depends on the directory you are using and the subject you are researching. None of the major directories use the same subject categories. In one directory, the term may be *Environment*; in another, the term may be *Ecology*.

In Chapter 1, we browsed Yahoo!, one of the most comprehensive directories on the World Wide Web. (We'll do more in Yahoo! in Chapter 4, "Directories and Virtual Libraries.") To illustrate the process of browsing in a detailed way, let's try an activity that will take you through a sample research problem in a different directory. We'll show you how easy it is to move from a broad subject category to a more specific one. We'll illustrate why browsing for information using directories can be a very satisfying way to do research on the WWW. In this activity, as in all the activities in the book, we'll give you a numbered list of each of the steps to follow and include the results you would have seen at the time this book was written.

 Tip

Remember that the Web is always changing and that your results may differ from those shown here. Don't let this confuse you. The activities demonstrate fundamental skills. These skills don't change, even though the number of results obtained or the actual screens may look very different.

Activity 3.1   ## Using a Directory to Browse for Information

Overview

In this activity, we'll access the search tool Magellan, **http://www.mckinley.com**, and use its directory to find resources on alternative energy. Magellan is a search tool that includes a search engine and a directory. You can access the directory by using the top-level subject headings that appear in Web Reviews. Web Reviews are collections of Web resources arranged by subject. The resources included in Web Reviews are each given an annotation and are rated using a four-star system. Web Reviews contains a small portion of the 50 million Web sites covered by the Magellan database. After we locate some links to alternative energy information by browsing Magellan's Web Reviews, we'll show you how to bookmark one of the useful resources we find.

We'll follow these steps:
1. Start the Web browser.
2. Go to the home page for Magellan.
3. Browse the Web Reviews directory.
4. Bookmark it!
5. End the session.

Don't forget to practice using the **Back** and **Forward** buttons to avoid losing your place.

Details

1   Start the Web browser.

✱*Do It!* Double-click on the **Netscape** icon.

2   Go to the home page for Magellan.

✱*Do It!* Point to the location field and click the (left) mouse button.

The URL of the current Web page will change color. Now you can type in the URL for Magellan.

✱*Do It!* Type **http://www.mckinley.com** in the location field and press `Enter`.

3   Browse the Web Reviews portion of Magellan.

Take a look at the list of subjects in Web Reviews, as shown in Figure 3.1.

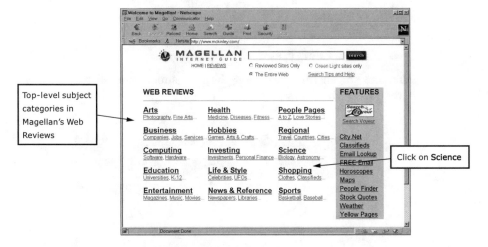

Figure 3.1—Web Reviews by Magellan

To access any of the resources in Web Reviews, you need to click on a top-level category. This will bring to your screen all kinds of resources available in that subject area. Since the types of resources we're looking for focus on alternative energy, we need to find a subject category that would be related to this. A logical choice is **Science**, since energy is usually studied as a physical science. Follow these steps:

✱*Do It!* Click on **Science**.

After the screen fills, you'll see more detailed subject categories, or *subcategories*, appear on your screen. If you scroll down a bit, you'll find that there are several reviewed Web sites listed. These are resources that have been placed in the general Science category. See Figure 3.2.

Chapter 3

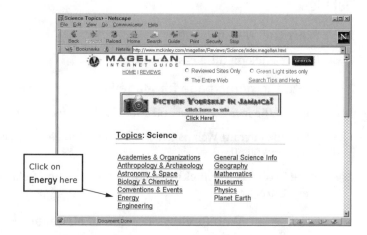

Figure 3.2—Subcategories Listed Under Science in Magellan's Web Reviews

To retrieve alternative energy Web sites, you'll need to click on a more specific subject category. The most logical one is **Energy**.

❋*Do It!* Click on **Energy**, as shown in Figure 3.2.

After the screen fills, note that the first subcategory listed is called **Alternative Energies**, as shown in Figure 3.3. There is another subcategory listed as well.

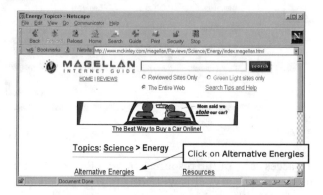

Figure 3.3—Subcategories of Energy in Magellan's Web Reviews

❋*Do It!* Click on **Alternative Energies**, as shown in Figure 3.3.

Figure 3.4 shows some of the alternative energy resources listed in Magellan's Web Reviews. The first one on the list, **Alternative Energy Engineering**, has received a four-star rating from the directory management at Magellan. Let's go ahead and open it.

❋*Do It!* Click on **Alternative Energy Engineering**, as shown in Figure 3.4.

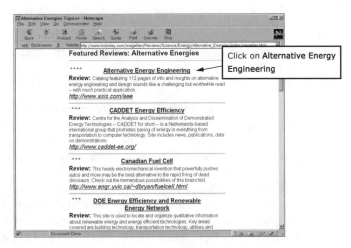

Figure 3.4—List of Resources in the Alternative Energies Subcategory

4   Bookmark it!

After you've found this great site, you may want to return to it again someday, so let's put it in your bookmark list.

✿*Do It!* Simply click on **Bookmarks** in the location toolbar and select **Add Bookmark**.

The title of the URL is automatically added to your bookmark list.

5   End the session.

You can end the session now, or you can stay online to do the next activity.

✿*Do It!* To end the session now, click on **File** in the menu bar and select **Exit** from the pulldown menu.

✿ Tip

Several times throughout this book we'll be asking you to make bookmarks to save the URL locations of valuable Web pages. You'll need to know how to delete bookmarks, especially if you're using a public computer. Follow these steps:

✿   Click on **Bookmarks** (which is located on the location toolbar in Netscape).

✿   Select **Edit Bookmarks**.

✿   Highlight the bookmark you want to delete by pointing to it.

✿   Click on **Edit** and drag the pointer to **Delete** and let go, or press the Delete key.

This should delete the bookmark. See Activity 2.2 for more information about bookmarks.

End of Activity 3.1

In this activity, we looked for an alternative energy resource by browsing a directory. In Magellan's Web Reviews, we started out by clicking on the top-level category **Science**, then we selected the subcategory **Energy**, and finally, **Alternative Energies**, to take us to our desired location. There, we found a list of several relevant resources. Each directory on the World Wide Web will approach a subject differently. For example, in LookSmart, **http://www.looksmart.com**, resources on alternative energies would be found using a completely different subject hierarchy. In LookSmart, the hierarchy looks like this:

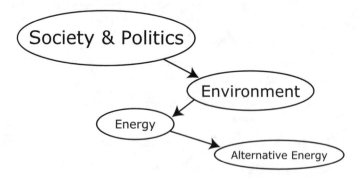

Browsing Versus Searching a Directory

It may be helpful to think of browsing a directory on the Web as similar to going through subjects in a card catalog. You may find exactly what you are looking for by browsing through many pages or cards filled with information, but then again, you may not. You may miss some related information, because your subject may appear in many different categories. For example, alternative energy resources appear in a subcategory of the Science category in Magellan's Web Reviews, but there are also resources on solar and other energies in a subcategory of the Life & Style category. Browsing a directory requires that you think categorically about the subject you are researching. You have to be careful about the direction in which you are going when you do a structured browse. Many directories have simple keyword-searching ability for just this reason. Keyword searching was created to help people find information without having to know ahead of time the category in which the information lies. Keyword searching helps us find Web information more quickly, just as computerized library catalogs have helped us find books more quickly.

If you don't want to take the time to browse categories in a directory, you may want to search the directory by keyword. Or you can do both. It is a good idea to use different tactics when looking for something on the Web. Keep in mind, however, that when you search most directories by keyword, you will find Web pages that have the word or words that you are searching for in their titles, annotations, or URLs, not in the Web pages themselves. In the next section, which focuses on virtual libraries, we'll explain how to search a directory using keywords.

Finding Information Gems in Virtual Libraries

Virtual libraries are directories that contain collections of resources that librarians or *cybrarians* have carefully chosen and organized in a logical way. The resources you find in a virtual library have been selected and placed there because of their excellence and usefulness. The Web pages included are usually evaluated by someone knowledgeable in that field. Typically, virtual libraries provide an organizational hierarchy with subject categories to facilitate browsing. Most include query interfaces in order to perform simple searches. Virtual libraries are great places to begin your research.

Here are several of the best-known virtual libraries on the Web:

- Argus Clearinghouse
  http://www.clearinghouse.net
- INFOMINE
  http://lib-www.ucr.edu
- Internet Public Library
  http://www.ipl.org
- Librarians' Index to the Internet
  http://sunsite.berkeley.edu/internetindex
- World Wide Web Virtual Library
  http://vlib.stanford.edu/Overview.html

The main difference between virtual libraries and the directories we discussed earlier in the chapter is that virtual libraries are much smaller, because the resources included are selected very carefully. The people who organize virtual libraries are usually on the lookout for three major types of information: *subject guides*, *reference works*, and *specialized databases*.

Subject Guides

A *subject guide* is a Web resource devoted to including hyperlinks to most, if not all, Web pages on a particular subject. For example, a resource devoted to listing Web pages on environmental ethics is a subject guide (see Figure 3.5).

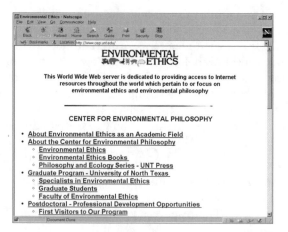

Figure 3.5—Subject Guide on Environmental Ethics

Reference Works

Another common type of resource collected by virtual libraries is reference works. A *reference work* is a full-text document with self-contained information. In other words, it doesn't necessarily contain hyperlinks to other resources.

A reference work on the World Wide Web is very similar to its print counterpart. A dictionary on the Web would look very much like a dictionary on a reference shelf. The only difference is that it would allow you to move around the document using hyperlinks instead of turning pages and looking in the index for related topics. There are encyclopedias, handbooks, dictionaries, directories, and many other types of reference works on the World Wide Web. Virtual libraries are also interested in including these types of works in their directories. Figure 3.6 pictures a reference work—the U.S. Postal Service's "Zip Code Lookup and Address Information."

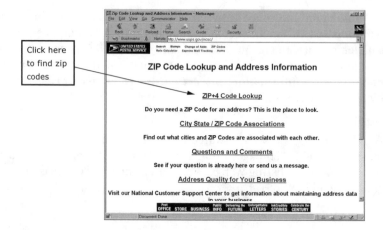

Figure 3.6—U.S. Postal Service's "Zip Code Lookup and Address Information"

Specialized Databases

Virtual libraries can be useful for finding *specialized databases* as well. A specialized database is an index that catalogs certain material, such as patent information, medical journal article citations, company financial data, court decisions, and so forth. Specialized databases can usually be searched by keyword. We'll discuss them in detail in Chapter 7. Figure 3.7 shows a specialized database—the IBM Patent Server.

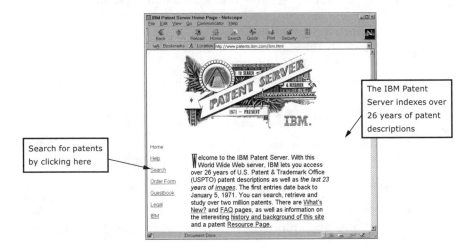

Figure 3.7—The IBM Patent Server

Now that you know what types of information are collected in virtual libraries, we'll show you how to find these information gems. Let's do an activity to illustrate how useful virtual libraries can be for your research.

Activity 3.2   Finding Resources in a Virtual Library

Overview

In the beginning of this chapter, we mentioned several research and reference questions to which the World Wide Web can provide answers. One of those questions was "What is the population of Egypt?" We will find the answer to this question by using the Internet Public Library (IPL), a virtual library maintained by librarians at the University of Michigan.

The IPL is organized much like a traditional library. It has a reference section, a youth section, and many others. If you can't find what you're looking for, you can submit the question to a real librarian who will email the answer back to you. You can browse the IPL or search its contents. Browsing is the easiest way to find information, however, because the search tool doesn't search the contents of the resources, only the titles of the resources and annotations attached to them.

In this activity, we'll first browse the IPL by subject. Because we're trying to find an answer to a reference question, we'll open the Reference Collection. Then we'll go to the Geography section, as the population of Egypt would likely be found in a geographic resource. We'll also open a reference work and look for the statistic we want by using the Find option in Netscape Navigator. After this, we'll show how to perform a keyword search in order to demonstrate the difference between searching and browsing in the IPL. We'll follow these steps:

1. Go to the home page for the Internet Public Library.
2. Open the Reference Collection.
3. Browse the Reference Collection.
4. Open *The World Factbook*.
5. Find the population of Egypt.
6. Search the Reference Collection.
7. Browse the results of the search.
8. End the session.

You'll see how quickly we can find not only the population of Egypt, but also other current information about that country. Let's get started!

Details

1   Go to the home page for the Internet Public Library. (We're assuming your Web browser is already started.)

❋*Do It!* Use the mouse to point to the location field and click the (left) mouse button.

The URL of the current Web page will change color. Now you can type in the URL for the Internet Public Library.

❋*Do It!* Type **http://www.ipl.org** in the location field and press Enter.

2   Open the Reference Collection.

❋*Do It!* First, click on **Reference** under the **Collections** heading.

Your screen will fill with a picture of a traditional library, complete with a reference librarian sitting at a desk, as shown in Figure 3.8.

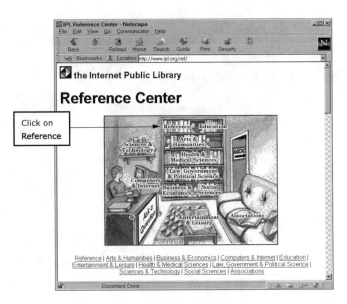

Figure 3.8—The Internet Public Library Reference Center

✿*Do It!* Click on **Reference** on the Reference Center page as shown in Figure 3.8.

3 Browse the Reference Collection.

✿*Do It!* After your screen fills, move down the list of subdivisions in the Reference section.

✿*Do It!* Click on **Geography**.

Why geography? This is a logical subcategory to look under to find information on population. After your screen fills, scroll down the list to find the most appropriate source that would contain the answer to this question. By reading the annotations attached to the reference sources, we determine that *The World Factbook 1997* would be a good choice, because it provides "quick facts on countries of the world." *The World Factbook*, authored and published by the U.S. Central Intelligence Agency, is updated annually. It's also available in printed form.

4 Open *The World Factbook*.

✿*Do It!* Click on **The World Factbook 1997**, as shown in Figure 3.9.

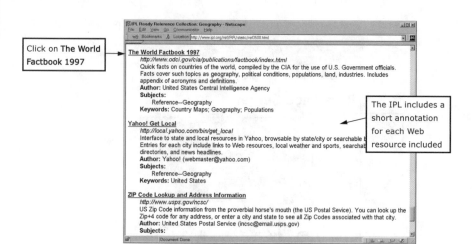

Click on **The World Factbook 1997**

The IPL includes a short annotation for each Web resource included

Figure 3.9—Geography Resources Listed in the Internet Public Library

Your screen will fill with several hyperlinks.

❀*Do It!* Click on **Countries**.

The screen that loads will be split into two frames. You'll need to scroll down the left frame to find the link for Egypt.

❀*Do It!* Click on **Egypt**.

Your screen should look like the one pictured in Figure 3.10.

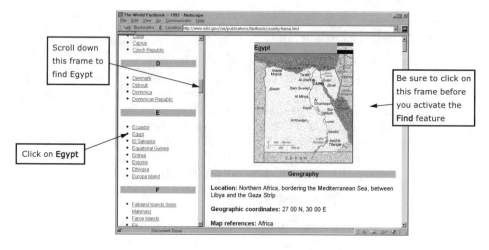

Scroll down this frame to find Egypt

Click on **Egypt**

Be sure to click on this frame before you activate the **Find** feature

Figure 3.10—Egypt in The World Factbook

5   Find the population of Egypt.

You could scroll down through the chapter on Egypt until you found population and other demographic statistics in the People section. Or you could follow these steps to find the population more quickly:

Do It! Point your mouse to **Edit** in the Netscape menu bar and choose **Find in Frame** (make sure you have clicked with your mouse on the right frame before you do this).

Do It! Type **population** in the pane next to **Find what**.

Do It! Click on **Find Next**.

This command will take you right to the statistic you want, as shown in Figure 3.11.

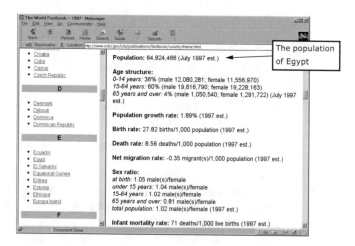

Figure 3.11—Demographic Information for Egypt from The World Factbook

6   Search the Reference Collection.

Now we'll show you how to search the Internet Public Library. We're going to type in the word **Egypt** first.

Do It! Click on the **Back** icon in the Netscape toolbar at the top of your screen until you are at the page that lists the resources in Geography.

At the bottom of the page, there is a form that you can use to do a search. You'll be searching only those Web pages in the IPL's Reference Collection.

Do It! Type in the word **Egypt** in the form provided. Click **Search**.

The search tool responds with some Web pages, but none of them is *The World Factbook*.

Do It! Highlight **Egypt** and try typing in **populations**, as shown in Figure 3.12. Click **Search**.

We may be tempted to type in *population* (without an *s* at the end), but if we go back and look at the annotation for *The World Factbook* in Figure 3.9, we notice that the word used is *populations*, not *population*.

Chapter 3

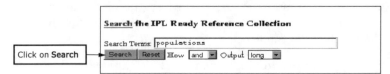

Click on **Search**

Figure 3.12—Searching the Reference Collection

7 Browse the results of the search.

The search tool responds with a collection of URLs that may be useful. Move down the list until you notice *The World Factbook*.

8 End the session.

You can end the session now, or you can stay online to do the next activity.

✷*Do It!* To end the session now, click on **File** in the menu bar and select **Exit** from the menu.

End of Activity 3.2

You can see from the preceding example that sometimes it is better to browse than to search a directory or virtual library. The search tool in the Internet Public Library doesn't find words that are in the body of the Web pages. The words indexed are in the Web pages' titles, their URLs, and their annotations. Because the word *Egypt* didn't appear in the title, URL, or annotation of *The World Factbook*, the search tool didn't locate it. We also pointed out that if we had typed *population* instead of *populations*, we wouldn't have had *The World Factbook* in the list of results.

Directories can be useful if you have a broad subject and aren't sure how to narrow down the search. They are also helpful if you want to get a general idea about existing resources that will help you focus your topic. By browsing a directory in the first activity, we quickly found Web pages that focused on alternative energy.

Virtual libraries are especially useful as starting points for research on a particular topic or as places to go for answers to quick reference questions. But if you want to zero in quickly on Web pages that are specifically related to your topic, or if your topic is multifaceted or extremely detailed, or if you are sure about the keywords you are going to use, a search engine is what you need. In the following sections, we'll explore search engines and give a brief overview of the most common keyword search features.

Searching the World Wide Web: Using Search Engines

Search engines are tools that use computer programs called *spiders* and *robots* to gather information automatically on the Internet. With this information, they create databases.

Spiders are computer programs that go out on the Internet and locate hyperlinks that are available to the public, such as WWW and *Gopher* documents. These spiders, or robots as they are commonly called, load these resources in a database, which you can then search by using a search engine. These spider, or robot, programs were created because the number of Internet documents increases so rapidly that people can't keep up with indexing them manually. Each of the major search engines attempts to do the same thing—namely, index as much of the entire Web as possible—so they handle a huge amount of data.

There are advantages to computer-generated databases. They are frequently updated, give access to very large collections, and provide the most comprehensive search results. If you are looking for a specific concept or phrase, a search engine is the best place to start. And you would be smart to look in more than one, because each engine gives different results.

Here are the major search engines:

AltaVista	**http://www.altavista.digital.com**
Excite	**http://www.excite.com**
HotBot	**http://www.hotbot.com**
Infoseek	**http://www.infoseek.com**
Lycos	**http://www.lycos.com**
Northern Light	**http://www.northernlight.com**
WebCrawler	**http://www.webcrawler.com**

 Tip

Finding search engines and other databases on the World Wide Web.

If you want to look for other search tools on the World Wide Web, or want to keep up-to-date with the new ones that have been added, there are two excellent places to go:

All-in-One Search Page	**http://www.albany.net/allinone**
The Internet Sleuth	**http://www.isleuth.com**

Both of these sites provide access to many databases and are usually referred to as *meta-search tools*, or more specifically, *all-in-one search tools*. We'll discuss these and similar services later in the chapter.

Search Engine Similarities

All of the major search engines are similar in that you enter keywords, phrases, or proper names in a ***search form***. After you click on **search**, **submit**, **seek**, or some other command button, the database returns a collection of hyperlinks to your screen.

The database usually lists them according to their ***relevance*** to the keyword(s) you typed in, from most to least relevant. Search engines determine relevance in different ways. Generally, they base this determination on how many times the search terms appear in the document.

All search engines have online help to acquaint you with their search options. Two common search options that most search engines support are ***Boolean searching*** and ***phrase searching***. We will briefly discuss these two options below. Then, in Chapter 5, "Search Strategies for Search Engines," we will cover these and other search options, which are available on many (but not all) search engines, including *relevancy ranking*, *field searching*, *truncation searching*, and *proximity searching*.

Boolean Operators

The Boolean operators are AND, OR, and NOT.

❀ The use of AND placed between keywords in your ***search expression*** will narrow the search results.

For example, *hiking AND camping* would narrow your search so that you would receive only those sites that have both the words *hiking* and *camping* in them.

❀ Placing an OR between keywords broadens your search results. For example, *hiking OR camping* would retrieve those sites that have either the word *hiking* or the word *camping* in them.

hiking AND camping   *hiking OR camping*

❀ The NOT operator will also narrow the search.

For example, *hiking NOT camping* would narrow your search so you would get all hiking that did not include camping.

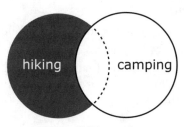

hiking NOT camping

❋ In some search engines, if nothing is typed between two words, you can assume an OR is between them. This is what we'd refer to as a default setting.

In order to override this setting, you'd either have to type AND between the words or put a **+** before both words.

Phrase Searching

❋ Searching by phrase guarantees that the words you type in will appear adjacent to each other, in the order you typed them.

❋ Let's say you are searching for information on global warming. If you typed in the two words *global warming* separated by a space, the system you're using may assume that you are in effect saying *global AND warming*, or in some cases (depending on the search engine), *global OR warming*. In the last case, your search results would not be very precise, because the words *global* and *warming* could appear separately from each other throughout the document.

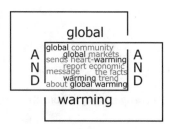

global AND warming

global OR warming

❋ Most search engines support phrase searching, requiring the use of double quotation marks around the phrase. We would type *global warming* in our example.

Chapter 3

Search Engine Differences

The major search engines differ in the following ways:

- Size of the index.
- Search options (many search engines support the same options but require you to use different *syntax* in order to initiate them).
- Speed.
- Update frequency.
- Relevance of the search results.
- Overall ease of use.

It is important to know these differences, because in order to do an exhaustive search of the World Wide Web, you must be familiar with the different search tools. You cannot rely on a single search engine to satisfy every query.

At this point it may be helpful to do a couple of activities to illustrate how search engines work. The first activity will focus on Boolean searching, and the second on phrase searching.

Activity 3.3 | ## Using Boolean Search Operators

Overview

Let's try to find Web pages on recycling plastic products. We'll use the search engine WebCrawler, which was one of the first to appear on the Web. To start, we will type in the keywords we want the Web pages to include. We'll examine the results and then check the help screen to find out how WebCrawler handles advanced search options. Then we'll do the search again using Boolean operators. We'll note how our search results were narrowed in size and how the contents of the pages were more relevant.

We'll follow these steps:

1. Go to the home page for WebCrawler.
2. Type in keywords and start the search.
3. Examine the search results.
4. Consult search help.
5. Modify the search by typing in a new search expression.
6. Examine the results.
7. End the session.

Ready? Let's start the engine!

Details

1   Go to the home page for WebCrawler. (We're assuming your Web browser is already started.)

❋*Do It!* Use the mouse to point to the location field and click the (left) mouse button.

The URL of the current Web page will change color. Now you can type in the URL for WebCrawler.

❋*Do It!* Type **http://www.webcrawler.com** in the location field and press ⌈**Enter**⌋.

2 Type in keywords and start the search.

❋*Do It!* Type the keywords **recycling plastic products** in the search form next to **Search**.

❋*Do It!* Now click on the **Search** button. Figure 3.13 shows the keywords typed in.

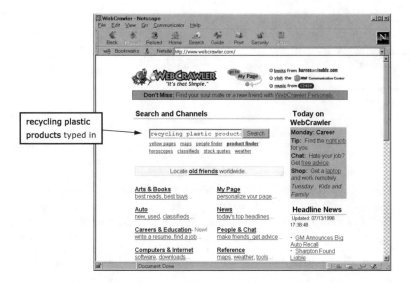

Figure 3.13—WebCrawler Home Page with Keywords Typed In

3 Examine the search results.

Notice the large number of hyperlinks retrieved by WebCrawler. They are listed according to their relevance to the search query, from most relevant to least relevant. After scrolling down and checking out some of the Web pages retrieved by this search, we start to think of other possibilities. What if there are some perfect hyperlinks out there that use the word *plastics* instead of *plastic*? How would we construct a search so we would get Web pages that included the words *recycling* and *products* and *plastics* or *plastic*? We're identifying the need to use Boolean operators, and we need to know whether WebCrawler supports Boolean searching. We hope that by using Boolean operators, we'll retrieve not only more relevant results but also fewer results. We could most easily find out whether WebCrawler supports Boolean searching by accessing its online help.

4 Consult search help.

✸*Do It!* Click on the **help** button on the upper right of the screen.

A partial list of the search help topics appears in Figure 3.14.

✸*Do It!* Click on **Advanced Searching**, as shown in Figure 3.14.

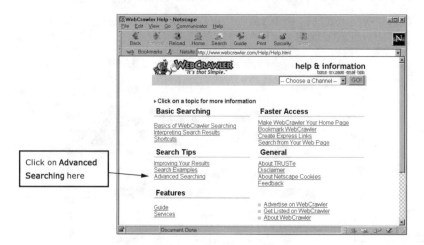

Click on **Advanced Searching** here

Figure 3.14—Help Topics in WebCrawler

We discover that WebCrawler does support Boolean searching. We can use AND, OR, and NOT. Farther down on the "Advanced Searching" page, we also learn that if there are ANDs and ORs in one search statement, then parentheses must be used to guarantee good search results.

✸*Do It!* Click on the **WebCrawler** icon at the top left of the screen.

You should now be back on the WebCrawler home page.

5 Modify the search by typing in a new search expression.

✸*Do It!* Type **recycling and products and (plastic or plastics)**, as shown in Figure 3.15.

This search expression will retrieve hyperlinks to those sites that have the words *recycling* AND *products* (must have both words) AND *plastic* OR *plastics* (must have either one).

✸*Do It!* Click on **Search**.

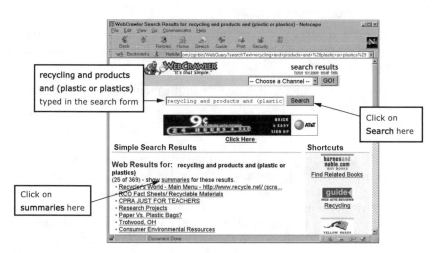

recycling and products and (plastic or plastics) typed in the search form

Click on **Search** here

Click on **summaries** here

Figure 3.15—Boolean Searching in WebCrawler

6   Examine the results.

Take a few minutes and explore the first Web pages retrieved. Notice that we received significantly fewer results by using the Boolean search operators.

❊*Do It!* To read the summaries or annotations of the Web pages, click on **summaries**, as shown in Figure 3.15.

Figure 3.16 shows the results with summaries, or annotations, attached. Note that you can also click on **Similar Pages** at the end of each annotation. This will lead you to other pages that are related to this particular page.

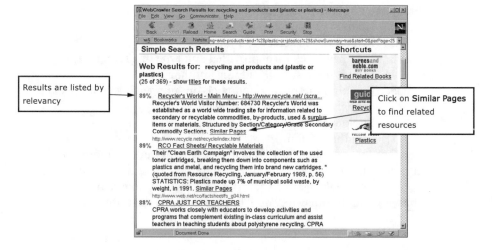

Results are listed by relevancy

Click on **Similar Pages** to find related resources

Figure 3.16—Hyperlinks to Recycling Plastics Information in WebCrawler

Chapter 3

7   End the session.

Wasn't that easy? Let's end this session and do another activity. You can stay online and continue to the next activity or end this session now.

❋*Do It!* To disconnect, click on **File** in the menu bar and select **Exit** from the menu.

End of Activity 3.3

In the last activity, we illustrated the importance of looking at a search engine's online help screen. This caused us to type in the search expression that gave us the most precise and relevant results. In the following activity, we'll use another search engine to show the phrase-searching feature. At the beginning of the chapter, we mentioned that the World Wide Web can help us find the answer to the question "What are the symptoms of decompression sickness?" We're going to look for that answer now by using the search engine Infoseek, **http://www. infoseek.com**. Infoseek is one of the more popular search engines. It also includes a browsable directory.

Activity 3.4   Using Phrase Searching to Find Information

Overview

In this activity, we will open Infoseek and look at the online help before we begin searching. We will type in the phrase *decompression sickness*, start the search, and then narrow the results to those which have the term *symptoms* included. We'll use the syntax that is particular to Infoseek and we will examine the results. We'll have you bookmark the best site we find so that you can start building your own reference library. We'll follow these steps:

1. Go to the home page for Infoseek.
2. Read the help screens in Infoseek.
3. Use the search form provided and type in a search expression.
4. Search the results by adding another term.
5. Examine the results and click on a hyperlink that appears to have the information you need.
6. Bookmark it!
7. End the session.

Once you see how easy it is to find an answer to a reference question on the World Wide Web, you may never want to comb through books or journals again. And after you make a bookmark to the site that provides the answer, you'll be able to flip to the information whenever you need it in a few seconds. Let's go find it!

Details

1   Go to the home page for Infoseek. (We assume your browser is already open.)

❋*Do It!* Use the mouse to point to the location field and click the (left) mouse button.

The URL of the current Web page will change color. Now you can type in the URL for Infoseek.

❋*Do It!* Type **http://www.infoseek.com** in the location field and press **Enter**.

2   Read the help screens in Infoseek.

❋*Do It!* Click on **Tips**, as shown in Figure 3.17.

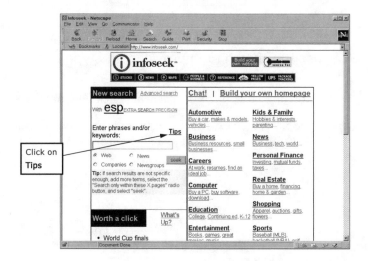

Figure 3.17—Infoseek Home Page

❋*Do It!* After your screen fills, click on **Quick Reference**.

Your screen should look like the one in Figure 3.18.

Notice that in Infoseek, you must place quotation marks before the first word and after the last word in the phrase you are searching for. This will ensure that the words in the phrase appear together. Note that you should also put a + before required words or phrases.

Chapter 3

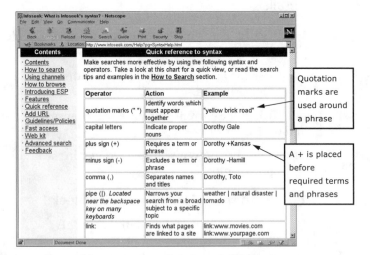

Figure 3.18—Infoseek Help

3 **Use the search form provided and type in a search expression.**

❈*Do It!* Scroll up to the top of the page and click on **Infoseek**.

❈*Do It!* Type the search expression **+ "decompression sickness"** in the search form provided and click on **seek**, as shown in Figure 3.19.

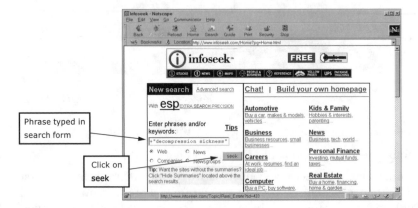

Figure 3.19—Phrase Searching in Infoseek

4 **Search the results by adding another term.**

Figure 3.20 shows the top of the screen where Infoseek indicates the number of results from this search. Infoseek provides the feature of being able to search only the results of your original search. This makes it easy for you to narrow your results. For example, in this activity, an appropriate word to add to our search expression might be *symptoms*. Let's try combining this word with the search results.

❁*Do It!* Type **symptoms** in the search form and click on the radio button next to **Search only within these 682 pages**, as shown in Figure 3.20.

❁*Do It!* Click on **seek**.

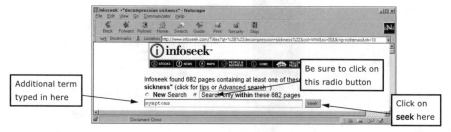

Figure 3.20—Search Results in Infoseek

5 Examine the results and click on a hyperlink that appears to have the information you need.

Your screen should look like the one pictured in Figure 3.21. The first Web page is the section of *The Merck Manual* that deals with the symptoms and signs of decompression sickness. *The Merck Manual* is a well-respected work published by Merck & Company. Let's take a look at it.

❁*Do It!* Click on **THE MERCK MANUAL - DECOMPRESSION SICKNESS;Symptoms and Signs**, as shown in Figure 3.21.

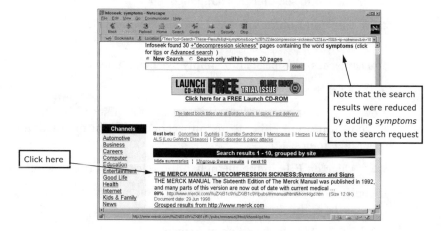

Figure 3.21—Results of Modified Search in Infoseek

A portion of this Web page is shown in Figure 3.22. It appears to be exactly what we're looking for.

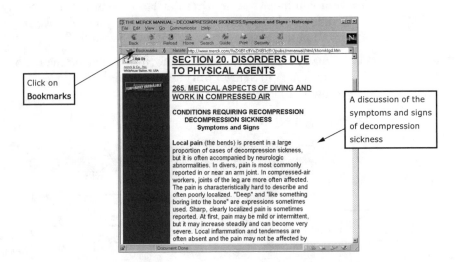

Click on
Bookmarks

A discussion of the
symptoms and signs
of decompression
sickness

Figure 3.22—Symptoms of Decompression Sickness

6   Bookmark it!

After finding this informative Web page, you may want to locate it again quickly, so let's put it in your bookmark list.

✸*Do It!* Point your mouse to **Bookmarks** in the location toolbar and click, as shown in Figure 3.22.

✸*Do It!* Point your mouse to **Add Bookmark** and click.

The URL's title is automatically added to your bookmark list. You can check the list to see that this happened.

✸*Do It!* Click on **Bookmark** again and see that the title of the location is there.

You can access this page later simply by clicking on it.

7   End the session.

Now that we've explored another dimension of searching the World Wide Web, it's time either to disconnect or to go to the next activity and cover new topics.

✸*Do It!* Click on **File** in the menu bar and select **Exit** from the menu.

If you're not using your own computer, you may want to delete your bookmarks at this time.

End of Activity 3.4

In this activity, we focused on the phrase-searching feature. Most search engines support this feature. You can see how important it is. Imagine if we were only able to search for decompression sickness without specifying that the two words appear next to each other in that order. We might get pages that had the word *decompression* in the first paragraph and *sickness* in the last paragraph, with no relationship between the words. In Chapter 5, we'll discuss this and other search features such as this in more detail.

In the next section, we'll talk about using meta-search tools. These resources allow you to use several search engine databases from the same Web site, or to do so simultaneously.

Using Several Search Engines Simultaneously: Meta-search Tools

We have mentioned the importance of looking in more than one search engine when trying to find relevant Web pages. Each search engine varies in size, indexing structure, update frequency, and search options. It can be confusing and time consuming to do your search in several databases, especially if you have to keep track of all of their differences.

To solve some of these problems, database providers have come up with meta-search tools. If meta-search tools allow you to use several search engines simultaneously, they are often called *parallel search tools* or *unified search interfaces*. Instead of building their own databases, meta-search tools use the major search engines and directories that already exist on the Internet and provide the user with search forms or interfaces for submitting queries to these search tools. Simply by submitting a query, the meta-search tool collects the most relevant sites in each database and sends them to the screen. Some sites merely list World Wide Web search tools with their search forms so you can search one at a time. These are called *all-in-one search tools*. Here are the most popular meta-search tools:

- All-in-One Search Page
  http://www.albany.net/allinone
- Dogpile
  http://www.dogpile.com
- Internet Sleuth
  http://www.isleuth.com
- MetaCrawler
  http://www.metacrawler.com
- SEARCH.COM
  http://www.search.com
- SavvySearch
  http://guaraldi.cs.colostate.edu:2000

The All-in-One Search Page is a service that provides an alphabetical list of Web search engines and directories, along with their search

Chapter 3

forms. Some of the search forms include the option of advanced searching, but some do not. Others offer the option of requesting the number of hits you want returned to you. See an example of the All-in-One Search Page in Figure 3.23.

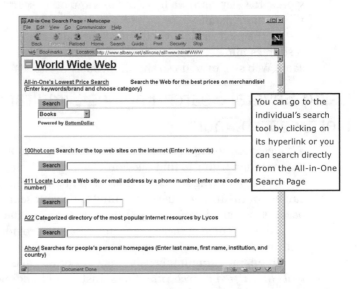

Figure 3.23—All-in-One Search Page

The All-in-One Search Page is a good site for you to find out what different search engines and directories are on the Internet. It's not the best place to learn about the different search tools, because help screens are not included, and not all the options are listed on the search interface form. You may not be able to extract the most relevant sites using All-in-One, because you won't be aware of the best search methods for each database. If, however, you are very familiar with a particular search engine's capabilities, All-in-One would be a good site to have in your bookmark list.

The Internet Sleuth allows you to search one database at a time or several at once. Like the All-in-One Search Page, the other meta-search tools listed won't allow you to use each individual search engine's capabilities to their fullest, because you will be using a search interface to search several databases at once. For this reason, simple searches work best.

It can be interesting to do a search in one of these meta-search tools and to notice what different hyperlinks the various search engines return to you. What is most relevant in one database is not considered as relevant in another. The following example will illustrate how a meta-search tool performs a search in several databases at once. We'll discover how and when these tools can be useful.

Activity 3.5   **Using a Meta-search Tool to Find Information**

Overview

We'll be using SavvySearch, a meta-search tool that includes not only the major Web search indexes and directories, but also indexes Usenet news, people, entertainment, and other topics. SavvySearch, like All-in-One, is available in multiple languages.

In this activity, we'll try to find information on campaign contributions to congressional candidates in the last national election. We want to keep the search simple, because we will be searching several databases at once, and meta-search engines have difficulty performing complicated searches in more than one database at a time. We will be typing in the words *congressional campaign contributions*.

We will take the following steps:

1. Go to the home page for SavvySearch.
2. Type the search expression in the search form.
3. Follow some of the hyperlinks returned by the databases.
4. Bookmark it!
5. End the session.

Let's find out how to use SavvySearch!

Details

1   Go to the home page for SavvySearch.

❀*Do It!* Use the mouse to point to the location field and click the (left) mouse button.

The URL of the current Web page will change color. Now you can type in the URL for SavvySearch.

❀*Do It!* Type **http://guaraldi.cs.colostate.edu:2000** in the location field and press Enter.

❀*Do It!* After the screen fills, click on **Search Form**.

2   Type the search expression in the search form.

SavvySearch supports Boolean searching by providing a pulldown menu under **Query options** and next to **Search for documents containing**, as shown in Figure 3.24. The options are as follows: **all query terms** (AND), **all query terms as a phrase**, and **any query term** (OR). We want all of the words to appear in the Web pages that are returned to us, but the words do not necessarily have to be in a phrase, so make sure **all query terms** is selected. After you select a Boolean operator and type your search terms, SavvySearch will use the search expression you typed in and will search three databases at a time.

❋*Do It!* Type **congressional campaign contributions** in the search form provided.

❋*Do It!* Choose **all query terms** from the pulldown menu located under **Query options**.

❋*Do It!* Click on **SavvySearch!** to start your search.

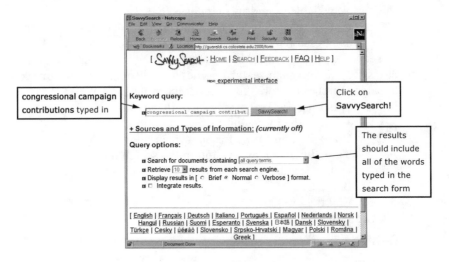

Figure 3.24—SavvySearch with Search Expression Typed In

3 Follow some of the hyperlinks returned by the databases.

After you submit your search expression to SavvySearch, results from three databases will come back and fill your screen. In our case, the three databases are Lycos, Yahoo!, and Infoseek. You may find that three different databases are searched when you do this activity. Look at the results that the services found for you. Notice that the Web pages that Lycos brought to your screen aren't the same ones that the other services generated. This proves that the search services have different ways of determining the relevance of documents that search tools find.

Figure 3.25 shows a portion of the search results. After looking at the results, we decide that the most promising one is first on the Yahoo! list. Although this resource has no title, the annotation describes the page as including political and campaign resources and the CAPWEB guide to the U.S. Congress. If you don't see this resource on your list of results, try to find another Web page that includes congressional campaign information and open it.

❋*Do It!* Click on the first result in the Yahoo! list, as shown in Figure 3.25.

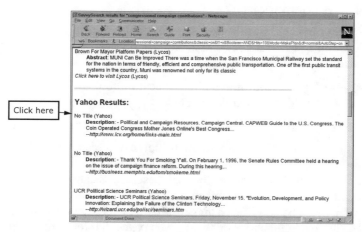

Figure 3.25—Partial Results from SavvySearch

If you scroll down through this page with the heading "Political and Campaign Resources," you'll discover many hyperlinks that will take you to information about different aspects of political campaigns. Take a look at the hyperlinks. Several of them may provide useful information. We'll try opening one of them to see what we can learn about congressional campaign contributions. **Vote Smart Web Project** looks promising. If you don't see **Vote Smart Web Project**, click on another hyperlink that looks useful.

✸*Do It!* Click on **Vote Smart Web Project**, as shown in Figure 3.26.

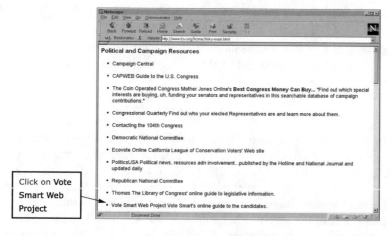

Figure 3.26—The "Political and Campaign Resources" Page

Take a look at this Web page to see what types of information it can provide. If you click on **Candidates & Elected Officials**, you'll find lots of information about campaign finances for each member of Congress.

4   Bookmark it!

Once you've found this great source of information, you don't want to lose track of it. Let's make a bookmark of the site so you can access it easily in the future.

❋*Do It!* Click on **Bookmarks** in the location toolbar. Point your mouse to **Add Bookmark** and click.

The title of the URL has now been added to your bookmark list.

After you've looked through the initial search results that SavvySearch returned, you could then ask the service to search more databases. They are listed at the bottom of the results screen, as shown in Figure 3.27. At this point, feel free to see what the other search engines have to offer, or go back to the earlier results (by clicking on the **Back** icon in the toolbar) and check out other Web pages that look interesting. Note that you can also search through Usenet archives by clicking on the category that has Deja News in it.

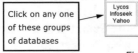

Each cell in the table below represents a parallel search among several internet search engines. The leftmost cell contains the group of search engines most likely to produce useful results and is invoked automatically. If you need more information, select another step, keeping in mind that the steps further to the right will probably produce less relevant results.

Click on any one of these groups of databases →

◻ Search Plan: congressional campaign contributions

Lycos Infoseek Yahoo	excite DejaNews Galaxy	Magellan FTPSearch95 WebCrawler	YellowPages shareware.com LinkStar	PointSearch

Integrate Results

Figure 3.27—SavvySearch's Expanded Search Capability

5   End the session.

When you've finished exploring SavvySearch, you'll want to disconnect from Netscape.

❋*Do It!* Click on **File** in the menu bar and select **Exit** from the menu. If you like, you can delete the bookmarks you've made.

That's all there is to it!

End of Activity 3.5

In this activity, we used SavvySearch. Meta-search tools such as this one can save you time because you can use several search engines or directory databases at once. The major drawback of using meta-search tools is that you can't use the individual databases to their fullest capabilities because the tool has to search more than one database at a time using a search query mechanism that will satisfy all of them. For example, Infoseek doesn't support full Boolean searching, whereas Excite does. In a meta-search tool, the search interface would need to be able to search both databases, so it may not support a feature that one has and the other doesn't have.

Summary

The World Wide Web is an immense collection of valuable information generated by such organizations as universities, corporations, hospitals, associations, and government agencies. Most countries and several languages are represented on the Web. In addition to this, hundreds of thousands of individuals, such as scholars, students, doctors, librarians, teachers, and virtually anyone who wants to contribute to this vast accumulation of resources, are adding their home pages to the Web every day, all over the world.

Finding information on the World Wide Web is becoming easier all the time. There are two basic ways to accomplish it: either you can browse or search directories, or you can search by keyword in search engines. Browsing directories can be a very effective way to find the resources you need, especially if you're sure of the general information you're seeking. Directories index neither all of the pages in the World Wide Web nor all of the words that appear in the Web pages they catalog, however, so if you need specific information, a search engine is the tool you'll want to use. Search engine databases aim to cover the entire Web, and most of them index every word in each Web page.

To illustrate the difference, let's say we wanted to find information on a multifaceted topic, like the regulation of food safety. We may find something about it by browsing in a directory, but we'd have to be sure of the category that included it. Would we look under science, health, or government? We could search the directory using the keywords *food*, *safety*, and *government*, but if these words didn't appear in the categories, Web page titles, or annotations, there would be no results. In a search engine database, by contrast, all we need to do is type *"food safety"* (as a phrase) and *government* in a search form. The search engine will then scan its database, which includes the full text of Web pages from the entire Web, and will return the pages that match the search expression.

A directory would be more likely used if we were looking for general information, for example, resources on the AIDS virus. Directories depend on human beings to create and maintain their collections, with virtual libraries being the most dependent on people. Virtual libraries are the best directories to go to for subject guides and reference works. Virtual libraries are similar to traditional libraries, in that the cybrarians who manage them select and catalog the Web pages that are included in their directories, much as librarians select and catalog materials that are included in their libraries.

Selected Terms Introduced in This Chapter

all-in-one search tool	Gopher
Boolean searching	hierarchy
browsing	keyword searching
directory	meta-search tool

parallel search tool
phrase searching
reference work
relevance
robot
search engine
search expression
search form
specialized database
spider

structured browse
subcategory
subject catalog
subject category
subject guide
syntax
top-level category
unified search interface
virtual library

4
Chapter

Directories and Virtual Libraries

In Chapter 3, "Using the World Wide Web for Research," we introduced different ways to investigate topics using the World Wide Web. One of the ways to find information is to browse directories. Directories, or subject catalogs, are especially useful for those with such general questions like "What resources does the World Wide Web have on the Human Genome Project?" and "What kind of information is available on distance learning?" Directories can also help you find the best resources on a particular topic. For example, they would help with the questions "What are the best sites on the topic of science education?" and "What are the most useful consumer resources on the Web?"

Virtual libraries are the most specialized of all the directories. They are therefore the best places to find sites that collect Internet resources on a particular topic. For example, if you wanted all the Web sites that focus on the Middle East and North Africa, a virtual library would be a good start. In the last chapter, we covered a virtual library—the Internet Public Library. In this chapter, we'll look at another one and show how to use it.

In Chapter 3, we also browsed Magellan's Web Reviews directory for information on alternative energy. In this chapter, we'll cover directories in more detail by discussing features that are common to all directories and by showing how directories can differ from one another. We also will walk you through several activities to show you how best to use directories on the World Wide Web.

The sections in this chapter are as follows:
  * Characteristics of Directories
  * Browsing and Searching Directories
  * Two Major Directories and How to Use Them
  * Virtual Libraries: Directories with a Difference

Chapter 4

Major Directories on the World Wide Web

* Galaxy

   http://galaxy.einet.net

* Infoseek

   http://www.infoseek.com

* LookSmart

   http://www.looksmart.com

* Lycos TOP 5 %

   http://point.lycos.com/categories

* Magellan Web Reviews

   http://www.mckinley.com

* NetGuide

   http://www.netguide.com

* WebCrawler Channels

   http://www.webcrawler.com

* Yahoo!

   http://www.yahoo.com

Characteristics of Directories

Directories are topical lists of Internet resources arranged in a hierarchical way. Although they are meant to be browsed by subject, directories can also be searched by keyword. They differ from search engines in one major way—the human element involved in collecting and maintaining the information. Directories are created and maintained by people, whereas search engines rely on spiders or robots to scour the Internet for links. There are a number of differences between directories. One way to determine directories' particular characteristics is to ask the following questions about each of them:

* Who selects the included Web resources—directory administrators or people in the Internet community?

* Who categorizes the Web pages and sites—the people who submit them or directory administrators?

* How are the results displayed—alphabetically, by relevance, or by type of Web page?

* Are the resources rated? Are they annotated? Are they reviewed?

Each directory differs from others mainly in the level of quality control involved in its management. For example, some directory managers have very little control over their collections, relying on Web page submitters to provide annotations and decisions about where their resource should be placed in the directory's hierarchy. Other directory managers are much more selective not only about which resources they include, but also about where in the subject hierarchy the pages will be located.

Some directory editors write detailed *annotations* of the pages. These annotations can be evaluative, descriptive, or both. Annotations are Web page descriptions that either the Web page submitter or the directory editor attaches to the Web pages. Many annotated directories also rate Web resources using criteria that vary from one directory to another.

There are also directories that are made up of the most popular Web pages found by programs that count how many pages have hyperlinks to these sites. Web pages that are popular may be very different from ones that are rated as excellent.

Of all the directories, virtual libraries rely most on human beings in selecting and controlling the resources included in their collections. Virtual libraries are organized in a way that tames the Internet's chaotic nature and thus attempts to create a more traditional "library-like" setting in which to do research.

The human element involved in creating and maintaining directories creates both advantages and disadvantages for the user. Some of the inherent strengths of directories can be weaknesses, and vice versa. We'll examine some of these strengths and weaknesses here.

Strengths

The major advantages of using directories are as follows:

- Directories contain fewer resources than search engine databases.
- Many directories rate, annotate, or categorize chosen resources.
- Directories increase the probability of retrieving relevant results.

Because directories rely on people to select, maintain, and update their resource lists, they contain fewer resources than search engine databases. This can be a plus, especially when you are looking for information on a general topic. It's a lot easier and less time-consuming to go through a list of 50 or so Web pages than to sort through the thousands of pages that a search engine may present. In addition, many directories rate, annotate, analyze, evaluate, and categorize the resources included, which helps you find resources of the highest quality.

Although we'll discuss the evaluation of Internet resources in detail later in the book, now is a good time to bring up the issue of quality control and filtering of WWW sites. With thousands of resources appearing on the Web each day, it is important that there are people working to determine which sites and Web pages on the World Wide Web have the highest quality. For example, if we want to find some of the

Chapter 4

best Web pages that focus on science education, we could try going to the Lycos TOP 5 % directory. Lycos TOP 5 % has an editorial staff that reviews Web pages and gives them ratings from 1 to 100 in the following categories: content, design, and overall. Figure 4.1 shows the results from choosing the top-level category **Education**, then clicking on **Educational Subjects**, and then on **Science Education**. You can browse through the list of annotated and rated resources until you find one or more that may be useful to you.

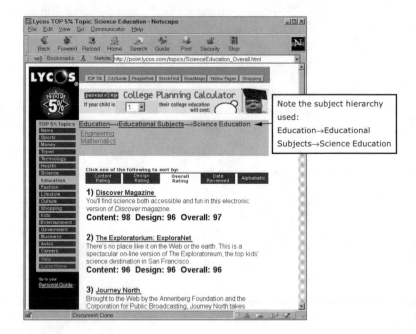

Figure 4.1—Rated/Annotated Science Education Sites: Lycos TOP 5%

Weaknesses

There are three major disadvantages inherent in World Wide Web directories. They are as follows:

- Arbitrary hierarchical arrangements.
- Infrequent updates.
- Subjectivity of rating and annotating resources.

One of the major disadvantages of using some directories is that the hierarchical arrangements may be arbitrary. For example, let's say we are looking for information on ozone depletion. We want to start by finding a few sites. We decide to use Yahoo!, one of the best-known directories on the Web.

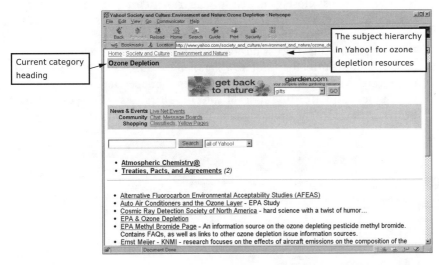

Current category heading

The subject hierarchy in Yahoo! for ozone depletion resources

Figure 4.2—Ozone Depletion in Yahoo!

Note in Figure 4.2 that **Ozone Depletion** is located under the subcategory or subheading **Environment and Nature**, which is located under the top-level category **Society and Culture**. The people who organized this directory chose this hierarchy. Another directory might place Ozone Depletion under the top-level category Science. The ability to search Yahoo! and most other directories by keyword solves this problem of arbitrary hierarchical arrangements.

Another drawback is that selecting, rating, and categorizing Web pages take a lot of time, so directories tend to be less up-to-date than search engine databases, which are constantly updated by computer programs that automatically gather new Web pages.

The third disadvantage inherent in some directories is also an advantage—the resources are chosen by people who subjectively decide which ones are best. What seems a good resource to one person may not to the next. This is why it is important for the directory management to have well-stated criteria for selecting and rating resources.

Browsing and Searching Directories

There are two ways to find information in directories. You can browse by subject or search by keyword. These will be discussed in the following section.

Browsing

Browsing a directory is not difficult. You simply click on a subject category that you think will contain the subject you are seeking. This will take you to another level in the hierarchy, where you will choose another subject from the list of subjects that appear on your computer screen. You then examine the choices that are returned to you and se-

Chapter 4

lect the one most closely related to your research topic. You continue this process until your screen fills with a list of resources that you can then examine to find the information you need.

Sometimes this process has two levels; other times it has several. It depends on the directory and how detailed the subject is. For example, if we were to search Magellan for resources about economics, we would start by clicking on the top-level category **Business**. **Economics & Statistics** is one of the subjects under this category, as noted in Figure 4.3.

The **Economics & Statistics** category is under **Business**

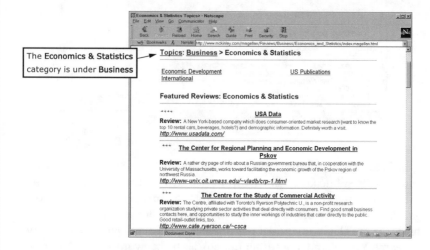

Figure 4.3—Topical Hierarchy in Magellan Web Reviews: Economics & Statistics

Now, let's try to find economics resources in Yahoo! The top-level category we need to click on is **Social Science**. Figure 4.4 shows that **Economics** is a subcategory of **Social Science**. Several subcategories under **Economics** cover specific aspects of the subject.

Economics is a subcategory of **Social Science**

These subcategories cover more specific aspects of economics

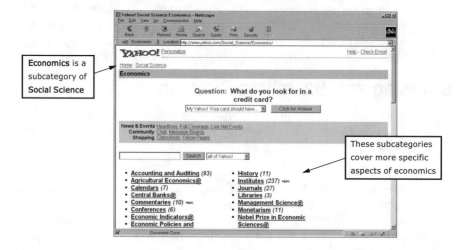

Figure 4.4—Economics Resources in Yahoo!

Tip

If you don't find any resources on the topic you are looking for while browsing, you can use the **Back** icon of your browser to return to another level. There you can try a different subject heading that may lead you to successful results.

Searching

By now, you can probably see the advantage of being able to search a directory. It may be difficult to determine where in a directory's hierarchy a particular subject will be found. Searching a directory is not the same as searching the Web using a search engine. The primary difference is that when you search a directory, you have access to only those resources that are included in the directory, not the entire Web. Also, in some directories (such as Yahoo!), you do not search the full text of Web pages; you search only the words in the URLs (Uniform Resource Locators), the titles of the Web pages, and annotations (if they exist).

Let's take the example of the topic of ozone depletion that we explored earlier in the chapter. If you recall, Yahoo! places Ozone Depletion under Society and Culture in its hierarchical arrangement. Let's now find Web pages in Yahoo! about ozone depletion by doing a search. By reading Yahoo!'s search options, we learn that phrase searching is a supported feature. Quotation marks must be placed around the words. Figure 4.5 shows the phrase entered.

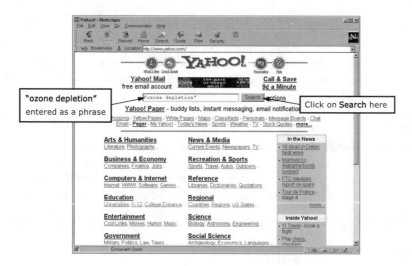

Figure 4.5—Keyword Search in Yahoo!

After we click on **Search**, the screen fills with the search results. Such a list of results is often referred to as a ***hit list***. Note in Figure 4.6 that Yahoo! delivers category matches and site matches. *Category matches*

Chapter 4

are categories or headings with the phrase *ozone depletion* in the category field. *Site matches* are sites with the phrase *ozone depletion* in their titles, pages, or annotations.

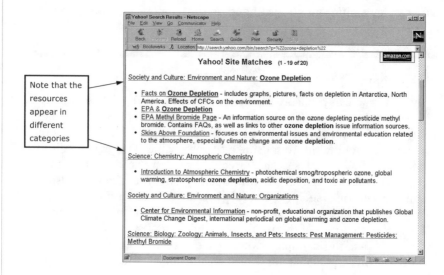

Note that the resources appear in different categories

Figure 4.6—Yahoo! Directory Search Results

Note the advantage of searching versus browsing in this example. This search produced sites on the subject of ozone depletion that are under different categories in the directory.

Two Major Directories and How to Use Them

In this section, we will discuss a couple of well-known directories, pointing out their differences, similarities, and special features by doing hands-on activities with them. The two directories we'll be using are Yahoo! and LookSmart.

❋ Tip

Remember that the Web is always changing and that your results may differ from those shown here. Don't let this confuse you. The activities demonstrate fundamental skills. These skills don't change, even though the number of results obtained or the actual screens may look very different.

Activity 4.1   Yahoo!

Overview

Yahoo!, **http://www.yahoo.com**, is the most comprehensive directory on the World Wide Web. Yahoo! relies on Web page submitters to annotate and categorize the resources that are included, so some sites have a brief descriptive note, and some do not. Some sites in Yahoo! will link to a review, but most will not. Yahoo! strives to be extensive; consequently, there is minimal filtering of resources. You can browse Yahoo! or search it by keyword. When you perform a search in Yahoo!, the first results are from the directory, listed by relevance to the search topics. At the same time, a search engine powered by Inktomi, the company that provides HotBot's search engine, will automatically perform your search for you. By clicking on **Web sites** at the top of the results screen, you'll see the results from the search engine listed.

In the following activity, we'll browse for information in Yahoo!, and then we'll search for the same information using the search query interface that Yahoo! provides. We'll be looking for some general information on the Human Genome Project. We don't know much about it and want to find a general information page. We'll follow these steps:

1. Go to the home page for Yahoo!
2. Browse Yahoo! for information on the Human Genome Project.
3. Bookmark it!
4. Search Yahoo! for information on the Human Genome Project.
5. Access the Web pages that the Inktomi search engine retrieved.
6. End the session.

Details

1   Go to the home page for Yahoo!

We're assuming your browser is already started.

❋Do It! Use the mouse to point to the location field and click the mouse button.

The URL of the current Web page will change color. Now you can type in the URL for Yahoo!

❋Do It! Type **http://www.yahoo.com**, and press Enter.

2   Browse Yahoo! for information on the Human Genome Project.

❋Do It! Click on **Science**, which is one of the top-level categories on Yahoo!'s list, as shown in Figure 4.7. Since the Human Genome Project is related to genetics research, this would be the most logical category to start with.

Chapter 4

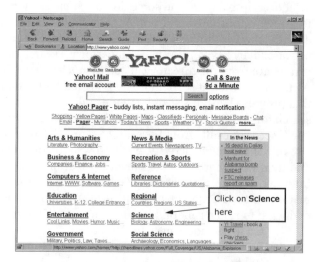

Figure 4.7—Top-level Category List in Yahoo!

❀*Do It!* Click on **Biology** from the list of subcategories.

❀*Do It!* Now click on **Genetics** from the list of subcategories that appear under **Biology.**

❀*Do It!* After the screen fills, click on the category **Human Genetics**, as shown in Figure 4.8.

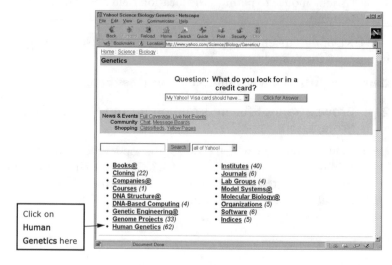

Figure 4.8—Subcategories of Genetics in Yahoo!

❀*Do It!* After the screen fills, click on **Genome Projects**.

Figure 4.9 shows the resources listed under **Genome Projects**. The top hyperlink, **Genome Databases@**, is a cross-reference to another category. Whenever you see a hyperlink with an @ sign after it, you'll know that this will link you to resources in another category. In this case, clicking on **Genome Databases@** would take you to resources that are located in the following hierarchy: Molecular Biology : Bioinformatic Servers : Genome Databases.

Note that in Figure 4.9 there are several genome project resources listed, and one of them is titled **Human Genome Project Information**. This may be the best place to start. If you can't locate this Web page, click on another that looks promising.

✿*Do It!* Click on **Human Genome Project Information** as shown in Figure 4.9.

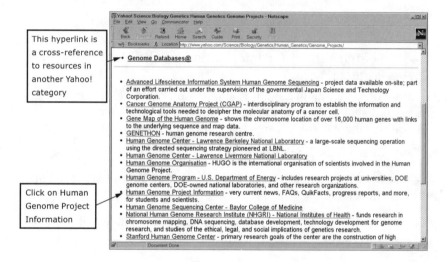

Figure 4.9—Results of Browsing Yahoo! for Resources

3 Bookmark it!

Now that you've found this informative site, you don't want to lose track of it. It's a good idea to place a hyperlink to it in your bookmark list.

✿*Do It!* Click on **Bookmarks** in the location toolbar. Point your mouse to **Add Bookmark** and click. Automatically, the title of the URL is added to your bookmark list. You can access this Web site at a later date by clicking on the title in your list.

Click on the **Back** icon to return to Yahoo!

Click on **Bookmarks** here to add this page to your list of bookmarks

Lots of good background information about the project is included

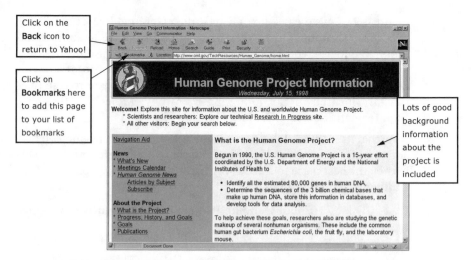

Figure 4.10—"Human Genome Project Information"

4   Search Yahoo! for information on the Human Genome Project.

Keyword searching in Yahoo! is simple. You can save time by doing a keyword search. You should keep your search terms broad, however, because Yahoo! doesn't search the words in the bodies of Web pages.

❁*Do It!* Click on the **Back** icon to return to Yahoo!

❁*Do It!* Return to Yahoo!'s home page by clicking **Yahoo!** at the top of the screen.

❁*Do It!* To discover what the search options are for Yahoo!, click on **options** next to the search form. See Figure 4.11.

Click **options** to find search tips in Yahoo!

Figure 4.11—How to Find Search Options in Yahoo!

Take a look at the "Search Options" page in Yahoo! (shown in Figure 4.12). If you click on **Advanced Search Syntax**, as shown in Figure 4.12, you'll learn that Yahoo! allows you to search for phrases by placing quotation marks around the words to be considered a phrase. We also learn that Yahoo! is case insensitive, so we don't need to capitalize the beginning letters of the words in the phrase.

❁*Do It!* On the "Search Options" page, point your cursor to the circle, or radio button, next to the method that reads **An exact phrase match** and click. Doing this makes it unnecessary to place quotation marks around the phrase. Next, point your cursor to the circle next to **Web Sites** and click.

✳️*Do It!* Type in the pane next to the **Search** button the search expression **human genome project** and press **Enter**. See Figure 4.12.

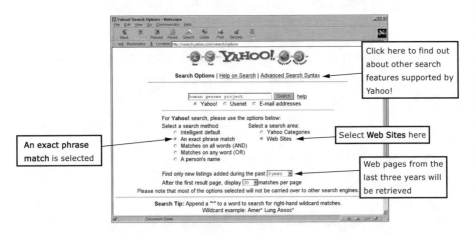

Click here to find out about other search features supported by Yahoo!

An exact phrase match is selected

Select **Web Sites** here

Web pages from the last three years will be retrieved

*Figure 4.12—Search Expression **human genome project** Entered*

This search will retrieve Web sites that have the phrase *human genome project* in their titles, URLs, or annotations. The search won't find the Yahoo! categories that match this phrase, only the sites. It will return the sites added in the past three years.

Note that the resources found are from different Yahoo! categories, as shown in Figure 4.13. Some of them are from the Business and Economy top-level category. The results are listed in order of relevance to the search topic.

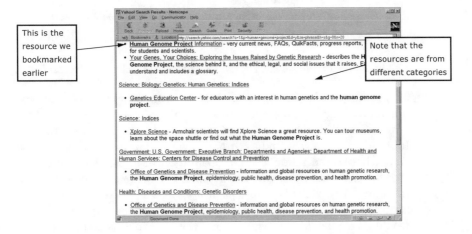

This is the resource we bookmarked earlier

Note that the resources are from different categories

Figure 4.13—Yahoo! Search Results

Chapter 4

5 Access the Web pages that the Inktomi search engine retrieved.

The sites that Yahoo! retrieved for us may be all we need, but let's say that after we read the short descriptions, we want to see what the entire World Wide Web has on this topic.

✿*Do It!* Click on the place where the words **Web Pages** appear, at the top of the screen, as shown in Figure 4.14.

Figure 4.14—Accessing Search Results from the Inktomi Search Engine

Automatically, the Inktomi search engine searches the entire Web for the search expression *human genome project.* The results are listed by relevance, as shown in Figure 4.15.

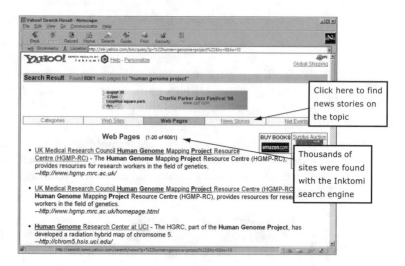

Figure 4.15—Results of the Search Request in the Inktomi Search Engine

As you can see, the Inktomi search engine found thousands of sites on this topic. This search engine uses a database that covers most of the World Wide Web, whereas Yahoo! covers only a small portion of it. The Inktomi engine also searches through every word in every page on the Web, whereas the Yahoo! search capability is limited to URL titles, category or Web site titles, and descriptions. Plus, we can't be sure if the Inktomi searched for *human genome project* as a phrase as we had it set up to be used in Yahoo! Perhaps the words were connected by OR, which would give much larger results. Since the pages are listed by relevancy, however, we can be sure that the first 10 or 20 resources listed will be highly relevant to your search request.

6 End the session.

You've learned a lot about Yahoo! Now it's time to discover the features of other directories. You can either end the session or continue to the next activity.

✿*DoIt!* To end the session now, click on **File** on the menu bar and select **Exit** from the menu.

End of Activity 4.1

In Activity 4.1, we saw the difference between browsing Yahoo!'s subject categories for a topic and performing a keyword search. A keyword search in Yahoo! looks for words that are in the URLs, the subject categories, and the titles of the Web pages. You can search the entire Web from Yahoo!, but to use a search engine's capabilities to the fullest, you should search directly from the search engine's home page. We'll show you how to do this in Chapter 5, "Search Strategies for Search Engines."

Activity 4.2   LookSmart

Overview

In this activity, we'll use LookSmart to find resources about distance learning in colleges and universities. LookSmart, like Yahoo!, is a directory that can be browsed by subject and searched by keyword. In a search, LookSmart will comb its Web pages first and at the same time, the AltaVista search engine will search the entire Web for the keywords entered. An interesting fact about LookSmart is that the HotBot search engine links to the LookSmart directory on its home page. Let's see how LookSmart works.

We'll follow these steps:
1. Go to the home page for LookSmart.
2. Browse LookSmart for distance learning resources.
3. Search LookSmart for Web pages on distance learning.
4. End the session.

Details

1 Go to the home page for LookSmart.

✿*DoIt!* Use the mouse to point to the location field and click.

The URL of the current Web page will change color. Now you can type the URL for LookSmart.

✿*DoIt!* Type **http://www.looksmart.com**, and press Enter.

2 Browse LookSmart for distance learning resources.

Take a look at the top-level subject categories that LookSmart provides on the left side of its home page. The most logical category to explore for distance learning resources for college students would be **Reference & Education**.

Chapter 4

❉*Do It!* From LookSmart's home page, click on **Reference & Education**, as shown in Figure 4.16.

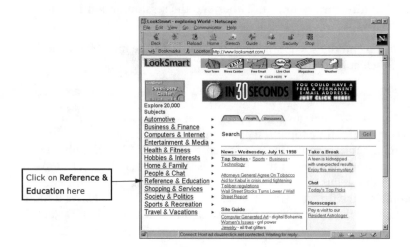

Figure 4.16—LookSmart's Home Page

❉*Do It!* Since we are interested in distance learning for college students, click on **Higher & Cont. Ed.** from the subcategories listed.

❉*Do It!* Now click on **Distance & Home Study**, as shown in Figure 4.17.

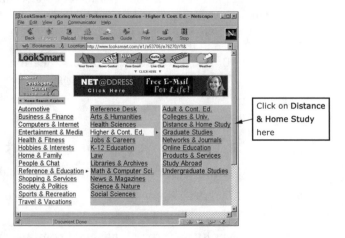

Figure 4.17—Browsing LookSmart's Directory for Distance Learning Resources

Note how LookSmart arranges its subcategories on the desktop. This design makes it easy to see where you are in the hierarchy, so you can quickly backtrack to related subject categories.

Figure 4.18 shows the list of resources in the **Distance & Home Study** category.

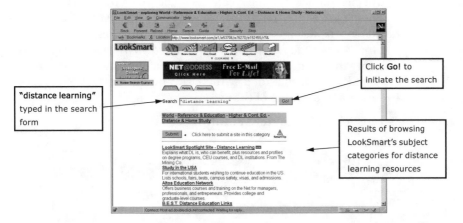

Figure 4.18—List of Resources in LookSmart's Distance & Home Study Category

3   Search LookSmart for Web pages on distance learning.

We found some useful distance learning resources by browsing, but perhaps there is a desire to retrieve documents from other categories. In order to do this, we'll need to perform a keyword search. Since distance learning should be searched as a phrase, we'll put quotes around the two words. (It should be noted that the same results were obtained without the quotation marks. The search help in LookSmart doesn't address this issue.)

❊Do It! In the search form provided, as shown in Figure 4.18, type **"distance learning"** and click on **Go!**

Partial results of this search are shown in Figure 4.19.

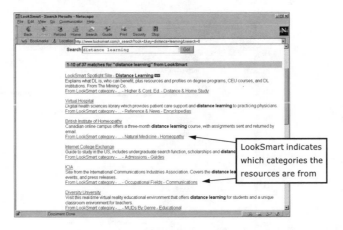

Figure 4.19—Results of Searching LookSmart for "distance learning"

Note that several of the pages are from different categories. There are four pages of results from LookSmart's directory. On the bottom of the fourth page, notice that the resources retrieved by the AltaVista search engine are introduced, as illustrated in Figure 4.20. An added feature of LookSmart makes it easy for you to focus on other aspects of the subject you've searched for. Let's say you wanted Web pages in LookSmart's directory that focused on how computers and the Internet contribute to distance learning. You could do this easily by clicking on **Computers & Internet** at the bottom of the page, as shown in Figure 4.20.

✳ *Do It!* Click on **Computers & Internet** as shown in Figure 4.20.

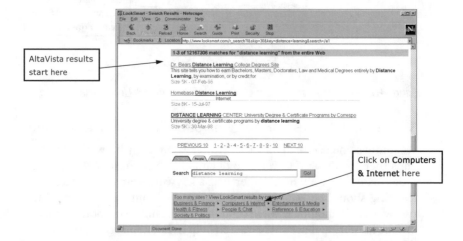

Figure 4.20—List of Results from LookSmart's Search Engine (AltaVista)

Figure 4.21 shows the results of this manipulation in LookSmart. These are resources that are located in the **Computers & Internet** hierarchy that also cover aspects of distance learning.

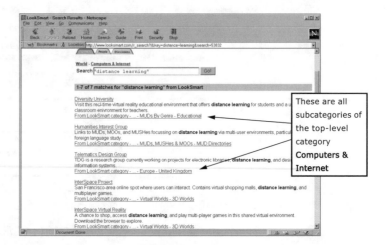

Figure 4.21—Computer-related Distance Learning Resources in LookSmart

4   End the session.

You can either end the session now or continue to the next activity.

❋*Do It!*   To end the session now, click on **File** on the menu bar and select **Exit** from the menu.

_____ End of Activity 4.2 _____

In Activity 4.2, we started looking for information on distance learning in higher education by browsing LookSmart. We found several Web sites that appeared to be useful. By searching LookSmart, we were able to find resources on distance learning that appeared in different categories, thereby increasing the chance of retrieving relevant results. LookSmart also supplied results from the AltaVista search engine. The main purpose of the activity was to show the different ways to manipulate a combination search engine–directory database to obtain as much information as possible.

Virtual Libraries: Directories with a Difference

Virtual libraries are directories with resources that information professionals, including librarians, have organized in a logical way. In Chapter 3, we looked closely at a virtual library—the Internet Public Library. Virtual libraries are often referred to as **annotated directories** as well. It is helpful to think of these specialized directories as being similar to libraries, because people who are committed to finding the very best resources on the Internet have carefully selected and maintained the resources in a virtual library. These people usually rate or analyze the resources and arrange them so they will be found easily.

The Major Virtual Libraries

❋   The Argus Clearinghouse
    http://www.clearinghouse.net
❋   Infomine
    http://lib-www.ucr.edu
❋   Internet Public Library
    http://www.ipl.org
❋   Librarians' Index to the Internet
    http://sunsite.berkeley.edu/internetindex
❋   World Wide Web Virtual Library
    http://vlib.stanford.edu/Overview.html

As we discussed in Chapter 3, there are three major types of resources that virtual libraries are most apt to contain: **subject guides**, **reference works**, and **specialized databases**. Subject guides are Web resources that include hyperlinks to sites on that particular subject. Reference works are full-text documents, such as dictionaries, encyclopedias, almanacs, and so forth. Specialized databases are searchable indexes that catalog certain types of material, such as journal article citations, financial data, and so forth.

It may be helpful to do an activity in a virtual library to show you how to obtain a subject guide. We will be using The Argus Clearinghouse for this activity.

Activity 4.3   The Argus Clearinghouse

Overview

Let's say you are interested in doing research on the Middle East. Unsure of which particular issue or country you are interested in researching, you would like to see a subject guide to the World Wide Web on the subject of the Middle East. A virtual library would be an excellent place to begin this search. Since The Argus Clearinghouse is a virtual library, let's start there.

The Argus Clearinghouse is a virtual library provided by Argus Associates. The resources included in The Argus Clearinghouse cover most subject areas. Subject specialists from all over the world write the subject guides, and subject specialists on the Argus staff rate and analyze each guide. You can browse and perform keyword searches in The Argus Clearinghouse. In this activity, we will illustrate how to browse the directory.

Let's explore The Argus Clearinghouse by following these steps:

1. Go to The Argus Clearinghouse.
2. Browse for subject guides on the Middle East.
3. Search for a Middle East subject guide.
4. End the session.

If you find a subject guide on the topic you are researching, it can save you a lot of time and energy by helping you navigate the Web's vast sea of information. Let's see what we find on the Middle East.

Details

1   Go to The Argus Clearinghouse.

❋*Do It!* Use the mouse to point to the location field and click.

The URL of the current Web page will change color. Now you can type in the URL for The Argus Clearinghouse.

❋*Do It!* Type **http://www.clearinghouse.net** and press ⏎ **Enter** .

See *The Argus Clearinghouse* home page in Figure 4.22.

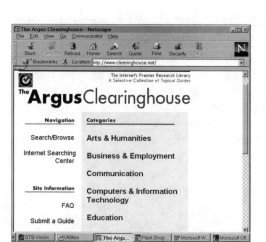

Figure 4.22—Top-level Subject Categories in The Argus Clearinghouse

2   Browse for subject guides on the Middle East.

❁*Do It!* Click on the top-level subject category **Places & Peoples**.

Wait until the screen fills with a list of subcategories.

❁*Do It!* Click on **Asia**.

There will be more subjects listed.

❁*Do It!* Click on **Middle East**.

Your screen should now look like the one in Figure 4.23.

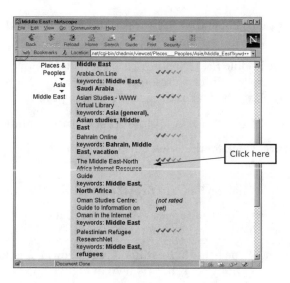

Figure 4.23—List of Subject Guides on the Middle East in The Argus Clearinghouse

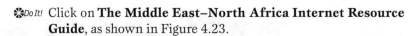

✺*Do It!* Click on **The Middle East–North Africa Internet Resource Guide**, as shown in Figure 4.23.

The screen will fill with information that the The Argus Clearinghouse provides, as shown in Figure 4.24. The Web page cites the guide's author, the organization with which he is affiliated, and ways to contact him. The clearinghouse also gives information about the rating system, the keywords attached to the guide, and the date when the guide was last checked for currency and accuracy. See Figure 4.24. You can now go to the subject guide by clicking on its URL.

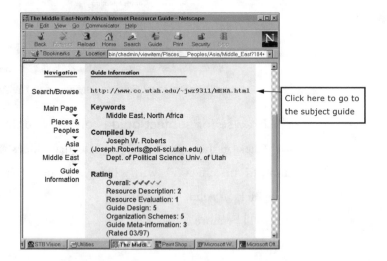

Figure 4.24—Information Page—Middle East-North Africa Resource Guide

✺*Do It!* Click on the URL for the Middle East–North Africa Internet Resource Guide.

The Middle East–North Africa Internet Resource Guide functions as a directory to Internet resources dealing with all aspects of that region. It is an excellent place to begin a research project on the Middle East.

3 Search for a Middle East subject guide.

✺*Do It!* Click on the **Back** button to return to The Argus Clearinghouse.

✺*Do It!* Click on **Search/Browse** under the **Navigation** section.

A search form will appear. We want to find a subject guide on the Middle East, so we enter that topic into the form.

✺*Do It!* Type **Middle East** in the search form, and then click on **submit search**, as shown in Figure 4.25.

Figure 4.25—Searching The Argus Clearinghouse for **Middle East**

The results of this search partially appear in Figure 4.26. We picked up one more subject guide by searching the guide rather than by browsing. This means that there was one guide that wasn't in the Middle East subject category. Can you determine which one it is?

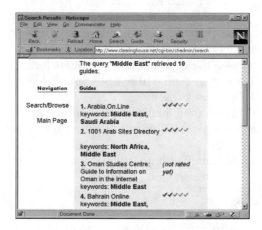

Figure 4.26—Results of Searching The Argus Clearinghouse for **Middle East**

4 End the session.

❊Do It! To end the session now, click on **File** on the menu bar and select **Exit** from the menu.

End of Activity 4.3

With The Argus Clearinghouse's search capability, we picked up one relevant subject guide that the structured browse didn't produce. This is another example of how keyword searching can enhance results. In Activity 4.3, we could easily see the difference between a virtual library and a Web directory such as Yahoo! A virtual library such as The Argus Clearinghouse is very selective about the Web resources that are included and the way they are rated. Keep in mind that virtual libraries are very small collections of Web resources, so they may not always have what you need.

Chapter 4

The Librarians' Index to the Internet

Overview

The Librarians' Index to the Internet (LII) is a virtual library that contains over 3,500 annotated and evaluated resources in most subject areas. The LII can be searched as well as browsed. The LII operates with a grant from the California State Library. It was initiated and is still maintained by Carol Leita, a librarian. The annotations are written by Ms. Leita and more than 30 other librarians from the state of California. The index is part of the Digital Library Sun SITE at the University of California, Berkeley. The Librarians' Index to the Internet is organized a lot like Yahoo!, so you should feel familiar with it quickly.

We're going to use the LII to find the "Blue Book" for automobiles. A virtual library is the best place to go to find a reference source like this. If you searched a search engine like AltaVista or HotBot for *blue book,* you could easily retrieve thousands of hits. The other advantage to using a virtual library for this type of information is that you may find other automobile resources for consumers that may be helpful. First, we'll browse the appropriate categories to locate it and then we'll search the directory by typing **blue book** in the search form.

We'll follow these steps:

1. Go to the Librarians' Index to the Internet.
2. Browse the library's directory for the Blue Book for automobiles.
3. Search the library's directory for the Blue Book.
4. End the session.

Details

1   Go to the Librarians' Index to the Internet.

❁*Do It!* Use the mouse to point to the location field and click.

The URL of the current Web page will change color. Now you can type in the URL for the Librarians' Index to the Internet.

❁*Do It!* Type **http://sunsite.berkeley.edu/internetindex** and press Enter.

See the *Librarians' Index to the Internet* home page in Figure 4.27.

2   Browse the library's directory for the Blue Book for automobiles.

Note that there is a top-level category in the LII for automobiles.

❁*Do It!* Click on **Automobiles**, as shown in Figure 4.27.

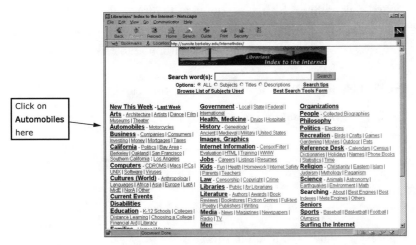

Click on **Automobiles** here

Figure 4.27—Home Page of the Librarians' Index to the Internet

Figure 4.28 shows a partial list of the resources in the Automobiles category. Note that the first three resources contain consumer information on both new and used cars. If you scrolled down the page, you'd find the Kelley Blue Book listed. For purposes of this activity, we'll search for the Blue Book to show you how it's done.

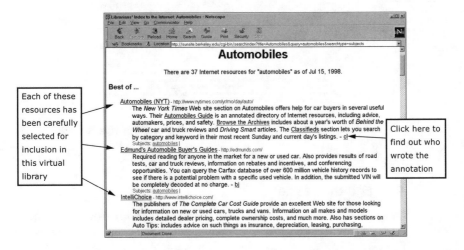

Each of these resources has been carefully selected for inclusion in this virtual library

Click here to find out who wrote the annotation

Figure 4.28—The Automobile Category in the Librarians' Index to the Internet

3   Search the library's directory for the Blue Book.

First, we need to return to the search form.

✤*Do It!* Click on the **Back** icon to return to the *Librarians' Index to the Internet* home page.

To determine the best way to search with any tool, it's always a good idea to read the help section.

121

❋*Do It!* Click on **Search tips**, as shown in Figure 4.29.

The search tips make no mention of supporting the phrase searching feature, so we'll just type in **blue book** without quotes and see what we get.

❋*Do It!* Click on the **Back** icon to return to the search form.

❋*Do It!* Type **blue book** in the search form and click on **Search**, as shown in Figure 4.29.

*Figure 4.29—Searching for **blue book** in the Librarians' Index to the Internet*

Figure 4.30 shows the result of this search.

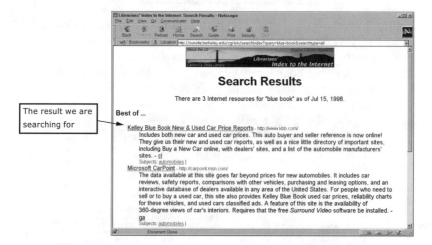

*Figure 4.30—Results of Search for **blue book** in the Librarians' Index to the Internet*

4   End the session.

❋*Do It!* Click on **File** in the menu bar and select **Exit** from the menu. If you like, you can delete any bookmarks you have made.

End of Activity 4.4

This activity showed how selective virtual libraries are. Virtual libraries are the places to go if you are looking for a reference source like a dictionary, handbook, encyclopedia, or special database. The Librarians' Index to the Internet is a good resource to have on your bookmark list.

Summary

Directories are topical lists of Internet resources, arranged hierarchically to facilitate browsing by subject. Most directories have a search capability, which can help you avoid occasionally becoming lost in arbitrary subject categories. Directories depend on the work of individuals who collect, categorize, maintain, and, in many cases, evaluate Web sites to make it easier for people to find what they are looking for. Directories vary in how they are organized, whether or not sites are evaluated, and, if they are, what criteria are used.

Because directories rely on people for their selections and maintenance, they are necessarily much smaller than the databases that search-engine spiders or robots create. This difference can be an asset in some cases and a detriment in others. When you are looking for a "few good sites" to start with, a directory can save you time, especially if your subject is broad and you're at the beginning of your research. Search engines are not meant to give you a few sites. They exist to bring everything to your screen that is on the World Wide Web and that fits your search expression. Search engines are best for finding very specific information or for researching multifaceted topics.

Virtual libraries are directories maintained by librarians, or cybrarians, who select materials for the directory based on their excellence and value to the Internet public, much as librarians in a traditional library do. Virtual libraries are the best places to find subject guides. These guides are usually maintained by people who are knowledgeable about the subjects covered.

It is a good idea to know how to use the different directories we covered in this chapter and to explore others. Keep one or two of your favorites in your bookmark list so you can find them quickly.

Selected Terms Introduced in This Chapter

annotated directory	reference work
annotation	specialized database
hit list	subject guide

5
Chapter

Search Strategies for
Search Engines

In Chapter 3, "Using the World Wide Web for Research," we introduced keyword searching in search engine databases. In this chapter, we'll cover searching these databases in detail. Why is it so important to learn how to search these databases? Search engines are the most powerful search tools on the World Wide Web, with the most popular being those that access the largest databases. Most of the major search engines claim to index the entire World Wide Web. Many also index Usenet newsgroups, FTP, and Gopher sites. None of the search engines are exactly alike. Some are better for certain kinds of information than others. Maybe you've tried a few search engines and have found that some engines retrieve too many documents that aren't at all what you wanted. Perhaps at other times they don't retrieve enough information. This chapter should clear up some ambiguities you may have about why some searches work well and others don't.

This chapter will include the following sections:
  * Search Engine Databases
  * Search Features Common to Most Search Engines
  * Output Features Common to Most Search Engines
  * A Basic Search Strategy: The 10 Steps

The Major Search Engine Databases on the World Wide Web

❄	AltaVista	**http://www.altavista.digital.com**
❄	Excite	**http://www.excite.com**
❄	HotBot	**http://www.hotbot.com**
❄	Infoseek	**http://www.infoseek.com**
❄	Lycos	**http://www.lycos.com**
❄	Northern Light	**http://www.northernlight.com**
❄	WebCrawler	**http://www.webcrawler.com**

Search Engine Databases

Knowing how search engine databases are indexed can help you select the most appropriate tool for your research needs, retrieve the most relevant information, and understand why results vary from one database to another.

Indexing

In Chapter 4, we discussed directories and how human beings control their contents. In directories, site managers and cybrarians assign keywords to Web pages. They describe the Web page with a few words. This *keyword indexing* enables you to find that page if any of the words you type in match the words used to describe the page.

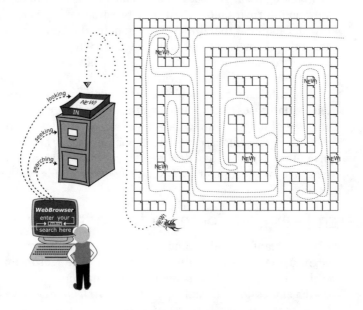

How a Spider Works—Searching the Internet for New Documents

In search engines, a computer program, called a spider or robot, gathers new documents from the World Wide Web. The program retrieves hyperlinks that are attached to these documents, loads them into a database, and indexes them using a formula that differs from database to database. The search engine then searches the database according to the request you enter. Although robots have many different ways of collecting information from Web pages, the major search engines all claim to index the entire text of each Web document in their databases. This is called *full-text indexing*. All of the major search engines are full-text databases.

Some robot programs are intuitive; they know which words are important to the meaning of the entire Web page, and some of them can find synonyms to the words and add them to the index. Some full-text databases, such as Excite, use a robot that enables them to search on concepts, as well as on the search query words. In some search engines, the robot skips over words that appear often, such as prepositions and articles. These common words are called *stop words*.

Some search engines allow Web page submitters to attach *meta-tags* to their pages. Meta-tags are keywords that describe the page but may not appear on the page. They appear only in the HTML source document. Meta-tags allow Web pages that don't have a lot of text in them to come up in a keyword search.

When to Use Search Engine Databases

Search engines are the best tools to use when you are looking for very specific information or when your research topic has many facets. We saw in Chapter 4 that directories are helpful when you are looking for general and single-faceted topics. Usually when you need information on a very detailed or multifaceted subject, however, a search engine will give you not only more information, but also the most precise and up-to-date information possible. Even though most of the major search engine databases attempt to index the entire Web, each one has a different way of determining which pages are most relevant to your search request. In one database, a relevant document may be fiftieth on the list; in another database, that document may be first. In order to retrieve the most relevant documents, you should become familiar with many search engines and their features.

Search Features Common to Most Search Engines

It's important to understand the different search features before you begin using a search engine for research. The reason for this is that each search engine has its own way of interpreting and manipulating search expressions. In addition, many search engines have *default settings* that you may need to override if you want to obtain the most precise results. Because a search can bring up so many words, it is very easy to have a lot of hits with few that are relevant to your query. This is called *low precision/high recall*. You may be satisfied with having very precise search results with a small set returned. This is defined as *high precision/low recall*. Ideally, using the search expression you enter, the search engine would retrieve all of the relevant documents you need. This would be described as *high precision/high recall*.

Search engines support many search features, though not all engines support each one. If they do support certain features, they may use different *syntax* in expressing the feature. Before you use any of these search features, you need to check the search engines' help pages to see how the feature is expressed, if it is supported at all. We will now list the most common search features and explain how each feature is used.

Boolean Operators

We discussed Boolean operators briefly in Chapter 3. Knowing how to apply Boolean operators in search expressions is extremely important. The diagrams show the different operators and how they are used.

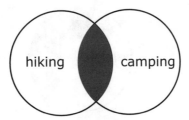

hiking AND camping

Use an AND between search terms when you need to narrow your search. The AND indicates that only those Web pages having both words in them will be retrieved. Some search engines automatically assume an AND relationship between two words if you don't type AND between them. This would be a default setting of the search engine.

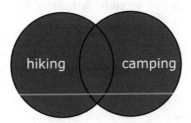

hiking OR camping

An OR between search terms will make your resulting set larger. When you use OR, Web pages that have either term will be retrieved. Many search engines automatically place an OR between two words if there is nothing typed between them. This would be a default setting of the search engine.

127

Chapter 5

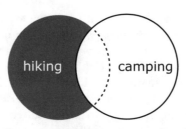

<u>hiking NOT camping</u>

The NOT operator is used when a term needs to be excluded. In this example, Web pages with both *hiking* and *camping* in them would not be retrieved. Some search engines require an AND in front of the NOT. In this case, the expression would be written like this: hiking AND NOT camping.

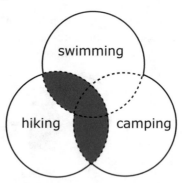

<u>hiking AND (camping OR swimming)</u>

This example shows **nested Boolean logic**. Use this logic when you need to include ANDs and ORs in one search statement. For example, say that there is a term that must appear in your results. You want to search for this term along with a concept that you can describe with synonyms. To do this, you would need to tell the search engine to find records with two or more synonyms and then to combine this result with the first term. In the example above, the parentheses indicate that *camping OR swimming* will be processed first, and that this result will be combined with *hiking*. If the parentheses were not there, the search engine would perform the search from left to right. All pages with both the words *hiking* and *camping* would be found first, and then all pages with the word *swimming* would be included. This would give you an unacceptable result, so you must be careful when using nested Boolean logic.

Implied Boolean Operators

Implied Boolean operators, or pseudo-Boolean operators, are short-cuts to typing AND and NOT. In most search engines that support this feature, you would type + before a word or phrase that must appear in the document and – before a word or phrase that must not appear in the document.

Phrase Searching

A *phrase* is a string of words that must appear next to each other. *Global warming* is a phrase, as is *chronic fatigue syndrome*. Use phrase-searching capability when the words you are searching for must appear next to each other and must appear in the order in which you type them. Most search engines require double quotation marks to differentiate a phrase from words searched by themselves. The two phrases mentioned above would be expressed like this: "global warming" and "chronic fatigue syndrome." Phrase searching is one of the most helpful search features, as it increases the chance that your search will have relevant results.

Proximity Searching

Proximity operators are words such as *near* or *within*. For example, you are trying to find information on the effects of chlorofluorocarbons on global warming. You might want to retrieve results that have the word *chlorofluorocarbons* very close to the phrase *global warming*. By placing the word NEAR between the two segments of the search expression, you would achieve more relevant results than if the words appeared in the same document but were perhaps pages apart. This is called ***proximity searching***.

Truncation

Truncation is the process of looking for multiple forms of a word. Some search engines refer to truncation as *stemming*. For example, if you were researching postmodern art, you might want to retrieve all the records that had the root word *postmodern*, as well as *postmodernist* and *postmodernism*. Most search engines support truncation by allowing you to place an asterisk (*) at the end of the root word. You would need to see the help screen in the search engine you are using to find out which symbol is used. For example, in this case we would type **postmodern***. Some search engines automatically truncate words. In those databases, you would type **postmodern** and be assured that all the endings would also be retrieved. In these cases, truncation would be a default setting of the search engines. If you didn't want your search expression to be truncated, you would need to override the default feature. You would find out how to do this by reading the search engine's help screens.

Wildcards

Using ***wildcards*** allows you to search for words that have most of the word in common, except for maybe a letter or two. For example, we might want to search for both *woman* and *women*. Instead of typing **woman OR women**, we could place a wildcard character (most often an asterisk) to replace the fourth letter. It would look like this: **wom*n**.

Field Searching

Web pages can be broken down into many parts. These parts, or *fields*, include titles, URLs, text, summaries or annotations (if present), and so forth. (See Figure 5.1.) *Field searching* is the ability to limit your search to certain fields. This ability to search by field can increase the relevance of the retrieved records. For example, let's say you wanted to search the Web for an image of a comet. You could, in the search engines that support this feature, limit your search results to Web pages that contain images that have the word *comet* in their file names.

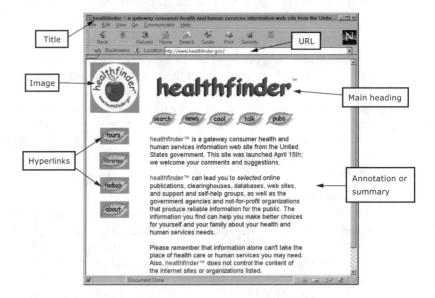

Figure 5.1—The Parts of a Web Page

Case Sensitivity

Case sensitivity is an important feature, especially if you are looking for proper names. Some search engines recognize capitalization, but some do not. If a search engine does recognize capitals, it can lead to a much more precise search, especially if you're looking for proper names such as *Sting, the Who,* or *Brad Pitt.* If the search engine you were using didn't recognize capitals, just think of the results you'd get by entering *sting* in the search query box.

Concept Searching

Concept searching occurs when a search engine automatically searches for Web pages that have similar terms to the ones you entered in the search query box. Excite supports this feature.

Limiting by Date

Some search engines allow you to search the Web for pages that were added to the database between certain dates. In *limiting by date*, you can find only the pages that were entered in the past month, in the past year, or in a particular year.

Output Features Common to Most Search Engines

The way a search engine displays results can help you decide which search engine to use. The following features are common to many engines, but as we saw earlier with the search features, the engines all have different ways of determining and showing these features.

Relevancy Ranking

Most search engines measure each Web page's relevance to your search query and arrange the search results from the most relevant to the least relevant. This is called *relevancy ranking*. Each search engine has its own algorithm for determining relevance, but it usually involves counting how many times the words in your query appear in the Web pages. In some search engines, a document is considered more relevant if the words appear in certain fields, for example, the title or summary field. In other search engines, relevance is determined by the number of times the keyword appears in a Web page divided by the total number of words in the page. This gives a percentage, and the page with the largest percentage appears first on the list.

Annotations or Summaries

Some search engines include short descriptive paragraphs of each Web page they return to you. These annotations, or summaries, can help you decide whether or not to open a Web page, especially if there is no title for the Web page or if the title doesn't describe the page in detail.

Results Per Page

In some search engines, the *results per page* option allows you to choose how many results you want listed per page. This can be a time saver, because it sometimes takes a while to go from page to page as you look through results.

Sorting Results

Some services allow you to choose how you want your results sorted— by relevance, URL, location, organization, folders, and so forth. This feature is known as *sorting*.

Duplicate Detection

It is not unusual to retrieve several instances of the same Web page in your results. Some search engines detect these duplicates and remove them. In meta-search engines or unified search interfaces, *duplicate detection* is a common feature.

Chapter 5

Modification of Search Results

Some search engines will insert a copy of your search request on the first page of your results to make it easier for you to modify the query if you so desire. With others, you may be required to return to the original search form before making this *modification of search results*. Some search engines allow you to search only the results of an earlier search, which can be extremely helpful.

Meta-tag Support

Some search engines acknowledge keywords that a Web page author has placed in the meta-tag field in the HTML source document. This means that a document may be retrieved by a keyword search, but that the search expression may not appear in the document.

A Basic Search Strategy: The 10 Steps

The following list provides a guideline for you to follow in formulating search requests, viewing search results, and modifying search results. These procedures can be followed for virtually any search request, from the simplest to the most complicated. For some search requests, you may not want or need to go through a formal search strategy. If you want to save time in the long run, however, it's a good idea to follow a strategy, especially when you're new to a particular search engine. A basic search strategy can help you get used to each search engine's features and how they are expressed in the search query. Following the 10 steps will also ensure good results if your search is multifaceted and you want to get the most relevant results.

The 10 steps are as follows:

1. Identify the important concepts of your search.
2. Choose the keywords that describe these concepts.
3. Determine whether there are synonyms, related terms, or other variations of the keywords that should be included.
4. Determine which search features may apply, including truncation, proximity operators, Boolean operators, and so forth.
5. Choose a search engine.
6. Read the search instructions on the search engine's home page. Look for sections entitled "Help," "Advanced Search," "Frequently Asked Questions," and so forth.
7. Create a search expression using syntax that is appropriate for the search engine.
8. View the results. How many hits were returned? Were the results relevant to your query?
9. Modify your search if needed. Go back to Steps 2 through 4 and revise your query accordingly.
10. Try the same search in a different search engine, following Steps 5 through 9 above.

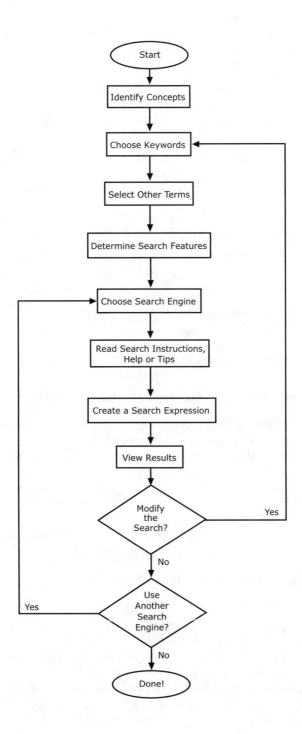

Basic Search Strategy

Chapter 5

Search Tips

If you feel that your search has yielded too few Web pages (low recall), there are several things to consider:

- ❋ Perhaps the search expression was too specific; go back and remove some terms that are connected by ANDs.

- ❋ Perhaps there are more terms to use. Think of more synonyms to OR together. Try truncating more words if possible.

- ❋ Check spelling and syntax (a forgotten quotation mark or a missing parentheses).

- ❋ Read the instructions on the help pages again.

If your search has given you too many results and many are unrelated to your topic (high recall/low precision), consider the following:

- ❋ Narrow your search to specific fields, if possible.

- ❋ Use more specific terms; for example, instead of *cancer,* use the specific type of cancer in which you're interested.

- ❋ Add additional terms with AND or NOT.

- ❋ Remove some synonyms if possible.

In order to explain these concepts in the most practical way, we'll do an activity in two full-text databases.

❋Tip

Remember that the Web is always changing and that your results may differ from those shown here. Don't let this confuse you. The activities demonstrate fundamental skills. These skills don't change, even though the number of results obtained or the actual screens may look very different.

Activity 5.1   Search Strategies in AltaVista and Northern Light

Performing a Search in AltaVista

Overview

In this activity, we are going to search for resources on a multifaceted topic. We want to find World Wide Web documents that focus on how self-esteem relates to young girls' likelihood of developing eating disorders. There has been a lot of research in the past 10 years about how changes in modern life have hurt teenage girls' development, and we'd like to see if any of this research has been published on the Web.

Following the steps of the basic search strategy, we need to examine the facts of our search, choosing the appropriate keywords and determining which search features apply. Then, we'll go to the search engine and read the search instructions. We'll explore AltaVista first. Then we'll perform the same search (using the appropriate syntax) in Northern Light. Let's see how these two search engines handle this multifaceted topic.

We'll follow these steps:

1. Identify the important concepts of your search.
2. Choose the keywords that describe these concepts.
3. Determine whether there are synonyms, related terms, or other variations of the keywords that should be included.
4. Determine which search features may apply, including truncation, proximity operators, Boolean operators, and so forth.
5. Choose a search engine.
6. Read the search instructions on the search engine's home page. Look for sections entitled "Help," "Advanced Search," "Frequently Asked Questions," and so forth.
7. Create a search expression using syntax that is appropriate for the search engine.
8. View the results. How many hits were returned? Were the results relevant to your query?
9. Modify your search if needed. Go back to Steps 2 through 4 and revise your query accordingly.
10. Try the same search in a different search engine, following Steps 5 through 9 above.

Details

1   Identify the important concepts of your search.

The most important concepts of this search are the development of eating disorders in adolescent girls and the way this is related to their lack of self-esteem.

2   Choose the keywords that describe these concepts.

The main terms or keywords include the following: teenage girls, self-esteem, and eating disorders.

3   Determine whether there are synonyms, related terms, or other variations of the keywords that should be included.

For teenage: adolescent, adolescence.

For eating disorders: anorexia nervosa, bulimia.

For self-esteem: self-respect.

4   Determine which search features may apply, including truncation, proximity operators, Boolean operators, and so forth.

When developing a search expression, keep in mind that you place OR between synonyms and AND between the different concepts, or facets, of the search topic. If you write down all the synonyms you choose, it may help with the construction of the final search phraseology. Table 5.1 shows the three major concepts, or facets, of the search topic with their synonyms connected with the appropriate Boolean operators. Keep in mind there can be different ways to express the same idea. For example, for the facet *teenage girls,* you could say *"teenage girls" or "adolescen* girls"* instead of *(teenage or adolescen*) and girls.* Note that by using the truncated word *adolescen,* we would retrieve the words *adolescent* and *adolescence.* Before you get online, take a few minutes to determine whether you have used all the search features that you possibly can. It can save you a lot of time in the long run.

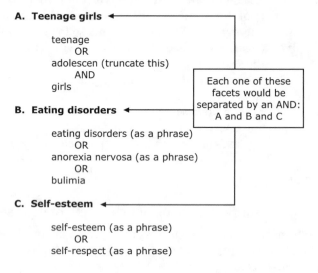

A. **Teenage girls**

    teenage
        OR
    adolescen (truncate this)
        AND
    girls

Each one of these facets would be separated by an AND: A and B and C

B. **Eating disorders**

    eating disorders (as a phrase)
        OR
    anorexia nervosa (as a phrase)
        OR
    bulimia

C. **Self-esteem**

    self-esteem (as a phrase)
        OR
    self-respect (as a phrase)

Table 5.1—Formulation of the Search Strategy

5   Choose a search engine.

In this activity, we are going to search AltaVista first. This search engine supports full Boolean searching, which is a search feature we need for this topic. AltaVista's advanced search mode has a large search form, which makes it easier to type in a lengthy search expression.

❉*Do It!* Click on the location field, type **http://www.altavista.digital. com**, and press ⏎**Enter**.

6   Read the search instructions on the search engine's home page. Look for sections entitled "Help," "Advanced Search," "Frequently Asked Questions," and so forth.

AltaVista has two search modes: simple and advanced. The simple search mode only supports implied, or pseudo-Boolean, searching. This means that you could perform an AND and NOT search by typing a **+** before the word if it has to appear in each of the results, and a **–** before words that you don't want in the results. Since our topic involves many ORs, we will need to do an advanced search.

When you open AltaVista, you will see the simple search form. You will need to go to the advanced search section. Then you will want to look at the search instructions for its advanced search capability.

❋*Do It!* Click on the hyperlink **Advanced**.

Your screen will fill with the advanced search form.

❋*Do It!* Click on the **Help** hyperlink.

❋*Do It!* Click on **Advanced Help**.

Scroll down the page until you see the advanced search example, as shown in Figure 5.2.

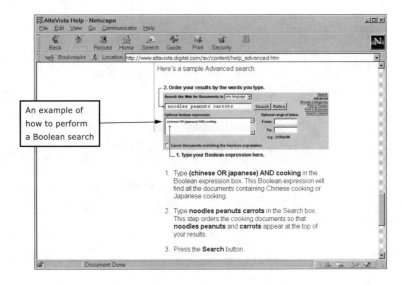

Figure 5.2—Help for Advanced Searches in AltaVista

After reading the extensive help screens in AltaVista, you can start determining how to construct your search expression. In addition to reviewing how to combine Boolean operators with phrases and parentheses, you'll need to find out how AltaVista truncates words. You'll also need to read the section on ranking, or ordering, your results. This is a crucial part of AltaVista's advanced search mode. You must type words in the search box that you want to have in the first documents returned to you. If you don't, the results will be listed in any order, and the first documents may not be as relevant as the last documents returned.

Chapter 5

7 Create a search expression using syntax that is appropriate for the search engine.

Now that you've read the search help, it's time to formulate the search expression. It will help to write it out before you type it in the search form. Here is a possible way to express this search:

(teenage or adolescen*) and girls and ("eating disorders" or "anorexia nervosa" or bulimia) and ("self-esteem" or "self-respect")

Keep in mind that you can always modify your search later. Let's try entering it in AltaVista's advanced search form.

❁*Do It!* Click on the **Back** icon twice to return to the advanced search form.

❁*Do It!* Enter the search expression in the form provided, as shown in Figure 5.3.

❁*Do It!* In the search box, type in the phrase **"eating disorders"** as shown in Figure 5.3.

Make sure all of the quotation marks are present and that you've closed all of the parentheses properly. Check your spelling and determine if you have the ANDs and ORs in the proper places.

❁*Do It!* Click on **Search**.

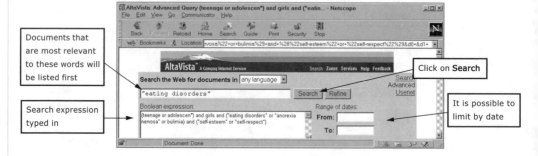

Figure 5.3—Advanced Search in AltaVista with Search Expression Entered

8 View the results. How many hits were returned? Were the results relevant to your query?

Note the number of hits this search has returned to your screen. Look at a few of the titles. Do they appear to be relevant? Figure 5.4 shows the first few. Because the Web is always changing, the results shown may not be the same ones that you retrieve.

❁*Do It!* Click on the title of the first result in the list.

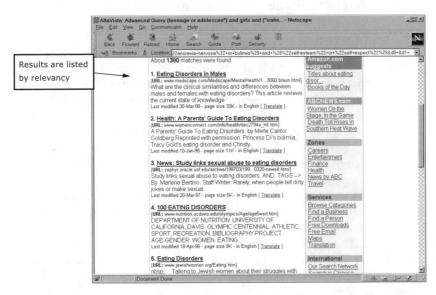

Results are listed by relevancy

Figure 5.4—Results of AltaVista Search

Examine the first page that appears on your screen. Is the information relevant to the search query? Scroll down to the bottom of the page and click on the arrows to see the next page of results, as shown in Figure 5.5. Look through the results on this page to determine whether they seem relevant.

Click here to go to the next page of results

Click here to go to the end of the results

Figure 5.5—Navigating Search Results in AltaVista

9 Modify your search if needed. Go back to Steps 2 through 4 and revise your query accordingly.

The results seem relevant, and the number of hits is an adequate set with which to work. You may, however, want to limit the results by date. You could do this by going back to the search query screen and typing a date in the space provided, shown in Figure 5.3.

10 Try the same search in a different search engine, following Steps 5 through 9 above.

Since our topic is multifaceted and requires a powerful search engine, we'll do the same search in Northern Light.

Chapter 5

Performing the Same Search in Northern Light

Overview

Northern Light, **http://www.northernlight.com**, is a full-text database that not only indexes World Wide Web documents, but also includes a fee-based database containing about a million articles from about 2,000 sources. These sources include journals, newspapers, books, and other types of publications. If you want to view a document from this special collection, you will be charged a fee. The cost ranges from $1 to $4 per item. You can subscribe to the service for a small monthly fee that covers the cost of obtaining up to 50 documents. Northern Light has another unique feature: the way results are organized. In addition to listing the results of your search by relevancy, Northern Light organizes the results for you in subject folders. These folders provide a way for you to screen, or filter, your results and can help with information overload. These folders are created anew with each search you perform, so the headings vary depending on the subject matter. There are four major types of folders: type, subject, source, and language. A type folder might be "press releases" or "job advertisements." A subject folder may be "global warming" or "epidemics." Source folders would resemble "www.globalchange.org" or "commercial sites." A language folder will group non-English language results together, which is another helpful feature. We'll follow these steps, which correspond to Steps 6 through 9 of the basic search strategy:

1. Read the search instructions on the search engine's home page. Look for sections entitled "Help," "Advanced Search," "Frequently Asked Questions," and so forth.
2. Create a search expression using syntax that is appropriate for the search engine.
3. View the results. How many hits were returned? Were the results relevant to your query?
4. Modify your search if needed. Go back and revise your query accordingly.
5. End the session.

Details

1 Read the search instructions on the search engine's home page. Look for sections entitled "Help," "Advanced Search," "Frequently Asked Questions," and so forth.

First we need to go to Northern Light.

❁*Do It!* Click on the location field, type **http://www. northernlight.com**, and press Enter.

❁*Do It!* Click on **HELP/HINTS** on Northern Light's home page.

Your screen should look like the one in Figure 5.6.

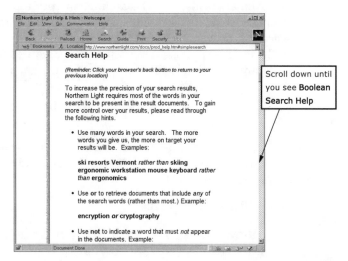

Figure 5.6—Northern Light Help

✿*Do It!* Scroll down the page until you see the hyperlink **Boolean Search Help**, and click on it.

Your screen should look like the one pictured in Figure 5.7.

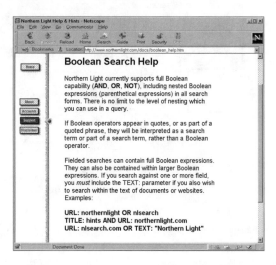

Figure 5.7—Boolean Search Help in Northern Light

2 Create a search expression, using syntax that is appropriate for the search engine.

✿*Do It!* After checking out the help pages, return to Northern Light's home page by clicking on **Home**, located on the left side of the screen.

Chapter 5

Now you are ready to start searching for your topic in Northern Light. We know that Northern Light supports phrase searching and Boolean searching, so we won't need to change our strategy. In fact, we can type in the exact search expression that was used in the AltaVista search. The only thing that is different is Northern Light's search form is much smaller than AltaVista's.

✷*Do It!* Type the following search expression in the search form provided:

(teenage or adolescen*) and girls and ("eating disorders" or "anorexia nervosa" or bulimia) and ("self-esteem" or "self-respect")

✷*Do It!* Click on **SEARCH**.

3 View the results. How many hits were returned? Were the results relevant to your query?

Look at the results of the search query, as shown in Figure 5.8. Your results may be different.

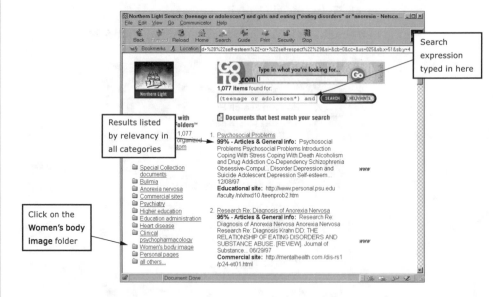

Figure 5.8—Northern Light Search Results

The results on the right side of the screen are listed by relevancy. Along the left side of the screen are Custom Search Folders. One of the folders looks particularly promising: **Women's body image**. Let's see what's inside this folder.

✷*Do It!* Click on the **Women's body image** folder, as shown in Figure 5.8.

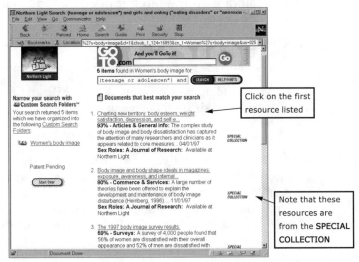

Figure 5.9—Items in Northern Light's Women's Body Image Folder

Figure 5.9 shows a partial list of the resources in this folder. Note that the first three resources are from the **SPECIAL COLLECTION**. This means that you will have to set up an account with Northern Light in order to read the full articles.

Let's access the first resource listed.

❋*Do It!* Click on the first resource listed, **Charting new territory: body esteem, weight satisfaction, depression, and self-e...**

Figure 5.10 shows a summary of this article, which is from the journal *Sex Roles: A Journal of Research*. There is a summary, or abstract, of the article. If you want to purchase this article, you'll need to click on the hyperlink **Purchase Document**.

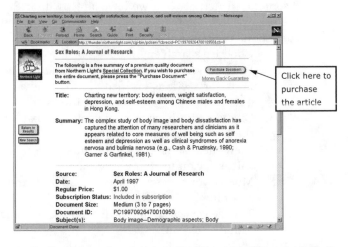

Figure 5.10—Summary of an Article in Northern Light's Special Collection

4 Modify your search if needed. Go back and revise your query accordingly.

5 End the session.

You can end the session now or continue to the next activity.

❀*Do It!* To end the session now, click on **File** on the menu bar, and select **Exit** from the menu.

End of Activity 5.1

As we saw in this activity, AltaVista and Northern Light handle multi-faceted search queries in much the same way. In some ways, the AltaVista search form makes it easier to perform a search. Because it is large you can type in a long search expression with ease (if you have read the search help carefully). Northern Light supports most of the same search features that AltaVista does. The two major differences are that Northern Light's results are organized into folders and its collection includes selective resources that you can pay for.

There are pros and cons to using any of the search engines. Sometimes it comes down to which service you are more comfortable with using. In the following two activities, we'll be searching for the same topic in two very different databases: Infoseek and MetaCrawler. Infoseek is a full-text search engine database, whereas MetaCrawler is a meta-search tool that allows you to search several search engines simultaneously. In performing searches in each of these indexes, we will follow the steps laid out in the basic search strategy.

Activity 5.2   Search Strategies in Infoseek

Overview

We'll be searching for the same information that we did in Activity 5.1—how self-esteem relates to teenage girls' likelihood of developing eating disorders. In Activity 5.1, we have already done Steps 1 through 4 of the basic search strategy, so we'll now do the following steps, which correspond to Steps 5 through 10 of the strategy:

1. Choose a search engine.
2. Read the search instructions on the search engine's home page. Look for sections entitled "Help," "Advanced Search," "Frequently Asked Questions," and so forth.
3. Create a search expression using syntax that is appropriate for the search engine.
4. View the results. How many hits were returned? Were the results relevant to your query?
5. Modify your search if needed. Go back and revise your query accordingly.
6. Try the same search in a different search engine.
7. End the session.

Details

1   Choose a search engine.

We'll be searching Infoseek, another popular search engine. Infoseek doesn't support Boolean searching as AltaVista and Northern Light do, but it does allow for the use of implied Boolean operators—the **+** and the **–**. These operators represent the Boolean AND and NOT, but there is no OR capability in Infoseek. This makes it difficult to search for synonyms. Infoseek does allow you to search the results of another search, which is one way around this limitation. Let's go to Infoseek and see how it handles our topic.

❊*Do It!* Click on the location field, type **http://www.infoseek.com**, and press **Enter**.

View the Infoseek home page, as shown in Figure 5.11.

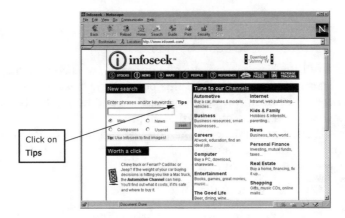

Figure 5.11—Infoseek's Home Page

2   Read the search instructions on the search engine's home page. Look for sections entitled "Help," "Advanced Search," "Frequently Asked Questions," and so forth.

❊*Do It!* Click on **Tips**, as shown in Figure 5.11.

❊*Do It!* Now click on **Quick reference**.

You can read through the tips if you like.

The "Quick reference to syntax" page appears in Figure 5.12. From reading the search tips, we determine the following:

❊   Infoseek supports phrase searching by requiring quotes to be placed around words that must be together or by placing hyphens between adjacent words.

❊   A **+** should be placed in front of a word or phrase that must be present in the Web pages found.

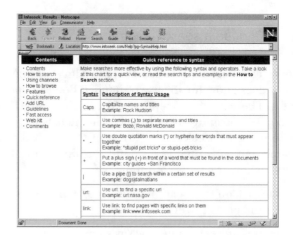

Figure 5.12—Search Help in Infoseek

3 Create a search expression, using syntax that is appropriate for the search engine.

Since full Boolean searching isn't supported, it's better to not type in too many words or phrases at this point. If we typed in **+ "anorexia nervosa" + bulimia + "self-esteem"** in addition to the two phrases below, we would be requiring that *all* phrases and words appear in the Web pages, which might give us too few results. It's best to start out with fewer terms at first and to see what results we obtain. We can always modify our results later.

❀*Do It!* Click on **Home** at the top of the page.

❀*Do It!* Type **+ "teenage girls" + "eating disorders"**, and click on **seek** as shown in Figure 5.13.

Type in search expression and click on **seek**

Figure 5.13—Search Expression Entered in Infoseek

4 View the results. How many hits were returned? Were the results relevant to your query?

This search retrieved some very relevant hits. A few of these results appear in Figure 5.14. Don't be surprised if you obtain different results.

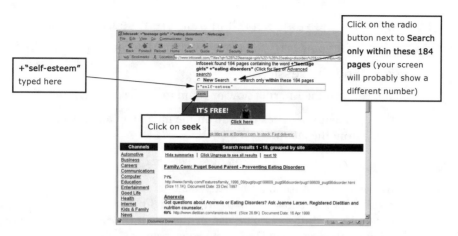

Figure 5.14—Results of Search in Infoseek with Added Keyword Phrase

5 Modify your search if needed. Go back and revise your query accordingly.

Infoseek allows you to search only the results of a search. Let's say that of the documents that the search retrieved, you want to know which ones have the phrase *self-esteem* in them. All that is required is to type **+ "self-esteem"** in the search form provided and to indicate that only these results should be searched. Let's do that now.

❂*Do It!* In the search form provided, type **+ "self-esteem"**, as shown in Figure 5.14.

❂*Do It!* Click on the button next to **Search only within these 184 pages**. Your screen will most likely show a different number of pages.

❂*Do It!* Click on **seek**, as shown in Figure 5.14.

Figure 5.15 shows the results of this modification. Remember that you may have different results, because the Web is always changing.

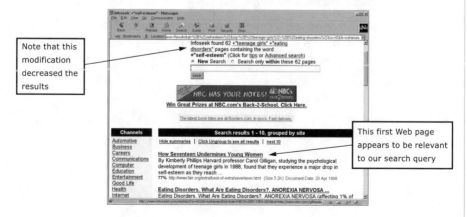

Figure 5.15—Results of Modifying the Original Search in Infoseek

6   Try the same search in a different search engine.

Next we're going to try the same search in MetaCrawler in Activity 5.3.

7   End the session.

You can exit the Internet now or go on to the next activity.

❀*Do It!* To exit now, click on **File** on the menu bar, and select **Exit** from the menu.

End of Activity 5.2

Infoseek proved to be an effective search engine. We obtained fewer results than in AltaVista or Northern Light, because there is no OR capability in Infoseek. The use of the Boolean OR expands results, whereas the use of AND or + narrows results.

Activity 5.3   Search Strategies in MetaCrawler

Overview

In this activity, we'll look for information on the same topic in MetaCrawler. As stated before, MetaCrawler is a meta-search tool. Also known as parallel-search tools or unified search interfaces, meta-search tools don't create their own indexes. They merely provide a search interface so that you can use several search engines and directories at the same time with one search expression. Currently, MetaCrawler searches five different databases: AltaVista, Excite, Lycos, WebCrawler, and Yahoo! Meta-search tools can be very useful for single-word subjects but unreliable for multiterm, multifaceted searches, such as the one we have been using in this chapter. Let's see how MetaCrawler handles our topic. We will be following Steps 5 through 10 of the basic search strategy, as we did in Activity 5.2.

Details

1   Choose a search engine.

Let's go to MetaCrawler.

❀*Do It!* Click on the location field, type in the URL for MetaCrawler, **http://www.metacrawler.com**, and press ⟨Enter⟩.

Your screen should look like the picture in Figure 5.16.

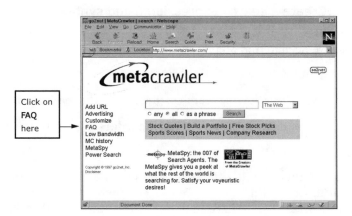

Figure 5.16—MetaCrawler's Home Page

2 Read the search instructions on the search engine's home page. Look for sections entitled "Help," "Advanced Search," "Frequently Asked Questions," and so forth.

In order to find out how to use MetaCrawler, read its documentation.

✱*Do It!* Click on **FAQ** on the left side of the screen, as shown in Figure 5.16.

✱*Do It!* Scroll down and click on the hyperlink **How can I refine MetaCrawler searches?**

Here you will notice that MetaCrawler uses implied Boolean operators (+ and –) and that phrase searching, using double quotation marks, is a supported feature. See Figure 5.17.

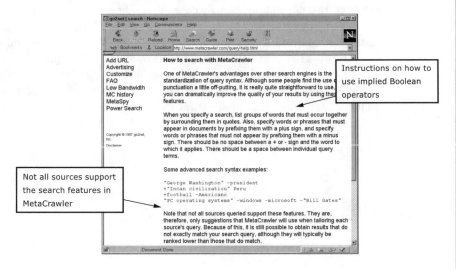

Figure 5.17—MetaCrawler Documentation

Chapter 5

3 Create a search expression using syntax that is appropriate for the search engine.

First, we need to find MetaCrawler's search form.

❀*Do It!* Scroll to the bottom of the FAQ page.

❀*Do It!* Type the following search expression in the search form:

+ "teenage girls" + "eating disorders" + "self-esteem"

❀*Do It!* Click on **all**.

By using this search expression and choosing **all**, you are telling MetaCrawler to find all the Web pages in which each of these three phrases occur. The + in front of each phrase indicates that the phrase *must* appear somewhere in the Web pages.

❀*Do It!* Click on **Search**.

This will initiate your search request. See Figure 5.18.

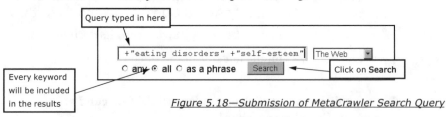

Figure 5.18—Submission of MetaCrawler Search Query

As MetaCrawler works to satisfy the search request, it will list on the screen the different search tools it has searched so far, along with the number of the results found in each one. You can't always rely on these results, however. If MetaCrawler says there are zero results in a certain database, this doesn't necessarily mean that there are zero results. Sometimes the search query in MetaCrawler doesn't coincide with the search features supported in the individual databases. When the results appear, they are listed by relevance and not by the search engine or directory in which they were found. MetaCrawler should detect and weed out duplicates. Figure 5.24 depicts how the results will be listed. Remember that your results may differ from the ones shown here.

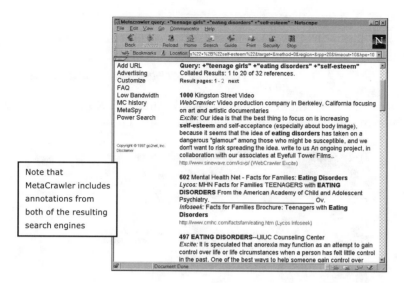

Note that MetaCrawler includes annotations from both of the resulting search engines

Figure 5.19—MetaCrawler Results

4   View the results. How many hits were returned? Were the results relevant to your query?

After looking through the results, we decide to modify our search to see if we can get more hits.

5   Modify your search if needed. Go back and revise your query accordingly.

Since MetaCrawler does not support nested Boolean searching, it may be unwise to add too many synonyms for the words we've already entered. We could add one more term, for example *bulimia,* and then change the search option to *any* instead of *all.* The danger would be that some of the results may not be as relevant as we would like. In effect, this would be the same as placing an OR between each word instead of an AND.

Let's modify our search by adding the extra keyword and changing the search options.

❋*Do It!* Scroll to the bottom of the page.

❋*Do It!* Place the cursor at the very beginning of the search query box and type **+ bulimia**. Make sure there is a space between bulimia and **+ "teenage girls"**.

❋*Do It!* Click next to **any**.

❋*Do It!* Click on **Search**.

The search query screen should look like the one in Figure 5.20.

151

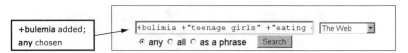

Figure 5.20—Modification of MetaCrawler Search

A partial list of the results appears in Figure 5.21. Notice how many more results resulted from changing the search options.

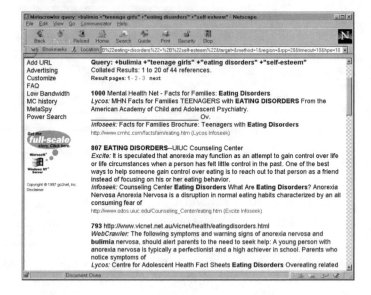

Figure 5.21—Results of Modifying Search in MetaCrawler

6   Try the same search in a different search engine.

If you like, you could try the same search in a different search engine on your own.

7   End the session.

✿*Do It!* Click on **File** on the menu bar, and select **Exit** from the menu.

End of Activity 5.3

In Activities 5.1, 5.2, and 5.3, we searched for information on the same topic in four different search engines. Each one had its own particular syntax and individual search and output features. We saw the importance of reading each search engine's documentation before going online. All of the search engines gave relevant results, but none of them gave the same results.

Summary

Search engines are tools that search databases. These search engines have been created by computer programs, commonly referred to as spiders or robots. These spiders go out onto the World Wide Web and put every single word of every Web page they find into a database. With the help of our search request, the search engine then searches this full-text database for us. Some databases are not full-text, but instead consist of selected words from Web documents.

In either case, each search engine accesses its database differently. Even though many search engine databases claim to cover the entire Web, the same search performed in more than one database never returns the same exact results. If you want to do a thorough search, you should become familiar with a few of the different search engines. Toward this end, it is important to understand the major search features, such as Boolean logic, phrase searching, truncation, and others before you get online. It is also necessary to read each search engine's documentation before you enter the search request in the query box. You may want to check the documentation often, since search engines are constantly changing their search and output features.

It can help to try your search in a meta-search tool if you're not overly concerned about obtaining precise and comprehensive results. That way, you can gather hits from several databases at once.

In this chapter, we introduced the basic search strategy, a 10-step procedure that can help you formulate search requests, submit them to search engines, and modify the results retrieved. We have focused on the major search engines on the World Wide Web, but there are several hundred smaller search engines on the Web that search smaller databases. We'll discuss these in some detail in Chapter 7, "Specialized Databases." In addition, there are other search engines that are not free to the public; they require passwords or subscription costs. Our intent in this chapter was to give you a foundation in searching any database, no matter whether it is large or small, fee-based or not. All of the steps in the basic search strategy apply to any database.

Selected Terms Introduced in This Chapter

case sensitivity	low precision/high recall
concept searching	meta-tag
default setting	modification of search results
duplicate detection	nested Boolean logic
field	proximity searching
field searching	relevancy ranking
full-text indexing	results per page
high precision/high recall	sorting
high precision/low recall	stop word
implied Boolean operator	syntax
keyword indexing	truncation
limiting by date	wildcard

6
Chapter

Using Search Engines

In this chapter, we'll continue to focus on searching databases, employing the 10-step basic search strategy described and used in Chapter 5. We'll do several activities that showcase search and output features that we didn't cover in earlier chapters. To refresh your memory, we list the strategy here.

Basic Search Strategy: The 10 Steps
1. Identify the important concepts of your search.
2. Choose the keywords that describe these concepts.
3. Determine whether there are synonyms, related terms, or other variations of the keywords that should be included.
4. Determine which search features may apply, including truncation, proximity operators, Boolean operators, and so forth.
5. Choose a search engine.
6. Read the search instructions on the search engine's home page. Look for sections entitled "Help," "Advanced Search," "Frequently Asked Questions," and so forth.
7. Create a search expression using syntax that is appropriate for the search engine.
8. View the results. How many hits were returned? Were the results relevant to your query?
9. Modify your search if needed. Go back to Steps 2 through 4 and revise your query accordingly.
10. Try the same search in a different search engine, following Steps 5 through 9 above.

We'll refer to the steps in the strategy as we go through each activity.

Tip

Remember that the Web is always changing and that your results may differ from those shown here. Don't let this confuse you. The activities demonstrate fundamental skills. These skills don't change, even though the number of results obtained or the actual screens may look very different.

Activity 6.1   Search Strategies in HotBot

Overview

In the first activity, we will look for recent information (that is, within the last six months) on the Shining Path, a revolutionary group in Peru. Before we get online, we will follow Steps 1 through 5 of the basic search strategy as we formulate the main ideas of our search.

- Steps 1 and 2: The important concepts and keywords are *Shining Path* and *Peru.*

- Step 3: Since the Shining Path is a revolutionary group in Peru, we'll want to include the phrase in Spanish, the primary language spoken in Peru. *Shining Path* in Spanish is *Sendero Luminoso.*

- Step 4: Since we don't want pages that have information about *Tupac Amaru*, another revolutionary group in Peru, we'll need to use the Boolean NOT operator. We'll also need to search with the phrases *Shining Path* AND *Sendero Luminoso,* if possible.

- Step 5: We'll choose HotBot, **http://www.hotbot.com**, a full-text database that is good for very specific searches because it supports full Boolean searching and has the capability to limit searches by date.

Now we're ready to go online and search HotBot. We'll follow these steps, which closely correspond to Steps 6 through 9 of the basic search strategy:

1. Go to the home page for HotBot.
2. Read the search instructions on HotBot's home page (Step 6).
3. Create a search expression using syntax appropriate for HotBot (Step 7).
4. View the results (Step 8).
5. Using the Find function, search a Web page for the keywords *Shining Path* or *Sendero Luminoso* (Step 8).
6. Modify the search by limiting it to educational sites only, and view the results (Step 9).
7. End the session.

Details

1 Go to the home page for HotBot.

❀*Do It!* Click on the location field, type **http://www.hotbot.com**, and press **Enter**.

2 Read the search instructions on HotBot's home page.

❀*Do It!* Click on **Help** as shown in Figure 6.1.

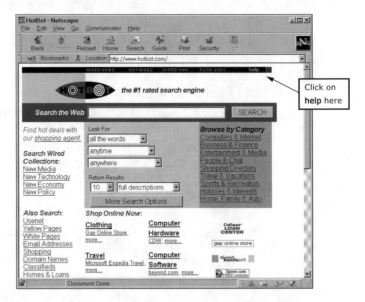

Figure 6.1—HotBot's Home Page

Your screen will fill with a list of common questions. Along the left side are several hyperlinks that will take you to other sections of the help page. One of the hyperlinks is **Search Tips**.

❀*Do It!* Click on **Search Tips**.

Your screen should include more hyperlinks.

❀*Do It!* Click on **Getting Started**, as shown in Figure 6.2.

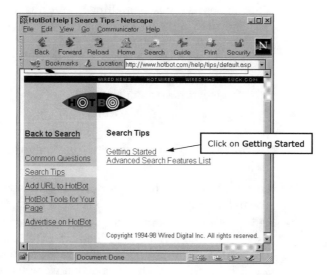

Figure 6.2—Search Tips in HotBot

The Getting Started section covers simple searches in HotBot, as shown in Figure 6.3. To read about advanced search features, click on the **Back** icon to return to the earlier window and select **Advanced Search Features List**.

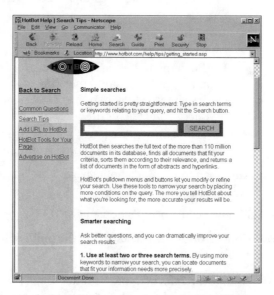

Figure 6.3—Simple Search Features in HotBot

After reading through all the help information, we can conclude that HotBot:

- ❋ supports phrase searching by offering the option **exact phrase** in the pulldown menu or by enclosing the phrase in quotation marks.
- ❋ supports Boolean searching by choosing words from the pulldown menus or by typing **and**, **or**, and **not**.
- ❋ supports nested Boolean logic.
- ❋ ignores case in most searches.

3 **Create a search expression using syntax appropriate for HotBot.**

You may want to review the section called "Search Features Common to Most Search Engines" in Chapter 5 before working on this step.

- ❋ Because we want pages that match the phrase *Shining Path* OR *Sendero Luminoso*, and that match the word *Peru* but NOT the phrase *Tupac Amaru*, we need to use nested Boolean logic. This means that we will use parentheses around the two phrases to separate the OR expression from the NOT, and parentheses around all three phrases to separate them from the word *Peru*. It would look like this: *((Shining Path or Sendero Luminoso) not Tupac Amaru) and Peru.* (Note: Since we are formulating a Boolean expression for this search, we need to use Boolean operators to exclude terms.)
- ❋ Since HotBot is not case sensitive, there is no need to capitalize proper nouns.
- ❋ HotBot supports phrase searching, so we will need to put quotation marks around the phrases. Now the search expression will look like this: *(("shining path" or "sendero luminoso") not "tupac amaru") and peru.*
- ❋ To search only those pages modified or indexed in the last six months, we need to choose from the pulldown options.

❋*Do It!* To return to HotBot's home page, click on the **Back to Search** button.

You will now be at HotBot's home page.

❋*Do It!* Choose **Boolean phrase** from the pulldown menu next to **Look For**.

❋*Do It!* In the search form, type the following: **(("shining path" or "sendero luminoso") not "tupac amaru") and peru**.

❋*Do It!* Choose **in the last 6 months** from the pulldown menu next to **anytime**.

Your screen should now look like the one pictured in Figure 6.4.

✱*Do It!* Click on **SEARCH**.

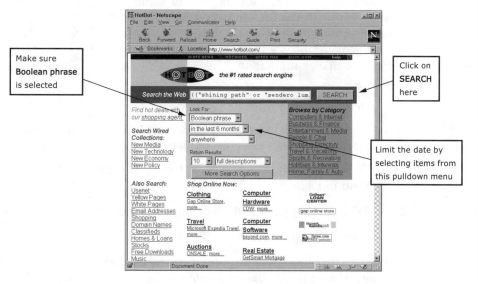

Make sure **Boolean phrase** is selected

Click on **SEARCH** here

Limit the date by selecting items from this pulldown menu

Figure 6.4—Search Request Entered

4   View the results.

The results of this search partially appear in Figure 6.5.

✱*Do It!* Click on a Web page that looks interesting and that does not have the search expression's keywords in the title or annotation.

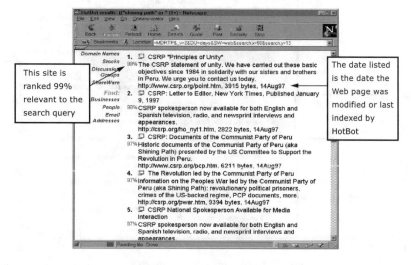

This site is ranked 99% relevant to the search query

The date listed is the date the Web page was modified or last indexed by HotBot

Figure 6.5—Partial List of Results in HotBot

Chapter 6

To go directly to the portion of a page that mentions the keyword(s) you searched for, you can use the Find function. To demonstrate how this works, you'll need to click on a Web page that doesn't have the search expression's keywords in the title or annotation. The reason for this is that you don't want to select a page that may have the keyword(s) only in the title or annotation.

5 **Using the Find function, search a Web page for the key-words** *shining path* **or** *sendero luminoso.*

Once you are in a Web page that looks interesting, try to find the words *shining path* in the page, as shown in Figure 6.6.

❋*Do It!* Click on **Edit** in the menu bar at the top of the screen. Choose **Find in Page**.

❋*Do It!* Type **shining path** in the pane next to **Find what**.

❋*Do It!* Click on **Find Next**.

Did you find the phrase *shining path*? If not, try to find the phrase *sendero luminoso*. One of these phrases should appear in the Web page. If they don't, the Web page publisher may have entered one or both of the phrases as meta-tags.

❋*Do It!* To remove the **Find** screen, click on **Cancel**.

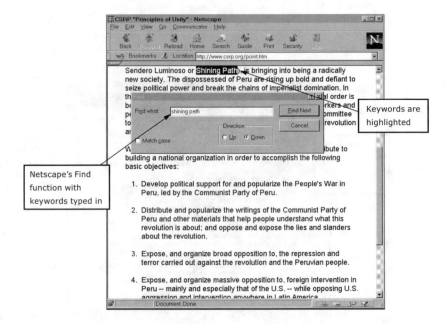

Figure 6.6—Using the Find in Page Option to Locate Keywords in Web Pages

6   Modify the search by limiting it to educational sites only, and view the results.

✿*Do It!* Click on the **Back** button in the toolbar to return to the search results.

✿*Do It!* Click on **Revise**.

You will return to the original search query screen.

✿*Do It!* Click on **More Search Options**.

✿*Do It!* Scroll down the page until you reach the Location/Domain section.

✿*Do It!* Click on the radio button next to **Domain** and type **.edu** in the form provided, as shown in Figure 6.7.

✿*Do It!* Scroll to the top of the page and click on **SEARCH**.

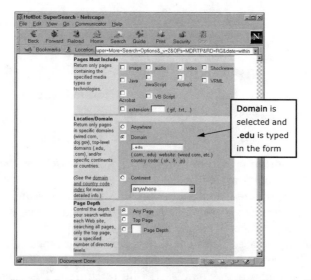

Figure 6.7—Limiting a Search to Educational Web Pages in HotBot

Modifying your search results by domain in this way will return only those Web pages that have URLs ending in **.edu**, which means that they will come from North American educational sites, as shown in Figure 6.8. This doesn't mean that every Web page is going to be authored by a university or college department, however. Many of them will be home pages of students and other people associated with academic institutions. Using this limiting device is just one way to help you narrow results.

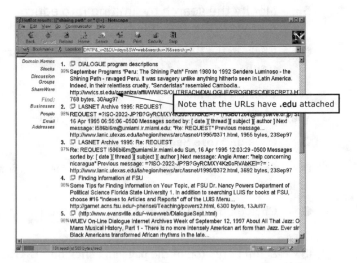

Figure 6.8—HotBot Results—Web Pages Originating from Educational Sites

7   End the session.

You can end the session now or stay online to do the next activity.

✸*Do It!* To end the session now, click on **File** on the menu bar and select **Exit** from the menu.

End of Activity 6.1

HotBot proved to be a good index to search for the topic we chose. It supports nested Boolean logic, phrase searching, and limiting by date. In the next activity, we'll use AltaVista to search for the same topic. AltaVista is one of the largest full-text databases, as is HotBot. It is also a good search engine to use when looking for specific information. We showcased AltaVista's advanced search mode in Activity 5.1. In this activity, we'll employ its simple search mode. This time, we won't focus on limiting by date as we did in HotBot. The simple search mode in AltaVista doesn't support date searching (although the advanced mode does). We'll demonstrate AltaVista's field-searching capability by limiting our results to those URLs that have a particular host name.

Activity 6.2	Search Strategies in AltaVista's Simple Search Mode

Overview

Since we already followed Steps 1 through 4 of the basic search strategy in Activity 6.1 by determining the keywords and search features (phrases, synonyms, Boolean logic, and so forth), and since we chose the search engine (Step 5), we can proceed to Steps 6 through 9. We will take the following steps in this activity:

1. Go to the home page for AltaVista.
2. Read the instructions for AltaVista's simple search mode (Step 6).
3. Create a search expression using syntax appropriate for AltaVista's simple search mode (Step 7).
4. View the results (Step 8).
5. Modify the search by limiting it to Web pages with **csrp.org** in the host name portion of the URLs, and then view the results (Step 9).
6. End the session.

Details

1 **Go to the home page for AltaVista.**

❋*Do It!* Click on the location field, type **http://www.altavista.digital. com**, and press **Enter**.

2 **Read the instructions for AltaVista's simple search mode.**

❋*Do It!* Click on **Help** on AltaVista's home page, as shown in Figure 6.9.

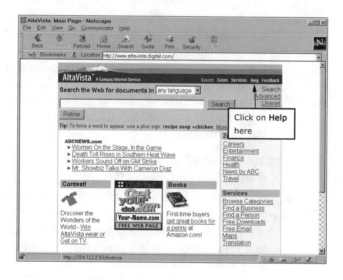

Figure 6.9—AltaVista Home Page

A partial list of the help topics available appears in Figure 6.10. AltaVista gives examples of the particular search features it supports.

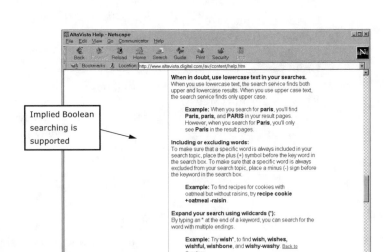

Implied Boolean searching is supported

Figure 6.10—Help for Simple Searches in AltaVista

After reading the search help screens, we determine that AltaVista

- supports phrase searching by requiring the user to enclose the words in quotation marks.

- uses implied Boolean operators (**+** and **–**) and not full Boolean logic (AND, OR, NOT).

- is case sensitive, so it recognizes capitalization. (In other words, if you don't capitalize the first letters in proper nouns, it will find matches for the words in lowercase and uppercase. If you use capital letters, however, an exact match will occur.)

3   Create a search expression, using syntax appropriate for AltaVista's simple search mode.

You may want to review the section called "Search Features Common to Most Search Engines" in Chapter 5 before working on this step.

- We want *Shining Path, Sendero Luminoso, Tupac Amaru,* and *Peru* searched as proper nouns, so we'll capitalize the first letters of these words.

- Since we are searching with the phrases *Shining Path, Sendero Luminoso,* and *Tupac Amaru,* we need to put quotation marks around them.

- Full Boolean logic is not supported, so we'll need to use implied Boolean logic. The phrase *Shining Path* must appear in the Web pages, so we'll put a **+** in front of this phrase. We may want *Sendero Luminoso* to appear as well, but it's not absolutely necessary, so we'll enter this without a **+** in front of it. Since there is no way in the simple search mode to place an OR between keywords or phrases, this is the best we can do. We also want the word *Peru* to appear, so we'll place a **+** in front of this word, as well. The phrase *Tupac Amaru* must not appear, so we need to place a **–** in front of this phrase. In essence, we are telling the search engine to return to our screen those Web pages that must have *Shining Path,* may have *Sendero Luminoso,* must have *Peru,* and must not have *Tupac Amaru* in them.

Now we're ready to type in the search expression.

🔆*Do It!* Click on the **Back** button in the toolbar.

🔆*Do It!* Type the following in the search form provided:

+ "Shining Path" "Sendero Luminoso" + Peru –"Tupac Amaru"

The search query is shown typed in Figure 6.11.

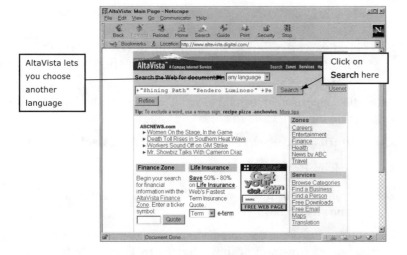

Figure 6.11—AltaVista Search Query Entered Using Implied Boolean Operators

🔆*Do It!* Click on **Search**, as shown in Figure 6.11.

4   View the results.

🔆*Do It!* The results appear in Figure 6.12. Scroll down the list of results until you find a Web page entitled **CSRP: Mumia Abu-Jamal on the Revolution in Peru**. Click on this title.

This Web page is published by an organization called the Committee to Support the Revolution in Peru (CSRP). It is important to find out who publishes Web pages so you can determine how objective or subjective the information is.

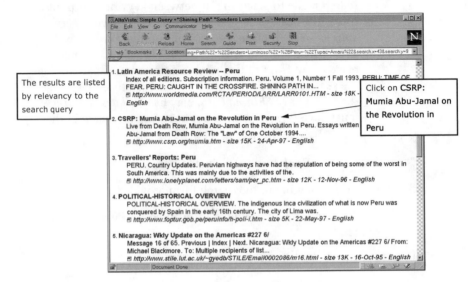

The results are listed by relevancy to the search query

Click on **CSRP: Mumia Abu-Jamal on the Revolution in Peru**

Figure 6.12—Results of AltaVista Search

5 Modify the search by limiting it to Web pages with **csrp.org** in the host name portion of the URLs, and then view the results.

AltaVista supports field searching. You'll need to refer back to the online help to find out how to do this.

✸*Do It!* Return to the search results page by clicking **Back**.

✸*Do It!* Click on **Help** at the top of the page.

✸*Do It!* Scroll down until you see a table entitled "Fancy Features for Typical Searches."

Figure 6.13 shows the portion of the help screen in AltaVista that describes how to constrain or limit searches by field. Note that you can search by host name. What this means is that you can search by the name of the organization, company, or educational facility by limiting your search to just those URLs with the name you are seeking. In our example, we want to examine the results for those Web pages that the CSRP has published. The CSRP is the host, and it is an organization. We know this by the **.org** in CSRP's URL.

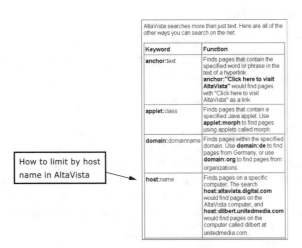

How to limit by host name in AltaVista

Figure 6.13—Field Searching Explained in AltaVista

To limit the results to just those Web pages that have **csrp.org** in the host name portion of the URL, we will first need to return to our original search query.

✹*Do It!* Click on **Back** once in the toolbar at the top of the screen.

✹*Do It!* Place your cursor at the end of the search expression (after **Tupac Amaru**), press the [Space Bar], and type **+ host:csrp.org**.

✹*Do It!* Click on **Search**.

View the results that appear on your screen after this modification. All of the Web pages returned should have **csrp.org** in the host name portion of their URLs, as shown in Figure 6.14.

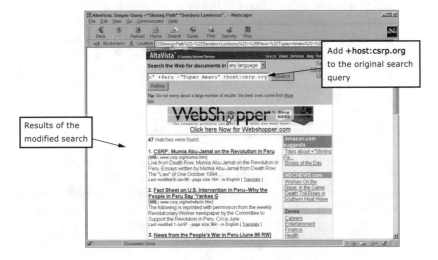

Add +host:csrp.org to the original search query

Results of the modified search

Figure 6.14—Limiting Search to URLs with ***csrp.org***

Chapter 6

6   End the session.

You can end the session now or stay online to do the next activity.

❋*Do It!*   To end the session now, click on **File** on the menu bar and select **Exit** from the menu.

End of Activity 6.2

In Activities 6.1 and 6.2, we focused on finding general information on a fairly obscure topic, the Shining Path. We discussed how to narrow results by excluding words that we didn't want in the search results, by limiting results by date, and by limiting the results to certain URLs. In the next section, we'll concentrate on searching for specific items, such as information about writers and their works, quotations, or specific lines of poetry.

Using Search Engines for Specific Information

When looking for specific information, you can use the basic search strategy, but you can employ it a bit more loosely than when you develop multifaceted searches. You'll need to prepare your search strategy before you get online by deciding whether there are name variations to include and determining what search features to employ, such as phrase searching, Boolean operators, and so forth. Choosing a database will be as important as it ever was; you'll want a database that supports features that will help you find the most precise results.

Full-text search engine databases (AltaVista, HotBot, Excite, Infoseek, and so forth) are the best places to go for specific information because almost every word in every page is indexed. In the following activity, we'll show you how to use search engines to find very specific information, such as proper names and quotations. When looking for information about a person, a quotation, or a line of poetry, it is essential to be exact when you type in the search request. If you are looking for a name, you also must include the different ways it might appear in the index you're searching. When you look for a quotation or line of text, it is again very important to know most of the major words in the phrase and to spell them correctly. The following activity is an excellent example of both of these types of searches.

Activity 6.3   Finding Specific Information in Excite

Overview

We're going to search Excite, **http://www.excite.com**. Excite is large and powerful and is mostly full-text, in that it ignores certain words, such as articles and prepositions. Excite supports concept searching; that is, the search engine automatically searches for synonyms of the words you enter. For example, if you asked for *teenager,* it might return results with the word *adolescent* as well.

In this activity, we are going to do a couple of different searches, one on a person's name and the other on a line of poetry. First, we'll search Excite's database for information, and hopefully for a bibliography, of the works of the writer Saki. Before going online, we have done our homework and have learned that Saki is also known as H.H. Munro, Hector Munro, or Hector H. Munro. After we do that search, we'll look for the poem with the line "Till human voices wake us, and we drown."

We'll follow these steps:

1. Go to the home page for Excite.
2. Read the search tips.
3. Formulate and enter the search expression.
4. View the results and access a Web page.
5. Search for the line of poetry "Till human voices wake us, and we drown."
6. View the results and access *The Love Song of J. Alfred Prufrock.*
7. End the session.

Details

1   Go to the home page for Excite.

❋*Do It!* Click on the location field, type **http://www.excite.com**, and press ⌑**Enter**⌑.

2   Read the search tips.

❋*Do It!* On Excite's home page, click **Search Tips**, as shown in Figure 6.15.

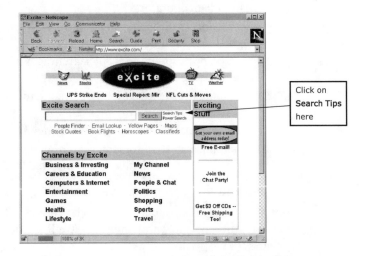

Figure 6.15—Excite's Home Page

The list of help topics in Excite appears in Figure 6.16. It's a good idea to read the help information thoroughly.

Chapter 6

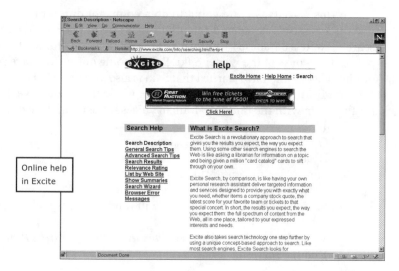

Figure 6.16—Help Screen in Excite

❋*Do It!* Read the section **What is Excite Search?** and click on the help topics that appear on the left.

After reading the help topics, we determine that Excite

❋ uses a program that performs searches by concept. This means that synonyms of the keywords you type in are automatically searched and retrieved.

❋ supports concept searching only when you use implied Boolean operators.

❋ supports full Boolean searching. AND, OR, and NOT must be in all capital letters.

❋ does not support concept searching when full Boolean searching is used.

❋ supports phrase searching by requiring that the phrase be enclosed in quotation marks.

❋ is case insensitive, so there is no need to capitalize.

❋ supports nested Boolean searching if you place parentheses around the words that are connected by AND or OR.

3   Formulate and enter the search expression.

Now we're ready to formulate the search expression by applying Excite's search features to our search question. We'll consider the following parameters:

❋ To retrieve all of Saki's names, we'll enter *Saki* and *Munro* connected by *OR*. This means that both of Saki's names may be retrieved. We'll disregard the first name Hector, since it may be listed as H.H. or Hector H.

❋ The names *Saki* and *Munro* can start with lowercase letters.

❋ There are two facets to our search—the writer's name and his works. Because both of these facets will be connected by an AND, and because both have synonyms that will be OR'd together, we need parentheses around each facet.

❋*Do It!* Click on the Excite logo in the upper-left corner to return to Excite's home page.

❋*Do It!* In the search form provided, type the following search expression:

(saki OR munro) AND (writings OR bibliography)

❋*Do It!* Click on **Search**.

4 View the results and access a Web page.

A partial listing of the search results appears in Figure 6.17.

❋*Do It!* Click on the first Web page to appear on the list, **H. H. Munro, Saki**. If this title is not in your list of results, choose a similar title.

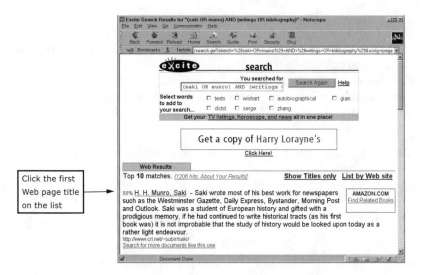

Click the first Web page title on the list

Figure 6.17—Results of Search for Saki's Writings or Bibliography

After your screen fills, scroll down the page until you see **A bibliography of Saki's works and related texts and movies**. If you click on the hyperlink **bibliography**, you'll have a list of Saki's works. See Figure 6.18.

Figure 6.18—First Page of "A Bibliography for Saki (H.H. Munro)"

5 Search for the line of poetry "Till human voices wake us, and we drown."

In looking for a line of poetry or a quotation, we want all of the words to be found together, not spread throughout a document, so the rules for phrase searching will apply. In Excite, small words such as prepositions and articles are not indexed, but the search engine will still locate the major words in a string. In this activity, we want to know which poem contains this line of poetry. Let's try typing in the phrase and see what we find. First, we need to return to the search query screen in Excite.

❋*Do It!* From the "Saki's Oeuvre" Web page, click on the **Back** button on the toolbar.

You should now be in Excite.

❋*Do It!* Click on the Excite icon in the upper-left corner.

You should be at Excite's home page with a blank search form.

❋*Do It!* Type in **"Till human voices wake us and we drown"**, and then click on **Search**.

6 View the results and access *The Love Song of J. Alfred Prufrock.*

A partial list of the results of this search appears in Figure 6.19. Several sites are listed. Scroll down until you find **The Love Song of J. Alfred Prufrock**.

❋*Do It!* Click on the title **The Love Song of J. Alfred Prufrock**, as shown in Figure 6.19.

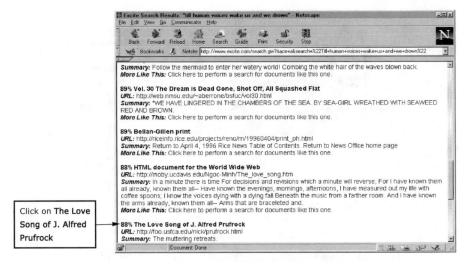

Click on **The Love Song of J. Alfred Prufrock**

Figure 6.19—Results of Search for Line of Poetry

Figure 6.20 shows the beginning of the poem that should include the line of poetry you're seeking.

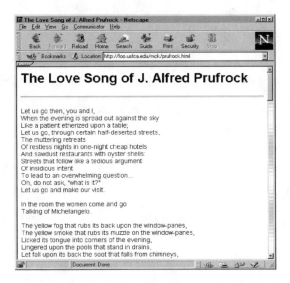

Figure 6.20—The Love Song of J. Alfred Prufrock

To find the line "Till human voices wake us, and we drown," we can use the Find in Page function.

❋*Do It!* Click on **Edit** in the menu bar. Choose **Find in Page**.

❋*Do It!* Type the words **human voices** in the search form next to **Find what**, as shown in Figure 6.21.

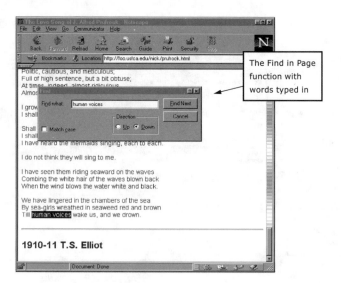

The Find in Page function with words typed in

Figure 6.21—Using the Find in Page Function to Locate a Line of Poetry

7   End the session.

❋*Do It!* To end the session, click on **File** on the menu bar and select **Exit** from the menu.

End of Activity 6.3

Activity 6.3 focused on finding specific information with search engines. Note that even though the topics were not multifaceted, you still benefited from using the search strategy discussed earlier in the chapter. Before you type a search expression, if you think of possible synonyms and phrases for even the simplest search topics, it can save you time and produce relevant results quickly.

Summary

This chapter continued Chapter 5's discussion of ways to use search engines' powers to their fullest. Formulating search expressions before you get online and keeping in mind the possible search features available to you are both of utmost importance. After you choose a search engine, you need to translate your search expression into the appropriate syntax for that search engine.

This chapter introduced several ways to search, including using implied Boolean operators and full Boolean capabilities, and limiting results by date and by certain parts of the URL. The examples showed how to search for specific information, including lines of poetry and titles of works. We also reviewed the Find in Page feature, which helps you locate search terms in the documents your search query returns.

7
Chapter

Specialized Databases

New databases containing public information or material not proprietary in nature frequently appear on the World Wide Web. These databases, many of which are maintained by government agencies and nonprofit organizations, can quickly provide you with a wealth of information that formerly was difficult or time-consuming to obtain.

Specialized databases are indexes that can be searched, much like the search engines explored in Chapters 5 and 6. The main difference is that specialized databases are collections on particular subjects, such as medical journal article abstracts and citations, company financial data, United States Supreme Court decisions, census data, patents, and so forth. You can find information in specialized databases that you often would not locate by using a global WWW search engine. If you know there is a specialized database on the subject you are researching, using that database can save you time and give you reliable, up-to-date information.

We covered subject guides in Chapters 3 and 4. The difference between a subject guide and a specialized database is that subject guides are collections of URLs in a particular area (many times these URLs are hyperlinks to specialized databases), whereas a specialized database contains the actual data or information you are seeking. Some specialized databases do contain hyperlinks to other specialized databases, however, if the two databases have related topics. One of the databases covered in this chapter has this feature.

This chapter will discuss such databases and will include the following sections:
* Overview of Specialized Databases
* How to Find Free Specialized Databases
* Using Specialized Databases

Chapter 7

Overview of Specialized Databases

Bibliographic and Full-text Databases

In this chapter, we'll show you two major types of databases: bibliographic and full-text. A ***bibliographic database*** includes citations that describe and identify titles, dates, authors, and other parts of written works. It doesn't contain the full text of the articles themselves. An example of a bibliographic database is MEDLINE, which we'll cover in Activity 7.1. A ***full-text database***, on the other hand, includes the entire text of the indexed works. A full-text database can contain financial, scientific, or other types of data. An example of a full-text database is *FindLaw: Supreme Court Opinions*, which we'll explore in Activity 7.3. The major difference between a bibliographic and a full-text database is that a bibliographic database describes an entity, whether it be an article, a book, a work of art, or any other product, whereas a full-text database includes a description *and* the work itself.

Proprietary and Free Databases

There are hundreds of ***proprietary***, or ***commercial***, ***databases*** on the World Wide Web, but these are available only if you or your organization has purchased access to them. For example, FirstSearch, DIALOG, STN, and Lexis-Nexis all provide proprietary databases.

Proprietary databases have certain value-added features that databases in the public domain do not have. Here are some examples of that enhanced content:

- Proprietary databases are likely to include extra information that helps the researcher. For example, most of the databases in FirstSearch (the Online Computer Library Center's (OCLC) proprietary database system) have links to library holdings. This means that if you find an article or book in a database provided by FirstSearch, such as MEDLINE, you can immediately find out which libraries own the material. Even though MEDLINE is available free to the public from the National Library of Medicine, you might prefer to use the FirstSearch version if you want to know who has the listed journal articles.

- Proprietary databases also allow you to download information easily. For instance, some of these databases include financial information that is commonly free to the public, but they charge for the use of their databases because they have made it much easier for the user to download the information to a spreadsheet program.

- Proprietary databases often index material that others do not. The information is distinguished by its uniqueness, its historical value, or its competitive value (for example, private company financial information).

❀ Proprietary database systems are more responsible to their users. Because they charge money, they are more apt to provide training and other user support, such as distributing newsletters that update their services.

Accessing Fee-based Databases

If you would like to have a list of the proprietary databases on the market, you might access "FACSNET: Directory of Database Services," **http://www.facsnet.org/report_tools/car/cardirec.htm**, a Web page published by the Poynter Institute for Media Studies. The people there have compiled a list of online databases that charge fees.

Remember, you can always ask a reference librarian at your local library about accessing proprietary databases. The library may have several databases on CD-ROM or may have purchased access to databases via the Internet.

The specialized databases covered in this chapter are all free and open to anyone.

How to Find Free Specialized Databases

Sometimes you'll stumble across specialized databases while doing a keyword search in a search engine. A database might pop up in the search results without your actually looking for it. Occasionally, a Web page will have a hyperlink to a database, or a friend or colleague will tell you about a particular site.

There is a more precise way to find them, but even this is not always foolproof. Virtual libraries, meta-search tools that include lists of databases, and directories are often the best sources to use when looking for specialized databases. If a specialized database isn't listed in one of these types of resources, you may find a database listed in a subject guide. It's important to keep in mind that if you don't find what you're looking for in one resource, that doesn't mean it doesn't exist. You may find it in another resource. The following tools are the most helpful in listing specialized databases and subject guides:

❀ Internet Public Library (IPL) Reference Center, **http://www.ipl.org/ref**, is a virtual library that provides a good starting point for finding reference works, subject guides, and specialized databases.

❀ Internet Sleuth, **http://www.isleuth.com**, is a meta-search tool. In other words, it is a collection of databases, with each database having a hyperlink and a search form attached. You can also search several databases simultaneously in the Sleuth.

❀ Librarians' Index to the Internet, **http://sunsite.berkeley.edu/internetindex**, is another virtual library. It is a searchable and browsable collection of Web resources, including subject guides and specialized databases, that librarians select and annotate.

LibrarySpot, **http://www.libraryspot.com**, lists quality reference resources, including specialized databases, and provides links to more than 2,500 libraries around the world.

 Yahoo!, **http://www.yahoo.com**, is one of the most popular and comprehensive directories on the World Wide Web. It is a good place to find subject guides (Yahoo! calls them *indices*) and specialized databases.

✱ Tip

A good way to keep up with new search tools, especially specialized databases, is to subscribe to *The Scout Report.* For information on how to subscribe to this valuable weekly publication, send email to **listserv@cs.wisc.edu** and type **info scout-report** in the body of the message. You can also visit the Web page, **http://www.scout.cs.wisc.edu/scout/report**, that provides the same list of new resources on the Web and includes hyperlinks to the reviewed titles. It also includes all of the previous *Scout Report*s.

Using Specialized Databases

Just as search engines do, specialized databases support different search features. Most of these databases support many of the same search features covered in Chapters 5 and 6, such as Boolean searching, truncation, and phrase searching. Many databases have search instruction pages, just as the major search engines do.

In this chapter, we'll be doing three activities that will familiarize you with some of the most useful types of databases on the World Wide Web. We've chosen databases from three subject areas: medicine, business, and law. We selected these three areas because the Web has become an excellent medium for research in these three fields. Much of the useful information needed for research in these fields is in the public domain. We'll search first for medical information. While you move through the activities, you may want to review the search features and the 10-step basic search strategy introduced in Chapter 5.

✱ Tip

Remember that the Web is always changing and that your results may differ from those shown here. Don't let this confuse you. The activities demonstrate fundamental skills. These skills don't change, even though the number of results obtained or the actual screens may look very different.

Searching for Medical Information

The World Wide Web is becoming an excellent source for health and medical information. Medical centers and physicians create home pages that discuss specific aspects of health care, and you can find these pages by doing searches in the major search engines. Medical reference books are also appearing on the Web. For example, the entire *Merck Manual of Diagnosis and Therapy,* **http://www.merck.com**, a well-known medical diagnostic handbook, is now online. You can also find citations to medical journal articles on the Web.

In the first activity, we'll look for a specialized database to help us find journal articles on a medical topic. In the example, we'll use the Librarians' Index to the Internet to help us find a hyperlink to MEDLINE, which is a bibliographic database devoted to medical journal literature. There are several ways to find hyperlinks to MEDLINE providers on the Web. Keep in mind that we are showing you only *one* way to do it.

Activity 7.1   Searching MEDLINE

Overview

We are doing research on Creutzfeldt-Jakob disease. This is the human disease that has been linked to eating beef from cows with bovine spongiform encephalopathy (BSE), commonly referred to as *mad cow disease*. We need to find recent articles from medical journals that would update our general knowledge of Creutzfeldt-Jakob disease, focusing on the connections between it and BSE.

We know that the National Library of Medicine publishes a database called MEDLINE, and we've heard that it may be available on the Web for free. How can we find it? Let's try the Librarians' Index to the Internet. After we find it, we'll access MEDLINE, search it, and view the results. We will take the following steps:

1. Go to the home page for the Librarians' Index to the Internet.
2. From the list of health and medicine resources, find and go to MEDLINE.
3. Look at basic search help.
4. Type in search terms and retrieve results.
5. Choose a citation from the list of results.
6. Display the full record of the selected citation.
7. End the session.

Details

1 **Go to the home page for the Librarians' Index to the Internet.**

❋*Do It!* Click on the location field, type **http://sunsite.berkeley.edu/ internetindex**, and then press **Enter**.

❋*Do It!* Click on **Health, Medicine** from the Librarians' Index to the Internet home page, as shown in Figure 7.1.

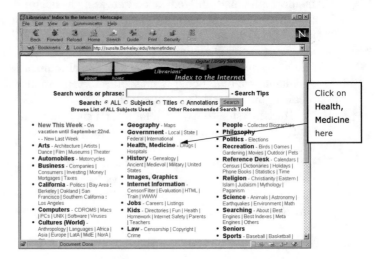

Figure 7.1—Home Page for the Librarians' Index to the Internet

2 From the list of health and medicine resources, find and go to MEDLINE.

❋*Do It!* Scroll down the list of resources until you find the "Databases" section. You'll see several different MEDLINE links.

❋*Do It!* Click on **Free MEDLINE: PubMed and Internet Grateful Med**, as shown in Figure 7.2.

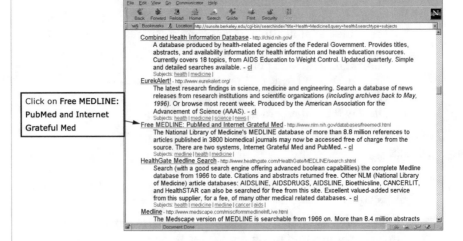

Figure 7.2—Health and Medicine Resources—Librarians' Index to the Internet

3   Look at basic search help.

Produced by the National Library of Medicine, MEDLINE is the premier database covering the fields of medicine, nursing, dentistry, veterinary medicine, and other health-related sciences. While MEDLINE does not include the full text of the journal articles it indexes, it does provide extensive abstracts of most articles. Figure 7.3 shows the NLM MEDLINE home page. There are two databases provided, PubMed and Internet Grateful Med. In addition to MEDLINE, HealthSTAR, PREMEDLINE, and AIDSLINE, this version of Internet Grateful Med (IGM) offers free access to AIDSDRUGS, AIDSTRIALS, DIRLINE, HISTLINE, and others. PubMed covers MEDLINE and PREMEDLINE only. We will be searching the PubMed database.

❄️*Do It!* Click on **PubMed**, as shown in Figure 7.3.

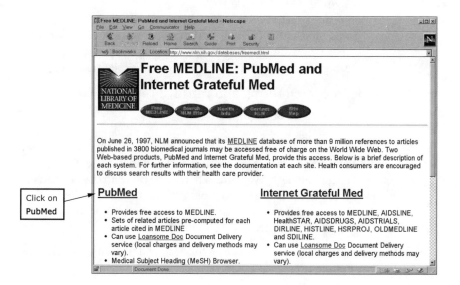

Figure 7.3—MEDLINE

There are several hyperlinks along the left side of the screen that will provide background information about this database. The "Overview" section tells us that PubMed is a project developed by the National Library of Medicine (NLM), which is located at the National Institutes of Health (NIH). The database consists of MEDLINE and PREMEDLINE. The MEDLINE file contains bibliographic citations and author abstracts from about 3,900 current biomedical journals published in the U.S. and 70 foreign countries. The file contains approximately 9 million records dating back to 1966. Most records are from English-language sources or have English-language abstracts. PREMEDLINE contains citation information and abstracts before the full records are prepared and added to MEDLINE.

Now that we know a bit more about what PubMed consists of, let's find out how to search it effectively by reading the help section.

For search help, we need to access the help section. **Help** is located below the **Overview** hyperlink on PubMed's main page.

✿*Do It!* Click on **Help**.

By reading the search help information, we discover the following:

- ✿ Boolean searching using operators other than AND is supported in the advanced search mode only.
- ✿ Boolean search operators (AND, OR, and NOT) must be capitalized.
- ✿ Phrase searching is supported by placing quotation marks around the phrase.
- ✿ PubMed is case insensitive.
- ✿ The advanced search mode allows you to limit your search to particular fields, such as individual journal titles, article types (for example, review articles and clinical trials), certain years, language, and many other specifications.

4   Type in search terms and retrieve results.

Now we're ready to do our search.

✿*Do It!* From the help screen, click the **Back** icon.

Since our search has two facets, Creutzfeldt-Jakob disease and bovine spongiform encephalopathy, we'll need to use the Boolean operator AND. We also want to limit our search to those articles that are in the English language. We learned from the help section that to limit results to those in certain fields, the advanced search mode must be used.

✿*Do It!* Click on **Advanced Search**, which is located along the left side of the screen.

Now you should be at a screen that looks like the one pictured in Figure 7.4.

Remember that PubMed is case insensitive so there is no need to capitalize proper nouns. Also note that we'll need to search for both of the concepts as phrases by placing quotation marks around each one.

✿*Do It!* Type **"creutzfeldt-jakob disease" AND "bovine spongiform encephalopathy"** in the search form.

✿*Do It!* Click on **Search**, as shown in Figure 7.4.

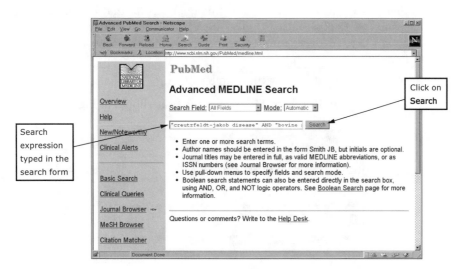

Figure 7.4—MEDLINE Search Query Entered

A "Current Query" information screen is shown in Figure 7.5. Note that you could add terms to the query by clicking on the pulldown menu arrow under **Add Term(s) to Query:** next to **Search Field:**. For example, if we wanted to limit our results to articles written in English, we could choose the **Language** field from the pulldown menu and type **english** in the search field next to **Enter Terms:**. Let's do that now.

❄️*Do It!* Click on the arrow next to the search form labeled **Search Field.**

❄️*Do It!* Type **english** in the search form labeled **Enter Terms**.

❄️*Do It!* Click **Search**, as shown in Figure 7.5.

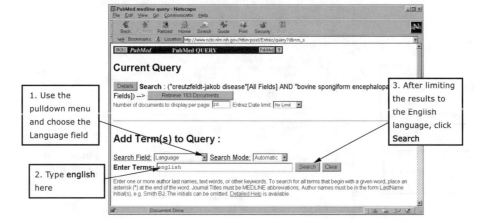

Figure 7.5—PubMed Query Report

Figure 7.6 shows the results of this query. Note that by limiting the results to English articles only, the number of results was decreased from 183 to 155. (*Note*: Your screen will most likely show different numbers.)

Now you'll want to view the search results.

✿*Do It!* Click on **Retrieve 155 Documents** as shown in Figure 7.6.

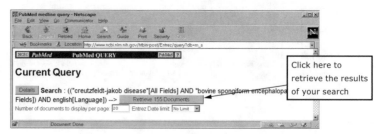

Figure 7.6—Results of PubMed Search

5   Choose a citation from the list of results.

A partial list of results is shown in Figure 7.7.

If you want to see a full record, you can click on the author hyperlink. If you'd like to see more than one record at a time, click on the boxes (radio buttons) next to the citations you wish to see.

In this example, we'll click on the citation that represents an article written by E. Girardi, et al.

✿*Do It!* Click on the hyperlink **Girardi E, et al.**, as shown in Figure 7.7.

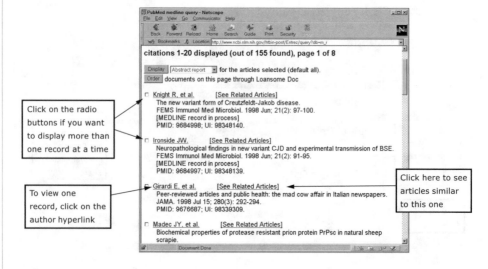

Figure 7.7—Partial List of PubMed Results

6   Display the full record of the selected citation.

Look at the portion of the record that appears in Figure 7.8.

❈*Do It!* Scroll through the complete record.

Note the detailed information that the abstract provides.

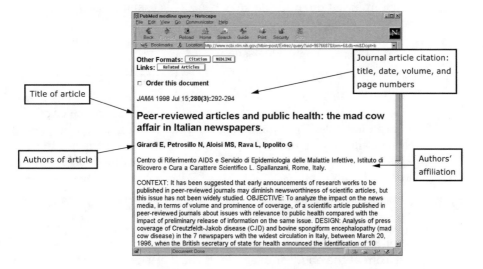

Figure 7.8—MEDLINE Record with Abstract

Let's say you wanted a copy of this article, which appears in *The Journal of the American Medical Association (JAMA)*. You could go about this in several ways:

- ❈ Find out if your local public or academic library carries this journal. If so, copy the article there.

- ❈ Call your local hospital and find out if it owns the journal and if the public is allowed to photocopy articles from its library.

- ❈ Initiate an interlibrary loan request from your library if the journal is not available from the previously mentioned sources.

- ❈ If your library has an agreement with Lonesome Doc, NLM's document delivery program, you can use that service to request documents.

7   End the session.

You can end the session now or stay online for the next activity.

❈*Do It!* To end the session now, click on **File** on the menu bar and select **Exit** from the menu.

End of Activity 7.1

MEDLINE is available on the World Wide Web through several providers. In our example, we chose PubMed through the National Library of Medicine because it is the official database and it doesn't require registration. Some database providers require you to register with them by filling out a form, usually including your email address and job title.

MEDLINE can provide you with the most up-to-date medical research information available anywhere. This example barely touches the surface of the searching possibilities in this database. Whether you're researching an illness or gathering information for a biology paper, MEDLINE is an invaluable resource.

Searching for Company and Industry Information

The World Wide Web has become a useful place to conduct business research. Most companies use their home pages as marketing or communications tools. These home pages may include annual reports, press releases, and biographies of the people in top-level management. Home pages may also include information about companies' products and services, including catalogs.

 Tip

If you want to find a company's home page but don't know the URL, you can often guess it by typing the company's name with **http://www.** at the beginning and **.com** at the end. For example, if you were looking for the home page for Sears, Roebuck, and Company, you could try typing **http://www.sears.com**. This is the correct URL for Sears, Roebuck, and Company. You could also use a search engine to look for the company's name, limiting the results to URLs that include **sears.com.**

If you want to do industry research, you can use business-related subject guides. These contain hyperlinks to businesses within the particular industry that interests you. You can easily find subject guides in virtual libraries and major directories.

You can also find business directories on the Web by using one of the virtual libraries or meta-search tools listed at the beginning of the chapter. Keep in mind that companies that provide the most financial information on the Web are usually publicly traded. Public companies are required to provide very detailed information about themselves to the U.S. government, whereas privately held companies are not. If a private company is listed in a nonproprietary (open-to-the-public) database, some financial information will be available, but not nearly as much as if it were a public company.

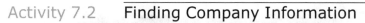
Activity 7.2   Finding Company Information

Overview

In this activity, we'll find information about a specific company. The company we'll be searching for is The Gap. Suppose you need to find a home page, address, annual report, 10-K report, and recent newspaper articles about this company. There are several company directories on the Web that would provide a starting place for this type of research. Virtual libraries and meta-search tools list databases by subject. You'll need to go to one to find company databases. In this activity, we'll go to the Internet Sleuth, **http://www.isleuth.com**, which is a meta-search tool. After we find a company directory that gives general information, we'll search it, using the interface that the Sleuth provides. We'll locate a Web page for the company and note that an annual report can be accessed from the page. After this, we will use the Sleuth again to help us find a link to the Securities and Exchange Commission's (SEC) EDGAR database. This database contains the full text of 10-K and other reports that public companies are required by law to submit to the SEC. Next, we'll go to *US Newspaper Archives on the Web,* **http://sunsite.unc.edu/slanews/internet/archives.html**, and search *The San Francisco Chronicle* and *Examiner* for articles on The Gap. The Gap's headquarters is located in San Francisco, so it makes sense for us to search that city's newspapers.

Let's get started!

We're assuming that you have a browser program set up on your computer, that you have a way of connecting to the Internet, and the browser is started.

We'll follow these steps:

1. Go to the Internet Sleuth and find a company directory.
2. Search Companies Online to find the company's address, home page, and other basic information.
3. Find a 10-K report for the company.
4. Find newspaper articles about the company.
5. Exit the Web browser.

Details

1   Go to the Internet Sleuth and find a company directory.

Do It! Click on the location field, type **http://www.isleuth.com**, and press Enter.

Along the left side of the Internet Sleuth's home page is a list of subject categories.

Do It! Click on **Business.**

Figure 7.9 shows how your screen should appear. Note the general business resources listed, each with a link to the resource and a search form that can search directly from the Sleuth's page.

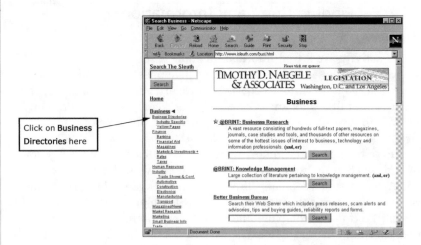

Figure 7.9—The Internet Sleuth's Directory of Business Resources

❀*Do It!* Click on **Business Directories**, as shown in Figure 7.9.

Figure 7.10 shows a partial view of the current screen. Scroll down until you come to **Companies Online**. You can click on **Companies Online** to go to its site, or you can search it from the Sleuth. Let's search it from the Sleuth's interface.

2 Search Companies Online to find the company's address, home page, and other basic information.

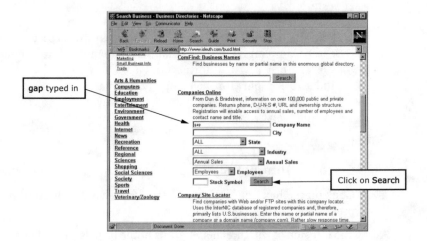

Figure 7.10—Searching Companies Online for Information About The Gap

❀*Do It!* Type **gap** in the **Company Name** field.

❀*Do It!* Click on **Search**, as shown in Figure 7.10.

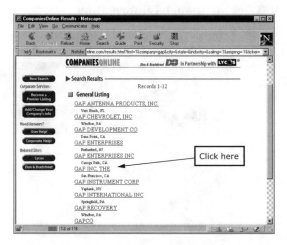

Figure 7.11—Results of Searching Companies Online for The Gap

Your screen will fill with companies that have the word *gap* in them, as shown in Figure 7.11. The hyperlink we need is **GAP INC, THE**.

❀*Do It!* Click on **GAP INC, THE**.

Figure 7.11 shows the entry for The Gap, Inc.

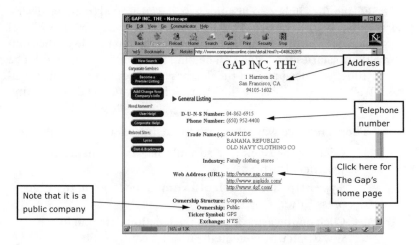

Figure 7.12—Entry for The Gap, Inc.

Note the information provided by Companies Online. Since companies often publish a great deal of information about themselves on their home pages, we would be smart to go to The Gap's home page.

❀*Do It!* Click on **http://www.gap.com/**, as shown in Figure 7.12.

Once you've accessed the home page, scroll down until you see the link **financial information**.

❋*Do It!* Click on **financial information**.

Figure 7.13 shows the "financial information" page for The Gap.

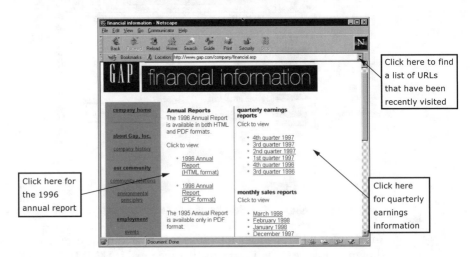

Figure 7.13—Financial Information for The Gap, Inc.

3   Find a 10-K report for the company.

The SEC requires public companies to make an annual financial disclosure, called a 10-K report. The 10-K not only gives recent financial information about the company, it also lists the top people in the company, their salaries, and stock ownership information. To obtain The Gap's 10-K, you need to find the database that contains this information. We'll need to go back to the Internet Sleuth and see if we can find it.

❋*Do It!* There are three ways to return to the Internet Sleuth:

❋   Click on the **Back** icon several times until you are at the Internet Sleuth.

❋   Type **http://www.isleuth.com** in the location field and press Enter.

❋   Click on the arrow next to the location field and locate **www.isleuth.com** on the list of recently visited Web pages, highlight it with your mouse, and click.

❋*Do It!* Once back in the Sleuth, type SEC in the search form under "Search The Sleuth."

We are searching the Sleuth because we don't know which category the database will be in. Scroll down the list of results until you locate **SEC EDGAR Archives**. Your screen should look like the one pictured in Figure 7.14. While we could search EDGAR from the search form provided in the Sleuth, let's go to the database and search it directly.

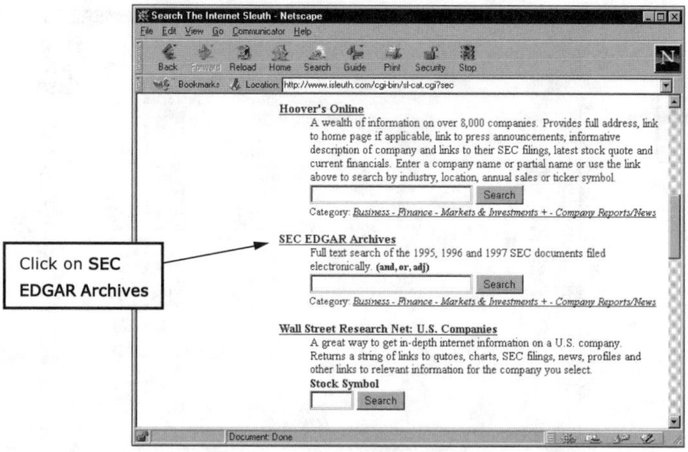

Figure 7.14—SEC EDGAR Archives Found in the Internet Sleuth

Do It! Click on **SEC EDGAR Archives**, as shown in Figure 7.14.

Your screen should look like the one pictured in Figure 7.15.

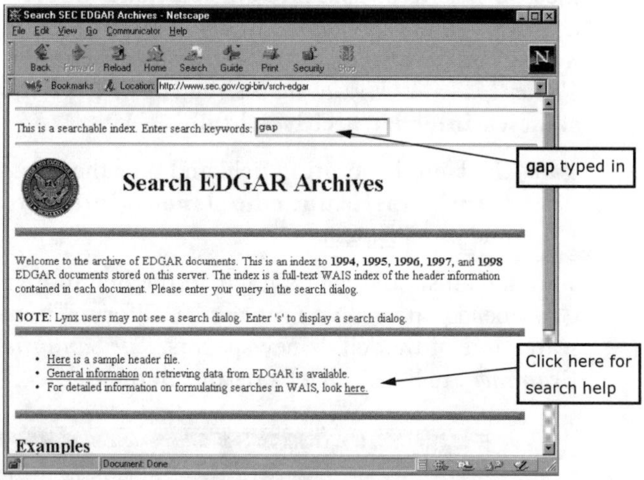

Figure 7.15—Searching EDGAR for The Gap

Do It! Type **gap** in the search form provided, and press **Enter**.

Figure 7.16 shows the list of reports filed with EDGAR for The Gap. Notice that the first report listed is a 10-K report. To view the report, click on **GAP INC** at the top of the screen.

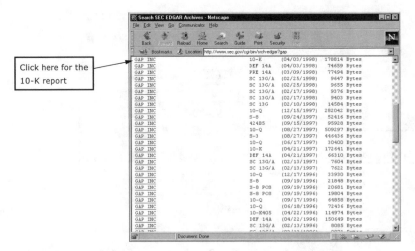

Click here for the 10-K report

Figure 7.16—Listing of SEC Reports for The Gap, Inc.

4   Find newspaper articles about the company.

We found a newspaper archive by returning to the Librarians' Index to the Internet, **http://sunsite.berkeley.edu/internetindex**, and browsing the "Media" category or by searching the database by typing **newspaper archives** in the search form. The site we found is called *US Newspaper Archives on the Web*, and its URL is **http://sunsite.unc.edu/slanews/internet/archives.html**.

❋*Do It!* Click on the location field and type the URL
http://sunsite.unc.edu/slanews/internet/archives.html, and press **Enter**.

Your screen should look similar to the one in Figure 7.17. Since The Gap's headquarters San Francisco, California, it may be a good idea to search one of that city's newspapers. *The San Francisco Chronicle* and *Examiner* are listed, so let's try one of them.

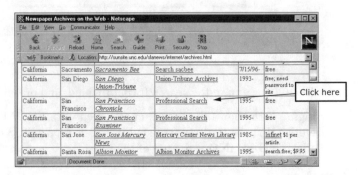

Click here

*Figure 7.17—*US Newspaper Archives on the Web

Do It! Click on **Professional Search** next to *San Francisco Chronicle.*

Note in Figure 7.18 that you can search the *Chronicle* and *Examiner* at the same time from this Web site. Note that there are search tips for searching this database. You must capitalize AND, OR , and NOT when using them in a search expression.

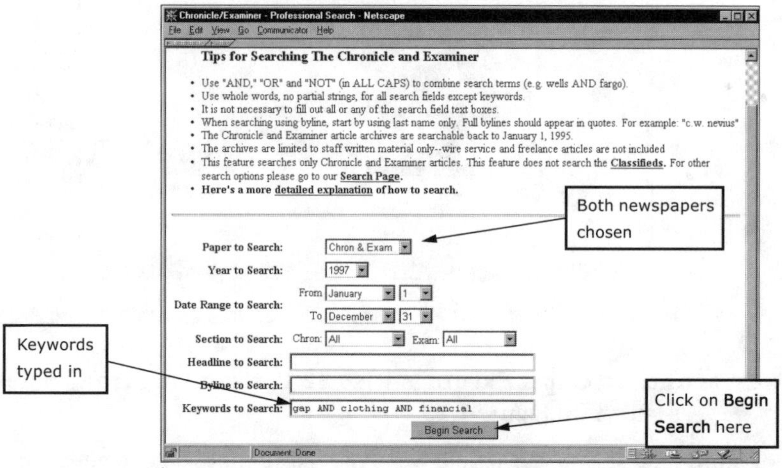

Figure 7.18—Searching the San Francisco Chronicle *and* Examiner

Do It! Use the pulldown menu next to **Paper to Search:** and choose **Chron & Exam**.

Do It! From the pulldown menu next to **Year to Search:** choose **1997**.

Do It! In the field next to **Keywords to Search:** type **gap AND clothing AND financial.**

Do It! Click on **Begin Search**.

Figure 7.19 shows the results of this search. We'll look for an article that provides sales information. If you don't have the same articles in your results list, click on an article of your choice.

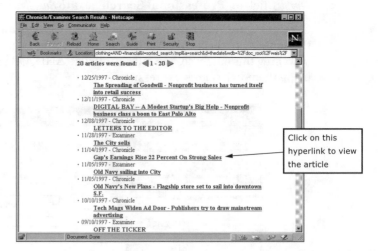

Figure 7.19—Results of Searching the Archive

✜*Do It!* Click on **Gap's Earnings Rise 22 Percent On Strong Sales**, as shown in Figure 7.19.

Figure 7.20 shows the article we chose. Note that you can get a copy of the article without the graphics and advertising by clicking on **printer-friendly version** on the right of the screen. There is also a link to information about the reporter that wrote the article.

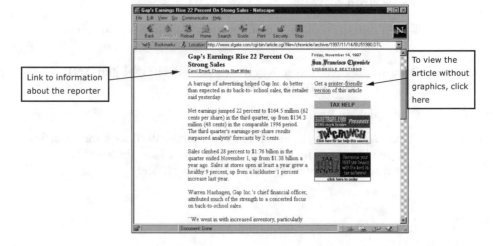

Figure 7.20—Newspaper Article from the San Francisco Chronicle

5 End the session.

Wasn't that simple? You can end the session now or stay online and proceed to the next activity.

❋*Do It!* To end the session now, click on **File** on the menu bar and select **Exit** from the menu.

End of Activity 7.2

This activity barely skimmed the surface of the business information available on the Web. We hope that it gave you an overview of what's involved with searching about a company from scratch. Using special databases for information like this can be more effective than searching with global search engines, since you can more precisely pinpoint the information you need.

Searching for Legal Information

Legal information is plentiful on the World Wide Web. The U.S. federal government has put much of its legal documentation up on the Web. For example, the *United States Code* (the text of current public laws enacted by Congress), the *Federal Register* (the daily report of new laws passed by government agencies), and the *United States Code of Federal Regulations* (the *Federal Register* codified by subject) are all on the Web in searchable form. A growing number of states publish their statutes or laws in collections similar to the *United States Code;* these are also available.

In addition to statutes or laws, court opinions from all jurisdictions are appearing on the World Wide Web. In this activity, we'll show how easy it is to get a full-text copy of a United States Supreme Court opinion.

Activity 7.3   Searching for United States Supreme Court Opinions

Overview

In this activity, we'll show how to obtain a copy of the Supreme Court opinion from the famous 1954 case Brown v. Board of Education. To find the database that indexes United States Supreme Court opinions, we'll use Yahoo! We could probably find this database by using the other resources listed at the beginning of the chapter as well. This activity will follow these steps:

1. Go to the home page for Yahoo!
2. Browse Yahoo!'s directory for databases on United States Supreme Court decisions.
3. Select **FindLaw: Supreme Court Opinions**.
4. Search FindLaw for Brown v. Board of Education.
5. Display the full text of the court opinion.
6. End the session.

Details

1   Go to the home page for Yahoo!

✺*Do It!* Click on the location field, type **http://www.yahoo.com**, and press [Enter].

2   Browse Yahoo!'s directory for databases on United States Supreme Court decisions.

✺*Do It!* From Yahoo!'s top-level subject categories or headings, click on **Law**, a subheading of **Government**.

✺*Do It!* From the list of subject categories that appear, click on **Judiciary and Supreme Court@**.

✺*Do It!* From this list of subject headings, click on **Supreme Court**.

✺*Do It!* Click on **Court Decisions**.

Your screen should look like the one in Figure 7.21.

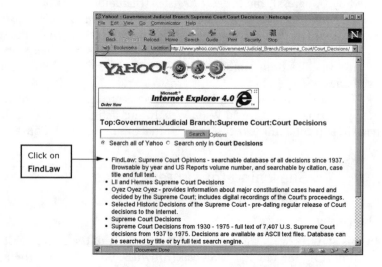

Figure 7.21—Results of Browsing for a Supreme Court Decisions Database

3   Select **FindLaw: Supreme Court Opinions**.

✺*Do It!* Click on **FindLaw: Supreme Court Opinions**, as shown in Figure 7.21.

Note that there are a few other databases that index full-text versions of United States Supreme Court decisions, but at the time of this writing, FindLaw appears to be the only one that indexes recent opinions.

Your screen should look like the one pictured in Figure 7.22. Note that FindLaw has a search help link (**options** next to the **Search FindLaw** button). If you wanted to search FindLaw by keyword, you'd be wise to look at the help pages. Because FindLaw has a "Party Name Search" category, we won't need to do a keyword search in the entire database.

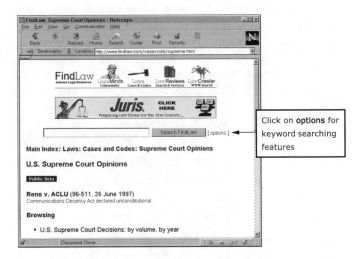

Figure 7.22—The FindLaw: Supreme Court Opinions *Site*

4   Search FindLaw for Brown v. Board of Education.

❉*Do It!* Scroll down the page until you come to "Party Name Search."

❉*Do It!* In the box under "Party Name Search," type the following:
Brown v. Board of Education.

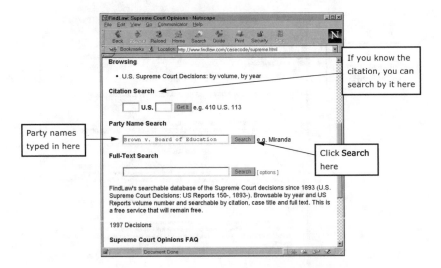

Figure 7.23—Party Names Entered

❉*Do It!* Click on **Search**.

Your screen should look like the one in Figure 7.24.

Chapter 7

FindLaw has returned a few citations that match our search request. We are interested in the 1954 case.

5 Display the full text of the court opinion.

✸*Do It!* As shown in Figure 7.24, click on **BROWN v. BOARD OF EDUCATION 347 U.S. 483 (1954)**.

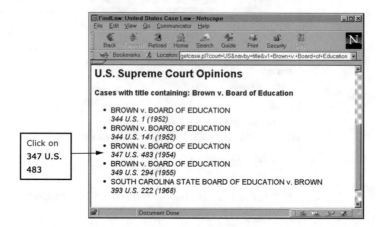

Figure 7.24—Results of Search for Brown v. Board of Education

The full text of the court opinion partially appears in Figure 7.25.

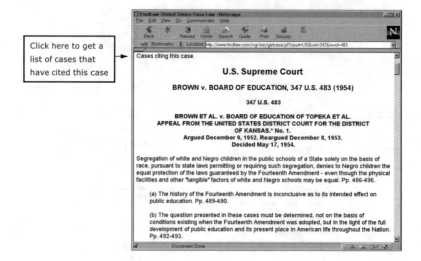

Figure 7.25—Full-text Opinion of Brown v. Board of Education

Moving from a court opinion to a related court opinion is very simple in a hypertext environment. Throughout the court opinion, you'll find links to related cases, as Figure 7.26 illustrates. Click on the hyperlink and you'll be taken to the full text of these related cases. Keep in mind, however, that the creators of FindLaw have not indexed all court opinions. They are in the process of adding more until they have the entire collection online. Even though there is a link to an opinion, the text of the opinion may not have been added to the database yet.

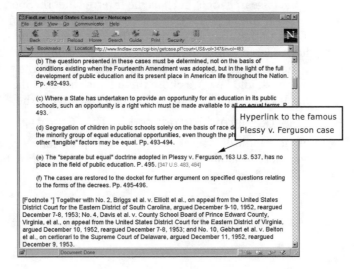

Figure 7.26—Hyperlinks to Related Court Opinions

6   End the session.

❋*Do It!* To end the session, click on **File** on the menu bar and select **Exit** from the menu.

End of Activity 7.3

In addition to providing the full text of United States Supreme Court opinions, FindLaw, **http://www.findlaw.com**, provides the full text of the United States Constitution, along with links to cited Supreme Court cases. The *United States Code* and the *Code of Federal Regulations* are also available through FindLaw. It has links to state law resources, as well as law school information. You can see the advantage of linking all of these resources in one database, as it is easy to read related material in a hypertext environment.

Summary

Specialized databases are searchable collections on particular subjects. The U.S. government and nonprofit organizations maintain many of the free, nonproprietary databases on the Web, but commercial databases are also starting to appear with greater frequency. The difference between a specialized database and a subject guide is that a subject guide is a collection of URLs in a particular subject area, whereas a database contains the actual data or information you are seeking. Many databases provide hyperlinks that take you from one related field to another. Some databases have hyperlinks to other specialized databases or related URLs as well.

You can easily find specialized databases by accessing virtual libraries or meta-search tools, such as the Internet Sleuth. Specialized databases are also found in subject guides. These databases are like search engines, in that they all support different search features. Most databases have search instruction pages that you should read before you start searching. This chapter focused on databases in the fields of medicine, business, and law. We chose these topics because the World Wide Web has become an excellent medium for research in these fields.

Selected Terms Introduced in This Chapter

bibliographic database

commercial database

full-text database

proprietary database

specialized database

8
Chapter

Searching Library Catalogs

In this chapter, we will discover the wealth of information to be found in library catalogs. Numerous types of libraries exist in the world, and every one has a catalog of its holdings. In addition to the large national libraries (such as the Library of Congress), academic libraries (such as the Harvard University Library), and public libraries (such as the New York Public Library), there are thousands of special libraries that are part of larger organizations, corporations, and government agencies. Most of the libraries in all of these categories, in the United States and in foreign countries, are rapidly making their catalogs accessible to the public through the Internet. Because of the World Wide Web's graphical interface and its hypertext environment, it is easy for people to access and use these catalogs.

This chapter will give you several ways to find library catalogs on the World Wide Web and provide you with pointers on how to use them most effectively.

It will include the following sections:
* Overview of the Development of Online Catalogs
* Characteristics of Online Library Catalogs
* Ways to Find Library Catalogs

Overview of the Development of Online Catalogs

For years, libraries kept track of their holdings by putting information about each item on cards. In recent years, libraries have been converting their card catalogs to *online catalogs*, commonly known as *OPACs (online public access catalogs)*. Each record in a library catalog contains information that is very useful to the librarian and the researcher. For instance, every record has a classification code, or call number, which is determined by whatever classification system the library has chosen to use. Most academic libraries use the *Library of Congress classification system*, whereas most public libraries use the *Dewey decimal classification system*. Because special libraries have collections that cover very specific subjects, some of them have invented their own classification systems to describe their materials better.

With the advent of OPACs, libraries have improved their service by allowing users to search their collections much more quickly and thoroughly. When a library's OPAC is available through the Internet, people can search that library's holdings from wherever they are. For several years, libraries have made their catalogs accessible via *Telnet*, a program that allows for remote login capability. Increasingly, libraries are converting their collections to *graphical user interface (GUI)* database systems. With these systems, one can use a mouse to point, click, and move through a library catalog in the World Wide Web's hypertext environment. There are still hundreds of library catalogs that are accessible only through Telnet programs. This chapter will focus just on those catalogs that are Web-based.

Why Search a Remote Library Catalog?

There are many reasons why you might need to search a library catalog remotely. For example, you may be traveling to a college or university library in another part of the country or the world, and you may want to know ahead of time what the library's holdings are on the topic you are interested in. There may be instances where you don't want to travel to the library at all. Perhaps you want to search a larger library collection than the one you have access to in order to know what has been published on a particular topic. You can then have an idea of what you want to request through interlibrary loan at the library you're affiliated with. There may also be situations where you want to search a *special collection* that is part of a larger library or a *special library* that collects information on a narrow subject and catalogs its holdings in greater detail than a larger library. There are several other reasons why you may need to search another library's catalog sometime. This chapter will give you several ways to find library catalogs on the World Wide Web and provide you with pointers on how to use them most effectively.

Characteristics of Online Library Catalogs

Library online catalogs provide more than library holdings information for books and journals.
By using online library catalogs, you can learn a good deal of information. You can determine whether a book is checked out and which books and articles have been placed on reserve. Library catalogs can tell you the different names periodicals have had in the past.

Each library catalog vendor offers different features.
Each time you search another library's catalog, you'll see different search features, because libraries don't all use the same software for their online catalogs. Each library chooses a *vendor*, or software company, to organize its records in that vendor's style. The catalogs' various search features are similar to those of search engines, which we discussed in Chapter 5.

Library catalogs are different from search engines.
Unlike Internet search engines, library catalogs do not usually index each word in every work that the library holds. Instead, they index the records of the library's collection.

Each record in a library catalog can be searched by field.
Each record in a library catalog has specific fields that are searchable. For example, subject headings, titles, authors, and so forth are fields. Some catalogs allow you to search by keyword. When you perform a keyword search, you are searching for words that appear anywhere in the records.

Full-text cataloging is possible.
More and more academic libraries are cataloging the full-text version of journals to which they have access via proprietary databases. For example, Project Muse is a collection of full-text journals published by Johns Hopkins University. If an academic library has purchased Project Muse, it may create a link from its OPAC to the full-text journal. If you are searching the library catalog remotely, you would probably not be allowed access to the full-text journals, because you would not be an authorized user of the service.

Special library collections can be searched.
You can use catalogs to search for materials in specialized libraries. You might want to search a special collection that is part of a larger library, or a special library that collects information on a narrow subject and catalogs its holdings in greater detail than a larger library. You may also wish to search for a *digital collection*. Many libraries have developed digital collections of such archival materials as photographs, records, manuscripts, and maps. You can find a few of these digital collections at the *LIBCAT* site, **http://www.metronet.lib.mn.us/lc/lc1.html**, which

we will visit in Activity 8.2. From the main page, click on **World Wide Web**. Scroll down until you find "Sampler: Exhibits and Image Archives."

In any of these situations, if you find a useful holding in a remote library, you can obtain that resource through interlibrary loan from your local library. It is also becoming easier for you to email records to yourself when you do searches in Web-based catalogs. Despite this ease of use, you might be looking for ways to save time when doing searches in library catalogs. Like search engines, library catalogs have faster response times in the early morning. It may also save time to search several libraries' catalogs at once. Some regions have set up a multilibrary consortium, which will have a catalog that contains the holdings of all the libraries in the group. You can find regional library consortia by looking in Libweb, **http://sunsite.berkeley.edu/libweb**.

Ways to Find Library Catalogs

The following sites are the most useful for finding library catalogs on the Web.

Libweb at Berkeley http://sunsite.berkeley.edu/libweb

Use Libweb to find all types of libraries. Some require you to use Telnet, and others allow you to use your Web browser. Be aware that the library catalogs for some of the libraries listed here are unavailable for remote use, especially those of foreign libraries. In some cases, the library's home page is all that is included.

LIBCAT http://www.metronet.lib.mn.us/lc/lc1.html

LIBCAT gives lots of information on searching library catalogs—Telnet and Web-based alike. Look here to find a list of special collections and the names of libraries in which they are located.

webCATS http://www.lights.com/webcats

Use webCATS for finding only Web-based library catalogs. You can also use it to search for libraries by vendor; that search would locate only library catalogs using the type of catalog software with which you are familiar.

We'll demonstrate how to find three different types of library catalogs and search them. In the first activity, we'll go to a national catalog, the Library of Congress. The second activity will take us to Brandeis University's library catalog. Finally, in the third activity, we'll search the special library catalog of the World Bank and IMF Libraries.

 Tip

Remember that the Web is always changing and that your results may differ from those shown here. Don't let this confuse you. The activities demonstrate fundamental skills. These skills don't change, even though the number of results obtained or the actual screens may look very different.

Activity 8.1   Using Libweb to Find a National Catalog

Overview

In this activity, we are going to search the national catalog of the United States—the Library of Congress. We will be searching for books about the Berlin Wall. If you want to find out almost everything that's been published on a certain topic, it's a good idea to start either with a large university library or the Library of Congress. To help us connect to the OPAC, we will go to Libweb, a service available through the University of California at Berkeley. We'll follow these steps:

1. Go to the home page for Libweb.
2. Select **The Library of Congress**.
3. Find the online catalogs and select a mode of searching.
4. Search for books on the Berlin Wall.
5. Print the list of records.
6. End the session.

Details

1   Go to the home page for Libweb.

❀*Do It!* Point to the location field and click. Type **http://sunsite. berkeley.edu/libweb** and press ⏎**Enter**.

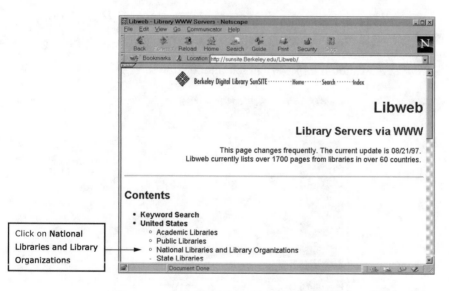

Figure 8.1—Using Libweb to Find Academic Library Catalogs

2   Select The Library of Congress.

❀*Do It!* Click on the hyperlink **National Libraries and Library Organizations**, as shown in Figure 8.1.

Your screen will fill with an alphabetical list of library names.

❄*Do It!* Scroll down until you see **Library of Congress**. Click on its hyperlink.

This will take you to *The Library of Congress* home page, as shown in Figure 8.2.

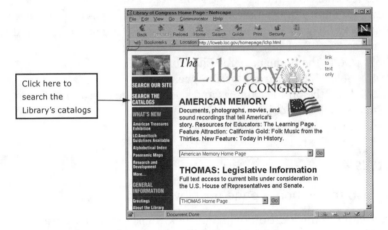

Click here to search the Library's catalogs

Figure 8.2—Home Page of the Library of Congress

3 Find the online catalogs and select a mode of searching.

❄*Do It!* Click on **SEARCH THE CATALOGS**, as shown in Figure 8.2.

Your screen should look very much like the one in Figure 8.3.

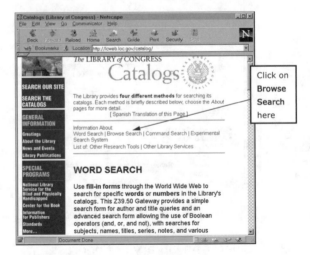

Click on **Browse Search** here

Figure 8.3—Library of Congress Catalogs

Since we are searching for a subject, we will select the **Browse Search** mode.

❋*Do It!* Click on **Browse Search**.

Your screen will look like the one in Figure 8.4. It supplies information about how to use Browse Search.

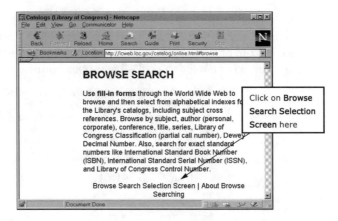

Figure 8.4—Information about Browse Search

❋*Do It!* Click on **Browse Search Selection Screen**, as shown in Figure 8.4. The screen that comes up will look like the one in Figure 8.5.

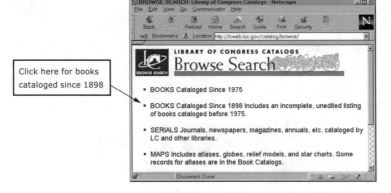

Figure 8.5—Browse Search Selection Screen

We can search for books cataloged since 1975, or we can search for books cataloged since 1898. Keep in mind that these are books *cataloged* since these years, not *published* since these years. Because we want a record of everything the library has on the topic of the Berlin Wall, we'll choose **BOOKS Cataloged Since 1898**, just to be on the safe side.

❋*Do It!* Click on **BOOKS Cataloged Since 1898**, as shown in Figure 8.5.

Your screen will fill with the types of searches you can perform in the catalog.

❀*Do It!* Click on **Subject**.

4   Search for books on the Berlin Wall.

Figure 8.6 shows the search query screen. Note the examples listed at the bottom of the screen. We can see that this catalog is not case sensitive; there is no need to capitalize proper nouns.

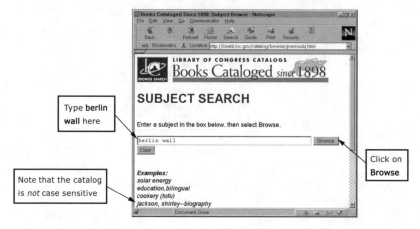

Figure 8.6—Search Form with Query Entered

❀*Do It!* Enter **berlin wall** in the search form provided.

❀*Do It!* Click on **Browse**.

The catalog has returned a list of *Library of Congress subject headings (LCSH)* that include the words *Berlin Wall*. (See Figure 8.7.) Select the records you want to see by clicking on the box next to each one.

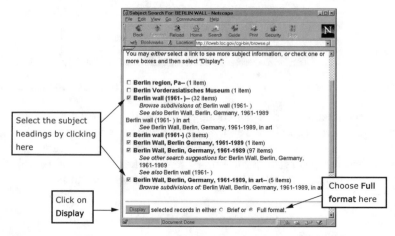

Figure 8.7—Subject Headings with the Words "Berlin Wall"

✸Do It! Click on the boxes next to the subject headings that contain the words *Berlin Wall* (note that the capitalization of *wall* is inconsistent—click on both upper- and lowercase versions).

✸Do It! Click on the button next to **Full format**. This will allow your records to be displayed with full information about each book.

✸Do It! Click on **Display**.

One of the records is displayed in Figure 8.8.

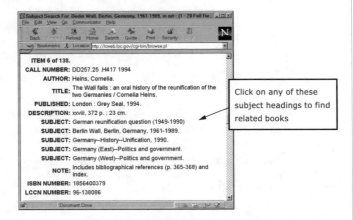

Figure 8.8—One Result of the Subject Search

5   Print the list of records.

If you would like to print the list of records, you can use the pulldown menu commands under **File**.

✸Do It! Click on **File**. From the pulldown menu that appears, choose **Print**. See Figure 8.9.

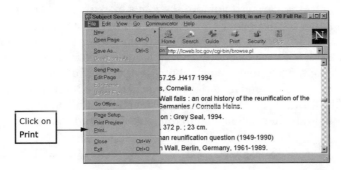

Figure 8.9—How to Print the Search Results

You will now be prompted to choose the pages you want to print, as shown in Figure 8.10. The default option is **All**. For this exercise, we don't want to print all of the pages.

Chapter 8

❋Do It! Click on the button next to **Pages**. Make sure the number **1** is in the first box. This will print only the first page.

❋Do It! Click on **OK**.

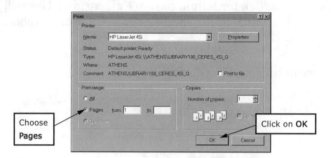

Figure 8.10—Print Screen

You could also download the records to a disk by choosing **Save As** from the **File** pulldown menu and inserting a disk in the A: drive of your computer. You would name your file "A:file-name," and the list of records would be downloaded to the disk.

6   End the session.

You can either end the session now, or you can stay online and continue to the next activity.

❋Do It! To end the session now, click on **File** on the menu bar and select **Exit** from the menu.

_____ End of Activity 8.1 _____

This activity showed how easy it is to search a Web-based library catalog. Searching a large library such as the Library of Congress can be a very good way to start finding materials on your topic. After doing such a search, you can try to obtain the items by requesting an interlibrary loan through your own library. The interlibrary loan office will find the materials for you and let you check them out for a period of time. Because the Library of Congress doesn't loan out its materials, the interlibrary loan personnel at your library will try to find the materials at a library that does lend materials. The availability of nonbook items, such as films, videos, and microform will depend on the individual libraries that hold the items. Some lend nonbook items and some do not.

Activity 8.2   **Using LIBCAT to Find Special Collections**

Overview

If you are doing research on a particular subject and want to gather virtually everything ever written on that subject, and in any format, a special collection can help you immeasurably. Many academic and public libraries across the country (and the world) maintain special collections on a myriad of subjects. Usually, items in a special collection do not circulate, so visitors can always find what they want on the library shelves. In addition to books, special collections may contain original letters, documents, sound recordings, audiotapes, and so forth. Special collections may also catalog privately published books and individual articles from obscure journals that may not be in libraries near you.

In this activity, we want to find books written in Spanish by the Spanish writer Felipe Alaiz on the Spanish Civil War. We want to find out if there is a library somewhere in the United States with a special collection on the Spanish Civil War. Since LIBCAT has a list of special collections that are included in libraries in the United States, we'll start there. We'll follow these steps:

1. Go to the home page for LIBCAT.
2. Search the list of special collections for the Spanish Civil War.
3. Connect to Brandeis University's library catalog.
4. Search by the author's name, Felipe Alaiz.
5. Do a related-subject search.
6. End the session.

Details

1   Go to the home page for LIBCAT.

Do It! Click on the location field, type **http://www.metronet.lib. mn.us/lc/lc1.html**, and press Enter.

2   Search the list of special collections for the Spanish Civil War.

Do It! Click on **Special Collections via Online Library Catalogs**, as shown in Figure 8.11.

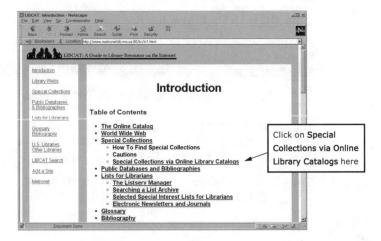

Figure 8.11—Introduction to LIBCAT

Chapter 8

Your screen will fill with a list of special collections arranged in alphabetical order by the collection name. The libraries that house the special collections are listed next to the collection names.

✹*Do It!* Scroll down the list until you find **Spanish Civil War**. Note that this special collection is located at Brandeis University, as shown in Figure 8.12.

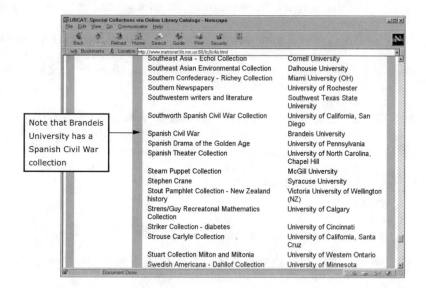

Figure 8.12—Spanish Civil War Collection at Brandeis University

3 Connect to Brandeis University's library catalog.

Scroll down to the bottom of the list until you see the menu options under **METRONET**.

✹*Do It!* Click on **US Libraries**. See Figure 8.13.

Figure 8.13—LIBCAT Options at the End of the Special Collections Page

You are now at the library catalog selection screen. You need to select the appropriate part of the alphabet for the library you want to search. Brandeis University would be found in the AB section.

✹*Do It!* Click on **AB** under "Table of Contents," as shown in Figure 8.14.

Click on **AB** here

Figure 8.14—Online Catalogs Listed in LIBCAT

You need to scroll down the list until you come to **Brandeis University**. You will see two entries for this school. One is the Web page for the university, and the other is its catalog.

✸*Do It!* Click on **Brandeis University (MA) WWW Catalog**, as shown in Figure 8.15.

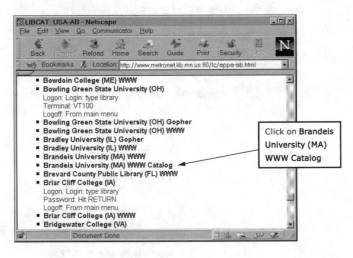

Click on **Brandeis University (MA) WWW Catalog**

Figure 8.15—Brandeis University on the LIBCAT List of Libraries

Now you are in LOUIS, Brandeis University's library catalog. As Figure 8.16 reflects, you can search by keywords, subject, title, author, call number, or in other ways. Help is also readily available.

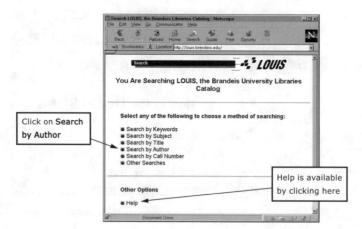

Click on **Search by Author**

Help is available by clicking here

Figure 8.16—Brandeis University's Library Catalog

4 Search by the author's name, Felipe Alaiz.

To begin an author search in LOUIS, you need to choose the **Search by Author** method.

❋*Do It!* Click on **Search by Author**, as shown in Figure 8.16.

❋*Do It!* In the search form provided, type in **alaiz, felipe**, as shown in Figure 8.17. Note in the instructions that LOUIS is not case sensitive, so there is no reason to capitalize the author's name.

❋*Do It!* Choose **am Books only** ("am" is an abbreviated code that the catalog uses to describes the field "Books") from the pulldown menu below the search query box.

❋*Do It!* Choose **spa Spanish** from the "Language" pulldown menu.

❋*Do It!* Click on **Begin Author Search**.

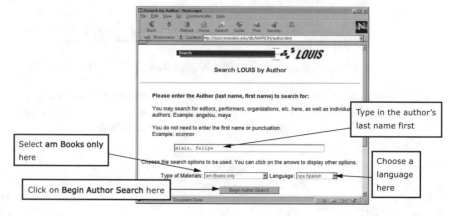

Type in the author's last name first

Select **am Books only** here

Choose a language here

Click on **Begin Author Search** here

Figure 8.17—Search Request Entered in LOUIS

5 Do a related-subject search.

Figure 8.18 shows the results of the search query. The catalog lists the author, title, and call number of each book retrieved.

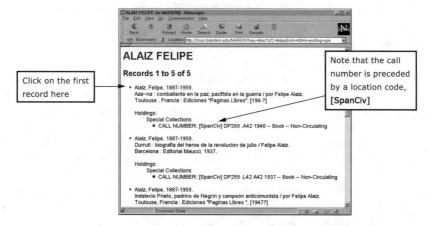

Click on the first record here

Note that the call number is preceded by a location code, **[SpanCiv]**

To see more descriptive information about the books, you'll need to click on the author-title record fields.

❀*Do It!* Click on the first record on the list.

Clicking on a record will give you a detailed description of the book, as shown in Figure 8.19. (Note that the first record on your screen may not be the same one chosen in this example.) This book is about someone named Manuel Azaña. If you wanted to find out more about him, you could click on the first subject heading—his name. If you clicked on the subject heading **Spanish Civil War Collection**, you would obtain a list of all the items in this collection.

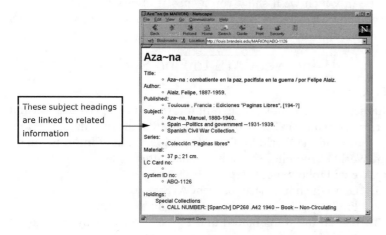

These subject headings are linked to related information

Figure 8.19—Full Description of the First Book Listed

6   End the session.

You can either end the session now or you can continue on to the next activity.

❊*Do It!* To end the session, click on **File** on the menu bar and select **Exit** from the menu.

End of Activity 8.2

Searching for items in a special collection proved to be quite simple. If this had been an actual research project, you would have been wise to print the search results. Then, you could have taken the citations with you when you traveled to the Brandeis library. You might also have checked to see if there were any items in the circulating collection at Brandeis that interested you. If so, you could have gone to your area library and submitted an interlibrary loan request for them.

In the following activity, we will search a special library catalog. Special libraries should not be confused with special collections. Special collections are materials that are part of a larger library, whereas special libraries are independent offices affiliated with organizations, such as associations, businesses, research institutes, and government agencies. Special libraries usually collect materials that are very pertinent to the type of business or research with which the parent organization concerns itself.

Special libraries frequently have much more detailed cataloging procedures than other libraries. For example, a university library catalog would rarely contain journal articles in its catalog. You would find only the title of the journal if it were in that library's collection. But special libraries will often catalog articles if they are specifically related to the parent organization's interests.

Some special libraries don't allow visitors. You'll need to read any stipulations about visitors in their home pages. Let's proceed to the next activity, in which we'll show you a special library catalog. Although Libweb and LIBCAT have links to special libraries, we'll use webCATS this time to start our search.

Activity 8.3   Using webCATS to Find Special Libraries

Overview

In this activity, we'll look for current information on privatization and government finance in Zimbabwe. We know that the International Monetary Fund and the World Bank publish a great deal of information on Third World economies, so we hope that either organization has a library. We will follow these steps:

1. Go to the home page for webCATS.
2. Find a special library that focuses on the topic.
3. Search the Joint Bank-Fund Library Network by the subject *Zimbabwe.*

4. Email selected records.
5. End the session.

Details

1 **Go to the home page for webCATS.**

✿*Do It!* Click on the location field, type **http://www.lights.com/ webcats**, and press ⏎**Enter**.

2 **Find a special library that focuses on the topic.**

✿*Do It!* Click on **Library-Type Index**, as shown in Figure 8.20. We need to click on this in order to see the list of libraries by type.

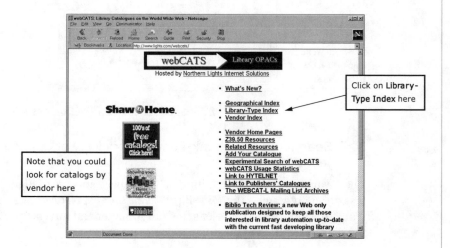

Figure 8.20—webCATS's Home Page

Next, we need to select special libraries.

✿*Do It!* Click on **Special** in "Library-Type Index," as shown in Figure 8.21.

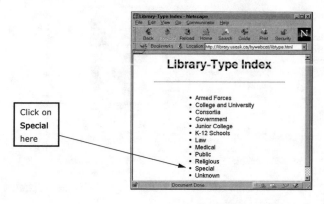

Figure 8.21—Library-Type Index in webCATS

Now your screen will fill with an alphabetical list of special libraries throughout the United States and the world.

❋*Do It!* Scroll down the list until you come to **World Bank and IMF Libraries (New York)**, and then click on it, as shown in Figure 8.22.

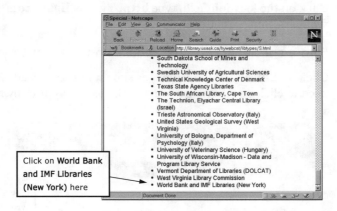

Click on **World Bank and IMF Libraries (New York)** here

Figure 8.22—List of Special Libraries in webCATS

3   Search the Joint Bank-Fund Library Network by the subject *Zimbabwe*.

The "World Bank and IMF Libraries" home page appears in Figure 8.23. It is officially named the *Joint Bank-Fund Library Network*. Before we search the library's catalog, let's find out some general information about the library.

❋*Do It!* Click on **About the Libraries**, as shown in Figure 8.23.

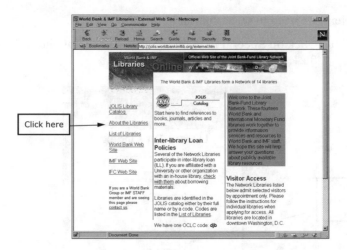

Click here

Figure 8.23—The "World Bank and IMF Libraries" Home Page

Your screen should appear like the one in Figure 8.24. There is a brief description of the roles and activities of the World Bank and the International Monetary Fund, and hyperlinks to these organizations' home pages are included as well. There is also information about the 14 libraries that make up the Joint Bank-Fund Library Network.

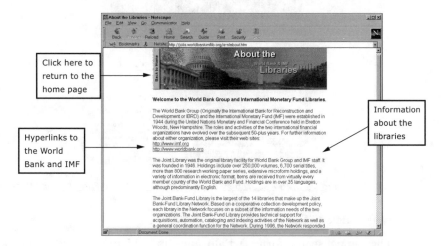

Figure 8.24—Information about the Joint Bank-Fund Library

❁*Do It!* Click on **Back to Home**, as shown in Figure 8.24.

❁*Do It!* From the home page, click on **JOLIS Library Catalog**.

❁*Do It!* Click on **Connect to the JOLIS Library Catalog**.

Your screen should look like the one in Figure 8.25.

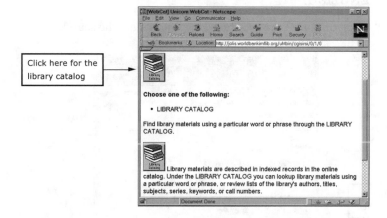

Figure 8.25—Accessing the Joint Bank-Fund Library Catalog

❁*Do It!* Click on the box that contains the picture of the stack of books and that is labeled **Library Catalog**, as shown in Figure 8.25.

You have several search choices available, as Figure 8.26 shows.

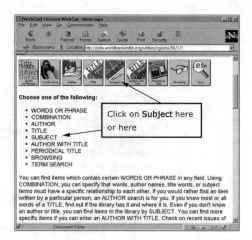

Figure 8.26—Search Choices in the Joint Bank-Fund Library Catalog

❉*Do It!* Click on **Subject**.

The subject search form partially appears in Figure 8.27. We are looking for all types of information, including journal articles, on the topic of *Zimbabwe*. We want to limit our information to resources published within the past two years.

❉*Do It!* Enter **zimbabwe** in the search query box next to **subject**.

❉*Do It!* Next to **pubyear**, type in **1996–1997**.

❉*Do It!* From the pulldown menu next to **language**, choose **ENGLISH**.

❉*Do It!* Click on the **Search Catalog** button to start the search.

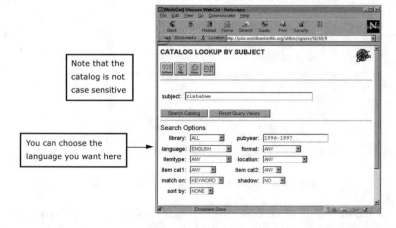

Figure 8.27—Search for the Subject Zimbabwe in the JOLIS Catalog

Partial results of this search appear in Figure 8.28. If we want to see more descriptive information about each item, we must click on the **View** icon connected to each record. We are interested in looking at the title **Rebirth of resistance: labour and structural adjustment in Zimbabwe**.

❋*Do It!* Click on the **View** icon next to the title **Rebirth of resistance: labour and structural adjustment in Zimbabwe**.

Click on
View here

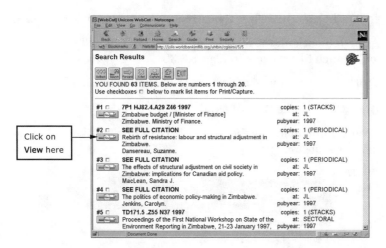

Figure 8.28—Results of Subject Search

Figure 8.29 shows the complete catalog record for this item. Note that this is an article in a journal titled **LABOUR, CAPITAL AND SOCIETY (CANADA)**. We know it is a journal article because a volume number and page numbers appear in the citation.

2. Click on **Print/Capture** here

1. Check this box to mark the item

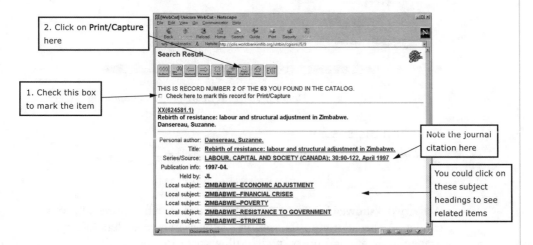

Note the journal citation here

You could click on these subject headings to see related items

Figure 8.29—Detailed Catalog Record of an Article

4   Email selected records.

The online catalog vendor that the Joint Bank-Fund Library uses makes it possible for the researcher to mark records for later printing or emailing. In this example, we will show you how to email a record to yourself.

✸*Do It!* Point at the box next to **Check here to mark this record for Print/Capture**, and click.

✸*Do It!* Click on the **Print/Capture** icon, as shown in Figure 8.29.

After you click on the **Print/Capture** icon, you will see a screen that looks much like the one in Figure 8.30.

✸*Do It!* Type your email address in the box next to **Email to**.

✸*Do It!* Click on the **E-Mail** icon.

Keep in mind that only the *records* you captured will be sent to you, not the actual documents.

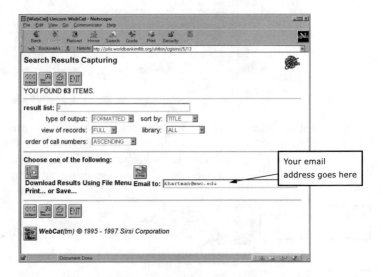

Figure 8.30—The "Search Results Capturing" Screen

5   End the session.

✸*Do It!* Click on **File** on the menu bar and select **Exit** from the menu.

End of Activity 8.3

Activity 8.3 showed how easy it is to locate and search a special library's catalog. A special library focuses on a subject in greater detail than an academic or public library, which allows you to find small pieces of information cataloged individually, including journal articles.

Summary

Libraries around the world are making their library catalogs compatible with the World Wide Web. These graphical user interface (GUI) systems have made it easier for people to search library catalogs from remote sites. The Web makes it possible for a library to integrate text, graphics, and other media and to include hyperlinks to outside resources. Hundreds of libraries have yet to migrate to Web-based systems and still use Telnet programs to enable access. This chapter focused on Web-based systems.

There are many reasons why you may want to search a library catalog remotely. You may need to visit a library collection that might contain useful research information, and you want to be sure of what's there before you go. You may also want to do an exhaustive search of your subject to find bibliographic records that you could then request through interlibrary loan from your library. There are many types of libraries and certain types are better for some topics than for others. This chapter covered some of the major library catalog–finding services on the World Wide Web which make it easy to find the different types of libraries and their catalogs.

Selected Terms Introduced in This Chapter

Dewey decimal classification
    system
digital collection
graphical user interface (GUI)
Library of Congress
    classification system
Library of Congress subject
    headings (LCSH)

online catalog
online public access catalog
    (OPAC)
special collection
special library
Telnet
vendor

9
Chapter

FTP: Searching Archives, Downloading Files

The Internet was primarily created so that researchers could exchange ideas and share the results of their work. It stands to reason, then, that one of the basic Internet services would be to enable people to copy files from one computer to another on the Internet. *FTP*, which stands for File Transfer Protocol, is that basic Internet service. It dates back almost to the beginnings of the Internet, the early 1970s, and it's used to share information in any type of file. Most of these files are publicly available through what is called *anonymous FTP,* since no special password other than *anonymous* is needed to retrieve the files. A computer system that allows others to connect to it through anonymous FTP is called an anonymous FTP site or an *FTP archive*. The collection of files available at an anonymous FTP site is also called an FTP archive.

This chapter will focus on using FTP and FTP archives as two more facets of doing research on the Web and using Web browsers. There will also be a brief introduction to using an FTP client (an FTP program on your computer) to upload and download files without using a browser.

The chapter will have the following sections:
* Understanding the URL Format for FTP
* Downloading a File by Anonymous FTP
* Locating FTP Archives and Other Sites for Finding Software
* Downloading and Working with Files from Software Archives
* Using an FTP Client Program

Web browsers and Web servers using HTTP (Hypertext Transfer Protocol) transfer files across the Internet. Hence, they allow the same sort of sharing as FTP. What is now the World Wide Web wouldn't have been possible without the notions associated with FTP and its use. In fact, one of the first search services available on the Internet (as of 1990) was designed to find files stored in FTP archives. Called Archie (short for *archive*, according to its originators), this service is still available. It works by indexing the titles of files in a database built from the entries in many FTP archives. This index, in turn, takes the form of a database. When a user supplies a search term, Archie displays the locations of matching files. When you think about it, you'll see that it works a lot like many of the search engines we've discussed in earlier chapters.

Do we still need to use FTP? Yes. FTP can be used to transfer any type of file. It's commonly used nowadays to distribute software throughout the Internet. Most of these software programs are available as **shareware**, which means that you retrieve (download) the program from an archive, use it, and purchase it if you find the program useful. FTP is an efficient way to transfer files when you know the exact name and location of the file—and that's all included in its URL. Using FTP, you can also transfer a file from your computer to another. This is called **uploading** a file. When you upload, you usually have to give a login name and password to the other computer system. This turns out to be a good way to work on one computer and transfer your work to another. Some people use this technique to update or create Web pages. They do their work on one computer and then transfer the files to a computer that acts as a Web server.

Understanding the URL Format for FTP

These days, much of the access to files by FTP is through a Web browser. As you know, that means you need to be familiar with the URL format for FTP. Here is the general form of a URL for anonymous FTP:

ftp://name-of-ftp-site/directory-name/file-name

Note the following features:

- The URL for anonymous FTP starts with **ftp://**.
- The name of the FTP site follows **//**.
- The directory name starts with the first single / and goes up to, but does not include, the last /.
- The name of the file follows the last /.
- All the slashes (/) go in the same direction and slant to the right.

Suppose a friend tells you, "I found this picture of Mars with great detail and colors. You can get it by anonymous FTP at the FTP site for the Jet Propulsion Laboratory, **ftp.jpl.nasa.gov**. You'll want to get the file **marglobe.gif**. It's in the directory **pub/images/browse**. There are also some animations at the same site in **pub/images/anim**." You'd like to view the image, and she's told you everything you need to retrieve it. The URL for that file is **ftp://ftp.jpl.nasa.gov/pub/images/browse/marglobe.gif**.

Matching this to the general form, we have the following:

You can also use a URL to refer to a directory. For example, if you enter the URL **ftp://ftp.jpl.nasa.gov/pub/images/browse**, the Web browser displays a list of all the files or subdirectories in the directory **/pub/images/browse**, as displayed in Figure 9.1. Each file or subdirectory is represented as a hyperlink, and you can view it by clicking on its name.

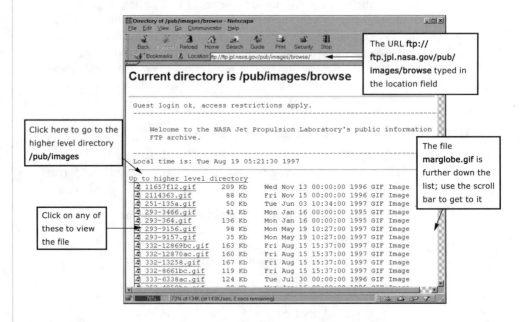

Figure 9.1—FTP Archive Displaying Directory Files

Downloading a File by Anonymous FTP

There are two ways to retrieve a file—that is, copy it from a remote site to the computer you're using.

Method 1: View the File First, and Then Save It Using the File Menu

If you type a file's URL or if you click on a hyperlink, the file will be transferred to the Web browser. This is useful if you want to view the file before you save it, but the file will be transferred to your computer first. If the browser is configured to display or play a file of that type, you'll see (and hear, if possible) the file's contents in the Web browser window. Some examples of files of this type are text files, Web pages that are text files with HTML commands, or GIF or JPEG image files.

The file may also be displayed in a window created by another program called a *helper application*. If there is no helper application installed to display the file, a message box pops up saying "No Viewer Configured for File Type." If the file is displayed in the browser window, select **Save As** from the **File** pulldown menu in the menu bar. This opens a **Save As** dialog box on the screen. Set the directory or folder name, and then click on the button labeled **Save**. If the file comes up in the window for another application, such as Microsoft Word, save it through the commands for that application. See the tip below to handle a file type that doesn't match any type that your browser can work with.

Method 2: Save the Hyperlink in a File Without Viewing It by Using the Right Mouse Button or Shift and Click

If there is a hyperlink to a file in the Web browser's window, you can save the hyperlink. To retrieve the file without viewing it, put the mouse pointer on the hyperlink and press the right mouse button. When a menu pops up, choose **Save Link As**. This opens a **Save As** dialog box on the screen. Set the directory or folder name, and then click on the **Save** button.

Another way to do this is to place the pointer on a hyperlink. Then hold down the **Shift** key, click on the hyperlink, and release the **Shift** key. This immediately opens a **Save As** dialog box. You can save it to a file you've specified on your computer.

✳ Tip

What to do when "No Viewer Configured for File Type" pops up.

The message "No Viewer Configured for File Type" means you've come across a file type that your browser doesn't know how to handle at the present time. Select the option that lets you **Save to Disk**. A **Save As** dialog box pops up, asking you to specify the folder in which you want to store the file. If you want to see or hear the file, then be sure you have any hardware and software you need to uncompress, display, or play the file after it has been transmitted. There are lots of variations and possibilities for the necessary equipment and programs, so we can't cover all of them here. But if you do have everything you need, you may want to configure the browser so that

Chapter 9

it knows what to do with files of that type in the future. In Netscape's online help, you can find instructions about informing Netscape about a particular helper application. Click on **Preferences** on the **Edit** pulldown menu in the menu bar, select the **Applications** panel, and click on the **Help** button if you're using Netscape 4. If you're using Netscape 3, click on **Options** in the menu bar, select **General Preferences**, choose **Helpers**, and click on the **Help** button.

The following activity goes through the steps involved in downloading a file by anonymous FTP when using a Web browser.

 Tip

Remember that the Web is always changing and that your results may differ from those shown here. Don't let this confuse you. The activities demonstrate fundamental skills. These skills don't change, even though the number of results obtained or the actual screens may look very different.

Activity 9.1   Retrieving a File by Anonymous FTP

Overview

In this activity, we'll retrieve the file that we mentioned previously, the one containing an image of Mars. We will retrieve the file using the two methods mentioned above to demonstrate how each is done.

Suppose the browser is already started and ready for use. First, using Method 1, we'll retrieve the file by typing the URL **ftp:// ftp.jpl.nasa.gov/pub/images/browse/marglobe.gif**. Web browsers can display files of this type. The file will be displayed, but it won't be saved into a file that we can use again until we select **Save As** from the **File** pulldown menu in the menu bar and set the folder and file name for it. In this case, we will view the file's contents before saving it.

Then we'll save the same file by using Method 2. We'll enter the URL for the directory that contains the file, **ftp://ftp.jpl.nasa.gov/ pub/images/browse**, find the file's hyperlink, and use the right mouse button to retrieve it. Retrieving a file this way is quicker, because the browser doesn't have to display it first.

Details

Method 1: View the File First

Type the file's URL in the location bar so that you can view the file.

Do It! Click on the location field, type **ftp://ftp.jpl.nasa.gov/pub/ images/browse/marglobe.gif**, and press ⌷Enter⌷.

Chapter 9

If the URL is correct and the image is still available, the browser will display the image of Mars.

You can now save this image in a file on your computer.

✸*Do It!* Click on **File** in the menu bar.

A menu pops up.

✸*Do It!* Select **Save As** from the menu.

A **Save As** dialog box appears, as shown in Figure 9.2.

The next step is to store the file in an appropriate folder or directory. You can save the file in the current folder. Alternately, you could select or create another folder to hold the image. Figure 9.2 shows the file being stored in a folder named **images**. Store the file wherever you'd like. It is a good idea to have one folder for all items of a similar type or a collection of files related to a project. That way it's easier for you to find the file the next time you want it.

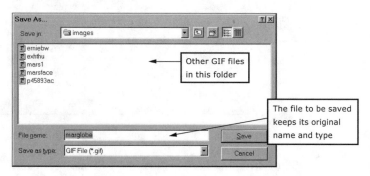

*Figure 9.2—Save As Dialog Box for Saving **marglobe.gif***

Once you have chosen an appropriate folder, you need to save the file.

✸*Do It!* Click on the button labeled **Save**.

Method 2: Save the Hyperlink in a File Without Viewing It

Go to the Web page with the hyperlink we want.

✸*Do It!* Click on the location field, type **ftp://ftp.jpl.nasa.gov/pub/images/browse**, and press Enter.

This connects you by anonymous FTP to the archive server at **ftp.jpl.nasa.gov** and displays the listings of the directory /**pub/images/browse**, as shown in Figure 9.1.

Find the entry for **marglobe.gif**. There are several ways to do this. You could browse the listings by pressing the down arrow key ↓ or the PgDn key or by using the vertical scroll bar. A more direct way is to use **Find** to let the browser locate it.

Chapter 9

❀*Do It!* Press Ctrl + F, or click on **Edit** in the menu bar and select **Find in Page**. Type the name of the file to retrieve, and then click on the button labeled **Find Next**.

❀*Do It!* The browser will take you to the first occurrence of whatever you entered, if that string is in the text portion of the Web page. If there are several items that match, press Ctrl + G to find the next until you reach the hyperlink. Press **Cancel** on the **Find** dialog box to move it off the screen.

You'll eventually reach the portion of the listing that resembles what is shown in Figure 9.3.

Directory listing—
here's the hyperlink
we want

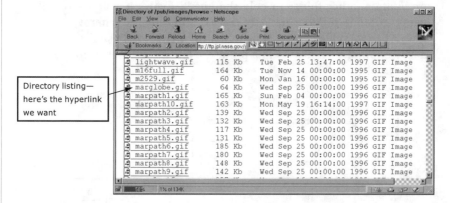

Figure 9.3—Directory Listing Showing Hyperlinks

The listing in Figure 9.3 contains an icon for each file. The icons here indicate that the files are images. This listing also contains the size of each file, the date it was last modified, and an annotation describing the file type.

You can now retrieve the file.

❀*Do It!* Move the cursor or mouse pointer to the name **marglobe.gif**. Press the right mouse button and select **Save Link As** from the menu.

❀*Do It!* A **Save As** dialog box appears, as shown in Figure 9.2. Select the proper folder or directory for the file and click on the button labeled **Save**. A box labeled **Saving Location** appears on the screen. That box keeps you updated about the progress of the transfer from the remote site to your computer.

Congratulations! You've successfully retrieved a file by anonymous FTP.

End of Activity 9.1

In Activity 9.1, we used a Web browser to retrieve a file through anonymous FTP. You go through the same steps to retrieve any type of file. In this case, because the image comes from NASA, it is available for your personal use. Before using it for any commercial purposes, be sure to obtain permission. You can retrieve files by anonymous FTP at no cost, but having retrieved a file doesn't give you the right to use it any way you'd like. The information in these files needs to be treated in the same way as information that's part of a book, newspaper, audio recording, or video recording.

Locating FTP Archives and Other Sites for Finding Software

FTP archives are collections of directories arranged according to some scheme. A common arrangement is for the top level to be arranged by the type of computer system (such as Mac, PC, and Unix) and for the levels below that to be ordered according to the type of software (such as games, utilities, and Internet). You start at the home, or root, directory and, by clicking on hyperlinks that represent folders or directories, you move or browse through the archive. Once you've located the file you want, you can download it using one of the methods described in Activity 9.1.

There are several well-established and reliable FTP archives in the world. The following list is representative of general purpose archives. The first has a search form available so you can find files in the archive. The second has a Web page interface that you use to go through the archives. The last is a more traditional type of listing; the items are well organized, but you have to find your own way.

- UIArchive, University of Illinois at Urbana-Champaign
  http://uiarchive.cso.uiuc.edu
- Wuarchive, Washington University in St. Louis
  http://ftp.wustl.edu
- Garbo archives, University of Vaasa, Finland
  ftp://garbo.uwasa.fi

Because millions of files are available through FTP, you can appreciate how difficult it is to find the name of a file and its archive without some automated search tool. In 1990, Peter Deutsch, Alan Emtage, and Bill Heelan at McGill University created a service named Archie and released it for public use. Archie is available with an interface specially designed for use with a Web browser. You enter the name or a portion of the name of the file you're looking for. Archie returns a collection of hyperlinks to files or directories that match the name used in the search box. For more information on using Archie, look at the home page for Archie at **http://www.bunyip.com/products/archie**. Here's a list of a few Archie servers. Try one!

✻ Archie Search at Bunyip
http://archie.bunyip.com/archie.html

✻ ArchiePlexForm at FUNET
**http://www.funet.fi/funet/archie/
archieplexform.html**

✻ FTP Search v4.0
http://ftpsearch.ntnu.no/ftpsearch

Using Archie is all well and good, provided you know the name or a portion of the name of the file you're seeking. Sometimes you need to guess what the name might be. But it can still be difficult. A better approach is to arrange files in categories according to their function—such as sound files, desktop utilities, games, HTML editors, and so forth—and a description of each. If there is a way to search the collection by file names and descriptions, then we have a more useful service.

Several of these software directories are available on the Web. Many of the files accessible through these sites are software, programs, or collections of programs and other files, which are distributed as shareware. The files are in either executable form (their names end with **.exe**) or compressed form (their names end with **.zip** or **.gz**). We explained these file types in Chapter 1, and we'll show you how to work with them in the next section. Here are a few sources on the Web that list FTP and software or shareware archives:

✻ Librarians' Index to the Internet
http://sunsite.berkeley.edu/internetindex,
then select **Computers, Software**

✻ nerd's HEAVEN: The Software Directory Directory
http://boole.stanford.edu/nerdsheaven.html

✻ Yahoo! Computers and Internet: Software: Shareware
**http://www.yahoo.com/computers_and_internet/
software/shareware**

Downloading and Working with Files from Software Archives

Several services on the Web act as archives and distributors of software in the form of shareware or *freeware* (software that may be used and distributed at no cost). Each service supplies links to the programs; when you click on the link, the software is transferred to your computer, essentially by FTP. In other words, you select the software you'd like, and you then use a Web browser to download it to your computer.

Shareware Often Comes in Packages

Most of the files in the archives are packages, or collections of related files. These are in packages because to install, run, and use a single program usually requires several files, such as program libraries, instructions for installing and registering the program, and online help files. When you retrieve these, you get all the files you need combined in one file, the package.

The files or packages are processed by a compression program, which reduces the total number of bytes necessary to represent the information in the package. Reducing the size of a file means it takes less time to download the file. Because of this compression, you must do two things to the package after you receive it: uncompress it and extract the individual files from the package.

Compressed files or packages have names that usually end in **.zip**. Two popular compression programs are PKZIP and WinZip (which are both shareware); these are also mentioned in Chapter 1. You will definitely want a copy of either of those utilities. As you might guess, they are both available in compressed format, as packages.

How can we extract the files necessary for those compression programs or similar packages? These and many other packages are in what is called a *self-extracting archive*. The package's file name ends in **.exe**. When you click on the name, it starts extracting its own components. For example, the software for the Netscape and Microsoft browsers are in that format.

This compressed format isn't used only with programs. Any single file or collection of files can be compressed and transmitted in that compressed format. In the course of writing this book, we used this technology. Because each chapter has so many images, the files were quite large. We put each chapter and the images into a single package and then compressed it using either PKZIP or WinZip. We used FTP to send the compressed packages to the publisher.

Downloading and Installing Software

Here are the steps involved in downloading and installing shareware or freeware programs and associated files:

* Find the program you want to retrieve in a software archive.
* Create a folder or directory to hold the program from the archive on your computer.
* Click on the hyperlink in the software archive to the program. As soon as you indicate where it should go using a **Save As** dialog box, it will be transferred to your computer.
* If the file name ends in **.exe**, then it's likely a self-extracting archive. Locate it using Windows Explorer and double-click on it. It will either install itself—follow the instructions—or it will extract its parts into the current directory.
* If the file name ends in **.zip**, then you have to use a program such as PKZIP or WinZip to extract the components. You usually select the folder or directory in which they will go.

* In either case, look for a file with a name similar to **Readme** or **Instructions** to see what steps you need to take to install the program or to work with the files in the package. In many cases, the extracted files need to go through some other processing by a program named **Setup** before they are ready to use.

* Be sure to check the program and associated files for computer viruses. Many of the archives check files for viruses before making them available to the public, but you ought to check them yourself.

Obtaining a Copy of PKZIP or WinZip

You can see from the above steps that you'll need a copy of PKZIP or WinZip, but you don't need both.

To get a copy of PKZIP, go to the home page for PKWARE, **http://www.pkware.com**. Spend a little time reading about PKZIP, the way it works, and file compression in general. Click on the hyperlink that takes you through the steps of downloading the software. Store it in a new folder only for PKZIP. Once it has finished downloading, there will be a new application (program) in the folder. Click on it and follow the instructions. It will install itself in a directory or folder. Once it's installed, go to that directory, using Windows Explorer, and read the file named **Readme**, which contains information about the files you've installed. The program's name is PKZIP; click on it when you need to use it.

To get a copy of WinZip, go to the home page for WinZip with the URL **http://www.winzip.com**. Spend a little time reading about WinZip, how it works, and about the topic of file compression. Click on the hyperlink that takes you through the steps of downloading the software. Store it in a new folder only for WinZip. Once it's finished downloading there will be a new application (program) in the folder. Click on it and it will lead you through the steps of installing the program in a folder on your computer. The name of the program is WinZip; click on it when you need it.

Acquiring Antivirus Software

You will also want a program that checks files for computer viruses. Several are available, and you can get shareware versions to evaluate and determine which you like best. One, F-PROT, makes its software free to individuals; commercial customers or organizations must pay for using it. Listed with F-PROT are two other sites that offer shareware versions of their antivirus and virus protection software:

* F-PROT, Data Fellows

  http://www.datafellows.com

* Symantec AntiVirus Research Center

  http://www.symantec.com/avcenter

* VirusScan for Windows 95, McAfee

  http://www.mcafee.com

If you don't have an antivirus program on your computer, visit one of the sites, download the most recent version, and install it. Any of the antivirus programs from the sites listed above come as compressed packages. Follow the same steps for installing these programs as for almost any other software that you download.

Using Software Archives and FTP Search Services

In an earlier section of this chapter, we listed the URLs of some lists of software archives or sites in which you find software to download through FTP.

What You'll Find in the Archives

Software archives maintain their own collections of files, and FTP archives have hyperlinks to the files, which are usually stored at the Web site for the person or organization that markets the software. Both types include a search form so you can search the collection for files, and several also have reviews, descriptions, and links to the software arranged into categories so you can browse the items accessible through the archive.

The files are usually arranged in categories according to the type of software, such as games, Internet, utilities, and personal use. Sometimes they are also arranged according to the type of operating system they're designed for, such as MS-DOS, Windows 3.x, Windows 95/NT, or Macintosh.

Some archives are dedicated to programs for a particular operating system, and some only to Internet software. Two examples are WinFiles.com, which specializes in software for Windows 95/NT systems, and TUCOWS, which has software to be used for working with the Internet. ZDNet Software Library is a good example of a full-featured software archive with extensive reviews of many of the items it lists.

Here's a list of a few archives:

General:

DOWNLOAD.COM	http://www.download.com
FILE MINE	http://www.filemine.com
FilePile	http://www.filepile.com/nc/start
SHAREWARE.COM	http://www.shareware.com
SNOOPIE File Search	http://www.snoopie.com
ZDNet Software Library	http://www.hotfiles.com

Specialized:

Stroud's Consummate Winsock Applications	http://cws.internet.com
TUCOWS	http://www.tucows.com
WinFiles.com	http://www.winfiles.com

Chapter 9

Before You Download

We're going to demonstrate downloading and installing some software in Activity 9.2. Before you download software, you need to answer a few questions for yourself.

Is the program appropriate for my computer system?

Most of the software archives include a description of the system requirements for the software you'll download. Check that you have enough memory (RAM) to run the program (some require 16 megabytes to run properly) and that you have the correct operating system. Software that's developed for a Windows 95 or Windows NT system won't work properly if it's installed on a system running Windows 3.1 or on a Macintosh system.

Do I have enough storage space on my disk to hold the software?

Again, look at the system requirements to see that you have enough disk space to hold the new program along with your other software.

Do I meet the licensing requirements?

Most software is available as shareware to anyone, but some software is available only to educational or nonprofit institutions. The software will likely come with a licensing agreement; you'll need to read this and decide whether to consent to it.

Do I have permission to install the software?

If you're working on your home computer, then there's probably no problem. However, if you're working on a computer that's owned by your school or company—and probably being shared by others—check local policies to see whether you may install new software on the computer.

Do I have the software I need to install the software?

Check to see if you have the proper software, such as PKZIP or WinZip, to extract the parts of the package. Oftentimes, this will be stated in the description of the software. Also look at the name of the package. If it ends with **.zip**, then you'll need a program such as the one we've mentioned to install it.

Will the software have a detrimental impact on other software on my computer?

This isn't always easy to answer until the software is installed, in which case it may be too late. Read as much as you can about the software before installing it to see if it will have a detrimental impact on existing programs or sys-

tem configuration. Be sure you can check it for viruses before installing it.

Will I be able to "uninstall" the program if things don't go well?
Most software nowadays comes with a program that makes
it easy to remove the primary program and all associated
files if and when you need to do this.

Now we'll go through some of the details involved in downloading
and installing software from an archive.

Activity 9.2   Downloading and Installing Software from a Software Archive

Overview

We've been searching for and finding information on the Web throughout this book. In many instances, we've added some resources to our
bookmark list. The list has grown and needs some organization and
management. We know we can do this through our browser, but we're
interested in seeing if there is some software that has better tools for
organizing and managing our bookmark collection. In this activity, we'll
go to one of the software archives, find something we'd like to try, check
to see that it's appropriate to download and install, and then go through
the steps necessary to install it. Here are the steps we'll follow:

1. Go to the home page for the ZDNet Software Library.
2. Search the library for software dealing with bookmarks.
3. Select software to download and check the system requirements.
4. Download the software.
5. Install the software.

Of course, we'll want to try the program at some point, but we won't
show that here.

Details

We'll assume that the Web browser is started and displayed on the screen.

1   Go to the home page for the ZDNet Software Library.

❋*Do It!* Click on the location field, type **http://www.hotfiles.com**,
and press **Enter**.

The ZDNet Library is a large, well-organized, and well-maintained software archive. We use the URL for its home page, **http://www.
hotfiles.com**, to access the software library or archive. The home page
appears in Figure 9.4. We're going to search for software dealing with
bookmarks in the next step. The term *bookmarks* is entered in the search
form in Figure 9.4.

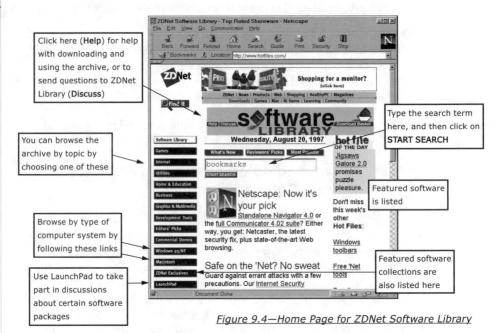

Click here (**Help**) for help with downloading and using the archive, or to send questions to ZDNet Library (**Discuss**)

You can browse the archive by topic by choosing one of these

Browse by type of computer system by following these links

Use LaunchPad to take part in discussions about certain software packages

Type the search term here, and then click on **START SEARCH**

Featured software is listed

Featured software collections are also listed here

Figure 9.4—Home Page for ZDNet Software Library

We see from the home page that we can search or browse the archive either by type of software or by type of computer system. Several types of software and individual programs are listed. For example, when we retrieved this page, there was a hyperlink to a collection of software titled **Internet Security ToolKit**. We also see there's a **Help** hyperlink so we can learn more about downloading and using this archive. We know from using other search services that it's a good idea to click on **Help** and to do some reading before we continue.

❀*Do It!* Click on the hyperlink **Help**.

This takes us to the help page for ZDNet Software Library. Read the section titled **Easy Download Guide**.

❀*Do It!* Click on the hyperlink **Easy Download Guide**.

We'll follow the steps listed there after we select the software to download. In the next step, we'll start searching for software that deals with bookmarks, but it's worth spending a little time to browse some of the categories.

2 Search the library for software dealing with bookmarks.

❀*Do It!* Go back to the home page for ZDNet Library.

❀*Do It!* Type **bookmarks** in the search box, and click on **START SEARCH**.

You can search for software by typing a keyword or phrase in the search box and clicking on the button labeled **START SEARCH**.

3 Select software to download and check the system requirements.

A portion of the Web page listing the search results appears in Figure 9.5. It's worth taking some time clicking on the hyperlinks for some of the packages to read the ZDNet Library reviews. In addition to a link to the review, we see the date the software was added to the archive, its rating, and the number of downloads (other folks retrieving the software) listed. To be specific we'll click on the hyperlink for **WebTabs v1.0**.

❀*Do It!* Click on the hyperlink for **WebTabs v1.0**.

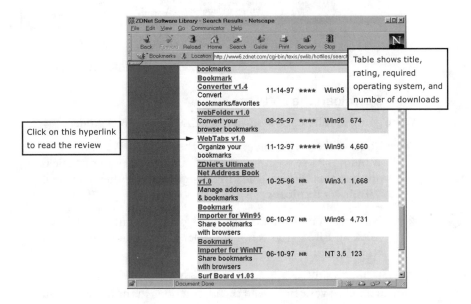

Figure 9.5—Web Page Showing Search Results

The Web page for WebTabs is shown in Figure 9.6. The entire Web page isn't shown there, but after reading all of it, we see that it is designed to run on a computer that uses a Windows 95 operating system and that in compressed form it takes up 2,303,081 bytes—roughly 2 megabytes. Once it's expanded, we can expect it to take up about twice as much space, and we need to decide if we have enough disk space to install it. If after reading the review we feel the software will be useful to us, it is appropriate for our computer, and we have enough space for it, then we can start downloading it.

Chapter 9

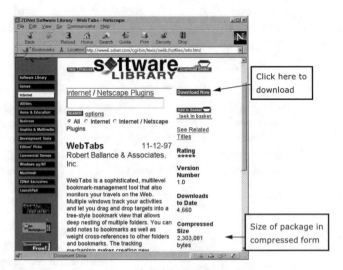

Figure 9.6—ZDNet Library Information About WebTabs

4   Download the software.

We're going to follow the steps in the ZDNet download guide.

❀*Do It!* First we'll create a folder to hold the package. We're using Windows 95 so we first activate Windows Explorer by clicking on the **Start** button, selecting **Programs**, and then choosing **Windows Explorer**.

❀*Do It!* We'll use Windows Explorer to display the contents of drive C:. Click on **File** in the menu bar, select **New**, and then click on **New Folder**.

The window you'll see appears in Figure 9.7. If you're using other soft-ware to manage your files, read the instructions in the download guide.

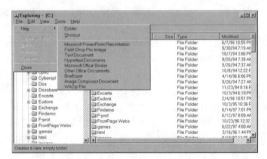

Figure 9.7—Creating a New Folder Using Windows Explorer

A new folder is created. We'll name it **WebTabs**.

❀*Do It!* Type **WebTabs** for the folder's name and press **Enter**.

Now we're ready for the second step in the download process. We can use the browser to transfer the file from ZDNet Library to our system. Be sure the Web page like the one in Figure 9.6 is displayed on your computer.

❋*Do It!* Return to the browser window and click on the hyperlink **Download Now**.

The browser will attempt to transfer the file to your computer using FTP. You'll likely get a dialog box message such as "Unknown file type" or some other warning. In any case we click on a button that lets us save the file to disk. If you were using a browser other than Netscape, you might get a different message. You want to save the file to your disk. Click on a button that lets you do this. A **Save As** dialog box will appear.

❋*Do It!* Use the controls in the **Save As** dialog box to select the folder **WebTabs**, as has been done in Figure 9.8. Then click on **Save**.

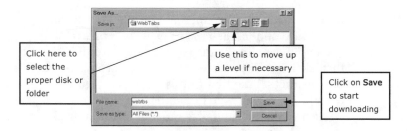

Figure 9.8—Save As Dialog Box with WebTabs as the Selected Folder

A window titled "Saving Location" pops up on the screen to show the estimated time it will take to download the file and the progress of the download. Depending on the speed of your modem, how busy the server is at ZDNet, and current Internet traffic, it could take a few minutes or longer (up to an hour in extreme cases) to download the file. Figure 9.9 shows the **Saving Location** box. It shows that the download is about 50 percent finished. We can estimate that it will take about 20 to 30 minutes for the download.

Figure 9.9—Saving Location Window Showing the Progress of the Download

When that box closes, we're ready to install the software.

5   Install the software.

Chapter 9

The downloaded file will be in the **WebTabs** folder we created on drive C:. To see what it looks like, use Windows Explorer to open the folder **WebTabs**.

❋*Do It!* Use Windows Explorer to open the folder **WebTabs**.

The listing indicates that the file is a compressed, or zip, file, as shown in Figure 9.10. It will appear this way if we've installed WinZip on our computer. If we had installed PKZIP instead, it would still be listed as a compressed file.

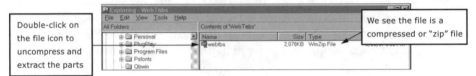

Figure 9.10—View of the Downloaded File

❋*Do It!* Double-click on the **webtbs** icon.

Double-clicking on the icon starts WinZip. If WinZip was installed with the Wizard option, then the software will take us step-by-step through extracting the parts of the package and installing the software. If not, then click on **Extract** to extract and uncompress the files. In either case, extract all the files to this directory. Figure 9.11 shows the contents of the folder **WebTabs** after the files have been extracted (and we've pressed the key **F5** to refresh the folder display).

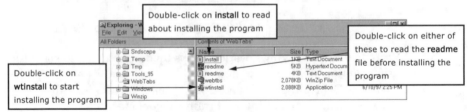

Figure 9.11—View of WebTabs after Extracting Files

Before going any further, we'll read some of the documentation that comes with the software.

❋*Do It!* Double-click on the icon for **readme**.

Double-clicking on either icon labeled **readme** allows us to read the contents of that file. It describes some of the program's features and requirements.

❋*Do It!* Double-click on the icon for **install**.

Double-clicking on the **install** icon opens a brief document that tells us about the installation file, **wtinstall**. The document also says that an uninstall program will be available so that we can remove the program and all its parts when we want to do this. We might, for example, decide that we don't want to purchase the program after the shareware trial period ends—after 30 days, in this case.

Now we're ready to install the program so that we can use it. When we double-click on the **wtinstall** icon, a program will start to lead us through the installation process. We will take all the usual options as the installation or setup program proceeds.

❋*Do It!* Double-click on the icon for **wtinstall**.

A setup program starts. When it finishes, the WebTabs program will be installed in the folder **C:\Program Files\WebTabs**, and **WebTabs** will be added to our **Start** menu. It's instructive to use Windows Explorer to see what's in the folder **C:\Program Files\WebTabs**. You'll see the program, and you need to click on its icon to start it. You will also see a program or application named **Unwise**; double-click on its icon to remove WebTabs from the system.

One more thing: Now that we've installed WebTabs, we don't need the files in the folder **C:\WebTabs** anymore. It's safe to delete that folder at this point.

<hr>

End of Activity 9.2

<hr>

In Activity 9.2, we downloaded and installed a program from a software archive. The steps we followed were fairly typical, although the details can change, depending on the program downloaded and the software archive used. We installed the program by clicking on an icon labeled **wtinstall**. In most other cases, we'll click on an icon labeled **Setup** or **Install**.

Using an FTP Client Program

In the examples and activities discussed so far in this chapter, we have used FTP through the Web browser. That may be all you need to search for and retrieve information from the Web or Internet using FTP. Sometimes, though, you may want to use an FTP program that's separate from the browser. To use an FTP program this way, you'll still need an Internet connection from your computer. The program you run will download files from a server or upload files from your computer to a server. This is the sort of client/server interaction we discussed in Chapter 1. The FTP program you use acts as a client.

When you work with an FTP client to contact another computer (called the *server* or *host*), you'll need to have certain pieces of information. The following list explains what you must know.

You'll need the Internet domain name or address of the server, or host.

The client uses the ***domain name*** to contact the server. Earlier in the chapter, in the section "Understanding the URL Format for FTP," we pointed out the domain name portion of a URL that implies the use of FTP.

If you're going to be downloading software, you'll need a user name and a password on the host.
If you're using anonymous FTP, the user name is *anonymous* and the password is your email address. If you're going to download some files from your user account on the server system, you'll use your assigned user name and password.

If you're going to be uploading files to another computer, you'll need a user name and password on the host.
The user name and password enable you to upload files to a directory or folder that isn't necessarily available to the public.

Of course, you'll also need an FTP client for your computer. Several are available as shareware, but one in particular is highly recommended. It's WS_FTP, and it's free for personal use. To get a copy appropriate for your system, go to the *Junod Software* home page, **http://www.gabn.net/junodj**. John A. Junod has written and continues to maintain WS_FTP. Several very good guides to using WS_FTP are available on the Web. Here's a short list:

* Installing and Configuring WS_FTP
  http://usats.com/learn/ftp.shtml

* WS FTP v4.5
  http://riceinfo.rice.edu/Computer/Facilities/Colleges/PC/WSFTP/WSFTP.html

* WS_FTP: A Quick Reference Guide
  http://anulib.anu.edu.au/courses/html/intro/48.html

We'll briefly go over how to use WS_FTP, but look at some of these guides for more help when you're ready.

First download and install the appropriate version of the software from Junod Software. Use the same techniques discussed in Activity 9.2.

Once the program is installed, start it by selecting it from the **Start** menu, clicking on an icon on your desktop, or clicking on an icon in a folder. Which one of these you choose depends on how it was installed. When it starts, a session profile pops onto the screen.

Figure 9.12 shows a session profile for connecting to a system with the host name (same as the domain name) **www.mwc.edu**. The user id or login name for this user is **ernie**. A password isn't typed in here; it will be typed in when the host system is contacted. If a password were saved with this profile, then anyone using the computer could access the files belonging to user **ernie** on **www.mwc.edu**. If this were to be an anonymous FTP session, then the box labeled **Anonymous** would be checked. You can select other servers with different profiles by clicking on the button to the right of the profile name.

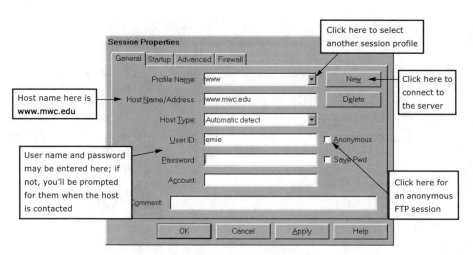

Figure 9.12—Sample Session Profile for WS FTP

To contact the host, click on the button labeled **OK**. Acting as a client, WS_FTP attempts to contact the host system. Another window pops up that shows whether the host has been contacted. The user then has control over the transfer of files.

Figure 9.13 shows the window that appears when WS_FTP starts an FTP session with **www.mwc.edu**. The left column lists the files in the current folder of your computer, the client. The right column lists the files in the directory with which you've connected on the host computer.

You can choose a file to transfer by selecting it from the appropriate column. You'll see that there are scroll bars to let you scroll through the list of files and directories on both the client and host computers. In each column, the subdirectories of the current directory are listed in the upper panel and the files are listed in the lower panel.

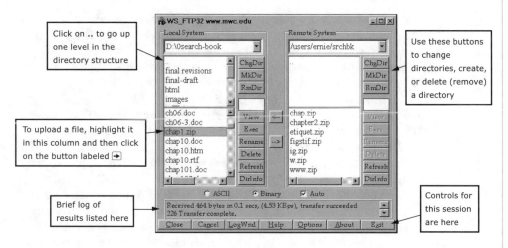

Figure 9.13—Session Window for WS FTP

Suppose we want to upload the file named **chap1.zip** from the client computer—that's the computer your using—to the host. We highlight **chap1.zip** as shown in Figure 9.13 and click on the button labeled ➡️. In doing so, we move the file from the client (listed on the left) to the host (listed on the right).

After we click on ➡️, another dialog box called *Transfer Status* pops up showing information about the transfer of the file from one computer to another over the Internet. Figure 9.14 shows the window for the upload we've been discussing. The items shown include the total number of bytes to transfer, the number transferred so far, the rate of transfer, how much time has been spent so far, and the estimated remaining time. That window will stay on the screen until the transfer is complete. You can stop the transfer by clicking on the **Cancel** button.

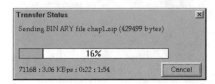

Figure 9.14—The Transfer Status Window

To download a file, select the directory on the local system that will hold the file, highlight the name of the file in the list on the right, and click on ⬅️.

WS_FTP is one example of an FTP client. It presents a graphical user interface for transferring files between a client and server. Other client programs have a strictly text-based interface. With those, you use a command *get*, as in **get etiquet.zip**, to download a file. You use the command *put*, as in **put chap1.zip**, to upload a file.

Summary

FTP stands for File Transfer Protocol. With FTP, you can share or copy files from one Internet site to another. Anonymous FTP is the term used when you copy a file from one computer to another without giving a login name or a password. Collections of files available by anonymous FTP are called anonymous FTP archives.

To retrieve a file by anonymous FTP through a Web browser, use a URL in the form **ftp://name-of-ftp-site/directory-name/file-name**. One example of such a URL would be **ftp://ftp.jpl.nasa.gov/pub/images/browse/marglobe.gif**. To browse a directory, use a URL in the form **ftp://name-of-ftp-site/directory-name**. An example would be **ftp://ftp.jpl.nasa.gov/pub/images/browse**. If the URL is for a file, the Web browser will attempt to display the file. You can then save it into a file on your computer. If you give the URL for a directory, the files and subdirectories of that directory will be displayed as hyperlinks. Put the mouse pointer on a hyperlink and press the right mouse button.

When a menu pops up, choose **Save Link As**. This opens a **Save As** dialog box on the screen. Set the directory or folder name, and then click on the **Save** button.

Literally trillions of bytes of information, programs, and resources are available by anonymous FTP. Archie, one of the first Internet search programs, is a tool specifically designed for searching anonymous FTP archives. When you supply a keyword, the names of the files, directories, and sites in the database are searched. Several other search services and software libraries search a database that holds descriptions and reviews of software available through anonymous FTP. Some of the software archives also have entries arranged by the type of program (for example, antivirus programs) or by the operating system (for example, Windows 95 or Macintosh).

Transferring a file from another computer to the computer you're using is called downloading. That's what you do when you retrieve a program from an FTP archive. Many of the programs depend on a number of auxiliary files to be run and used effectively, such as online help. These files are put together into a package, and the contents are compressed to allow for easier and faster storage and transfer.

After you retrieve one of these packages of software, you need to process it to extract the components. If the package name ends with **.exe**, then it's a self-extracting archive. Click on the name of the package, and it will unpack itself. If the name ends with **.zip**, you'll need to use a program, such as PKZIP or WinZip.

Once the files are extracted, you will run a program (application) to install the program. To be safe, you'll also want to scan the software for computer viruses before you install it. Look for a file with a name such as **Readme**, and read it before you install the program. It may help you decide whether the program is appropriate for you and your computer system. Finally, look for a program—often named **Setup** or **Install**— that you'll run to install the program.

An FTP client program is run on your computer to exchange files with another computer that acts as the host, or server. This program is not usually part of the Web browser. To access another computer through FTP, you need to give the client program the Internet domain name for the host computer. That's the part of the URL that immediately follows **ftp://**. For example, in the URL **ftp://ftp.jpl.nasa.gov/pub/images/ browse/marglobe.gif**, the domain name is **ftp.jpl.nasa.gov**. Once connected, you can upload files from your computer to the host or download files from the host to your computer. You can do either one by using a graphical interface provided by the client or by using the commands *put* and *get*.

Selected Terms Introduced in This Chapter

anonymous FTP	FTP archive
domain name	shareware
freeware	upload

10
Chapter

Finding Email Addresses,
Phone Numbers, and Maps

Your Web browser and some of the services on the World Wide Web make it relatively easy to find email addresses and phone numbers for people, businesses, and government agencies. Finding a phone number or street address without using the Web involves searching through the appropriate phone book(s), dialing 411 for Information, and paying charges for the service. Alternately, it would mean searching the CD-ROMs that list phone numbers and addresses.

Using the Web to find an address or phone number is usually much more direct. Through the Web browser, you search a large collection of data. Using the browser this way demonstrates some of the advantages of using a computer and an electronic database to search for information. The search is based on fields or portions of a form you complete. After you give the necessary information and click on a button, millions of entries in the database are searched to give results matching your request. You can select the results you want to use.

This chapter includes two activities. In one, you will find information about an individual. In the other, you will use a service to obtain information (including maps and driving directions) about a business.

This chapter will include the following sections:
  * Advantages and Disadvantages of Using These Services
  * Privacy and Ethics Issues
  * Keeping Current: White Pages and Map Web Services

There are several services for finding information about people or businesses, and their Web sites are relatively easy to locate. One way is to open the Web page for the Netscape guide to finding people; its URL is **http://home.netscape.com/netcenter/whitepages.html**. If you're using Netscape 4, you can get to it by clicking with the right mouse button on **Guide** in the command toolbar and selecting **People** from the menu. The browser returns a window similar to the one shown in Figure 10.1. Because these services are used to look up addresses and phone numbers, they're often called *people finders* or **white pages services**.

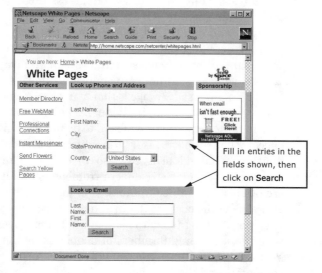

Figure 10.1—Netscape "People" Web Page

If you try more than one service, you'll notice that they are similar. They all search their databases using the information you enter into fields in a form. Each field holds a specific type of information that matches entries in the database. For example, typing **El Paso** in the field labeled **Last Name** isn't likely to help you find information about an address in El Paso. The database will instead be searched for people whose last name is El Paso. This type of searching, which is based on the entries or values of specific predefined categories, is called *field searching*.

Advantages and Disadvantages of Using These Services

The white page services give you fast access to very large databases of email addresses, phone numbers, street addresses, and other information. Some services also provide maps, driving directions, and information about businesses in a specific area. Here are several good reasons to use these services:

Chapter 10

- You met people at a conference, business meeting, or another situation, and you want to get in touch with them again.
- You wonder which of your old or current friends have email and what their addresses might be.
- You're applying for a job or interviewing at a company, so you want the company address, a map of the surrounding area, information about the community in which it's located, and directions by car.

You use your Web browser to access these services and information. That means you can use the tools and techniques you have already acquired and don't need to learn how to work with an entirely new program or interface to the database. Also, you can use the browser to save, print, or email your search results if you want to take them with you. As you can see, there are many advantages to using such services.

The main disadvantage is that many times, you can't find the information you'd like for an individual. The overwhelming majority of entries in these databases are related to businesses. Listings for individuals appear when people register (give information about themselves) in these directories. Individual listings also come from addresses people use when they post an article on Usenet or from membership or mailing lists that are often related to computers. It is impossible to find a directory of everyone with access to the Internet—there's no central control of registry service for Internet users, and no single agency could keep pace with the increasing numbers of people using the Internet and World Wide Web. Sometimes you can only find information for folks who use computers and the Internet, or information that may be out-of-date or inaccurate. On the other hand, these services may be the only means of finding someone's email address quickly. The surest way, if you can do it, is to ask people directly for their email addresses!

Now we'll show you how to use one of the white pages services to find an email address, street address, and phone number.

❋ Tip

Remember that the Web is always changing and that your results may differ from those shown here. Don't let this confuse you. The activities demonstrate fundamental skills. These skills don't change, even though the number of results obtained or the actual screens may look very different.

Activity 10.1 Finding an Individual's Email Address, Phone Number, and Mailing Address

Overview

In this activity, we'll use the Web service Four11 to search for an individual's email address, specifically that of Ernest Ackermann. We'll also follow a link that would give us his phone number. You could follow the steps we go through here to search for anyone's email address, phone number, or mailing address. The details may be different if you're using something other than Four11, but the steps will almost be the same. Here are the steps we'll take:

1. Go to the home page for Four11.
2. Fill in the form.
3. Activate the search and note the results.
4. Search for a phone number and note the results.

Details

We assume you've started Netscape or another browser.

1 Go to the home page for Four11.

Do It! Click on the location field, type **http://www.four11.com**, and press **Enter**.

The home page for Four11, with the information necessary for our search, appears in Figure 10.2. We've noted a number of features or options. Take a few moments to see what's available at this Web site. Click on the hyperlink **Help/FAQ** to learn more about using the service, and don't be shy about trying interesting links. Note that there are links to other types of directories. There is also a link that allows you to register or add information about yourself.

❋ Tip

Remember that anyone on the Web can access this information, so don't include information that you wouldn't feel comfortable or safe sharing with any stranger browsing through this database.

Before we move on, note that Four11 has a link to its acceptable use policy. You can find it by looking at the links under Help/FAQ. This policy addresses issues about commercial use of the database information, privacy, and the accuracy of the information users provide.

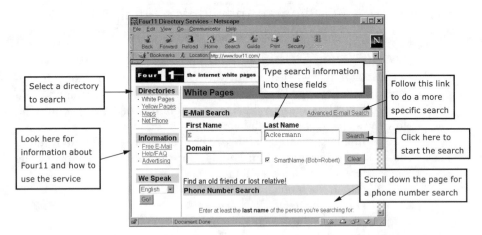

Figure 10.2—Home Page for Four11

2   Fill in the form.

Figure 10.2 shows information entered into some but not all of the fields. When you use Four11, you can fill in as few or as many fields as you wish. Filling in more fields makes your search more specific and restricted. If we fill in only the **Last Name** field, we get too many responses (more than 5,000 in this case!). Regardless of how many records are found, Four11 lists no more than 200. Follow the link **Advanced E-mail Search** to go to a form that has more fields and lets you be more specific.

❋*Do It!* On the Four11 home page, type **E** into the **First Name** field and **Ackermann** into the **Last Name** field. Note that **Ackermann** ends with *two* n's.

You probably noticed that we only put an initial in the First Name field. Four11 treats entries in the name fields as being the beginnings of names; if you enter *Johns* as a last name, you will also receive results for *Johnson*. If we knew that Ackermann had an email address at an educational institution then we would put **edu** in the domain field. This might be too restrictive so we'll leave it blank. We'll receive information about all the people who are listed in the Four11 database with first names starting with *E* and last names starting with *Ackermann*.

3   Activate the search and note the results.

❋*Do It!* Click on the button labeled **Search**.

Clicking on the **Search** button sends the search request to Four11 for processing. Within a few seconds, depending on how heavily the Internet is being used, the Four11 server sends another Web page to your browser. The new page has the search results. Figure 10.3 shows the results of our search.

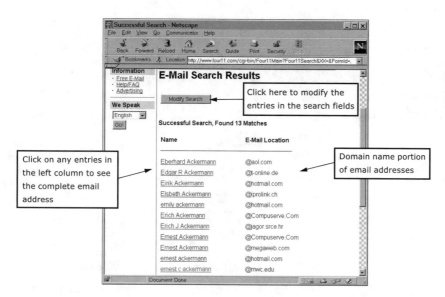

Figure 10.3—Results of Search for Email Address

Figure 10.3 shows four entries with the first name **Ernest** and the last name **Ackermann**. Does this guy have four addresses, or are they addresses for different people? We can't tell from here, but we can use the domain name or email location information to help us choose. Since the Ackermann we're looking for works at Mary Washington College, we might try the **@mwc.edu** listing first. (Except for the possible waste of time, there's no harm in trying all of them.)

 Tip

Before following one of these links, you ought to know that our search criteria may not yield any results or may give too many results. If we don't get any results, we might want to make the search more general by not filling in so many fields. If we get too many results, then we need to make the search more specific, usually by providing more information in the fields. To change entries in the search fields, you click on the **Modify Search** button.

Do It! Click on the link **ernest c ackermann**.

Clicking on the link **ernest c ackermann** brings up a Web page, shown in Figure 10.4. Relatively speaking, it gives a lot of information about Ackermann, including his email address, a link to his home page, and alternate email addresses. There's so much available on him because he registered with Four11 and supplied this information. Otherwise, the page would hold little more than his email address.

Click on **White Pages** or **Yellow Pages** to search for other telephone numbers and mailing addresses

Click here to search for a telephone number and mailing address for the name **ernest c ackermann** associated with this email address

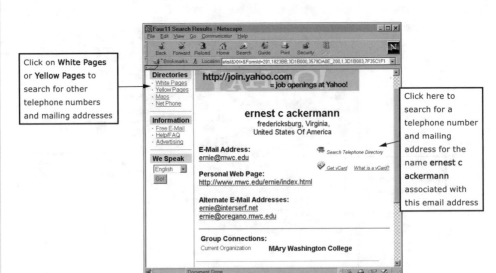

*Figure 10.4—Four11 Search Results for **ernest c ackermann***

4 Search for a phone number and note the results.

❀*Do It!* Click on the telephone icon to the left of **Search Telephone Directory**.

You click on the telephone icon to reach the Four11 Web page with the person's telephone and address information. That brings up a Web page with the person's name, along with city, state, and zip code information. The Web page for this example appears in Figure 10.5.

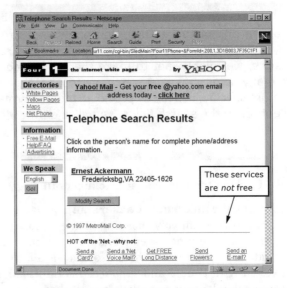

Figure 10.5—Four11 Web Page for U.S. Telephone Directory

To obtain complete address information, click on the name. Check the Four11 help page to see if this search service provides information only from U.S. phone books—a common practice. As with the email address search, several types of services may be listed.

End of Activity 10.1

In Activity 10.1, we looked for an individual's email and street address using Four11, one of many search services. Other services may be somewhat different, but they will be similar enough that you'll be able to use them.

Privacy and Ethics Issues

In Activity 10.1, you saw how easy it is to find an individual's email address, phone number, or mailing address. Services such as the one you used make it possible to search a centralized collection of millions of records in seconds. This capability raises a number of questions related to privacy and the ethical use of the information in such records. An example of such a question is this: Where does the information in these databases originate? Most of the services obtain their information from public sources, such as published phone books and registration lists for online services. All services encourage individuals to register with them. If you register, you must provide information about yourself. In return, you gain access to some features not available to the general public. Some services only list information provided by registered users or by those who have supplied data on another voluntary basis.

What control does an individual have over the information in these databases? Much of it comes from public sources, such as phone books, so accuracy and issues of whether a listing appears at all sometimes need to be addressed at the source of the information. You can request that you not be listed in such services. Most of the online white pages services make it relatively easy for you to do that. The problem is that you have to send an email request or fill out a form for *each* service. There's no way to ask that information about yourself be hidden or removed from every service.

Can users perform so-called reverse searches? For example, can they type in a phone number and find the name and address of the person with that number? This feature isn't available in most services, but it is available in some. Using this capability would help someone identify a person based on the phone number. Services in which the user pays a fee for searching often permit these reverse searches. These include CD-ROM-based databases that give full access to phone book information.

Questions related to ethical use of the information almost all deal with using the information for online junk mail—mass mailings related to commercial activity. Such unsolicited email (usually advertising something or soliciting money) is called *spam*. Phone listings in online databases could also be used to generate lists for commercial calls for telemarketing.

Most of the services on the Web include a policy statement saying that the information they provide isn't to be used for commercial purposes, but the services don't police the people searching their databases. In their statements, they only promise to respond to complaints from others. It's really up to individuals to protect their privacy and to demand ethical behavior on the Web and Internet.

Before registering for one of these services, you need to read policies about how your personal information will be used. You can usually find such policies by clicking on hyperlinks labeled **Help**, **About**, **Acceptable Use Policy**, or **FAQ** from the service's Web page. Here are two examples of policy statements:

- Four11 Acceptable Use Policy
  http://www.four11.com/cgi-bin/Four11Main?Aup
- WhoWhere? Usage Agreement
  http://www.whowhere.com/Agree

Some services make it more difficult than others to obtain a long list of email addresses or phone numbers. As we saw in Activity 10.1, Four11 doesn't give direct access to a list, but the service we'll use in Activity 10.2—InfoSpace—does provide this access. Mailing addresses and phone numbers are available in other forms, such as commercial (but not very expensive) CD-ROM-based products. Anyone interested in large-scale mailings or telemarketing would probably use those products to procure lists of phone numbers or addresses.

The questions raised by the use of this technology are typical of what we need to be aware of and concerned about as more information becomes readily available through the use of computers, networks, and other technologies. There are lots of advantages to using these tools, but we need to think about, and act on, the ramifications of making this type of information so easily accessible.

Activity 10.2 Search for a Business Address, a Phone Number, a Map, and Driving Directions

Overview

In this activity, you will find information about a specific business. You will use techniques that you can later apply when finding the same types of information about other organizations or government agencies.

Suppose you've got a job interview scheduled with Netscape Communications Corporation in Mountain View, California. You'd like to know the address and phone number of the office, and it would help to have a map of the area. It would also be nice to know a little about the community. No problem! We'll go to the InfoSpace Web site, find its business section, and search for Netscape's address and phone number. Once you have that information, you'll use InfoSpace's hyperlinks to find the following things: a map showing the business's location, the names and types of businesses in the area, some background information about the city, and even driving directions!

You'll follow these steps:

1. Go to the home page for the InfoSpace Web site.
2. Follow the hyperlink to the business phone directories.
3. Search for the business's address and phone number.
4. Follow hyperlinks for more information.

You follow the same steps to get information about any business.

Details

We assume your Web browser is already started.

1 Go to the home page for the InfoSpace Web site.

✳Do It! Click on the location field, type **http://www.infospace.com**, and press **Enter**.

A portion of the InfoSpace home page appears in Figure 10.6. It has links to different types of information. These include telephone directories and lists of email addresses for individuals, businesses, and the government at city, county, state, and federal levels; lists of Web pages, fax numbers, and toll-free phone numbers for businesses; directories for businesses and other information about localities; and "yellow pages" for the United States and Canada.

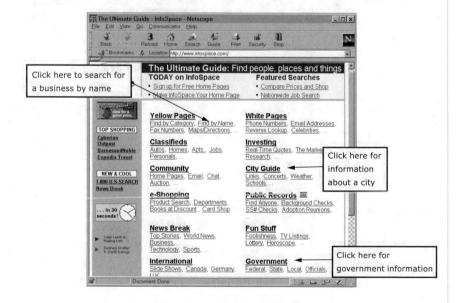

Figure 10.6—Portion of InfoSpace's Home Page

257

2   Follow the hyperlink to the business phone directories.

❉*Do It!* Click on the hyperlink **Find by Name** in the **Yellow Pages** section.

Figure 10.6 shows where to click. A few seconds after you click on this hyperlink, another Web page will be displayed. There, in the three fields of a search form, you will type the name and address (if you know it) of the business for which you're seeking information. Figure 10.7 shows the completed search form. It isn't necessary to fill in all of the fields, but the less information you give here, the more general the search will be and the more items it will return. InfoSpace returns at most 100 items, and they're listed 10 per page. Since InfoSpace sometimes changes the design of its Web pages, what you see may not look exactly as it's shown here, but you'll be able to find your way.

3   Search for the business's address and phone number.

With the hyperlinks in Figure 10.7, you can also search for businesses by category and by proximity to an address. You can get directions to a business as well.

❉*Do It!* Complete the form by typing **Netscape Communications** in the field labeled **Business Name** and **Mountain View** in the field labeled **City**. Select **California** from the list of states.

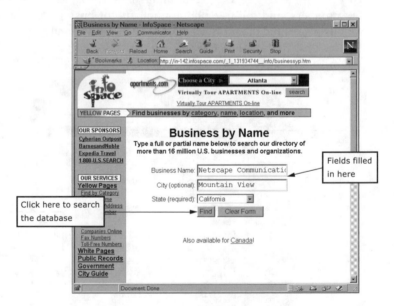

Figure 10.7—InfoSpace Search Form for Business by Name

❉*Do It!* Click on the button labeled **Find**.

Clicking on **Find** sends your information to the database. The results appear shortly and are shown in Figure 10.8.

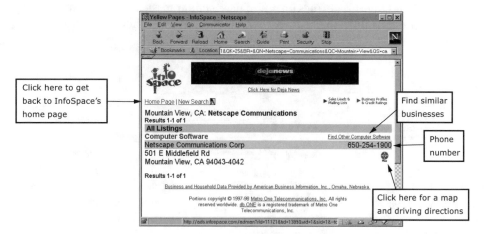

Click here to get back to InfoSpace's home page

Find similar businesses

Phone number

Click here for a map and driving directions

Figure 10.8—Search Results from InfoSpace

4   Follow hyperlinks for more information.

To save space here, we won't show what happens if you follow all the possible links. Try a few to see what type of information you can find.

❋*Do It!* Click on the hyperlink labeled **Map**.

This hyperlink brings up a map of the region. The Web page holding the map has controls, so you can zoom in or zoom out for more or less detail about the region. In some cases, you'll want to print the map to take with you on your travels.

You can get driving directions to the company by clicking on the hyperlink **Directions** on the page with the map.

❋*Do It!* Click on the hyperlink labeled **Directions**.

This hyperlink brings up a Web page in which you give a starting address. The address you've selected is used as the destination address. Click on one more hyperlink to obtain detailed driving directions. You may want to print these or email them to someone else (yourself too!).

To find out about the city in which the company is located you'll follow a link labeled **City Guide**. First you may have to go back to the infospace home page.

❋*Do It!* Click on the hyperlink labeled **Home Page**.

❋*Do It!* Click on the hyperlink labeled **City Guide**.

This hyperlink takes you to a Web page with a search form. There, you type in the name of a city, state, and maybe a zip code. Once you have completed the search form, click on the button labeled **Find**.

❋*Do It!* Enter **Mountain View** and **California** into the search form, and click on the hyperlink labeled **Find**.

This hyperlink brings up a Web page similar to the one in Figure 10.9. It contains links to local weather, businesses, and other resources.

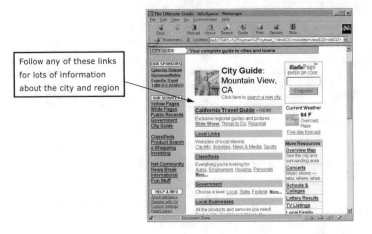

Figure 10.9—Links to Local Information in InfoSpace

End of Activity 10.2

In Activity 10.2, you used search forms provided by InfoSpace to obtain information about a business. You'd go through similar steps and have many of the same options (for example, seeing a map and getting driving directions) if you used InfoSpace to find the address of an individual or government agency. You could also click on the hyperlink labeled **Government** in Figure 10.6 to obtain information about government agencies, services, offices, and officials. Figure 10.10 shows the result of clicking on this hyperlink. You can get information about government at the national, state, and local levels, and you can also get information about embassies in Washington, D.C.

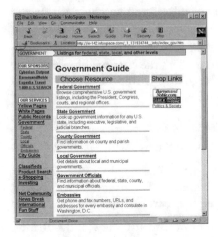

Figure 10.10—InfoSpace Government Information Web Page

Keeping Current: White Pages and Map Web Services

In this chapter we've featured some white pages services and saw in Activity 10.2 a way to find a map of an area. Some links to Web pages that list white pages services and map services are given here.

Lists of White Pages Web Services

Several Web pages contain lists of the white pages services discussed in this chapter. To see what new features these services offer, you need to check these sites occasionally. Here's a selected list of resources to keep you current on the topic of white pages services:

* Flip's Search Resources
  http://aa.net/ ~ flip/search/search.html
* People Search: Looking for Someone?
  http://home.sprynet.com/sprynet/kenkirk/people1.htm
* SEARCH.COM
  http://www.search.com
* Yahoo! Reference: White Pages
  http://www.yahoo.com/Reference/White_Pages

Map Services

In Activity 10.2 we used InfoSpace to find a map of the area surrounding an address. There are several map services on the Web. To see what new features these services offer, you need to check these sites occasionally. Here's a selected list of resources:

DeLorme CyberMaps	**http://www.delorme.com/cybermaps**
Excite Maps	**http://city.net/indexes/top_maps.dcg**
Lycos RoadMaps	**http://www.lycos.com/roadmap.html**
MapQuest	**http://www.mapquest.com**
Yahoo! Maps	**http://maps.yahoo.com/yahoo**

Try one the next time you need a map or driving directions.

Summary

Several services that let you search for email addresses, phone numbers, mailing addresses, and other information about individuals and businesses are available on the World Wide Web. The services are available as Web pages, so you use your browser for searching them. They provide electronic access to the white pages (and in some cases the yellow and blue pages) of a phone book. The difference here is that you

Chapter 10

can also search for email addresses. Plus, instead of searching an individual phone book, you can search a very large collection of phone books.

Although various services provide different features, you use them all in about the same way. In each case, you complete a form by entering names, addresses, or other information in fields. Then, you click on a button on the Web page. The information you have supplied is passed to the service, and its database is searched based on the entries in the fields. For example, the entry in the Last Name field is matched with the last names in the database. This is an example of field searching. Once the results are displayed, you select the relevant information from a list. Some services have separate directories for individuals, businesses, and government. Some provide maps, while others give different features. As more people use these tools, we're likely to see more similarities between the services.

The advantages of using these tools are that we can search millions of records in a matter of seconds. We use our Web browser to do it, which means that we don't necessarily have to learn a new interface to the data or new techniques to work with results. We can save, print, or email the results in the same way as with any other Web page.

The disadvantages are that the available information may not be up-to-date or complete. Plus, having rapid access to this type of information raises questions about privacy and the ethical use of this information. Most services have a hyperlink from their home pages that takes you to a policy statement regarding these issues. You need to be aware of your rights and responsibilities when you register with or use these services. Also, be sure not to give these services information that wouldn't be safe to share with a complete stranger. Putting information on these services is like tacking it up on thousands of bulletin boards throughout the world.

Several Web sites list hyperlinks to these white pages services, or "people finders" as they're sometimes called. You can access some of the major lists by clicking on the **People** directory button in the Netscape browser. You could also look in the Reference section of Yahoo!

Selected Terms Introduced in This Chapter

field searching	white pages service
spam	

$$11$$
Chapter

Searching Email Discussion Group Archives and Usenet Newsgroup Archives

Email and Usenet news are two popular uses of the Internet. In fact, email is *the* most popular, and both show some of the unique features of communication on the Internet. With no difference in effort, one person can send a message to one or thousands of people, and one person can receive information on a topic or an answer to a question from anywhere on the Internet. People have been using email since the beginning of the Internet, and those with common interests have formed email *discussion groups*—also called ***interest groups***, ***mailing lists***, or ***listservs***—based on specific topics. ***Usenet***, which originated independently of the Internet, is a system for exchanging messages called ***articles*** arranged according to specific categories called ***newsgroups***. The articles or messages are passed from one system to another, not as email between individuals. Group discussions take place as individuals compose and post messages, answer questions, and respond to other people's statements.

In this chapter, we'll concentrate on finding discussion groups and newsgroups that deal with specific topics and determining the resources available through the groups. We'll also cover ways of searching archives of Usenet articles. We will give a brief overview of how to access and use the two forms of group discussion—email discussion groups and Usenet newsgroups. There are some differences in the methods and tools you use to work with each. The last section of the chapter covers an important topic: proper etiquette or behavior in a discussion group or newsgroup.

The chapter will include the following sections:
* Email Discussion Groups
* Usenet Newsgroups
* Etiquette in a Discussion Group or a Usenet Newsgroup

To get more detailed information on using discussion groups and newsgroups, see Chapters 4 and 5 in *Learning to Use the World Wide Web* by Ernest Ackermann and the Web pages accompanying those chapters at **http://www.mwc.edu/ernie/Lrn-web04.html** and **http://www.mwc.edu/ernie/Lrn-web05.html**.

Both email discussion groups and Usenet newsgroups allow for group communication. The primary difference is that you must first subscribe to or join an email discussion group, whereas anyone with a *newsreader*—such as the one included with Netscape—can browse and interact with a newsgroup. Both email discussion groups and Usenet newsgroups give you valuable resources when searching for information on specific topics or seeking answers to questions. Here are a few reasons that these resources are so helpful:

- The group itself. The articles or messages posted to discussion groups and newsgroups are sometimes read by thousands or millions of people throughout the world. Replying to messages, giving help, and supplying accurate information when possible are part of Internet culture. Although it's unreasonable to expect group members to do your research for you, the group can be very helpful.

- The discussions—the messages or articles—are often archived and can be searched and retrieved.

- The collections of frequently asked questions (FAQs) and periodic postings on a specific topic are usually compiled and updated by volunteers.

Email Discussion Groups

Email discussion groups are made up of people anywhere on the Internet who agree to communicate about a certain topic using email. The group named "Herb," for example, supports discussions about the use of herbs and spices in cooking. Anyone can join or subscribe to the list. Discussions are usually on the main topic, but messages on other topics are usually tolerated or redirected to other groups. Each message sent to the group's address is routed, virtually immediately, through email to all group members. In this section we'll cover the details of working with discussion groups. We'll use the term *discussion group* or *list* to refer to any of these types of groups. Some of the topics we'll cover are:

- Essential Information About Discussion Groups
- Ways to Join, Contribute to, and Leave a List
- Ways to Find and Retrieve a Group's Archives
- Ways to Locate Discussion Groups About Specific Topics
- Sources of Information About Discussion Groups on the Internet

Essential Information About Discussion Groups

It's All Done by Email

Email is the medium for all communication in a discussion group. Using email, a person makes a request to join, or *subscribe* to, a group. That person then shares in the group discussions. Any message sent to the group is broadcast via email to all group members; these discussions are public. There is an exception, however; some groups are moderated, in which case a message sent to the group is first routed to the ***moderator***. Some groups are very large, with thousands of subscribers. Some are very diverse, with members throughout the world. An active group generates several email messages per day.

You Decide How Much You Want to Participate

Being a member of a discussion group means that you can join in discussions, ask questions, help others with questions, make announcements related to the group, or just see what others are talking about. You'll find members with all levels of experience. You don't have to respond to every message; you can simply read or even ignore some of the discussions. It's usually a good idea just to read messages when you first join a group, so you can get an idea of the discussion's general tone and level. Some folks use the term ***lurking*** to describe this act of observing discussions. Lurking is just fine; it may be exactly what you want.

When Everything Goes Well, the Group or List Is Managed by Software

Most of the management of a list—tasks such as adding new members or subscribers and removing members who choose to leave (or ***unsubscribe*** from) a list—is handled automatically by software. A program runs on the computer that serves as the host system for the list. The software maintains the files associated with the list and responds to commands from the membership. These requests for service are handled by commands you send to an email address, called the ***administrative address***, which passes the command on to the software managing the list. Because these requests are satisfied automatically by a computer program, the requests need to be in a specific form that the software can understand.

Know the Difference Between the Group or List Address and the Administrative Address

When you're a member of a list, you need to know two addresses, and you need to know when to use them.

1. The address of the group, sometimes called the ***list address*** or ***group address***, is what you'll use to communicate with the group. When you send email to this address, the mail is delivered to all group members.
2. The address you use to request services or to give commands to the software managing the list is sometimes called the *administrative address*. With this address, you can subscribe, unsubscribe, receive several messages in one email as a digest, retrieve a list of members, request archives, and so on. This is the same address you use to join the list.

It's easy to make a mistake and confuse the two addresses. If you send a request to the wrong address, a member of the list will usually remind you of the correct address. If you send a message that's passed on to the managing software but was meant for the members of the list, you'll usually get a reply back indicating that the message wasn't in the proper form.

Each Group Has a Name
The name of a discussion group is usually part of the group address. Here are some examples:

- One list about noncommercial aspects of photography is called photo-l. The list address is **photo-l@csuohio.edu**.

- One list used for announcing new or changed Web sites and other resources is net-happenings. Messages are submitted to the moderator who then passes them onto the group. The messages are labeled with a category such as "BOOK," "COMP," "K12," or "SOFT." Net-happenings is a service of Internet Scout Project in the Computer Sciences Department at the University of Wisconsin, Madison, and the list moderator, Gleason Sackman. The list address is **net-happenings@cs.wisc.edu**.

- One of several lists used for practicing working with a discussion group is called test-listproc. The list address is **test-listproc@listproc.mwc.edu**.

Remember: Never Send a Message to Join (Subscribe) or Leave (Unsubscribe) a Discussion Group or List Address
Use the administrative address for these. Below, we'll point out some ways of finding the names and administrative address for a list.

Getting Help and a List of All Commands
Send the simple message

help

to the administrative address. You'll receive by email a list of all the commands you can use with the list. This works for any type of software managing a list. Some lists also provide a reference card (via email) that explains all the commands. If the managing software is Listserv, send the command

info refcard

to the administrative address of any system that supports Listserv.

Ways to Join, Contribute to, and Leave a List
Several different types of software are used to manage a mailing list. The most common ones are Listproc, Listserv, and Majordomo. Most of the commands are the same for the different types of lists. We'll work with one type, Listproc, and use the list test-listproc. This list was set up for people to learn about using a discussion group, so feel free to practice with it.

Here is the information you'll need about this list:

List Name: **test-listproc**
Administrative Address: **listproc@listproc.mwc.edu**
List Address: **test-listproc@listproc.mwc.edu**

To Join a Discussion Group or Mailing List, Send Email to the Group's Administrative Address

The body of the message should contain only *subscribe,* the list name, and your full name. Using the example, you would send email to **listproc@listproc.mwc.edu** with the following message:

subscribe test-listproc *your-full-name*

For example: **subscribe test-listproc chris athana**

What Happens Next?

If you've used the proper address and the list still exists, you ought to receive a response from the software managing the list within a few minutes, hours, or maybe a day or two. The response will either say that you've succeeded in subscribing or ask you to confirm your request to join. To confirm, you usually just have to reply *OK* in the body of the message. If the address isn't correct, you'll probably have your mail returned as undeliverable, or you'll get email saying that the list doesn't exist at the site. Look up the address once more and try again.

Let's assume you've succeeded in subscribing and that you've received email about the list. In most cases, you'll receive an email message welcoming you to the list. *Save the welcome message!* It usually contains important information about unsubscribing from the list and about other commands with which you can request services. It also tells you how to get more information. Once again, save that message! You'll probably need it in the future.

To Leave, or Unsubscribe from, a Discussion Group or Mailing List, Send Email to the Group's Administrative Address

The body of the message should contain only *unsubscribe* and the list name. Using the example, send email with the message

unsubscribe test-listproc

to **listproc@listproc.mwc.edu**. Some lists allow you to unsubscribe from or send a message to the list only from the same address you used to join or subscribe to the list. That is a strict policy; some users access the Internet from a network of systems, and they may not always be using a system with the same address. If you have problems sending or posting a message to a list, try posting a message from the address you used to subscribe to the list.

To Post a Message, Question, or Reply to the Group, Send Email to the List Address

Using the example, send email to **test-listproc@listproc.mwc.edu**.

One Other Address You May Need Is That of the List Owner or Moderator

You'll probably get that address with your "welcome to the group" email. Write to the owner or moderator when you have questions about the nature of the list, if you think something is wrong with the list, or if you want to volunteer to help the moderator. Send special requests or questions you can't resolve to the address of the list owner, administrator, or moderator.

Ways to Find and Retrieve a Group's Archives

Most discussion groups keep archives of the messages posted to the group. They sometimes contain useful information, so you'll want to know how to gain access to and retrieve files from the archives.

Searching the Archives by Topic

Many lists are *archived*, which means that collections of past messages are kept so that members can retrieve them. These are usually categorized only by date, so it may be difficult to search the archives for messages related to a specific subject. Some progress is being made in this area. The University of Buffalo, for example, provides a forms-based interface for searching the archives of the lists hosted there. Use the URL **http://listserv.acsu.buffalo.edu/archives** to try this service. Some lists also keep FAQ collections about the topics discussed on the list and other files useful to the group members. To get a list of the names of the files in a group's archives, send email containing the command

index *list-name*

to the list's administrative address. Substitute the name of a specific list for *list-name*. For example, to get the archives for the list test-listproc, send the message

index test-listproc

to **listproc@listproc.mwc.edu**.

Retrieving a File from the Archives

You can retrieve any of the files in the list's archives by sending a command to the administrative address. You might see something in the archives you'd like to retrieve, or someone may tell you about a file in a list's archives. The precise commands you use may differ from one type of list to another. For specific instructions, send the command **help get** or **help send**.

   You either use the command **get** or the command **send** to retrieve a file from an archive (depending on the type of software that manages the list). Include the list name and the file name. Table 11.1 lists the commands to use for each type of software, along with an example. Substitute the specific list name for *list-name* and the specific name of a file for *file-name*. Remember to send your commands to the administrative address for the list.

List Type: **Listproc**
Command: **get *list-name file-name***
Example: **get photo-l photo-l.sep-25**

List Type: **Listserv**
Command: **get *file-name file-type list-name***
Example: **get aou101 txt birdchat**
Note: Listserv software requires you to specify the type of file. This file type appears in the list of files in the archive.

List Type: **Majordomo**
Command: **get *list-name file-name***
Example: **get f-costume topics**

Table 11.1—Retrieving a File

Ways to Locate Discussion Groups About Specific Topics

There are more than 80,000 email discussion groups, with more added each day. A group named new-list carries announcements of new lists. To join the list, send email to **listserv@hypatia.cs.wisc.edu** with the message

sub new-list *your-first-name your-last-name*

The number of discussion groups and the rate of increase make it almost impossible to keep current with the available groups. It's probably more important (and certainly more practical) for you to know how to find the names of lists that focus on a topic that interests you.

You're likely to hear about some lists from your correspondents on the Internet. You'll also see lists mentioned if you read Usenet news. To find lists by topic you can use one of the following services. When you use these services you type in a keyword or phrase, and the software searches a database of list names, descriptions, and associated addresses. You'll get the information you need (list name, address for joining the list, address of the list, address of the list owner or moderator, etc.) for the appropriate lists.

- CataList, **http://www.lsoft.com/lists/listref.html**, a catalog of listserv lists. CataList allows you to search or browse the database of the more than 10,000 lists that use Listserv.

- Liszt, the mailing list directory, **http://www.liszt.com**.

- Publicly Accessible Mailing Lists, **http://www.neosoft. com/internet/paml**. This Web page, maintained by Stephanie da Silva, has names, addresses, and information about lists available through the Internet.

- Reference.COM, **http://www.reference.com**. This Web site lets you search for discussion groups, Usenet newsgroups, and archives of selected discussion groups and newsgroups.

The lists section of tile.net, **http://tile.net/lists**. Click on the hyperlink **Search** to search for lists. In this case, the search brings back all the information you need to join a list, along with hyperlinks that make it easy to subscribe.

In the next activity, you will practice using one of these services. When you use such services, you will type in a keyword or phrase, and the software will search a database of list names, descriptions, and associated addresses. You'll obtain the information you need (list name, address for joining the list, address of the list, address of the list owner or moderator, and so forth) for the appropriate list.

Tip

Remember that the Web is always changing and that your results may differ from those shown here. Don't let this confuse you. The activities demonstrate fundamental skills. These skills don't change, even though the number of results obtained or the actual screens may look very different.

Activity 11.1   Finding a Discussion Group

Overview

One of the most comprehensive collections of discussion groups that's been designed for searching through the Web is *Liszt, the mailing list directory*. The site is relatively easy to use and gives useful information about the discussion groups in its database. We can search by typing one or more keywords into a form. Liszt allows for Boolean expressions and has instructions clearly available through hyperlinks on the home page. A subject guide to selected discussion groups is also on the home page.

We'll follow these steps:
1. Go to the home page for Liszt.
2. Search for discussion groups dealing with business ethics.
3. Browse the results to learn about the discussion groups found and how to subscribe.

Details

We assume that the Web browser is already started and is available on the screen.

1   Go to the home page for Liszt.

Do It! Click on the location field, type **http://www.liszt.com**, and press Enter.

Using this URL, we go to the home page for Liszt. A portion of it appears in Figure 11.1. Like other Web or Internet services, Liszt regularly improves or expands its service. The Web pages you see may be different from these, but they will be similar.

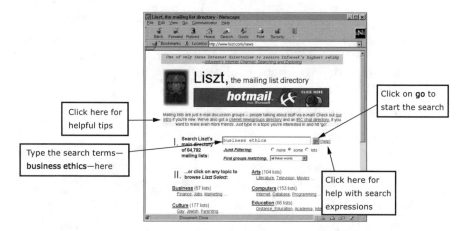

Figure 11.1—Liszt's Home Page: Searchable Directory, Email Discussion Groups

2   Search for discussion groups dealing with business ethics.

Liszt's home page has a place next to the button labeled **go** for you to type keywords or a Boolean expression. You can also use an asterisk (*) in a word as a wildcard. Click on the hyperlink **help** for complete information about search expressions. Here, we'll type **business ethics**, as shown in Figure 11.1 and we'll click on **go**.

✹*Do It!* Type **business ethics** in the form and click on the **go** button.

By default, Liszt searches its database for descriptions of discussion groups that contain *all* the terms. A portion of the Web page showing the search results appears in Figure 11.2. Your results may not be exactly the same as these.

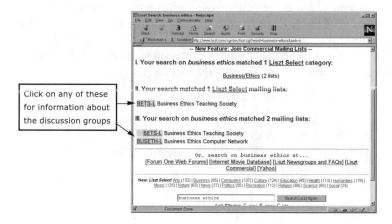

Figure 11.2—Search Results Using "business ethics"

3   Browse the results to learn about the discussion groups found and how to subscribe.

Figure 11.2 shows a portion of the Web page that holds the search results. Although this book does not reflect it, the results are color coded, indicating how much information is available. (The system is explained on the Web page.) Clicking on any of the results brings up an intermediate page with links for more information. We will click on the second one, **BUSETH-L**.

❋*Do It!* Click on **BUSETH-L**.

Figure 11.3 shows a portion of the page that appears.

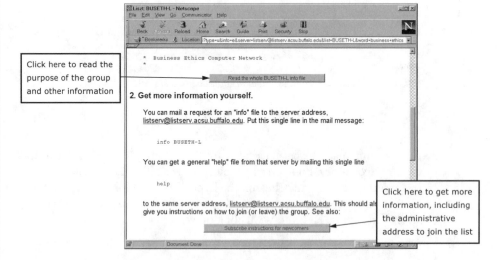

Figure 11.3—Web Page About the Discussion Group BUSETH-L

Clicking on the button labeled **Read the whole BUSETH-L info file** brings up the same thing you would see if you sent a request for information to the administrative address. This information usually includes a statement of the list's purpose and the name and email of the person in charge of the list. Clicking on the button labeled **Subscribe instructions for newcomers** yields that information, including the administrative and list addresses for the discussion group.

❋*Do It!* Click on **Subscribe instructions for newcomers**.

Figure 11.4 shows a portion of the Web page that tells how to subscribe to the list. Read through the information on the Web page before subscribing to any list. There's more useful information further down the Web page.

Information about subscribing to the group

Click here to send email to the administrative address

Pay attention to this. It's important!

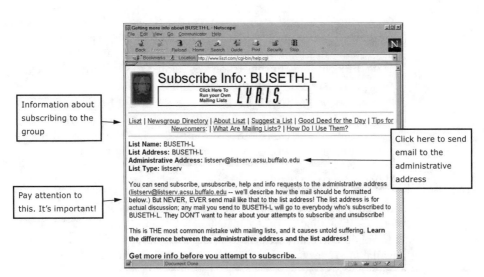

Figure 11.4—Information About Subscribing to the Discussion Group

You can join the list at this point by clicking on the hyperlink that represents the administrative address. When you have finished with this page, press the **Back** icon in the command toolbar to return to the list of discussion groups in Figure 11.2. Look at these lists, or search for more.

End of Activity 11.1

Activity 11.1 showed how to use Liszt to search for discussion groups based on a topic. For each group found, we could have retrieved information about the group and ways of subscribing. Liszt has discussion groups or mailing lists arranged into a subject directory. In addition, Liszt makes it possible to search for Usenet newsgroups. You can use the other search services mentioned in this chapter in a similar manner.

Sources of Information About Discussion Groups on the Internet

For more information on discussion groups, you may want to consult the following Web resources.

❋ *Discussion Lists: Mailing List Manager Commands*, by James Milles, contains information about working with discussion lists, interest groups, and mailing lists. The file is available by email and on the Web. To retrieve it by email, send the message

get mailser cmd nettrain

to **listserv@listserv.acsu.buffalo.edu**. To retrieve it through your Web browser, use the URL **http://lawwww.cwru.edu/cwrulaw/faculty/milles/mailser.html**.

* *Email Discussion Groups and Lists - Resources,* **http://www. webcom.com/impulse/list.html**. This page has a summary of the basic commands for discussion groups and links to lots of other resources related to searching, finding, and using discussion groups or lists.

* *Internet Mailing Lists Guides and Resources,* **http://www. nlc-bnc.ca/ifla/I/training/listserv/lists.htm**. This comprehensive resource is maintained by the International Federation of Library Associations and Institutions.

Usenet Newsgroups

Another popular means of exchanging information is Usenet news. Sometimes it's called *Netnews* or just *News*. Usenet was originally created for people to share information on Unix computer systems. Now it's available to everyone through the Internet. You use Usenet news for the same reasons you use a discussion group—to exchange or read information about specific topics. Here are some ways in which Usenet news differs from discussion groups:

* With Usenet, you have access to many groups. Some sites carry hundreds or thousands of groups; others carry fewer groups or different ones, depending on the policies and procedures of that site.

* Messages to a group aren't exchanged between individuals using email; instead, messages are passed from one computer system to another.

* You use software called a *newsreader* to read and manage the news (articles) available through Usenet, instead of using your email program or sending commands to a remote site.

Usenet is similar to a bulletin board system (BBS), except that most bulletin boards are managed by one person and are run on one computer. With Usenet, there is no single person, group, or computer system in charge. All the computers and people that are part of Usenet support and manage it. Usenet is a community with its own generally agreed-upon code of etiquette. Involving thousands of computers, hundreds of thousands of messages, and millions of people, Usenet is very large. Once you become comfortable with Usenet news, you'll find that it helps you find answers to different types of questions, get help on a variety of topics, and keep up with what's happening in the world and on the Internet.

In addition to the articles in each newsgroup, many newsgroups have FAQs available. Volunteers maintain these collections of commonly asked questions. Several search engines give the option of searching archives of articles or postings to Usenet news. Later in this chapter, we'll take a detailed look at using one of those—Deja News.

We don't have space here to go into all of the details of using a newsreader and working with Usenet news. We will give enough information to get you started, but for more information, you ought to look at Chapter 5 of *Learning to Use the World Wide Web* by Ernest Ackermann or visit the Web page **http://www.mwc.edu/ernie/Lrn-web05.html**. Here's a list of the topics we'll cover in this section.

- Essential Information About Usenet News
- Organization of Usenet Articles
- FAQs
- Ways to Locate Newsgroups About Specific Topics
- Sources of Information About Usenet News on the Web
- Ways to Search Usenet Archives

Essential Information About Usenet News

It's not easy to define Usenet because it's so diverse. Instead, we'll try to describe how it works and how to work with it.

- Usenet is made up of computers and people that agree to exchange or pass on collections of files.

- Each file is called an article and belongs to one or more newsgroups. There are newsgroups on all sorts of topics. Some are specialized or technical groups, such as comp.protocols.tcp-ip.domains (topics related to Internet domain style names). Some deal with recreational activities, such as rec.outdoors.fishing.saltwater (topics dealing with saltwater fishing). One, news.newusers.questions, is dedicated to questions from new Usenet users.

- People at each site can read the articles, ignore them, save or print them, respond to them through email to their authors, or *post* their own articles. *Posting* means composing either an original article or a response to someone else's article, and then passing it on to Usenet.

- There are thousands of computers involved, and an estimated 15 to 30 million people participate in Usenet news.

- In order to read or post articles, you need to use a program called a *newsreader*. A Web browser often has a newsreader included with it. Netscape Communicator, for example, includes a newsreader you access by selecting **Collabra Discussion Groups** from the pulldown menu **Communicator** in the menu bar. Communicator provides at least three other ways of getting there—if you want to use the newsreader, click on **Help** in the menu bar and check the appropriate sections of the online guide.

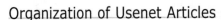

Chapter 11

Organization of Usenet Articles

All articles belong to one or more newsgroups. Many newsgroups have a charter that states the newsgroup's purpose and the topics discussed within the group. An article is either a follow-up to another article or a new piece on a different topic. Posting an article to more than one newsgroup is called *cross-posting*.

Threads

There may be several articles on the same topic in a single newsgroup. If each of the articles has been posted as a follow-up to some original article, then the collection of these articles is called a *thread*. You'll probably want to have the articles arranged into threads. It really helps to have this sort of organization for a collection of articles in a particular group. You follow a thread by reading the articles one after the other.

Newsgroup Categories

Each newsgroup has a name that gives the topic or topics for the articles in the group. The groups are arranged or named according to a hierarchy. When you look at the name of a newsgroup, you'll see that it usually consists of several words or names separated by periods. The first part of the newsgroup name is the name of the top level of the hierarchy. As you move to the right, the names become more specific. Here is a nice long name: rec.music.makers.guitar.acoustic.

Starting on the left, rec is the name of a top-level group; it includes groups that deal with artistic activities, hobbies, or recreational activities. The next name, music, indicates that the group addresses topics related to music. The next, makers, tells you that this group is about performing or playing music, rather than reviewing music or collecting recordings, for instance. The last two names, guitar and acoustic, pretty much nail this down as dealing with discussions or other matters related to playing acoustic guitars. To give you a feeling for this naming scheme, here are a few other groups in the rec.music hierarchy: rec.music.makers.piano, rec.music.makers.percussion, rec.music. marketplace, rec.music.reggae, rec.music.reviews.

There are more than 15,000 newsgroups and several major, top-level categories. We won't list the categories here. A complete list, *Master List of Newsgroup Hierarchies,* **http://home.magmacom.com/ ~ leisen/master_list.html**, is maintained by Lewis S. Eisen.

What Is a Newsreader?

A newsreader is the interface between a user and the news itself. It allows you to go through the newsgroups one at a time. Once you've chosen a newsgroup, it allows you to deal with the articles it contains. The newsreader keeps track of the newsgroups you read regularly, as well as the articles you've read in each newsgroup.

Here, we'll talk about using the newsreader included with Netscape Navigator. There are a number of other newsreaders available. A popular one is Free Agent, **http://www.forteinc.com/agent**, and WinVN.

Starting the Newsreader. In Netscape Communicator, click on **Communicator** in the menu bar, and then select **Collabra Discussion Groups** from the pulldown menu. (Check the online help from your browser for other ways to access Usenet news.) A window called the **Netscape Message Center** will open, listing your mailboxes and the name of the news server or servers. Click on the name of a news server to see a list of newsgroups. (If neither newsgroups nor a news server is listed, then you need to check that the entries in the Groups Server category in Preferences are set properly—that's covered below.) Then select a newsgroup. If you want one that isn't listed, you can subscribe to it by clicking on **File** in the menu bar and selecting **Subscribe to Discussion Groups**; these menus are available only in the Netscape Message Center window or the Netscape Discussion window. It may take some time—perhaps a few minutes—for the list of all newsgroups to be retrieved from the server. You'll see them in the newsgroup pane as documents and folders; the folders represent the categories in the Usenet hierarchy. Select the ones you'd like to look at regularly by clicking on the box to the right of a newsgroup's name. Once you select a group, a Netscape Discussion window pops up. It has two panes: one for the list of articles and the other to read a selected article. An example of that window is shown in Figure 11.5.

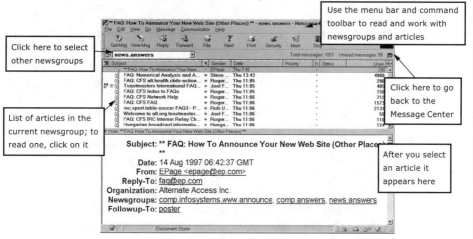

Use the menu bar and command toolbar to read and work with newsgroups and articles

Click here to select other newsgroups

Click here to go back to the Message Center

List of articles in the current newsgroup; to read one, click on it

After you select an article it appears here

Figure 11.5—Sample Netscape Discussion Window—Newsgroup news.answers

Setting News Preferences. The computer you're using needs to contact a news server (sometimes called an NNTP server) to receive and interact with Usenet news. **NNTP** stands for **Network News Transport Protocol**, the protocol used to exchange Usenet news. Your newsreader needs to have the Internet name or IP address of that computer. This may already be set on your computer, or you may have received instructions about how to do it. If you can read Usenet news, then you don't have to worry about this. To set news preferences, click on **Edit** in the menu bar, then click on **Preferences**, select the category

Chapter 11

Mail & Groups, and finally select **Groups Server**. It's crucial that this is filled in correctly so you can work with Usenet news. The pane just below **Discussion groups (news) server** must be filled in with the Internet domain name or IP address of a news server. The name or IP address that goes here depends on how your Internet services are provided. You should get this information from your Internet provider or someone in your organization. You probably won't have to change other entries in this panel.

Posting an Article. Posting an article means composing an article—a message, a question, a great discourse on some deep philosophical or extremely important political topic—and distributing it to a newsgroup. Usenet is a fairly open forum. But some topics are not appropriate for some newsgroups. Before you post anything, read "A Primer on How to Work with the Usenet Community," **ftp://rtfm.mit.edu/pub/usenet/ news.announce.newusers/A_Primer_on_How_to_Work_With_ the_Usenet_Community**. You'll also find this posted in news.announce.newusers. When using Netscape News (Collabra), you post a new article to the current newsgroup by clicking on the icon labeled **New Msg** in the command toolbar. To post a follow-up to the current article, click on the icon labeled **Reply**.

FAQs

Many newsgroups have volunteers who put together and maintain a collection of common questions and answers. Most newsgroups have FAQs that are very informative and useful. You can find them posted either in the newsgroup for which the FAQ was created or posted to news.answers.

Be sure to consult the FAQ for information before you post a question to a newsgroup. It may be embarrassing for you if you post a question to a newsgroup and receive several replies (or follow-ups) letting you (and everyone else reading the newsgroup) know that you should read the FAQ before asking other questions. It could also be annoying to other group members to see questions that could be answered with a little research beforehand. Some places to look for FAQs (other than the newsgroup) are **ftp://rtfm.mit.edu/pub/usenet-by-group** and **http://www.cis.ohio-state.edu/hypertext/faq/usenet/top.html**.

Ways to Locate Newsgroups About Specific Topics

There are thousands of newsgroups. How can you find out which to read or which ones even exist? To find the groups your server carries, you select **Show All Newsgroups** from the pulldown menu **Options** in the menu bar of the news window.

There are several lists of newsgroups available through Usenet. Keep your eye on the newsgroups news.answers, news.lists, or news.groups so you can read or save these listings when they appear (usually monthly).

Some Web sites enable you to search for newsgroups. For the sites we'll mention, use the URL to bring up a Web page. On that page, enter a keyword or phrase, click on a button labeled **Search**, and then work with the results. In both cases, if a newsgroup is found, click on its name to read articles in the group. Whether that's successful depends on whether your news server is set up to receive that newsgroup. Here are the Web sites:

❋ Deja News, **http://www.dejanews.com**. Deja News was originally developed to read archives of news articles. It also allows keyword searching for newsgroups.

❋ Liszt's Usenet Newsgroups Directory, **http://www.liszt. com/news**. The searching results in a list of newsgroups, each with a brief description.

❋ Reference.COM, **http://www.reference.com**. Searching here brings up a list of newsgroups. Clicking on a name gives a brief description of the groups and the average number of articles posted daily.

❋ tile.net/news, **http://tile.net/news**. Searching here brings up a list of newsgroups. Clicking on the name of a newsgroup takes you to a page that tells about the amount of articles posted daily and what percentage of Usenet sites carry the group. There's also a form that lets you search Lycos using newsgroup names as keywords.

Sources of Information About Usenet News on the Web

Some of the best information about Usenet is part of Usenet itself. There are several newsgroups that a beginning or infrequent user should browse. These newsgroups include information about Usenet, FAQ lists for Usenet and several newsgroups, and articles that will help you use Usenet. Here are the newsgroups:

news.announce.newusers　　This newsgroup has explanatory and important articles for new or infrequent Usenet users.

news.answers　　This newsgroup is where periodic Usenet postings are put. The periodic postings are primarily FAQs. This is often the first place to look when you have a question.

news.newusers.questions　　This newsgroup is dedicated to questions from new Usenet users. There is no such thing as a "dumb question" here. You ought to browse this group to see if others have asked the same question that's been bothering you. Once you get some expertise in using Usenet, you'll want to check this group to see if you can help someone.

The articles you will want to read are posted in news.announce.newusers. Here's a list:

- A Primer on How to Work with the Usenet Community
- Answers to Frequently Asked Questions About Usenet
- Hints on Writing Style for Usenet
- How to Find the Right Place to Post (FAQ)
- Rules for Posting to Usenet
- Usenet Software: History and Sources
- Welcome to news.newusers.questions
- What Is Usenet?

Links to these articles and other resources about Usenet are available on several different Web pages. Here's a short list of some good general resources:

- Chapter 5 Usenet—Reading and Writing the News
  http://www.mwc.edu/ernie/Lrn-web05.html
- Usenet Info Center Launch Pad
  http://sunsite.unc.edu/usenet-i/home.html
- news.newusers.questions Links Page
  http://web.presby.edu/ ~ nnqadmin/nnq/ nnqlinks.html

Ways to Search Usenet Archives

Several of the major search engines include options for searching Usenet news. Some of these are listed in Table 11.2.

Name	URL	Way to Search Usenet Archives
AltaVista	**http://www.altavista. digital.com**	Select Search Usenet
HotBot	**http://www.hotbot.com**	Select Also Search Usenet
Infoseek	**http://www.infoseek.com**	Select Newsgroups

Table 11.2—Search Engines That Have Options for Searching Usenet Archives

There are also a few search engines dedicated to searching archives of Usenet news. Here are two.

1. Deja News, **http://www.dejanews.com**. This was the first search engine devoted to Usenet. In addition to searching, it allows you to post articles, browse, and find newsgroups.

2. Reference.COM, **http://www.reference.com**. This allows searching for newsgroups and discussion groups. You browse and post to newsgroups only if you register (free) with Reference.COM.

Most of these keep archives of Usenet articles for six months to a year, so they're useful for finding information that's being discussed currently or relatively recently.

Now we'll do an activity in which we'll search for Usenet news articles using Deja News.

Activity 11.2   Searching Usenet News Using Deja News

Overview

To use Deja News to search for Usenet articles on a specific subject, we'll use a key phrase, and Deja News will report back a list of articles. We'll be able to read any of the articles, and we'll note the names of the newsgroups that hold the articles in case we want to read other articles in that group. We'll also see the email address of each article's author; this address is part of every article posted to Usenet. We could send email to the authors if we had questions or comments about what they wrote, thereby taking advantage of their expertise. In this activity, we'll also look at the features and options available to us when we use Deja News.

We'll search using the phrase *Appalachian banjo music*. Why? You've always been interested in music, and you like different types of music. Now you want to listen to and maybe play banjo tunes and music—specifically, Appalachian banjo music. We'll use Deja News to search Usenet news for recent articles on this topic. Here are the steps we'll follow:

1. Go to the home page for Deja News.
2. Search for articles using the phrase *Appalachian banjo music*.
3. Browse the results.
4. Note the names of newsgroups and authors' email addresses.
5. Explore some of Deja News's features.

Details

We assume you've already started the Web browser.

1   Go to the home page for Deja News.

❋*Do It!* Click on the location field, type **http://www.dejanews.com**, and press **Enter**.

Using this URL, we go to the home page for Deja News. The home page with the search terms entered appears in Figure 11.6. Remember, though, that Deja News may have changed the look of its home page when you try this.

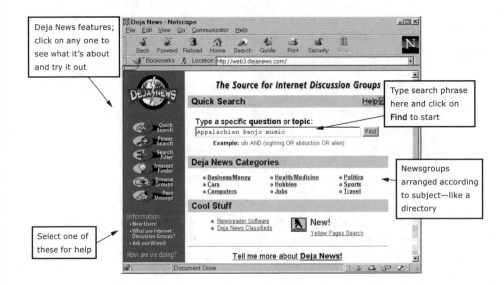

Deja News features; click on any one to see what it's about and try it out

Type search phrase here and click on **Find** to start

Newsgroups arranged according to subject—like a directory

Select one of these for help

Figure 11.6—Deja News's Home Page

2   Search for articles using the phrase *Appalachian banjo music.*

❊*Do It!*   Type **Appalachian banjo music** just below **Type a specific question or topic** and click on the button labeled **Find**.

In Figure 11.6, we've shown where to type in the search phrase and where to click to start the search. You'll find that a "quick search" looks for articles that contain *all* the words in your search phrase, but not necessarily in the order you've typed them. Click on the hyperlink **Quick Search** to get some more information about how Deja News works. To search using other features or options, click on **Power Search**.

3   Browse the results.

Figure 11.7 shows the search results. At almost any other time, we would expect different results, so use these as a guide. There are 16 relevant articles retrieved from the Deja News database; if there are more, they appear 20 per page. For each article in the list, we have the date it was posted, its "score," the subject, the newsgroup to which it was posted, and the author's email address. For reasons of privacy, we've purposely not shown the entire email address of each author here. It does appear on the Web page, however. After the list of articles, near the bottom of the Web page (not shown here), there is a form to let you search again or refine your search. There is also a link to a larger database holding older articles. Click on the hyperlink **Help** for more information about interpreting the results.

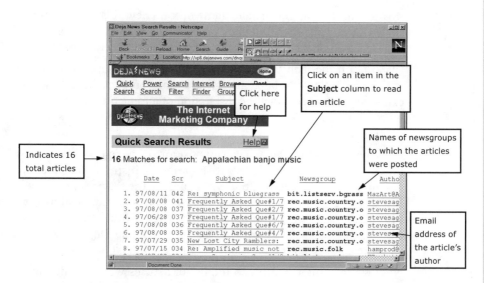

Figure 11.7—Results of Search Using the Phrase Appalachian banjo music

We can read any article, but let's look at the second one to be specific; it's a portion of a FAQ.

✱*Do It!* Click on the subject listed for the second article in Figure 11.7.

Clicking on the subject in the listing brings up a Web page that contains the article, as shown in Figure 11.8. This happens to be a portion of the FAQ for the newsgroup rec.music.country.old-time.

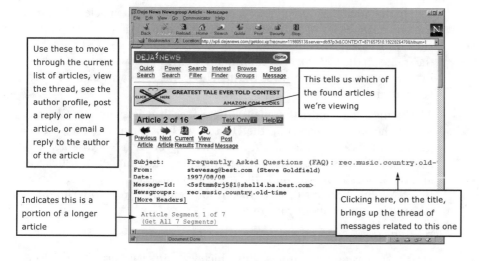

Figure 11.8—Portion of the FAQ for the Newsgroup rec.music.country.old-time

If you want to read the article, then you can view this Web page in the same way as any other. You click on the icons across the top of the Web page to reach other articles in the current list or to return to the list.

Clicking on the icon labeled **View Thread** brings up a Web page in which the thread of related articles are represented as hyperlinks. You can read them and follow the discussion of a topic on Usenet. Try this with another article in the list, one that's not a FAQ. It's likely to be more lively.

Clicking on **Post Message** lets you post an article to the newsgroup of the current article. This comes with appropriate instruction and reminders from Deja News about appropriate uses of the service and etiquette. If you register with Deja News, you give them your email address and they send you a small file that identifies you to them whenever you contact their service. There's no fee involved, and Deja News says it won't use or sell your email address for commercial purposes.

Now we're going to return to the list of articles we found during the search.

✻*Do It!* Click on the icon labeled **Current Results**.

From there, you can read other items in the hit list or take note of the newsgroups and addresses listed.

4   Note the names of newsgroups and authors' email addresses.

Clicking on the icon labeled **Current Results** takes us back to the list of articles shown in Figure 11.7.

The listing includes the name of a newsgroup for each article. We can use our newsreader to browse any of these groups. Another way is to click on **Browse Groups** and then enter the name of a newsgroup in the frame on the page that appears. You'll get a list of newsgroups. Clicking on any one lets you browse the articles in the same way as with the current hit list.

The listing also includes the email address of each article's author. Clicking on the address brings up the Deja News "author profile" for that person. That's a summary of information from the Deja News database about articles posted by this author, including the number of articles and the names of newsgroups in which you can find this author's articles. You might want to save the author's email address to write for more information about your topic.

5   Explore some of Deja News's features.

Deja News has several features with which you can set criteria for searching and for reading or posting articles to Usenet. They're listed either along the top or down the side of each page. We won't go into all the details here. Instead, we'll list and briefly describe some of the features.

Deja News lists features that let you browse the Usenet hierarchies of newsgroups, read articles in a newsgroup, and post articles. Once you register, Deja News offers you many of the features of a newsreader.

There are several features for searching. We used **Quick Search** above. There's also **Power Search**, with which you can specify whether to use all or any of the terms in the search phrase, Boolean search expressions, the dates of articles, the number of items listed per page, and other options. You can also set a **Search Filter** that obtains matches only from specific newsgroups, authors, dates, and subjects. **Interest Finder** lets you search by topic and gives you a directory of newsgroups arranged by subject. **Browse Groups** lets you read messages from groups in which the newsgroups are arranged according to the Usenet hierarchy. You have to go through three Web pages, for example, to reach the articles in the group rec.bicycles.off-road. You can type the name of a newsgroup here to see if Deja News makes it available. There's also a link to a page from which you can post articles to Usenet.

The features page also contains links to extensive help in using and explaining Deja News and Usenet. One page that is worthy to note is "Search Language Help," **http://www.dejanews.com/help/ help_lang.shtml**. That page gives all the details you need to form a search phrase using Boolean expressions, wildcards, parentheses, or proximity searching (when you want to look for words next to or near each other). You can also use expressions that allow for context searching, such as searching for a specific word in the newsgroup name or author field.

Take some time to explore these features. There's lots of useful information available about Usenet and lots of ways to use Deja News.

End of Activity 11.2

In Activity 11.2, we used Deja News to search the archives of Usenet articles. When you type in a keyword or phrase, a list of articles appears. You then select articles to read. You can also click on the author's address to see what other articles by that author are available. Deja News offers several other services, including a search for newsgroups and a good introduction to using Usenet, reading news, and posting articles.

Etiquette in a Discussion Group or a Usenet Newsgroup

Rules	Reasons
Spend some time getting to know the group.	When you first join a discussion group, take a little time to see the types of items discussed and the tone of the discussion. Read the articles in a

newsgroup before posting. You may also find that the questions you have are currently being answered.

Write easy-to-read messages.

The material you write to the group should be grammatically correct, concise, and thoughtful. Check your spelling too. It's a lot easier to read something that is well written, and many group members may not have the time to deal with long-winded, incorrect writing that does not make a clear point. If the posting must go on for several screens, it's a good idea to summarize it and to invite others to ask you for more information.

When responding to something from the group, include only the pertinent portions of the original message.

Let's say that a group member starts a discussion and writes something about 40 lines long. You want to respond, but only to one portion of it. In your follow-up message, include just the portion that's relevant to your response.

When you ask group members any questions, post a summary of the responses you receive.

With this summary, everyone in the group benefits from the responses to your question. Naturally, this applies only if you get several responses and if the answers to the question are of general interest.

Posting or sending a message to the group is a public act.

Everything you write to the group may be distributed to all group members or posted worldwide through Usenet. If the group is moderated, your messages may be read first by the moderator and then passed on to the group. If you're working with a list that isn't moderated (most aren't), your messages go directly to the group. Don't embarrass yourself. A friend, relative, or supervisor may also be a member of the list.

Group members are people like yourself and need to be treated with respect and courtesy.

Respond to messages as if you were talking face-to-face. A member may be from a different culture, may not be familiar with your language, and may have different views and values from your own. Don't respond too quickly to something that upsets you, and don't criticize others too hastily or without good reason. It's better to think before you write than to be sorry afterward.

Avoid sarcasm and be careful with humor.

You are communicating entirely by your words. You don't have the benefit of facial expressions, body language, or tone of voice to let somebody know you're only kidding when you make a sarcastic remark. Group members will appreciate well-written, humorous pieces or responses, but be sure your writing will be interpreted that way.

Think about whether a response to a message should go to the group or to an individual.

Messages to the list should be of general interest. They may be requests on your part for advice or for help in solving a problem. You'll know the email address of the person who made the original request, and you can send a response to that person if it's appropriate.

If you're working with an email discussion group, remember to send messages going to the entire group to the list address. Send commands or requests to be interpreted by the software managing the list to the administrative address.

Over the years, several documents have been developed about proper Usenet etiquette. These are regularly posted in news.announce.newusers, news.answers, or news.newusers.questions. Here is a list of some that you ought to read:

- A Primer on How to Work with the Usenet Community
- Emily Postnews Answers Your Questions on Netiquette
- Hints on Writing Style for Usenet
- How to Find the Right Place to Post (FAQ)
- Please Read Before Posting
- Rules for Posting to Usenet
- A Weekly FAQ on Test Postings

Summary

Both email discussion groups and Usenet news are examples of group communication on the Internet. They're useful and valuable as sources of information for two reasons:

- The people who participate in them are a ready source of information.
- The groups often keep archives of files, FAQs, and periodic postings that can sometimes be retrieved and searched.

Email discussion group members communicate via email, with messages broadcast to all group members. In Usenet, people communicate via articles or files that are posted to Usenet newsgroups. Anyone with access to Usenet can access the articles. In both cases, messages can be read, replied to, or posted.

Several thousand discussion groups are available and active on the Internet. They may be called mailing lists, discussion groups, listserv lists, or interest groups. Regardless of the name, each consists of a group of members anywhere on the Internet. This way, communities or collections of people can discuss items related to a common topic, find information about the topic, make announcements to the group, or ask questions and receive help from other group members. The large number of lists guarantees a wide range of topics. The groups are particularly useful to people who want to discuss issues with a large or diverse group. The groups extend any resources beyond a local site.

You send messages to the list by using the list address. Commands and requests for service are usually sent to the administrative address. For example, the list photo-l, which deals with a variety of topics related to photography, has **photo-l@csuohio.edu** as the list address and **listproc@csuohio.edu** as the administrative address. You use this second address to join a list, leave or unsubscribe from a list, request archived files from the list, and get a roster of the members of the list. Be sure you use the correct address when you communicate with the group or list. Most lists also have a person designated as the list owner, list administrator, or moderator. That person is in charge of the list, and you send him or her email if you have problems using the list or questions about the operation of the list. Some lists are moderated. Messages sent to these lists first go to moderators, who decide whether to pass the messages on to all group members.

The lists can be thought of as communities of people sharing common interests. There are generally accepted rules of behavior or etiquette for list members. These include providing appropriate, thoughtful, and concise messages to the group, providing a summary of the responses received in answer to a question, and communicating with other group members in a civil and respectful manner.

Several "lists of lists" and other documents related to using discussion groups are available as part of the World Wide Web. There are also services on the Web that help you find discussion groups and search or retrieve groups' archives.

The news is a collection of messages called articles. Each is designated as belonging to one or more newsgroups. These articles are passed from one computer system to another. There are several thousand newsgroups, all arranged into categories. Users at a site can usually select any of the groups that are available and can often reply to, follow up, or post an article. Some estimates put the number of participants at more than 40 million worldwide.

Usenet is a community of users helping each other and exchanging opinions. A code of behavior has developed. The rules are, of course, voluntary, but users are expected to obtain copies of some articles about working with Usenet and to follow the rules. Several newsgroups carry regular postings of articles meant to inform the Usenet community. These are often found in the groups news.announce.newgroups, news.announce.newusers, and news.answers.

You use software called a newsreader to work with the articles and newsgroups in Usenet news. Several different newsreaders are available. The one you use will depend on your preferences and what's available on the system with which you access Usenet.

You'll probably find Usenet a valuable resource for information on a wide array of topics. It can be enjoyable to read and participate in the discussions. Services are available on the World Wide Web to search for newsgroups related to a specific topic and to search for articles that contain keywords or phrases.

Selected Terms Introduced in This Chapter

administrative address	moderator
archived	Network News Transport
article	Protocol (NNTP)
cross-posting	newsgroup
discussion group	newsreader
group address	post
interest group	subscribe
list address	thread
listserv	unsubscribe
lurking	Usenet
mailing list	

12
Chapter

Evaluating Information
Found on the WWW

As you've seen in previous chapters, you can find information on the World Wide Web on all sorts of topics. You've also seen that the information can come from different types of sources, such as online magazines and other periodicals, news agencies, government agencies, companies, nonprofit organizations, educational institutions, and individuals. Information abounds; it's possible for anyone with the appropriate computer, the right software, and an Internet connection to make information available on the Web.

When we access or retrieve something on the World Wide Web, we need to decide whether the information is useful, reliable, and appropriate for our purposes. This is particularly true when we're using Web or Internet resources for research, which should be based on accurate, trustworthy, and authoritative sources. Of course, we need to assess the veracity of information from other sources as well, including printed material, broadcast media, and communication with individuals. Information that appears in print often has been reviewed and checked for correctness before publication, but outlandish stories, incorrect information, and hoaxes have certainly been published. Information on radio and television is usually checked for accuracy, but that's not always the case.

In this chapter, we'll look at some issues related to evaluating resources on the World Wide Web. The chapter will include these sections:
* Reasons to Evaluate
* Guidelines for Evaluation
* Information on the World Wide Web About Evaluating Resources

Reasons to Evaluate

We use the information we've found on the Internet or Web for a variety of purposes. Sometimes we use it for entertainment, recreation, or casual conversation. When we use the information for research, we have to be sure the information is reliable and authoritative. That puts us in the position of having to verify information and make judgments about whether it is appropriate. We need to think critically, as opposed to using information just because it's available to us or published on the Web.

In some situations, we don't have to do that work on our own. Some information is screened before it comes to us. When we retrieve information from an academic or research library, either by using the Web or by visiting in person, we rely on professional librarians who have evaluated and selected the material. Information in a database that's been prepared by a scholarly or commercial organization is often evaluated and checked for correctness before it's made available. Articles and reports published by scholarly organizations, research labs, and government agencies often go through an independent review process before being published. Some librarians and other information specialists have established virtual libraries on the Web where they review, evaluate, and list reliable sources of information on the World Wide Web. Here are some of those virtual libraries:

- The Argus Clearinghouse
  http://www.clearinghouse.net
- Internet Public Library
  http://www.ipl.org
- Librarians' Index to the Internet
  http://sunsite.berkeley.edu/internetindex

It's useful to visit these sites to find information that's been reviewed by someone else. Still, when you deal with any information you find on the Web or in a library, it is up to you to be skeptical about it and to assess whether it's appropriate for your purposes. For example, if you want information before buying a CD player, then product announcements from manufacturers will give you some data, but the announcements will probably not be the right source for impartial brand comparisons. If you're researching techniques for advertising electronic consumer products, then the advertisements might be good resource material; if you are writing about the physics involved in producing sound from audio CDs, however, these ads may not be authoritative sources.

The nature of the Internet and the World Wide Web makes it easy for almost anyone to create and disperse information. People also have considerable freedom and variety in the formats with which they publish information on the Web. A person who wants to sell a product or disseminate propaganda can make material appear to be part of a well-researched report. A quotation attributed to English dramatist Thomas Dekker (1572?–1632?), a contemporary of William Shakespeare, is particularly applicable here: "A mask of gold hides all deformities." Thinking critically about information and its sources means being able to separate facts from opinions. We have to be able to verify information and know its source, we have to determine whether the facts are current, and we need to know why someone offered the data at all. After considering these issues, we can decide whether the information is appropriate for our purposes.

Guidelines for Evaluation

In this section, we will first list guidelines or criteria that you can use for evaluating information. Then, we will indicate how you can apply these guidelines to documents and other information that you retrieve from the Web or the Internet.

Guidelines

To help you develop guidelines for evaluating sources, we will pose the sorts of questions you might ask when assessing information.

Who Is the Author or Institution?

- If an individual has written the resource, does it give biographical information about the author? That information could include any of the following: educational and other credentials, occupational position, institutional affiliation, and address.

- If an institution has written the resource, does it give information about that institution, including its purpose, history, and street address?

- Have you seen the author's or institution's name cited in other sources or bibliographies?

- What clues does the URL give you about a source's authority? A tilde (~) in a Web page's URL usually indicates that it is a personal page, rather than part of an institutional Web site. Also, make a mental note of the domain section of the URL, as follows:

  - **.edu**, educational. (Can be anything from serious research to zany student pages.)
  - **.gov**, governmental. (Is usually dependable.)
  - **.com**, commercial. (May be trying to sell a product.)
  - **.net**, network. (May provide services to commercial or individual customers.)
  - **.org**, organization. (Is a nonprofit institution; may be biased.)

⁂ If the page is part of a larger institution's Web site, does the institution appear to filter the information that appears at its site? Was the information screened somehow before it was put on the Web?

How Current Is the Information?

⁂ Is there a date on the Web page that indicates when the page was placed on the Web?

⁂ Is it clear when the page was last updated?

⁂ Is some of the information obviously out of date?

⁂ Does the page creator mention how frequently the material is updated?

Who Is the Audience?

⁂ Is the Web page intended for the general public, or is it meant for scholars, practitioners, children, and so forth? Is the audience clearly stated?

⁂ Does the Web page meet the needs of its stated audience?

Is the Content Accurate and Objective?

⁂ Are there political, ideological, cultural, religious, or institutional biases?

⁂ Is the content intended to be a brief overview of the information or an in-depth analysis?

⁂ If the information is opinion, is this clearly stated?

⁂ If information has been copied from other sources, is this acknowledged? Are there footnotes, if necessary?

What Is the Purpose of the Information?

⁂ Is the purpose of the information to inform, explain, persuade, market a product, or advocate a cause?

⁂ Is the purpose clearly stated?

⁂ Does the resource fulfill the stated purpose?

Discussion and Tips

We will now discuss the criteria we have listed and indicate how you can verify information obtained from the Internet.

Who Is the Author or Institution?

If you're not familiar with the author or institution responsible for producing the information, you'll need to do some checking to determine whether the source is reliable and authoritative. You can't consider a resource reliable if you don't know who wrote it or what institution published it. If a Web page doesn't contain the name of the author or the institution, and if there are no hyperlinks to Web pages that give that information, then you should be suspicious of its content.

Chapter 12

Tip

Look for the name of the author or institution at the top or bottom of a Web page.

Being suspicious doesn't mean that you must disqualify the information. For example, the Web page "The VENONA Project," **http://www.nsa.gov:8080/docs/venona/ddir.html**, doesn't say who has sponsored the information. But if you look at the URL, you can see that the information is provided through the Web server with the Internet domain name **www.nsa.gov**. This indicates that it's supplied by a government organization, which means that it's usually suitable for research purposes. We'll do some more sleuthing in Activity 12.1, and we'll start with this Web page.

On the other hand, if the information is provided by a commercial site (its URL will contain **.com**, as in **www.greatplace.com**) or if it's on a personal Web page (its URL will contain a tilde, as in **mary.mwc.edu/ ~ ernie**), then we may need to do further checking.

Tip

To find out about the sponsor, go to the home page for the site that hosts the information.

Regardless of whether the Web page contains the sponsor's name, we can investigate further by looking for more information about the author or institution. For example, consider the document "CDT Children's Privacy Issues Page," **http://www.cdt.org/privacy/children**. Looking at that Web page, we can see that the Center for Democracy and Technology (CDT) has made it available. There are hyperlinks from that Web page to the home page for CDT. You can follow the hyperlinks to find out more about the CDT, or you can go to the home page by typing the URL **http://www.cdt.org** in the location panel and pressing **Enter**. When you can't find your way to a home page or to other information, try using a search engine, directory, or other service to search the Web or Usenet.

Tip

To find further information about the institution or author, use a search engine to see what related information is available on the Web.

Chapter 12

 Tip

Use Deja News or another tool to search Usenet archives. That way, you can find other information about the author or institution. If an individual is the author, you can see what sorts of articles they've posted on Usenet.

If you're searching with Deja News, use the URL **http://www.dejanews.com**. Type the author's name in the search panel. If a list of articles comes up, click on the author's name in the Author column to read articles that the author has posted to Usenet. To read more about working with Deja News's Author Profile Help, use the URL **http://www.dejanews.com/help/help_ap.shtml**.

 Tip

Remember that the Web is always changing and that your results may differ from those shown here. Don't let this confuse you. The activities demonstrate fundamental skills. These skills don't change, even though the number of results obtained or the actual screens may look very different.

Activity 12.1 Using a URL and Search Engines to Investigate a Resource

Overview

In this activity, we'll seek further information about a resource we've come across on the Web. Let's assume that we've found or retrieved the Web page shown in Figure 12.1. Its title is "The VENONA Project," but it doesn't contain the name of the author or institution providing the information. To find more information, we will do the following steps:

1. Use parts of the URL to find further information about this resource.
2. Use a search engine to learn more about this resource.

Details

1   **Use parts of the URL to find further information about this resource.**

Here is the URL for the Web page shown in Figure 12.1:

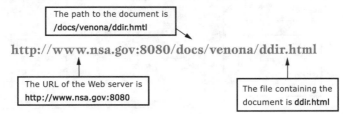

We can see that the URL for the Web server that makes this document available is **http://www.nsa.gov:8080**. The path to the document is **docs/venona/ddir.html**. Finally, the name of the file containing the document is **ddir.html**.

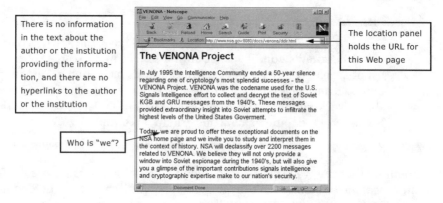

Figure 12.1—Web Page for the VENONA Project

To obtain more information about the document, we'll first use the URL without the path or file name. That may give us a Web page with links to this document and to other related Web pages.

❊*Do It!* In the location panel, type **http://www.nsa.gov:8080**, and press **Enter**.

Another way to get the same result is to click on the location panel to the right of the URL. The panel will turn blue. Click again so that the cursor is just to the right of the URL (just past **html**). Use **Backspace** to erase characters until only **http://www.nsa.gov:8080** is left, and press **Enter**. The Web page in Figure 12.2 will be displayed in a few seconds.

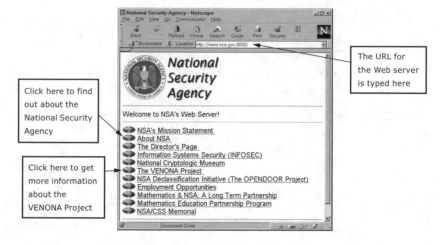

Figure 12.2—Home Page for the National Security Agency

We see that the URL **http://www.nsa.gov:8080** has led us to the home page of the National Security Agency. The NSA has therefore made the information available. What is the NSA? The seal on the page leads us to believe it's an agency of the U.S. government. To find out more, we'll click on the hyperlink labeled **About NSA**.

✿*Do It!* Click on the hyperlink **About NSA**.

Clicking on the hyperlink brings up a Web page describing the NSA; we won't show it here. We read there that the NSA is a part of the U.S. Department of Defense. That indicates that the information we find at this site is authoritative.

Now we will try to find out more about the VENONA Project.

✿*Do It!* Click on the toolbar button labeled **Back** to return to the NSA's home page.

You should be back at the home page.

✿*Do It!* Click on the hyperlink **The VENONA Project**.

Clicking on this hyperlink takes us to the Web page for the project. We show a portion of this Web page in Figure 12.3. The page starts with such a large colorful image that you might mistake it for a commercial site advertising a movie.

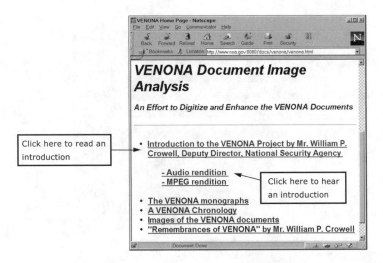

Figure 12.3—Home Page for the VENONA Project

We'll follow the first hyperlink to see what we can find out about the VENONA Project.

✿*Do It!* Click on the hyperlink **Introduction to the VENONA Project by Mr. William P. Crowell, Deputy Director, National Security Agency**.

Following that link takes us to the Web page we were first considering—Figure 12.1! Now we know the author, William P. Crowell, and the sponsoring institution, the National Security Agency. You can follow the hyperlinks on the VENONA home page (Figure 12.3) to find out more about the project.

2   Use a search engine to learn more about this resource.

First, we'll see what information we can find on William P. Crowell. We're going to use HotBot because it has the option to treat the search phrase as a name.

❋*Do It!* Go to HotBot's home page by typing **http://www.hotbot.com** in the location panel and pressing **Enter**.

We are now at HotBot's home page, as Figure 12.4 reflects. Enter the search query by following the next instructions.

❋*Do It!* Using the pulldown menu indicated in Figure 12.4, set the option to search for **the person**.

❋*Do It!* Type **William P. Crowell** in the search phrase panel.

❋*Do It!* Select **brief descriptions** as a display option.

We'll select this display option here, just so we can show more results in Figure 12.5.

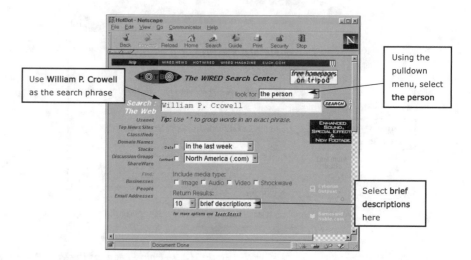

Figure 12.4—HotBot's Home Page with the Search Query Entered

Once the options and search phrase are set, we're ready for HotBot to search its database.

❋*Do It!* Click on **SEARCH**.

Our results partly appear in Figure 12.5. Yours may differ.

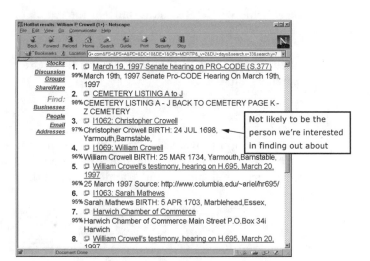

Figure 12.5—A Portion of HotBot's Search Results

Using HotBot to search for the person William P. Crowell gives several results. Some of the results listed in Figure 12.5 deal with people who lived in the seventeenth and eighteenth century, so they wouldn't be appropriate because the VENONA Project took place during the 1940s. You may wonder why the Web pages titled **1062: Christopher Crowell** and **1063: Sarah Mathews** turned up at all. Remember that search engines usually index the full text of a Web page. Therefore it's enough for the name William Crowell to appear anywhere on a Web page for the page to turn up in the list of results. Another item is a listing for a chamber of commerce, so it doesn't apply to the NSA's work. Checking some of the other links, we confirm that William Crowell was Deputy Director of the NSA and that he's particularly well qualified in the areas of cryptography and electronic intelligence gathering.

Now we'll use search engines to see if there's other information on the Web related to the VENONA Project. This will help us to evaluate the information available through the NSA. First we'll search HotBot's index for information about VENONA, and then we'll search using WebCrawler. Both use full-text indexing for documents, but they use different methods for relevancy ranking, so we're likely to see different results.

❋*Do It!* Go to HotBot's home page by typing **http://www.hotbot.com** in the location panel and pressing **Enter**.

❋*Do It!* Using the pulldown menu to the right of the words **look for**, as shown in Figure 12.4, set the option to search for all the words, any of the words, or exact phrase.

We have to use one of those search options since our search phrase is a word, *VENONA,* not a person's name.

❋*Do It!* Type **VENONA** in the panel as the search phrase.

❋*Do It!* Select **brief descriptions** as a display option.

Once the options and search phrase are set, we're ready for HotBot to search its database.

❋*Do It!* Click on **SEARCH**.

The first few search results appear in Figure 12.6. Most of the links go to information provided by NSA. You'll want to check the first link, **VENONA – Soviet Espionage against the US Atomic Program**, to see if it's helpful. You should examine some of the others as well.

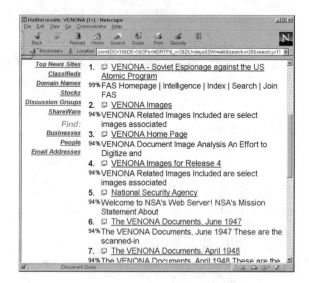

Figure 12.6—Results of Search for Exact Phrase VENONA

Now we'll use WebCrawler to see what information we can find about VENONA.

❋*Do It!* Go to WebCrawler's home page by typing **http://www. webcrawler.com** in the location field and pressing **Enter**.

❋*Do It!* Type **VENONA** in the search phrase panel.

The Web page with searching options set appears in Figure 12.7.

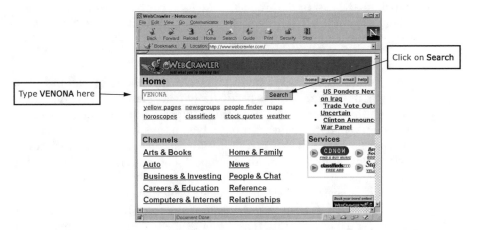

Figure 12.7—WebCrawler's Home Page with the Search Query Entered

Once the options and search phrase are set, we're ready for WebCrawler to search its database.

❋*Do It!* Click on **Search**.

The first few search results appear in Figure 12.8. If we were to follow the first two, we'd see they are linked to the NSA, but there are several others listed that don't go directly to the NSA.

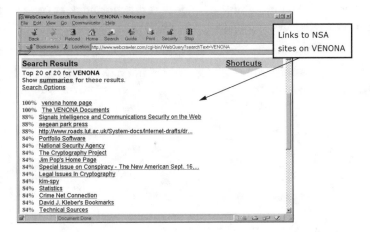

Figure 12.8—WebCrawler's Search Results

We leave it to you to explore and read some of the other links. Remember to think critically about and evaluate the information you find.

End of Activity 12.1

In Activity 12.1, we started with a Web page and used its URL to find the organization that published the Web page and to whom we could attribute the text in the Web page. We used HotBot to find information about the author. Then we used HotBot and WebCrawler to find additional information about the topic.

How Current Is the Information?

In some cases, it's important to know whether the information you're using is up-to-date. This is particularly true when you're using information that contains statistics. If the information is of the type that is frequently updated—for example, a FAQ or a news report—then try to be sure you have the most recent information. Check the date on the Web page, and if it's more than a month old, search for a more recent version.

A well-designed Web page indicates when the information was last updated, often at the top or bottom of the page. If that date isn't displayed, you may be able to find the date on which the Web page was last modified on the server. If you're using Netscape Navigator, click on **View** in the menu bar and select **Page Info**. That will tell you the date of the last modification to the file. If you're using Microsoft Internet Explorer, put the cursor on the Web page in the browser window. Then click the right mouse button and select **Properties** to obtain the same information. We show this in detail in Chapter 13.

Tip

Check the top and bottom of a Web page for the date on which the information was last modified. If no date is present, look at **Page Info** if you're using Netscape, or **Properties** if you're using Microsoft Internet Explorer.

Email messages and Usenet news articles usually have the date on which the message was posted. This information is part of the message or it's in the header information, as shown here.

```
Subject: Re: Agape on the Internet: A Preach
From: Ernest C Ackermann <ernie@paprika.mwc.edu>
Date: 1997/03/30
Message-Id: <199703301552.KAA13690@eagle>
Newsgroups: bit.listserv.nettrain
```

Date posted ►

Who Is the Audience?

Web pages are sometimes written to give information to a specific group: the general public, researchers and scholars, professionals in a specific field, children, potential customers, or others. Try to determine the intended audience, as that may have an impact on whether the information is relevant or appropriate for your purpose. Suppose you are preparing a report on sustainable forest management. An appropriate information resource, whether in print or on the Web, is one that is written for your level of expertise and for the expertise of your audience. The Web page "Forest Service Mission, Vision, and Guiding Principles," United States Department of Agriculture Forest Service, **http://www.fs.fed.us/intro/mvgp.html**, might be useful for a general overview of the issues and principles involved in forest management. On the other hand, the Web page "Alternatives to Methyl Bromide: Research Needs for California," **http://www.cdpr.ca.gov/docs/dprdocs/methbrom/mb4chg.htm**, is more appropriate for a specialized audience.

Is the Content Accurate and Objective?

Determining whether information is accurate and objective is easy if we can find corroborating sources for it. Before using information that makes claims or contains statistics, we need to be sure they can be substantiated. In the best situations, claims or statistics on Web pages are supported by original research or by hyperlinks or footnotes to the primary sources of the information. Sometimes, however, one has to check several sources to verify the accuracy and objectivity of a source. This can involve a lot of work, but it's worth it, because you end up with solid, factual results.

Take, for example, the following quotation:

> Women make up more than half of the undergraduate enrollments in higher education for every racial/ethnic group in the United States. Among black students, women comprise more than 60 percent of the undergraduate enrollments. Foreign students are the exception; women comprise less than one-half of foreign undergraduate enrollments (45 percent). Students with disabilities make up about 6 percent of all students enrolled in postsecondary institutions; 5.7 percent of all students who major in S&E fields and 6.6 percent of students who major in non-S&E fields (NCES, 1995a).

This quotation has been taken from "Undergraduate Science and Engineering Students and Degrees," **http://www.nsf.gov/sbe/srs/seind96/ch2_undr.htm#p1**, which the National Science Foundation published in December 1996. It may be viewed as accurate and objective, because it is part of a report that underwent a prepublication review by the National Science Foundation, an independent U.S. government agency. Furthermore, there is a citation—NCES, 1995a—for the statistics. Checking the included footnotes tells us that NCES is an abbreviation for the National Center for Educational Statistics. Enrollment figures are available through a hyperlink (not shown here) in the report.

The following statements are presented for contrast to show information that would likely be less reliable:

We're losing our freedom—with the government's help. Right now one out of every four Americans legally owns a firearm, and yet the government is spending more than one-third of its budget to ban firearms. In 1996, only 1.25 percent of all deaths were attributed to the use of guns, but guns were used in over 83 percent of all crimes. The government is going after the wrong group. Most crimes—74.56 percent—are committed by illegal minorities. The government wastes billions of dollars ($2.7 billion in 1995) to keep guns away from Americans, but studies show that money would be better spent in supporting firearm safety training and increasing the size and effectiveness of the immigration service.

This is unreliable for several reasons; the statistics aren't corroborated, the language suggests an ideological bias, and none of the claims are supported by citations or footnotes. We wrote this to give a contrasting example; it doesn't represent our views or those of the publisher.

What Is the Purpose of the Information?

When you're evaluating information that you've found on the World Wide Web, the Internet, or in print, you need to consider its purpose. Information on the Web can be produced in a variety of formats and styles, and the appearance sometimes gives a clue to its intent. You probably know that information in a glossy brochure is usually produced with the intent of selling a product, concept, or cause. Similarly, Web pages aimed to market something are often designed in a clever way to catch our attention and emphasize a product. For example, see the home page for Ford in the United States at **http://www.ford.com/us**. Since there's considerable freedom in publishing information on the Web and the Internet, it's not too difficult to mask the purpose of information through its appearance. A person who wants to sell a product or promote a cause can present information in a format that makes it appear to be part of a well-researched report. It's your job, then, to concentrate on the content and to determine the purpose of the information so you'll feel comfortable using it for research or other purposes.

Activity 12.2 **Applying Guidelines to Evaluate a Resource**

Overview

In this activity, we'll apply the guidelines for evaluating information on the Web. If we were researching a topic related to teaching or distance education, we might come across a Web page called "Tools For Teaching: The World Wide Web and a Web Browser," **http://www.mwc.edu/ ~ernie/facacad/WWW-Teaching.html**. This is the Web page we'll evaluate in this activity. We'll go through the guidelines by answering each of the following questions:

1. Who is the author or institution?
2. How current is the information?
3. Who is the audience?
4. Is the content accurate and objective?
5. What is the purpose of the information?

In this activity, we'll be able to obtain answers in a rather direct way. It's not always so straightforward, but this is meant to be a demonstration. In your own work, you may have to be more persistent and discerning.

Details

We'll assume your Web browser is already started. You get to the Web page discussed in this activity by typing in its URL, **http:// www.mwc.edu/ ~ ernie/facacad/WWW-Teaching.html**.

1   Who is the author or institution?

Figure 12.9 shows the beginning of the Web page we're considering. The author's name is at both the beginning and end of the page, as shown in Figures 12.9 and 12.10. We can see that the author is affiliated with the computer science department at Mary Washington College. The page has hyperlinks to the author's home page and to this college. If we viewed his home page, we'd see that he's written at least two books on using the Internet and the World Wide Web and he has developed several Web pages for the courses he teaches. If we followed the links **Department of Computer Science** and **Mary Washington College**, we'd see that he is a professor of computer science at a state-supported college in Virginia. These help establish the author's credentials, which influence our assessment of the resource we're considering.

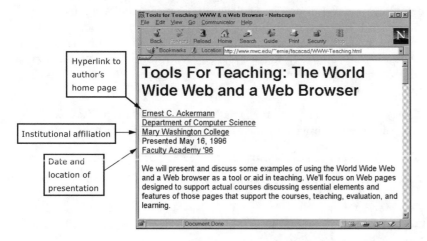

Figure 12.9—Beginning of "Tools For Teaching" Web Page

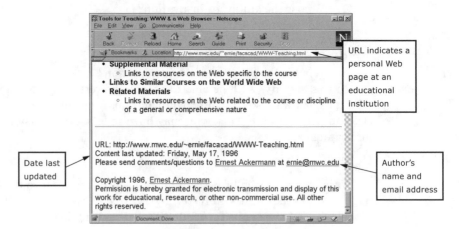

Figure 12.10—End of "Tools For Teaching" Web Page

We can search the Web for other information about the author or for hyperlinks to resources that cite his work. One way is to use HotBot, as we did in Activity 12.1, to search for the person Ernest Ackermann. When this was tried, HotBot returned more than 300 results. Many referred to pages he had written, several related to courses he teaches, and more than 50 were from other sources citing his work.

Another way is to use Deja News to see what work of his is available on Usenet. The second activity in Chapter 11 showed you how to use Deja News to find information on a topic. You could find any newsgroups to which Ackermann posts messages by searching the Deja News archives; you would use *Ernest Ackermann* as the search string. Your results would likely be extremely different from any we would show here, because by default, Deja News searches a collection of articles that's at most a few months old. You could select an option to bring up entries going back a few years, but that's likely to give you postings in a wide variety of newsgroups. It may help to use Deja News's Author Profile for a summary of the names of newsgroups to which the author contributes. We'll try that now.

✹*Do It!* Go to the home page for Deja News by typing **http://www. dejanews.com** in the location field and pressing Enter.

✹*Do It!* Type **Ernest Ackermann** in the search form.

✹*Do It!* Click on the button labeled **Find**.

This starts the search using the Deja News database. Results will be displayed in a format similar to that shown in Figure 12.11. The first three articles were not posted by Ackermann, so we've hidden the addresses in Figure 12.11.

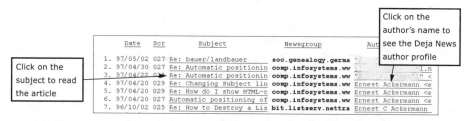

Click on the author's name to see the Deja News author profile

Click on the subject to read the article

	Date	Scr	Subject	Newsgroup	Aut
1.	97/05/02	027	Re: bauer/landbauer	soc.genealogy.germa	
2.	97/04/30	027	Re: Automatic positionin	comp.infosystems.ww	
3.	97/04/22	027	Re: Automatic positionin	comp.infosystems.ww	
4.	97/04/20	029	Re: Changing Subject lin	comp.infosystems.ww	Ernest Ackermann <e
5.	97/04/20	029	Re: How do I show HTML-c	comp.infosystems.ww	Ernest Ackermann <e
6.	97/04/20	027	Automatic positioning of	comp.infosystems.ww	Ernest Ackermann <e
7.	96/10/02	025	Re: How to Destroy a Lis	bit.listserv.nettra	Ernest C Ackermann

Figure 12.11—Excerpt of Deja News Search Results

To read any of the articles, click on the entry in the **Subject** column. For a summary of the newsgroups to which Ackermann has posted messages, click on the entry in the **Author** column. Reading some of the articles he's written and noting the newsgroups to which he posts may give you some clues about whether to consider his work credible.

In this case, we see that Ackermann has posted several of the articles listed. Reading them, we can see that the first few are posted to **comp.infosys.www.authoring.html** and that the last is posted to **bit.listserv.nettrain**. If we think it's necessary, we can obtain more information about the newsgroups themselves by using tile.net or Liszt, as described in Chapter 11. The first group deals with writing or authoring Web pages, and anyone may post to it. Nettrain addresses issues related to training or teaching others to use the Internet and the World Wide Web. It's a moderated group, so the posting goes through an initial screening to see if it's appropriate.

Searching for postings to Usenet tells us that the author is interested in writing Web pages and teaching and training people to use the Internet and the Web. This gives us a positive indication about the resource we've found, as it deals with a related topic—using the Web for instruction.

We can use the URL as a clue to a source's authority. In this case, the URL is **http://www.mwc.edu/ ~ ernie/facacad/WWW-Teaching.html**. The domain name **www.mwc.edu** ends with **.edu**, so the site hosting the page is an educational institution in the United States. If this were an educational institution in another country, the domain name would end with a two-letter abbreviation for the country and probably wouldn't have **edu** in its name. The tilde (~) in the URL indicates that this page was most likely posted by the author, rather than being officially posted by the institution. Therefore, the URL alone tells us that this resource was published on the Web by an individual at an educational institution in the United States. To find out more, the best bet is to visit the Web site. Visiting the site with the URL **http://www.mwc.edu** and following appropriate hyperlinks would tell us that the institution is a liberal arts, state-supported college in Virginia. Since the Web resource deals with teaching, it seems appropriate for it to be available at such a site.

Chapter 12

2   How current is the information?

In Figure 12.9, we see that the material about teaching with the Web was presented on May 16, 1996, and in Figure 12.10, we see that it was last updated on May 17, 1996. Any information about a specific technology may be relevant for about two years after the last update. Information related to the contents of Web pages or the teaching practices and methods applicable to teaching with the Web will probably be relevant for more than two years after the date of publication.

3   Who is the audience?

In Figure 12.9 we see the hyperlink **Faculty Academy '96**. Following that link takes us to a document holding the proceedings of Faculty Academy '96, which was held at Mary Washington College in Fredericksburg, Virginia. Reading through the proceedings, we see that the resource we're considering was presented at a conference about using technology in the instructional program at an educational institution. From this information and from reading the resource we're considering, we see that the audience consists of educators who want to use technology, specifically the World Wide Web, to support instruction.

4   Is the content accurate and objective?

As we read the Web page we're considering, we see that the language is not inflammatory. It is, in fact, rather objective. It lists several references, which may be checked to corroborate the information present. It also provides links to other Web resources on the same topic. We can conclude that the information presented is accurate and objective.

5   What is the purpose of the information?

The page states that it relates to using the World Wide Web and a Web browser to teach. Reading the Web page, which contains recommendations for using the Web as an instructional tool, we see that this is the case.

Conclusion

The Web page we're considering was written by a college professor with experience related to the topic. It's relatively current. Furthermore, it was presented at a conference related to using technology in instruction. We may conclude that it is an authoritative and objective source of information.

End of Activity 12.2

In Activity 12.2, we used the guidelines in this chapter to evaluate a Web page. We used a variety of Web and Internet resources to establish the identity and suitability of the author, and we considered other issues related to whether the information was reliable and appropriate.

Information on the World Wide Web About Evaluating Resources

There are several good resources on the World Wide Web to help you evaluate information. They give in-depth information about critically examining documents that appear on the Web or in print, and they offer other guidelines and suggestions for assessing Internet and Web resources.

Guides to Evaluating Library Resources

❈ "Evaluating What You Have Found," University of Waterloo Library
http://www.lib.uwaterloo.ca/howto/howto28.pdf

❈ "How to Critically Analyze Information Sources," Reference Services Division of the Cornell University Library
http://www.library.cornell.edu/okuref/research/skill26.htm

Brief Guides to Evaluating Web Resources

❈ "Evaluating the Documents You Have Found on the World Wide Web," Gillian Westera
http://www.curtin.edu.au/curtin/library/staffpages/gwpersonal/senginestudy/zeval.htm

❈ "Evaluating World Wide Web Information," D. Scott Brandt, Purdue University Libraries
http://thorplus.lib.purdue.edu/library_info/instruction/gs175/1gs175e/evaluation.html

❈ "Practical Steps in Evaluating Internet Resources," Elizabeth Kirk, Milton S. Eisenhower Library, Johns Hopkins University
http://milton.mse.jhu.edu:8001/research/education/practical.html

❈ "Significance," Iowa State University
http://www.public.iastate.edu/ ~ CYBERSTACKS/signif.htm

❈ "Thinking Critically about World Wide Web Resources," Esther Grassian, UCLA College Library
http://www.library.ucla.edu/libraries/college/instruct/critical.htm

Chapter 12

Extensive Guides to Evaluating Resources on the World Wide Web

❋ "Criteria for evaluation of Internet Information Resources," Alastair Smith, Department of Library and Information Studies, Victoria University of Wellington, New Zealand
http://www.vuw.ac.nz/ ~ agsmith/evaln/index.htm

❋ "Evaluating information found on the Internet," Elizabeth Kirk, Milton S. Eisenhower Library, Johns Hopkins University
http://milton.mse.jhu.edu:8001/research/education/net.html

❋ "Kathy Schrock's Guide for Educators—Critical Evaluation Surveys," Kathleen Schrock
http://www.capecod.net/schrockguide/eval.htm

❋ "Evaluating Web Resources," Jan Alexander and Marsha Tate, Wolfgram Memorial Library, Widener University
http://www.science.widener.edu/ ~ withers/webeval.htm

Bibliographies for Evaluating Web Resources

❋ "Bibliography on Evaluating Internet Resources," Nicole Auer, Virginia Polytechnic Institute and State University
http://refserver.lib.vt.edu/libinst/critTHINK.HTM

❋ "Evaluating Web Sites for Educational Uses: Bibliography and Checklist," Carolyn Kotlas, Institute for Academic Technology
http://www.iat.unc.edu/guides/irg-49.html

❋ "Information Quality WWW Virtual Library," T. Matthew Ciolek
http://www.ciolek.com/WWWVL-InfoQuality.html

❋ "Web Evaluation Techniques: Bibliography," Jan Alexander and Marsha Tate, Wolfgram Memorial Library, Widener University
http://www.science.widener.edu/ ~ withers/wbstrbib.htm

Summary

The World Wide Web gives us access to a great variety of information on many different topics. When we want to use the information or resources we find on the Web for information or research purposes, we need to exercise some care to be sure it's authentic, reliable, and authoritative. We need to be equally cautious when we use information from other sources.

Print sources that are available to us through a research or academic library have often been put through a screening process by professional librarians. There are several virtual libraries on the Web, and it's useful to consult some of these libraries when doing research. Information in such libraries tends to be evaluated before it's listed. Plus, by consulting these libraries, we can also observe how librarians and other information specialists evaluate resources.

It pays to be skeptical or critical of information we want to use. It's relatively easy to publish information on the Web, and it can be presented in such a way as to hide its intent or purpose. Generally, as we evaluate documents, we also learn more about the topic we're considering. Assessing resources, then, makes us more confident of the information and helps us become better versed in the topic.

We need to use some general guidelines or criteria when evaluating information or resources. In this vein, we should ask the following questions about whatever information we find:

- Who is the author or institution?
- How current is the information?
- Who is the audience?
- Is the content accurate and objective?
- What is the purpose of the information?

Various strategies will help us find answers to the questions. Here are some of those tips:

- Look for the name of the author or institution at the top or bottom of a Web page.
- Go to the home page for the site hosting the information to find out about the organization.
- To find further information about the institution or author, use a search engine to see what related information is available on the Web.
- Use Deja News or another tool to search archives of Usenet articles. This way, you can find other information about the author or institution. If an individual has written the article, you can see what other articles they've posted on Usenet.
- Check the top and bottom of a Web page for the date on which the information was last modified or updated. If no date is present, look at Document Info if you're using Netscape, or Properties if you're using Microsoft Internet Explorer.

There are a number of Web resources that can help us evaluate information and that discuss issues related to assessing documents.

13
Chapter

Citing Web and Internet Resources

It's necessary to cite your sources when you write a research report. That way, others who read your work can check the resources you've used. They can view or read the original sources to check for accuracy, to see excerpts or ideas in the context of the original piece, or to obtain more information. You'll also want to cite resources to let people know where they can find information on the Internet or the Web, whether you're preparing a formal research paper or writing email to a friend.

There are several guidelines and styles for citing works correctly. No one uniform style has been adopted or is appropriate in every case. The same situation exists for citing works that appear in print; you may be expected to follow APA or MLA style, for instance. You need to adopt a style for your own work and communications, and you should check with whoever is directing the research—your editor, instructor, or publisher—to see what citation style is required.

In the last few years, people have been citing resources that they find on the Web or through the Internet. The styles used for citing electronic works sometimes differ from those of citations for printed works, which have a long tradition of specific formats. Citations for works in print or on the Web have a number of common elements. These include the author's name, the work's title, and the date on which the cited work was published or revised.

In this chapter, we'll discuss the formats for different types of URLs and suggest citation styles for various resources. Specifically, this chapter will contain the following sections:
    * URL Formats
    * Styles for Citing Web Resources
    * Information on the Web About Citing Electronic Resources

Unlike citations for printed works, a citation for a Web or Internet resource must have information about how to access it. That's often indicated through the work's URL (Uniform Resource Locator). In addition to telling you where to access a work, a URL serves to retrieve the work. For that reason, we have to be precise about all the symbols in the URL and about capitalization.

There are other differences as well. Works that appear in print—such as books, essays, articles, or songs—have a definite publication date associated with them. Documents on the Web sometimes include information about when they were first created or last revised, but not always. Add to that the fact that authors can revise work on the Web at any time. It may therefore be more important to cite the date on which a work was viewed or retrieved.

URL Formats

Everything on the Web has a URL, indicating where something is located and how to access it. We've seen lots of URLs throughout this text. Here are some examples:

http://www.loc.gov	The home page for The Library of Congress
http://vlib.stanford.edu/ Overview.html	The World Wide Web Virtual Library arranged by subject
http://home.netscape.com/ escapes/search	The Web page you see when you click on **Search** in the Netscape command toolbar
ftp://ftp.jpl.nasa.gov/pub/ images/browse	The NASA Jet Propulsion Laboratory's directory of image files from JPL space missions

You'll find it helpful to think of a URL as having the following form:

how-to-get-there://where-to-go/what-to-get

You probably already know some ways in which URLs are used. For example, all hyperlinks on Web pages are represented as URLs. Entries in bookmark and history files are stored as URLs. You type in a URL when you want to direct your browser to go to a specific Web page. When you cite a resource on the World Wide Web, you include its URL. You'll also want to include the URL when you're telling someone else about a resource, such as in an email message. Here's an example:

> If you haven't already seen this fabulous page, you must
> look at it. It's called "A Business Researcher's Interests"
> and is hosted by @BRINT. The URL is:
> **http://www.brint.com/interest.html**
> It's one of the best subject guides I've ever used.

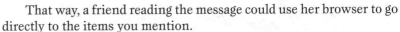

That way, a friend reading the message could use her browser to go directly to the items you mention.

By providing the name of a Web server and the name of a file or directory holding certain information, a URL tells you how to retrieve the information; from the URL alone, you know which Internet protocol to use when retrieving the information and where it's located. If only a server name is present, as in **http://www.loc.gov**, then a file will still be retrieved. Web servers are configured to pass along a certain file (usually named **index.html** or **index.htm**) when the URL contains only the name of the server or only the name of a directory. Table 13.1 lists different types of URLs that you're likely to use when citing resources from the World Wide Web. The URLs are arranged by Internet protocol.

Resource or Service	Beginning of URL	Example	Description
Web page	**http://**	**http://nmaa-ryder.si. edu/artdir/treasures. html**	Selections from the permanent collection of the National Museum of American Art
FTP	**ftp://**	**ftp://ftp.jpl.nasa. gov/pub/images/ browse**	A directory of images from NASA Jet Propulsion Laboratory's public information FTP archive
Gopher	**gopher://**	**gopher://wiretap. spies.com**	Internet Wiretap

Table 13.1—Types of URLs Arranged by Protocol

It's important to be precise when you write URLs, because a Web browser uses the URL to access something and bring it to your computer. More specifically, the browser sends a request extracted from the information in the URL to a Web server. Remember, we're talking about having one computer communicate with another; as amazing as some computer systems are, they generally need very precise instructions. Therefore, you have to be careful about spaces (generally there aren't blanks in a URL), symbols (interchanging a slash and a period won't give appropriate results), and capitalization.

Here's an example. In Chapter 12 we examined the Web page called "Tools For Teaching: The World Wide Web and a Web Browser," with the URL **http://www.mwc.edu/ ~ ernie/facacad/WWW-Teaching. html**. Replacing the uppercase T in Teaching with a lowercase t and writing the URL as **http://www.mwc.edu/ ~ ernie/facacad/ WWW-teaching.html** will cause the browser to give the following response:

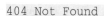
```
404 Not Found

The requested URL /~ernie/facacad/WWW-teaching.html
was not found on this server.
```

That tells us that the name of the Web server, **www.mwc.edu**, was correct but that there was something wrong with the rest of the URL.

Styles for Citing Web Resources

When you're looking for the proper way to cite resources in a report or research paper, you must first see if there is a required or accepted citation style. If you're preparing a report or paper for a class, then check with your instructor. If you're writing for a journal, periodical, or some other publication (either in print or electronic form), then see if the editor or publisher has guidelines.

Proper format for citations from printed sources is very well established. Two commonly used formats are APA (American Psychological Association) style and MLA (Modern Language Association) style. Each of these organizations publishes a handbook or publication guide. At the time of this writing, however, only the MLA has adopted a style that completely addresses citations for electronically printed works. To see the MLA style guidelines go to the Web page "MLA Style," **http://www.mla.org/main_stl.htm**.

There are a number of issues involved in citing Web or Internet resources. For instance, they may be updated or modified at any time, they may not have a title or major heading, and they don't have page numbers. Thoughtful people have been working to expand existing standards. There are several very good guides to specific citation styles for electronic resources, and some are listed in the section "Information on the Web About Citing Electronic Sources" in this chapter. A few books have been published on the topic; the Internet Public Library has a short list in the books section of its Web page "Citing Electronic Resources," **http://www.ipl.org/ref/QUE/FARQ/netciteFARQ.html#books**. One of the first books written on this subject (it's been revised since it was first published) is *Electronic Styles: A Handbook for Citing Electronic Information,* Xia Li and Nancy Crane, Information Today, 1996. There is an accompanying Web site at **http://www.uvm.edu/ ~ xli/ reference/espub.html**. Another is *Online! A Reference Guide to Using Internet Sources,* Andrew Harnack and Eugene Kleppinger, St. Martin's Press, Inc., 1998; there is an accompanying Web site at **http:// www.smpcollege.com/online-4styles ~ help**.

There are some differences of opinion about the format of citations for Web and Internet items. Some say to include a URL in angle brackets (< >), and others do not. Some people advise including the place of publication if the Web resource is a copy of a printed work. Several say to put the date of last revision and to place in parentheses the date on

Chapter 13

which you accessed the document, whereas others do not make this recommendation. There is, however, considerable agreement on the basic information to be included in a citation to a Web resource. We need to remember that the World Wide Web is a relatively new concept, and an even newer resource for researchers and other scholars. It's reasonable to expect some differences in style.

 Tip

When you have specific questions about citing Internet and Web sources, check some of the Web resources listed in this chapter, and be sure to check with whoever is going to be evaluating or editing your work.

You'll see that the guidelines for citations or references to Web or Internet resources all contain two dates: the date of publication or revision and the date of last access. The reason we need both dates has to do with the nature of digital media as it's made available or published on the Web. Works in print form are different from digital works; printed documents have a tangible, physical form. We all know we can pick up and feel a magazine or journal in our hands, or we can use a book or periodical as a pillow. It's pretty hard to do that with a Web page! This tangible nature of a printed work also gives an edition or revision a certain permanent nature. It's usually possible to assign a date of publication to a work, and if there are revisions or different editions of a work, it's possible to date and look at the revisions. If a new edition of a printed work exists, it doesn't mean that older editions or versions were destroyed.

The situation is different for Web documents and other items in digital form on the Internet, for several reasons. They don't have a tangible form. It's relatively easy for an author to publish a work (the work usually only needs to be in a certain directory on a computer that functions as a Web server). It's easy to modify or revise a work. Furthermore, when a work is revised, the previous version is often replaced by or overwritten with the new version. Because of this last point, the most recent version may be the only one that exists. The version you cited might not exist anymore. It is therefore necessary to include the date you accessed or read a work listed in a citation or reference. You may also want to keep a copy of the document in a file (save it while browsing) or print a copy of it to provide as documentation if someone questions your sources.

In some cases the first date of publication or posting on the Internet (not only the date of last revision) is important as well. A periodical was recently the focus of a $1 billion libel lawsuit. The suit was filed one year to the day after an article appeared in print format. It turns out the article was available online one day earlier than the print version. Since the statute of limitations for libel suits is one year after publication, lawyers for the periodical asked a trial judge to dismiss the case since the suit was brought a day after the article was first published. At the time of this writing, the case is still unresolved.

To find the date a work was last revised, see if the date is mentioned as part of the work. You'll often see a line like

Last modified: Wednesday, January 15, 1998

in a Web document. If a date of last revision isn't included, or if you want to verify the date, you can usually determine when the file holding the document or item was last modified. Here are some ways.

* If you're using Netscape Navigator, click on **View** in the menu bar and select **Page Info**. That will tell you the date on which the file was last modified, as well as the document's title, as shown in Figure 13.1.

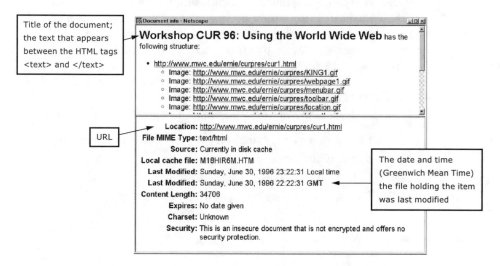

Figure 13.1—Netscape Document Info for a Web Page

* If you're using Microsoft Internet Explorer, with the cursor on the Web page in the browser window, click the right mouse button and select **Properties**. That tells the document's title and the date on which the Web page was viewed. The date after **Updated:** shows when the page was last modified. Note that the date after **Modified:** is not when the source file was last modified, as shown in Figure 13.2.

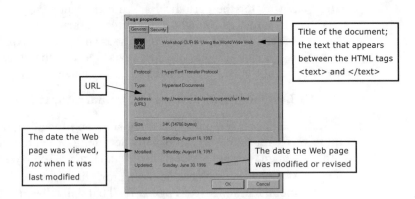

Figure 13.2—Microsoft Internet Explorer Page Properties for a Web Page

Here we'll give some models for citations. These models are meant to include the basic information needed to cite a work so that someone using the citation can access the resource. It would be presumptuous for us to claim to give definitive formats here. We will concentrate on describing ways to find the necessary information for a citation. For simplicity's sake, we won't put angle brackets around URLs and won't put the date of last access in parentheses.

Web Pages

A citation for a Web page contains certain parts in the following order:

- Name of author or authors—if known
- Title of the work—in quotes, if known
- Title of the Web page—in italics, if applicable
- Date of last revision—if known
- URL
- Date accessed

We will now show you how to examine Web pages so that you can identify these citation elements and write citations. Figure 13.3 shows parts of a sample Web page with its citation.

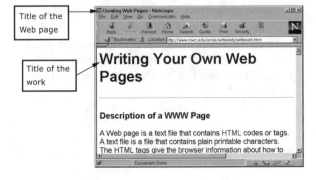

Ackermann, Ernest. "Writing Your Own Web Pages." *Creating Web Pages.*
23 October 1996.
http://www.mwc.edu/ernie/writeweb/writeweb.html
10 February 1998.

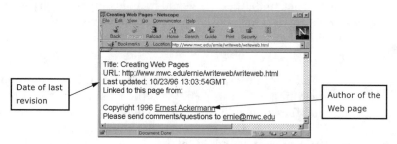

Figure 13.3—A Web Page and Its Citation

In the citation, note that the URL is on a separate line with no period at the end. We do this for clarity; we don't want a reader to think that a period is the last character in the URL. We'll follow this convention for the other formats we give in this chapter. Some authorities require the URL to be surrounded by angle brackets. This method would also clearly set off the characters in the URL.

We looked at the very end of the document to determine the author's name. Not every Web document includes the author's name. If it weren't part of the document, we wouldn't include it.

We found the date of the last revision at the end of the document as well. You could also determine that date by looking at Page Info or Properties, as we mentioned earlier.

We determined the work's title by using the major heading that appeared when we viewed the document with a browser. The Web page title, cited in italics, comes from the title at the top of the browser window. That's the same title that would show up as a hyperlink in the search results if you had used a search engine. The title is specified in the HTML source for the page and doesn't necessarily show up in the text of the document as you view it with a browser. The following is a portion of the HTML code for the Web page cited above. It's here in case you're curious about how the title of a page is specified.

The exact text of the title of a Web page is surrounded by the tags < TITLE > and < /TITLE > in the HTML source for the page. The source for this page, for example, begins with

```
<HTML>
<HEAD>                          Title of the Web page
<TITLE>Creating Web Pages</TITLE>
</HEAD>
<BODY>                          Title of the work
<P>
<B><H1>Writing Your Own Web Pages</H1></B><HR>
```

If the Web page title is the same as the title of the work—see the Web page with the URL **http://www.mwc.edu/ernie/vas96.html**, for example—then we would include only the work's title, and we would put it in quotes. If there is no apparent title of the work (in other words, no major heading), then we would include only the Web page title, and we would style it in italics. If there is neither a major heading nor a Web page title, then you'll have to come up with some descriptive title.

FTP Resources

FTP stands for File Transfer Protocol. Before World Wide Web browsers came into popular use, FTP was the most popular way to retrieve and send files from one computer to another on the Internet. Anonymous FTP allows people to retrieve files without supplying a secret login name or password. Hundreds of thousands of files on the Web are available by anonymous FTP. It's an efficient and reliable way to transfer files.

Within the context of using a Web browser, you often access a file through anonymous FTP by clicking on its name in a list of file names. You can specify a file that is available by anonymous FTP or an anonymous FTP site by using a URL. For example, the Electronic Frontier Foundation (EFF) makes many files available by anonymous FTP through the system **ftp.eff.org**—here the URL is **ftp://ftp.eff.org**. ACLU Briefing Paper Number 5, "Drug Testing in the Workplace," is accessible using the URL **ftp://ftp.eff.org/pub/Privacy/Medical/aclu_drug_testing_workplace.faq**.

A citation for a file available by anonymous FTP contains certain parts in the following order:

- Name of author or authors—if known
- Title of the work—in quotes, if known
- Date of last revision—if known
- URL
- Date accessed

The work mentioned above would be cited in this way:

American Civil Liberties Union. "ACLU Briefing Paper Number 5, Drug Testing in the Workplace." 19 November 1992.
ftp://ftp.eff.org/pub/Privacy/Medical/aclu_drug_testing_workplace.faq
13 February 1998.

Note that there are periods after each of the items, except for the URL, and that the URL is on a separate line.

If there's no obvious title for a file, as in the case of a file that holds an image, then use the file name as the name of the work. An example is the file that holds an image of Mars, cited in the following way:

"Mars1.gif." 16 January 1995.
ftp://ftp.jpl.nasa.gov/pub/images/browse/mars1.gif
13 May 1998.

Gopher Resources

Two or three years before Web browsers became popular, Gopher was one of the easiest ways to retrieve information and access Internet services. Gopher lets you select items from a menu or list. Each item on a menu could be a file, an Internet service, or a link to another menu. Gopher was very popular because it was easier to navigate through the resources on the Internet with it than with other tools, such as anonymous FTP. Because of its popularity, a great many documents were (and still are) available through Gopher.

You can access Gopher by using a Web browser. The URL for a Gopher resource starts with **gopher://**. For example, the URL for the Gopher server called AskERIC is **gopher://ericir.syr.edu**. AskERIC is the Internet-based education information service of the Educational Resources Information Center (ERIC).

When you cite a resource available by Gopher, as with other forms of citations, you use a URL. These are the items to include when citing a Gopher resource:

- Name of author or authors—if known
- Title of the work—in quotes, if known
- Date of last revision—if known
- URL
- Date accessed

Here's an example:

Shultz, Michael T. "Significant Figures." May 1994.
gopher://ericir.syr.edu:70/00/Lesson/Subject/Math/cecmath.42
15 February 1998.

All items except for the URL are followed by periods.

Email Resources

We'll discuss writing citations for two types of email resources: email sent to an individual and email messages distributed through a discussion group. The main reason for the distinction is that discussion groups usually keep past messages in archives so the message cited can be retrieved.

In either case, a citation will include the following items:

- Name of author
- Subject of the message—in quotes
- Date the message was sent
- Author's email address
- Date accessed

All of these are usually displayed by the software you're using to read email; these are available as standard headers in a message.

We alter this boilerplate format, depending on which type of email message we're citing. These are the items to include in the citation of an email message to an individual:

- Name of author
- Subject of the message—in quotes
- Date the message was sent
- *Type of communication: personal, distribution list, professional*
- Author's email address
- Date accessed

The italicized line represents the only addition to the standard format. Here are some examples of such citations:

Mills, C. "Getting gigs in Nashville." 13 May 1996. Personal.
cc@digicool.com
13 December 1996.

Ackermann, E. "Working on post-tenure review." 02 February 1997.
Distribution list.
ernie@mwc.edu
04 February 1997.

Hartman, K. "Changes in search engines." 13 November 1996. Professional.
khartman@mwcgw.mwc.edu
21 November 1996.

A citation for email that was generated in a discussion group or listserv needs to include the discussion group's address. If the message can be retrieved through an archive, the citation needs to include the URL of the Web page that allows access to the archive. Here are the items included in a citation for an email message distributed through a discussion group:

- Name of author
- Subject of the message—in quotes
- Date the message was sent
- Author's email address
- *Address of discussion group*
- *"via" plus URL of archive—if known*
- Date accessed

Again, the italicized lines represent deviations from the standard format. Here's an example of this sort of citation:

Ackermann, E. "Re: Bookmark files with Netscape 2.0." 7 March 1996.
ernie@mwc.edu
nettrain@ubvm.cc.buffalo.edu
via http://listserv.acsu.buffalo.edu/cgi-bin/wa?S1 = nettrain
14 February 1997.

Usenet Articles

Usenet news consists of a collection of articles, each part of a specific
newsgroup. The articles, like email messages, have headers that will
give us the information we need for the citation. These are the items to
include in the citation of a Usenet article:

- Name of author
- Subject of the message—in quotes
- Name of the newsgroup
- Date the message was sent
- Author's email address
- Date of access

Here's an example:

Ackermann, E. "Question about keeping Bay plant indoors." rec.gardens.
3 December 1995.
ernie@mwc.edu
13 February 1997.

Electronic Journals

In this section, we'll consider electronic journals that are accessible
through a Web browser. Since we can access FTP and Gopher resources
through a Web browser, this includes journals that are accessible by
FTP or Gopher. An article in an electronic journal can be cited very
much like any other WWW resource. If we're making a citation to an
article in a journal, then it's reasonable to include the journal name and
the volume and issue information. If you were citing a resource from a
printed journal, you would also include page numbers, but that does
not apply in this case. The URL gives the location of the article. The
citation, then, will include the following elements:

- Name of author or authors—if known
- Title of the work—in quotes, if known
- Title of the journal, volume number, issue number, and
  date of publication—in italics, if applicable
- Date of last revision—if known and if different from the
  date of publication above
- URL
- Date accessed

Here are two example citations of articles from electronic journals:

Harnack, A., and Kleppinger, G. "Beyond the MLA Handbook: Documenting Electronic Sources on the Internet." *Kairos: 1.2. Summer 1996.* June 11, 1996.
http://english.ttu.edu/kairos/1.2/inbox/mla.html
10 February 1997.

Agre, P. "Designing Genres for New Media: Social, Economic, and Political Contexts." *The Network Observer: 2.11. November 1995.*
http://communication.ucsd.edu/pagre/tno/november-1995.html#designing
14 February 1997.

Information on the Web About Citing Electronic Resources

There are several very good Web pages with information about citing Web and other electronic resources. The following two Web pages have links to several other sources on the subject:

- "Citing Electronic Sources" **http://www.csbsju.edu/library/internet/citing.html**

- "Citing Electronic Resources," Internet Public Library **http://www.ipl.org/ref/QUE/FARQ/netciteFARQ.html**

The Web pages in this list contain information about specific styles for citations:

- "Bibliographic Formats for Citing Electronic Information," Xia Li and Nancy Crane
  http://www.uvm.edu/ ~ ncrane/estyles

- "MLA Style," Modern Language Association of America
  http://www.mla.org/main_stl.htm

- "CITING INTERNET - APA Style," Maryann Readal and Susan Goodwin
  http://www.nhmccd.cc.tx.us/contracts/lrc/kc/CitingElecSources-apa.html

- "MLA Electronic Citation Examples—Internet/Westlaw," Peggy Whitley
  http://www.nhmccd.cc.tx.us/groups/lrc/kc/mla-internet.html

- "The Columbia Guide to Online Style: MLA-Style Citations of Electronic Sources," Janice R. Walker
  http://www.cas.usf.edu/english/walker/mla.html

These two Web pages contain good, thoughtful discussions about citing work from Web or other electronic sources:

* "Citing Electronic Information in History Papers," Maurice Crouse
  http://www.people.memphis.edu/ ~ mcrouse/ elcite.html

* "Electronic Style—What's Here," George H. Hoemann
  http://funnelweb.utcc.utk.edu/ ~ hoemann/whats.html

Summary

Citing references or writing a bibliography is usually part of creating a research report. You provide citations so others may check or examine the resources used in the report. There are several agreed-upon styles for citing documents in print format. With the use of resources from the Web or the Internet, it becomes necessary to have a uniform format for citing these resources. This chapter presents a set of formats for documenting or citing information obtained from the Web or the Internet.

Citations to documents and other information found on the Web or the Internet always include the URL, or Uniform Resource Locator. A URL includes the names of the Web server and the file or directory holding the information. The URL therefore tells you which Internet protocol to use to retrieve the information and where it's located. You need to be precise in terms of spelling and capitalization when writing a URL, as a computer will be interpreting it. We listed URL formats for common Web or Internet services.

There is no uniform agreement on how to cite information from the Web or Internet. Most suggest that a citation include the author's name, the work's title, the date the information was last revised, the date the information was accessed, and the URL. The date of access is included because it's relatively easy to modify information on the Web and the information may not always be the same as when it was accessed for research. We discussed methods for determining the date of access and the title of a Web document.

The chapter concluded with a list of Web resources that provide more information about citing sources and some suggestions for specific formats.

14
Chapter

Putting It All Together:
Two Sample Research Projects

In this chapter, we will bring together most of the important skills introduced in this book. We'll accomplish this by doing two separate projects. The first one involves using several different types of search tools to research a broad topic that we'll narrow as we go along. The second project is also broad, but it is much more focused from the outset; we know what we need to find, and we'll look for it using an approach and resources that we won't have used in the first project.

We'll go through the following major steps involved in using the World Wide Web for research:
* Search a Directory to Find Resources
* Find and Search a Specialized Database
* Formulate and Submit a Search Query to a Search Engine
* Locate and Search a Library Catalog
* Search a Usenet Archive
* Evaluate the Resources Found
* Cite the Sources in a Bibliography

Project 1—Finding Resources for a Research Paper

In the first project, we'll research the topic of women in computing. This topic is fairly broad. Although we aren't sure exactly what we want to focus on, we do want to know why there are so few women in this field. We'll start by looking at the topic broadly, and we'll narrow the focus as we go along. We may end up choosing a particular aspect of the topic that we didn't know about beforehand.

We'll go through the following major steps:

A. Search a directory to find resources.
B. Find and search a specialized database.
C. Formulate and submit a search query to a search engine.
D. Locate and search a library catalog.
E. Search a Usenet archive.
F. Evaluate the resources found.
G. Cite the sources in a bibliography.

 Tip

Remember that the Web is always changing and that your results may differ from those shown here. Don't let this confuse you. The activities are meant to demonstrate fundamental skills. These skills don't change, even though the number of results obtained or the actual screens may look very different.

Activity 1-A   Search a Directory to Find Resources

Overview

Before starting this section, you may want to review Chapter 4. We'll need to find a subject guide for the topic. A subject guide lists several types of resources on a topic and can thereby provide an overview of the subject. The best place to obtain a subject guide is a directory or virtual library. In this project, we'll use a directory. Let's try one of the most comprehensive directories on the Web—Yahoo! Why? Because Yahoo! is so large, it is likely to have some Web pages on women in computing.

Follow these steps:

1. Go to the home page for Yahoo!
2. Search Yahoo! for the concept *women and computing.*
3. Follow hyperlinks that appear to be helpful.
4. Bookmark a useful Web page.

Details

1   Go to the home page for Yahoo!

Do It! Click on the location field, type **http://www.yahoo.com**, and press **Enter**.

Chapter 14

2   Search Yahoo! for the concept *women and computing*.

You should be on Yahoo!'s home page.

Since we're going to do a keyword search, let's see what our options are.

Do It! Click on **options**, located next to the **Search** button on Yahoo!'s home page.

Do It! Under **Select a search method**, select **Matches on all words (AND)**.

Do It! Click on the circle next to **Web Sites**.

Do It! Type **women computing** in the search form and click on **Search**.

Your screen should look like the one in Figure 14.1.

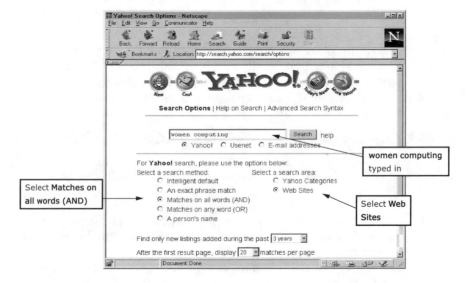

Figure 14.1—Yahoo! Search Options Page

You could also get the same results by typing **women and computing** in the search query box on Yahoo!'s home page.

3   Follow hyperlinks that appear to be helpful.

The search results should appear, as in Figure 14.2. Scroll down until you find some Web pages that look interesting. There are several hyperlinks to investigate. Several Web pages do not turn out to be relevant. **Women and Computing** looks more promising.

Do It! Click on **Women and Computing**, as shown in Figure 14.2.

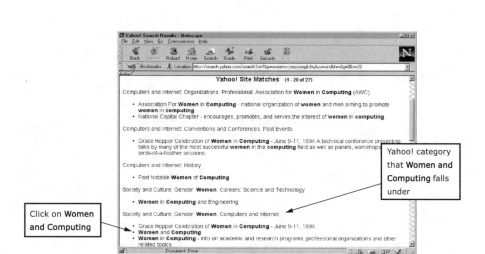

Yahoo! category that **Women and Computing** falls under

Click on **Women and Computing**

Figure 14.2—Women and Computing Search Results in Yahoo!

Figure 14.3 shows a portion of the Web site that appears. "Women and Computing" is a subject guide and information page put out by CPSR. By scrolling to the bottom of the page and clicking on **CPSR Home Page**, we find out that *CPSR* stands for Computer Professionals for Social Responsibility. The page has a collection of hyperlinks, called Gender Pages Index, on the topic of women in computer science, engineering, and related technical fields. Let's open the first Gender Page listed.

❋*Do It!* Click on **General Resources for Women**, as shown in Figure 14.3.

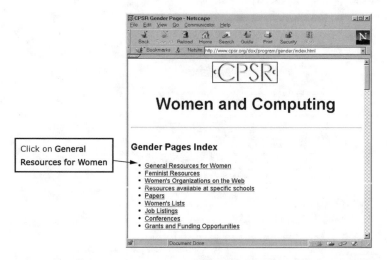

Click on **General Resources for Women**

Figure 14.3—CPSR's "Women and Computing" Page

The page that comes up appears in Figure 14.4 with the heading "General Resources for Women."

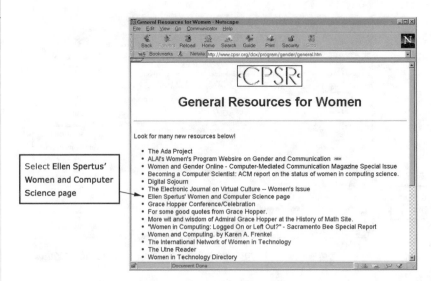

Select **Ellen Spertus'
Women and Computer
Science page**

Figure 14.4—CPSR's List of General Resources for Women

We could try many of the hyperlinks listed under this heading. Let's try
Ellen Spertus' Women and Computer Science page.

❋*Do It!* Click on **Ellen Spertus' Women and Computer Science
page**.

A portion of this page appears in Figure 14.5. "Women and Computer
Science" is a subject guide with links to journal articles, associations,
and other types of resources covering the subject of women and computer science.

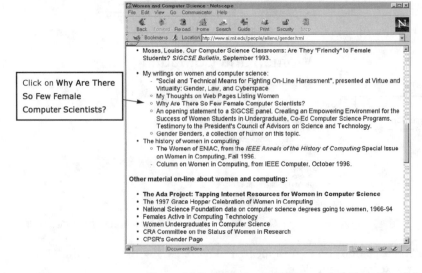

Click on **Why Are There
So Few Female
Computer Scientists?**

Figure 14.5—Ellen Spertus' Women and Computer Science Page

Notice in Figure 14.5 that Ms. Spertus has listed several hyperlinks to her own writings. The article "Why Are There So Few Female Computer Scientists?" appears to be exactly what we want.

✸*Do It!* Click on **Why Are There So Few Female Computer Scientists?**

An abstract of this article appears in Figure 14.6.

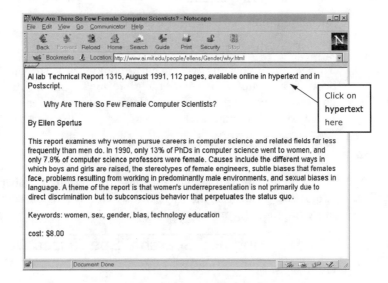

Figure 14.6—Abstract of the Article

The next step is to find out something about the author. You'll need to find a hyperlink that takes you to biographical information. In this example, you'll need to go back to the list of Ellen Spertus' writings that appears in Figure 14.5.

✸*Do It!* Click on the **Back** icon in the toolbar.

✸*Do It!* Now click on the hyperlink **Creating an Empowering Environment for the Success of Women Students in Undergraduate, Co-Ed Computer Science Programs**.

An essay should appear on your screen with the hyperlink **Ellen Spertus**.

✸*Do It!* Click on **Ellen Spertus**.

We find out from reading Ms. Spertus' home page that she obtained her Ph.D. in electrical engineering and computer science from MIT in 1997, and that she won an award for this article in 1991. By knowing something about the author, you can better evaluate the quality of the information.

Chapter 14

❈*Do It!* Return to the abstract of "Why Are There So Few Female Computer Scientists?" by clicking **Back** on the toolbar twice, and then clicking on its hyperlink again.

Although the abstract provides useful information, we may want to read the entire article. We can do this by clicking on the word **hypertext**, as shown in Figure 14.6.

❈*Do It!* Click on **hypertext**.

You should now have the entire article.

4 Bookmark a useful Web page.

To save this hyperlink, you need to bookmark it so you'll be able to access it at a later time. (After the project is finished, you may want to go back and delete the bookmark. Refer to Chapter 2 for instructions on how to delete bookmarks.)

❈*Do It!* Point to **Bookmarks** in the location toolbar and click. Point to **Add Bookmark** and click.

If you were doing an actual research project, you'd probably want to explore all or most of the hyperlinks that have appeared so far. We'll move on, though, and try to find a journal article on the topic.

Activity 1-B Find and Search a Specialized Database

Overview

We're looking for a database that indexes journal articles. As we discussed in Chapter 7, one of the best sources for such databases is the Internet Sleuth. We'll use the Internet Sleuth to find a journal article database, and then we'll search it, following these steps:
1. Go to the home page for the Internet Sleuth.
2. Use the Internet Sleuth's directory to find a database that indexes journal articles.
3. Go to the CMP Technology Database.
4. Search for the keywords *women AND computer.*
5. Bookmark an article.

Details

1 Go to the home page for the Internet Sleuth.

❈*Do It!* Click on the location field, type **http://www.isleuth.com**, and press **Enter**.

You should now be at the Internet Sleuth, as shown in Figure 14.7.

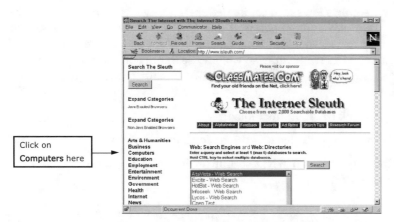

Figure 14.7—The Internet Sleuth

2   Use the Internet Sleuth's directory to find a database that indexes journal articles.

The Internet Sleuth's directory is on the left side of the screen. Of the major subject headings, we could look under **Women** (a subheading of **Society**) and **Computers**.

❉*Do It!* Scroll down until you find **Society**. Click on it. Then click on **Women**.

Scroll down the list of databases. Although there are several databases listed that may provide useful information, none of them specifically mentions indexing journal articles. Let's try **Computers**.

❉*Do It!* Locate **Computers** in the directory and click on it.

3   Go to the CMP Technology Database.

Scroll down the list of databases until you see **CMP Technology Database**. This database consists of more than 100,000 articles. We could search the database from the Internet Sleuth or we could click on its hyperlink and search the database directly. For this exercise, we'll search it directly.

❉*Do It!* Click on **CMP Technology Database**.

4   Search for the concept *women AND computer*.

The first thing to do in any database is to find out what search techniques are used.

❉*Do It!* Click on **Search Help**.

From the help page, we learn that the CMP Technology Database's searchable index, called TechSearch, supports some simple search features, including the ability to AND words together. Although it's not explicitly mentioned, it appears that AND should be capitalized, since the example shows it in capital letters. Since we want articles with the words *women* and *computers* or *computer science,* we need to search the word *computer* by itself. There is no mention about whether the database supports truncation, so we'll try searching on the singular form of *computer* and see if the database automatically truncates the word for us.

❋*Do It!* Click **Back** on the toolbar.

You should now be back at the screen shown in Figure 14.8.

❋*Do It!* Type **women AND computer** in the search form, and click on **Search**.

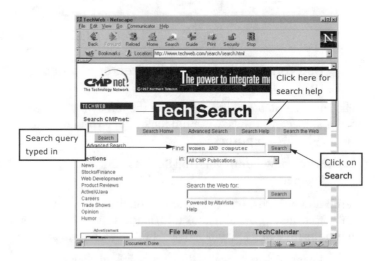

Figure 14.8—Query women AND computer—*CMP Technology Database*

Several article titles will appear. Part of this list appears in Figure 14.9.

Figure 14.9—Journal Article Titles Found in CMP Technology Database

🏵*Do It!* Scroll down the list until you see **Introducing girls to high-tech careers is 'Awsem'**. You'll need to go through several pages. Let's read the article.

🏵*Do It!* Click on **Introducing girls to high-tech careers is 'Awsem'**.

The full text of the article appears and is partially shown in Figure 14.10.

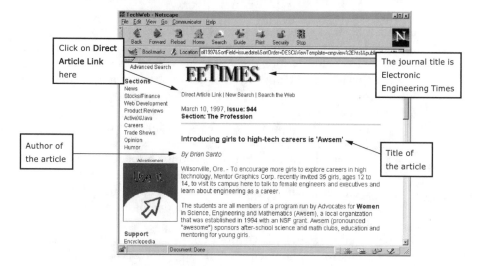

Figure 14.10—Full Text of an Article Found in CMP Technology Database

5   Bookmark an article.

This seems to be a useful journal article. Let's bookmark it for later use. Since the primary reason we're bookmarking items we find is so we can show how to cite these resources in a bibliography, you may want to save this article with a shorter URL that is easier to deal with. This database allows this by providing a *Direct Article Link*. Let's try it.

🏵*Do It!* Click on **Direct Article Link**, as shown in Figure 14.10.

🏵*Do It!* Click on the URL that's provided.

Your screen should fill with the same article but with a different URL. Now we're ready to bookmark it.

🏵*Do It!* Point to **Bookmarks** in the location toolbar and click.

🏵*Do It!* Point to **Add Bookmark** and click.

Several other articles in the list look like they'd be appropriate. If this were an actual project, you would read them. After reading a few articles, you may be ready to formulate a search request and submit it to a search engine database.

Chapter 14

Formulate and Submit a Search Query to a Search Engine

Overview

Before working on this section, you may want to go back and review Chapter 5. If you typed **women in computing** in a full-text search engine, you could easily get several thousand hits. With a few other keywords and a more pointed search, you can narrow the search considerably and retrieve more relevant results. In terms of the given topic, you may want to focus your research on how gender bias has affected career choices for women starting when they were schoolgirls.

For this part of the project, we'll use the basic search strategy that we introduced in Chapter 5. We'll follow the first nine of the 10 steps. These are the steps to take:

1. Identify the important concepts of your search.
2. Choose the keywords that describe these concepts.
3. Determine whether there are synonyms, related terms, or other variations of the keywords that should be included.
4. Determine which search features may apply, including truncation, proximity operators, Boolean operators, and so forth.
5. Choose a search engine.
6. Read the search instructions on the search engine's home page. Look for sections entitled "Help," "Advanced Search," "Frequently Asked Questions," and so forth.
7. Create a search expression using syntax that is appropriate for the search engine.
8. View the results. How many hits were returned? Were the results relevant to your query?
9. Modify your search if needed.

Details

1 Identify the important concepts of your search.

We want to focus on the gender bias and stereotypes in our society that seem to thwart girls' abilities to study engineering and computer science later in life.

2 Choose the keywords that describe these concepts.

The main terms or keywords are *girls, gender, bias, stereotypes,* and *computer science.*

3 Determine whether there are synonyms, related terms, or other variations of the keywords that should be included.

Synonyms for girls: women, female.

Synonyms for computer science: computing, computers, engineering.

4 **Determine which search features may apply, including truncation, proximity operators, Boolean operators, and so forth.**

Synonyms are connected by OR because any of the keywords are acceptable in the results. *Computer science* should be searched as a phrase, and *stereotypes* should be truncated so that alternative endings to the word will appear in the search results as well. This is one example of how this search could be worked out:

- girls **OR** women **OR** female
  AND
- gender
  AND
- bias
  AND
- "computer science" **OR** comput* (truncating this will get computers and computing) **OR** engineering
  AND
- stereotyp* (to retrieve stereotypes, stereotypical, stereotyping, and so forth)

5 **Choose a search engine.**

We require a search engine that supports Boolean searching (both simple and nested), truncation, and phrase searching, so we'll use AltaVista.

❋*Do It!* Click on the location field, type **http://www.altavista.digital. com**, and press **Enter**.

6 **Read the search instructions on the search engine's home page. Look for sections entitled "Help," "Advanced Search," "Frequently Asked Questions," and so forth.**

Since our search requires the nested Boolean search feature, we'll have to use AltaVista's advanced mode. The advanced mode also provides a big search query box that makes it easier to type a multifaceted search query. To refresh your memory about how AltaVista's advanced searching works, we'll look at the search instructions.

❋*Do It!* Click on the **Advanced** button.

Your screen will fill with the advanced search form.

❋*Do It!* Click on the **help** button.

Read the instructions.

7 Create a search expression using syntax that is appropriate for the search engine.

Now that you've familiarized yourself with the search features, we're ready to formulate the search expression. Here is one way to express this search:

(girls or women or female) and gender and bias and ("computer science" or comput* or engineering) and stereotyp*

You can always modify your search at a later time. Let's see what Web pages this search expression retrieves.

❋*Do It!* Click on **Back** to return to the advanced search page.

❋*Do It!* Type the search expression in the box provided, as shown in Figure 14.11.

Make sure all of the parentheses are closed properly and that you spell the words correctly.

❋*Do It!* In the ranking field, type **girls**.

❋*Do It!* Click on **Search**.

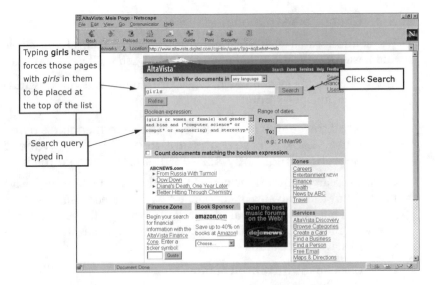

Figure 14.11—Search Query Entered in AltaVista's Advanced Search Mode

8 View the results. How many hits were returned? Were the results relevant to your query?

The results appear to be relevant to the query we entered, as shown in Figure 14.12.

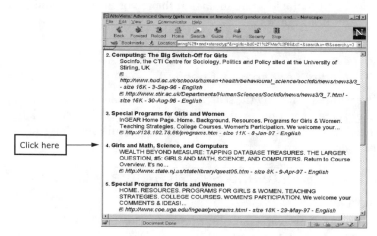

Figure 14.12—Prominent Search Results in AltaVista

Let's open a Web page to see how useful it may be.

✿*Do It!* Click on **Girls and Math, Science, and Computers**, as shown in Figure 14.12.

Part of this page appears in Figure 14.13.

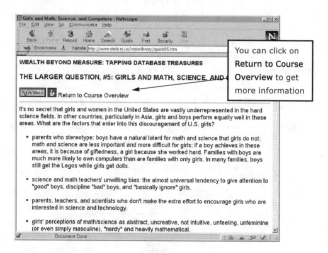

Figure 14.13—Girls and Math, Science, and Computers

The New Jersey State Library published this page as part of a course designed for school library media specialists. How do we know this? When we click on **Return to Course Overview**, as shown in Figure 14.13, we find a course description and the name and biographical information of the person who created it.

This page will help our research, so we'll want to bookmark it for later use.

❈*Do It!* Point to the location toolbar at the top of the screen and click on **Bookmarks**.

❈*Do It!* Point to **Add Bookmark** and click.

9   Modify your search if needed.

If we wanted to modify the search results, we could go back to the search query screen and type in another keyword. We could also click on **Refine**. AltaVista would provide keywords. We could add those keywords and redo the search.

Activity 1-D   **Locate and Search a Library Catalog**

Overview

For this section, you may want to review Chapter 8. We'll find a Web-based library catalog and look for books about women in computing. Specifically, we want books on the gender bias against girls, as that seems to be one of the main reasons that more women don't go into computer and engineering fields. In order to obtain the largest number of books on this topic, we'll want to search a sizable library catalog, specifically one from a large research university. We'll follow these steps:

1. Open the location for webCATS.
2. Find a large university library catalog.
3. Search the ALADIN catalog for *women* and *computer science*.
4. Browse the list.
5. Email a record that appears to be useful.

Details

1   Open the location for webCATS.

❈*Do It!* Click on the location field, type **http://www.lights.com/webcats**, and press **Enter**.

You should be at the webCATS home page, as in Figure 14.14.

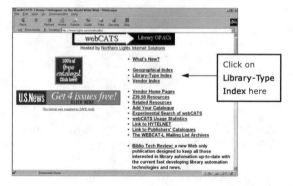

Figure 14.14—webCATS's Home Page

2   Find a large university library catalog.

To find a university library catalog, we first need to open the Library-Type Index.

❀*Do It!* Click on **Library-Type Index**, as shown in Figure 14.14.

The screen will fill with different categories. You want to select the category for college and university libraries.

❀*Do It!* Click on **College and University**.

The screen will fill with the names of hundreds of colleges and universities with Web-based library catalogs. Scroll down until you come to George Washington University.

❀*Do It!* Click on **George Washington University (Washington, D.C.) (via ALADIN)**, as shown in Figure 14.15.

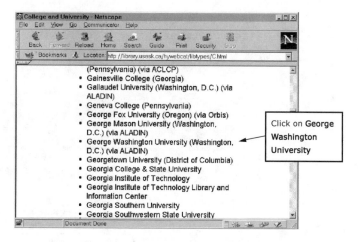

Figure 14.15—Partial Listing of College and University Libraries in webCATS

Your screen should look like the one in Figure 14.16.

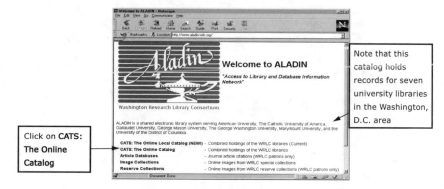

Figure 14.16—The ALADIN Catalog: Washington Research Library Consortium

Chapter 14

3 Search the ALADIN catalog for *women* and *computer science*.

Note that the ALADIN catalog holds library records for seven university libraries in and around Washington, D.C. Of the choices offered in Figure 14.16, you want to search the online catalog.

✸*Do It!* Click on **CATS: The Online Catalog**.

You may get a screen with some text that explains the changes that are being made to this catalog. If you get this screen, simply click on **continue**.

You will now be at the ALADIN database search query screen, which appears in Figure 14.17. Since we aren't sure which subject headings are attached to books on this subject, it's a good idea to start with a keyword search. Make sure **Keyword(s)** is selected, as shown in Figure 14.17.

✸*Do It!* Type **women computer science** in the box under **Enter search word(s) or phrase**.

✸*Do It!* Click on **Begin Search**.

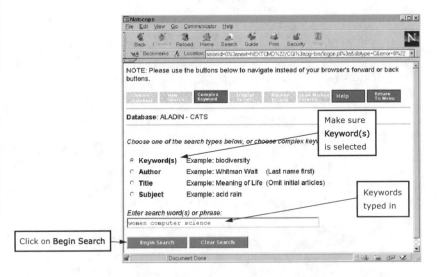

*Figure 14.17—Keywords **women computer science** Entered in ALADIN Form*

4 Browse the list.

Partial search results are listed in Figure 14.18.

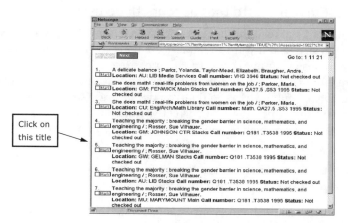

Figure 14.18—Results of Keyword Search in ALADIN

On the first page, a title that looks particularly useful is **Teaching the majority: breaking the gender barrier in science, mathematics, and engineering**. Note that a few copies of this book are listed. They are in different libraries. Next to **Location**, letters indicate which library holds the books. For example, GW is George Washington University, GM is George Mason University, and so forth.

To read a full description of this book, we need to click on its title.

✳️*Do It!* Click on **Teaching the majority: breaking the gender barrier in science, mathematics, and engineering**.

Figure 14.19 shows some of the descriptive information that has been included in this database for this book, which is a collection of several authors' writings on gender and the teaching of mathematics and other sciences. The contents section lists all the chapter titles and chapter authors. By reading the chapter titles, you can determine whether the book covers the type of information you're seeking. This book in particular seems to have some useful information.

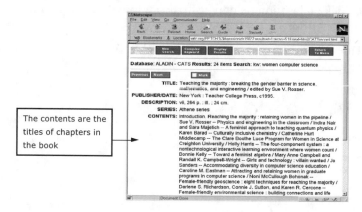

Figure 14.19—Detailed Information About the Book's Contents

5   Email a record that appears to be useful.

If you'd like to read this book, you'll need to see if your library owns it. If it doesn't, you'll want to request the book through interlibrary loan or purchase your own copy. In either case, you'll need to document accurate information about the book, including the author, title, publisher, and date of publication. So that you don't forget something important or write something down incorrectly, you could bookmark the record or email it to yourself. To email the record to yourself, you'll need to go back to the previous screen and follow these steps:

❋*Do It!* Click on **Mark** next to the record, then click on **Show Marked Records** at the top of the screen.

❋*Do It!* Click **E-mail**, type your email address in the space provided, and click on **Submit**.

Activity 1-E   **Search a Usenet Archive**

Overview

Now we're ready to find out what other people have to say informally about women in computing. The best way to find out what's being discussed is to search a Usenet or email discussion group archive. For this project, we'll use Deja News, a search service that specializes in searching newsgroup articles. You may want to refer to Chapter 11 for more in-depth information about searching Deja News. This section will cover the process very briefly.

We'll follow these steps:
1. Open the location for Deja News.
2. Search for articles using the keywords *girls computers technology.*
3. Browse the results and bookmark an article.

Details

1   Open the location for Deja News.

❋*Do It!* Click on location field, type **http://www.dejanews.com**, and press Enter.

The Deja News home page with the search terms entered appears in Figure 14.20.

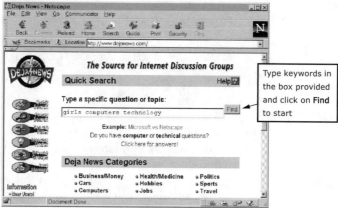

Figure 14.20—Deja News's Home Page with Keywords Entered

2   Search for articles using the keywords *girls computers technology*.

❋*Do It!*   In the search form provided, type the following keywords, as shown in Figure 14.20: **girls computers technology**, and click on **Find**.

We want each of these words to appear in the articles. By clicking on **Help** at the top of the Deja News home page, and then clicking on the hyperlink **New Users**, you'll see some search examples to help you understand how Deja News works.

3   Browse the results and bookmark an article.

Figure 14.21 shows the search results, which list several articles. We've chosen not to show the authors' entire email addresses for privacy reasons.

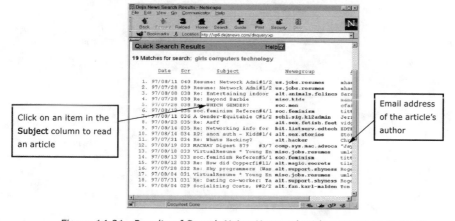

Figure 14.21—Results of Search Using Keywords girls computers technology

❋*Do It!* Browse the list and click on any articles that look interesting.

❋*Do It!* Bookmark an article of your choice.

Activity 1-F   Evaluate the Resources Found

Overview

We've gone through the most important research skills, and we've collected some Web pages that appear to be useful. Now it's time to go back to the pages we bookmarked and look at them again. We'll evaluate their usefulness to our research and determine whether they are worthy of our project. You may want to refer to Chapter 12 before doing this activity. We've bookmarked four references in this exercise. If this were an actual research project, you'd want to read and evaluate each Web page carefully before citing it in your bibliography. To save space, we'll take one of the resources and run it through the evaluation criteria introduced in Chapter 12. We'll follow these steps:

1. Go to your bookmark list and select "Why Are There So Few Female Computer Scientists?"
2. Evaluate this resource using the evaluation guidelines.

Details

1   Go to your bookmark list and select "Why Are There So Few Female Computer Scientists?"

❋*Do It!* Point to the location toolbar and click on **Bookmarks**.

❋*Do It!* Drag the mouse down until you come to **Why Are There So Few Female Computer Scientists?** Click on the title.

Figure 14.22 shows the Web page that appears.

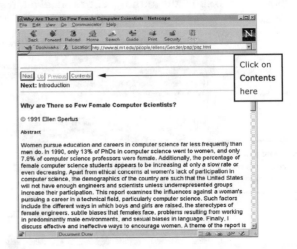

Figure 14.22—Why Are There so Few Female Computer Scientists?

Before proceeding any further, scroll down the page pictured in Figure 14.22 and note that this paper is labeled **MIT Artificial Intelligence Laboratory Technical Report 1315**. We can also verify by looking at the URL that the author is affiliated with MIT.

To see the contents of the research paper, you can click on the hyperlink shown in Figure 14.22.

❋*Do It!* Click on **Contents**.

The paper's contents appear in Figure 14.23. These are hyperlinks to all the major parts of the paper.

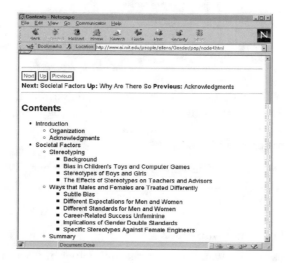

Figure 14.23—Contents of the Research Page

2 Evaluate this resource using the evaluation guidelines.

Now that you have the paper on your computer screen, we'll go through the evaluation guidelines one by one.

Who Is the Author or Institution?

Earlier in the chapter, on page 331, we found out that Ellen Spertus, the paper's author, obtained her Ph.D. in electrical engineering and computer science from MIT in 1997.

How Current Is the Information?

We can note from the page shown in Figure 14.22 that the paper's copyright is 1991.

❋*Do It!* Scroll down the **Contents** page (Figure 14.23) until you find the hyperlink **References**, as shown in Figure 14.24.

❋*Do It!* Click on **References**.

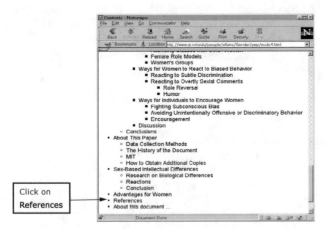

Figure 14.24—A Hyperlink to the References

You'll find that most of the references date from the late 1980s through 1991. When you cite this page in the bibliography, you'll need to state when the page was last updated. To determine this, access the **Page Info** screen in Netscape.

❋*Do It!* Click on **View** in the Netscape menu bar, and choose **Page Info**. This screen will indicate when the page was last modified.

Who Is the Audience?

Because the Web page is a research paper, it is explicitly intended for scholars and educators. As the paper was placed on the Web, we can infer, however, that Ms. Spertus has widened her audience to include students, parents, and anyone else who is interested in this subject.

Is the Content Accurate and Objective?

The author cites others' research in the thesis and gives each author a hyperlink, so you can go directly to the list of references at the end of the paper to the full bibliographic information of the cited author's work. Finding cites to others' research is a good indicator that the material is objective and well documented, not just the writer's opinion.

What Is the Purpose of the Information?

The intention is to document, with actual research, the reasons women are underrepresented in engineering and computer science. Acknowledging that women's underrepresentation in these fields raises ethical concerns, the author also points out that fuller participation from all segments of society would strengthen these fields of study. The paper's major purpose is to educate people about this situation and to offer solutions.

Activity 1-G Cite the Sources in a Bibliography

Overview

Now you'll need to pull all of your resources together and cite them properly in a bibliography, or a *webliography,* as they're sometimes called. Here are the steps to follow:

1. Open your bookmarks.
2. Determine how to cite each resource properly.
3. Assemble the citations in a bibliography.

Details

1 Open your bookmarks.

❋Do It! While in Netscape, click on **Bookmarks** in the location toolbar, and move the pointer to the bookmarks.

❋Do It! Select each bookmark in turn, starting with **Why Are There So Few Female Computer Scientists?**

2 Determine how to cite each resource properly.

We'll use the guidelines from Chapter 13 to cite the resources properly.

Resource: Why Are There So Few Female Computer Scientists?

Type of resource: Web page

- **Name of author:** Spertus, Ellen
- **Title of the work (in quotes):** "Why Are There So Few Female Computer Scientists?" (Since the title of the work and the title of the Web page are the same, we need only the title of the work.)
- **Date of last revision:** 28 January 1995 (To find this, click on **View** in the menu bar and select **Page Info**.)
- **URL:** http://www.ai.mit.edu/people/ellens/Gender/pap/pap.html
- **Date accessed:** 21 April 1997

Resource: TechWeb

Type of resource: Electronic journal

- **Name of author:** Santo, Brian
- **Title of work (in quotes):** "Introducing Girls to High-Tech Careers Is 'Awsem'"
- **Title of the journal, volume, issue, and date (in italics):** *Electronic Engineering Times, March 10, 1997*
- **Date of last revision:** Not available

Chapter 14

✲ **URL:** http://www.techweb.com/se/ directlink.cgi?EET19970310S0124
✲ **Date accessed:** 21 April 1997

Resource: Girls and Math, Science, and Computers
Type of resource: Web page

✲ **Name of author:** Kay, Linda
✲ **Title of the work (in quotes):** "Wealth Beyond Measure: Tapping Database Treasures"
✲ **Title of the Web page (in italics):** *Girls and Math, Science, and Computers*
✲ **Date of last revision:** 9 April 1997
✲ **URL:** http://www.state.nj.us/statelibrary/quest05.htm
✲ **Date accessed:** 15 April 1997

Resource: Usenet article of your choice (this is a sample citation)
Type of resource: Usenet article

✲ **Name of author:** Hartman, Karen
✲ **Subject of the message (in quotes):** "Girls and Mathematics"
✲ **Name of the newsgroup:** soc.feminism
✲ **Date the message was sent:** 13 April 1997
✲ **Author's email address:** khartman@mwc.edu
✲ **Date accessed:** 3 May 1997

3   Assemble the citations in a bibliography.

Now that we've determined the elements in each citation, we need to gather the citations into a bibliography. Remember the book we found in the ALADIN library catalog? Let's say we found a copy of the book, read it, and wanted to cite it in our bibliography. We would cite it properly by using a style manual and including a citation in our list of Web resources. You'll find that book included in the following list of sources.

Bibliography
Hartman, K. "Girls and Mathematics." soc.feminism. 13 April 1997.
khartman@mwc.edu
3 May 1997.

Kay, Linda. "Wealth Beyond Measure: Tapping Database Treasures."
Girls and Math, Science, and Computers. 9 April 1997.
http://www.state.nj.us/statelibrary/quest05.htm
15 April 1997.

Rosser, Sue V., ed. *Teaching the Majority: Breaking the Gender Barrier in Science, Mathematics, and Engineering.* New York: Teacher College Press, 1995.

Santo, Brian. "Introducing Girls to High-Tech Careers Is 'Awsem.'" *Electronic Engineering Times, March 10, 1997.* Date of last revision not available.
http://www.techweb.com/se/directlink.cgi?EET19970310S0124
21 April 1997.

Spertus, Ellen. "Why Are There So Few Female Computer Scientists?" 28 January 1995.
http://www.ai.mit.edu/people/ellens/Gender/pap/pap.html
21 April 1997.

Project 2—Using the Internet for Market Research

This project focuses on using the Web for market research. Let's say you have come into some money. You want to make a sound investment, and you've always wanted to own a bookstore. You've read that one of the fastest growing areas in the country, specifically on the East Coast, is Fredericksburg, Virginia. All you know about the area is that it is 50 miles south of Washington, D.C. You want to research the following:

- How is the bookstore industry faring in the United States?
- Is the Fredericksburg, Virginia, bookstore market saturated?
- What types of people buy the most books? Couples with no children? Couples with children? Single people?
- What does the Fredericksburg area look like demographically? How many people live there? What is the population growth projected to be in the next few years? What is the educational background of the people there?
- What is the business climate of the area? What is the unemployment rate?

We'll look for this information by taking the following steps:
   A. Search a virtual library.
   B. Search a specialized database.
   C. Perform a search in a search engine.
   D. Evaluate the resources found.
   E. Cite the resources found.

Chapter 14

Activity 2-A   Search a Virtual Library

Overview

The best place to find free information about industries is through trade association Web pages. Such pages can provide a wealth of information about the industry they cover, gleaned from a myriad of sources to which you may not have access. Some association Web pages provide links to other related sites and resources, as well as publishing their own research.

There are several ways to find association Web pages. You could do a keyword search in a search engine. For example, you could search for *bookstores and association* or *"bookstore industry"*. It may be difficult, however, to find an association quickly using this method. The best place to go for a resource like this is a virtual library. Why? As you may remember, virtual libraries make it their priority to list specialized databases on the Web. They also try to list resources that will help people doing serious research.

In this part of our project, we'll search a virtual library for a database on associations, search this database, and find an association that involves the bookstore industry. We'll search the association's Web page for information about the bookstore market. We'll follow these steps:

1. Go to the Librarians' Index to the Internet and search for associations.
2. Select "Associations on the Net," an Internet Public Library database.
3. Search for and select an association that involves the bookstore industry.
4. Browse BookWeb, the American Booksellers Association's Web page.
5. Bookmark some useful information about the bookstore industry.

Details

1   Go to the Librarians' Index to the Internet and search for associations.

❀*Do It!* Click on the location field, type **http://sunsite.berkeley.edu/ internetindex**, and press **Enter**.

We want to find any special databases that focus on associations. In this virtual library, we're only searching for words in the titles of Web pages, annotations, and URLs—not in the Web pages themselves.

❀*Do It!* Type **associations** in the form next to **Search words or phrase**, as shown in Figure 14.25.

❀*Do It!* Click on **Search**.

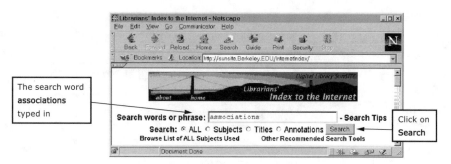

Figure 14.25—Librarians' Index to the Internet Home Page

Figure 14.26 shows the search results. Note that there is a database entitled **Associations on the Net**, which the Internet Public Library has assembled.

2   Select "Associations on the Net," an Internet Public Library database.

❋*Do It!* Click on **Associations on the Net**, as shown in Figure 14.26.

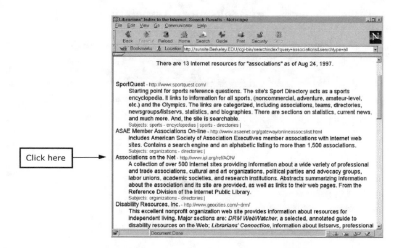

Figure 14.26—Search Results in the Librarians' Index to the Internet

3   Search for and select an association that involves the bookstore industry.

You should now be in "Associations on the Net."

❋*Do It!* Scroll down until you come to a search form.

❋*Do It!* Type **bookstores** in the search query box and click on **Search**, as shown in Figure 14.27. (Since all the resources in this database are association Web pages, you don't need to type in the word *association*.)

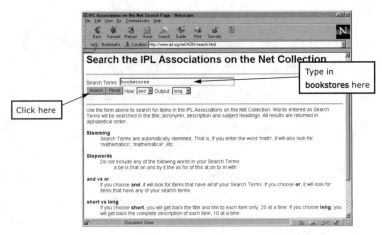

Figure 14.27—"Associations on the Net" Search Form

The search results appear in Figure 14.28. The first resource listed, **American Booksellers Association (ABA)**, looks like the Web page we've been seeking.

❀*Do It!* Click on **American Booksellers Association (ABA)**.

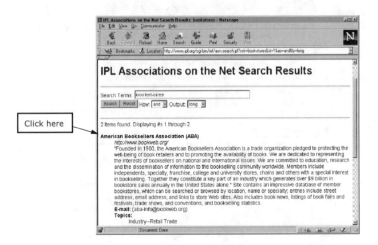

Figure 14.28—"Associations on the Net" Search Results

4   Browse BookWeb, the American Booksellers Association's Web page.

Your screen should now show the home page of the American Booksellers Association's BookWeb. You'll need to scroll down until you see **Contents**. Since we want to find out something about the bookstore industry and we're not sure where to begin, let's try the Reference Desk.

❀*Do It!* Click on **Reference Desk**.

Figure 14.29 shows a picture of it. We'd like to find out if the Fredericksburg area is already one of the top U.S. book markets, so we are especially interested in the link to **Top U.S. Book Markets**, as shown in Figure 14.29.

❋*Do It!* Click on **Top U.S. Book Markets**.

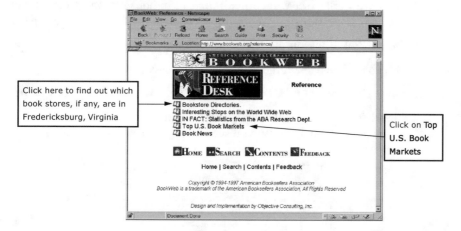

Figure 14.29—"Reference Desk" Page of BookWeb

When your screen fills, you'll see a list of the cities with the number of bookstores in each, along with the 1992 sales in thousands of dollars. See Figure 14.30. For each sales amount listed, you would add three zeros to get the accurate amount spent on books for that particular year. The cities are ranked from highest to lowest sales figures. If we want to know if Fredericksburg is on the list, we need to use the Find feature.

❋*Do It!* Click on **Edit** in the menu bar. Choose **Find in Page**.

❋*Do It!* Type **Fredericksburg** in the query box next to **Find what**.

❋*Do It!* Click on **Find Next**.

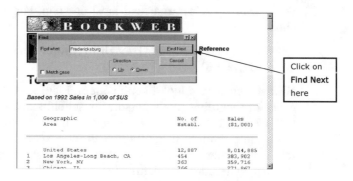

Figure 14.30—Using the Find Feature to Locate Fredericksburg

After you click on **Find Next**, the Find function will return with the message "Search String Not Found!" This means that Fredericksburg is not on the list of the top U.S. book markets.

✳*Do It!* Click **OK** to close the "Search String Not Found!" message box. Close the Find in Page dialog box.

Next, we want to see what other information BookWeb can give us about the bookstore industry. We need to go back to the Reference Desk page.

✳*Do It!* Click **Back** on the Netscape toolbar.

You should be back at the BookWeb Reference Desk.

✳*Do It!* Click on **IN FACT: Statistics from the ABA Research Dept**.

Figure 14.31 shows a partial listing of the information that is provided. Scroll down the page until you see a list of topics.

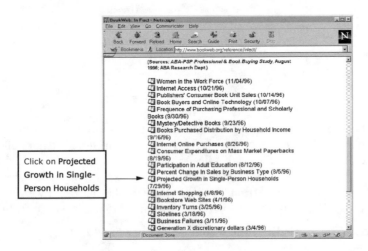

Figure 14.31—List of Research Topics on the Bookstore Industry

We could select several items, and if this were an actual research project, you'd want to select and read most of them. For our purposes, we'll choose one.

✳*Do It!* Click on **Projected Growth in Single-Person Households (7/29/96)**.

Your screen should look like the one in Figure 14.32. Note the significance of including single-person household statistical information in this Web page. Single people, or people living alone, tend to purchase more books than those in other types of households. The Web page also tells us that there is going to be an increase of single-person households in the next decade. Our picture doesn't show the source of this information, but if you scrolled down to the end of the page, you'd find that the U.S. Department of Commerce, the Bureau of the Census, and the ABA

Research Department supplied these facts. This statistical information can give us clues as to what to look for in the next step, when we'll search for demographic data on the Fredericksburg area.

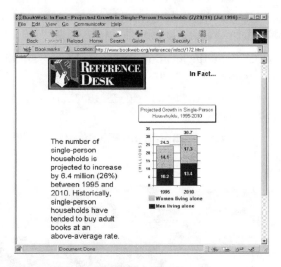

Figure 14.32—U.S. Census Statistics on Single-Person Households

5 **Bookmark some useful information about the bookstore industry.**

Before you leave this very useful site, you should bookmark it so you can return to it later and cite it in your bibliography. First, return to the home page.

❋*Do It!* Scroll down to the bottom of the page and click on **HOME**.

❋*Do It!* Now point to the location toolbar and click on **Bookmarks**.

❋*Do It!* Point to **Add Bookmark** and click on it.

Activity 2-B   Search a Specialized Database

Overview

While looking for marketing information about bookstores in BookWeb, we noted that some of the demographic statistics came from the U.S. Bureau of the Census. In this section, we will locate the U.S. Bureau of the Census database and search it for demographic information about Fredericksburg, Virginia. We'll follow these steps:

1. Return to the Librarians' Index to the Internet and search for demographic data.
2. Select the U.S. Bureau of the Census.
3. Search for demographic data on Fredericksburg, Virginia.
4. Bookmark the demographic information.

Details

1   Return to the Librarians' Index to the Internet and search for demographic data.

The best way to return to the Librarians' Index to the Internet is to type the URL for its location.

✸*Do It!* Click on the location field, type **http://sunsite.berkeley.edu/ internetindex**, and press Enter .

You should be at the home page for the Librarians' Index to the Internet, as shown in Figure 14.33.

✸*Do It!* Type **demographic data** in the search query box and click on **Search**.

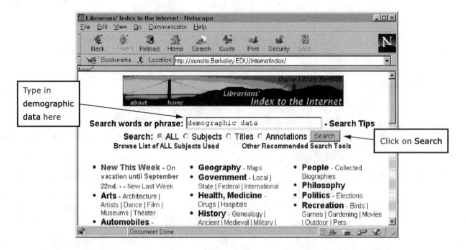

Figure 14.33—Librarians' Index to the Internet with Search Query Entered

2   Select the U.S. Bureau of the Census.

The search results appear in Figure 14.34. The best source on this list is the **U.S. Bureau of the Census**. Remember that much of the statistical information we found in the American Booksellers Association's Web page came from the U.S. Bureau of the Census.

✸*Do It!* Click on **U.S. Bureau of the Census**.

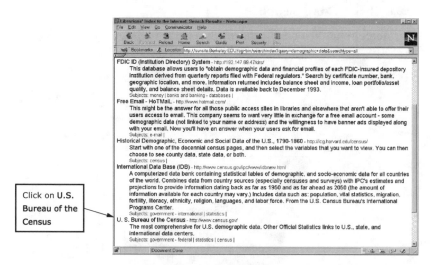

Click on **U.S. Bureau of the Census**

Figure 14.34—Search Results with U.S. Bureau of the Census Selected

Your screen should look like the one in Figure 14.35. This is an official U.S. government Web page. The United States takes a census of population and housing every 10 years. The last one was done in 1990. Entire books have been written on the U.S. Census and how to understand it. We'll barely touch the surface here. Suffice it to say that having this information in digitized form will make it much easier for the public to find demographic information. Census information, hypertext, and graphical imaging go together quite nicely.

Click on **Search**

Figure 14.35—U.S. Census Bureau Home Page

❋*Do It!* From the U.S. Census Bureau home page, click on **Search**.

Your screen will fill with a list of different types of searches you can do. We could do a place search, but for educational purposes let's try a map search.

✿*Do It!* Click on **Map Search**.

Your screen should look like the one in Figure 14.36. As Fredericksburg is in Virginia, we want to select Virginia, as shown in Figure 14.36.

✿*Do It!* Click on **VA**.

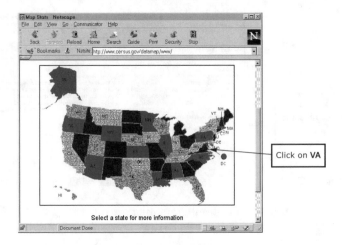

Figure 14.36—U.S. Census Bureau Map of the United States

3 Search for demographic data on Fredericksburg, Virginia.

Your screen will fill with a map of Virginia separated into parts. We know that Fredericksburg is 50 miles south of Washington, D.C., so we can make an educated guess that Fredericksburg would be in the state's northern section.

✿*Do It!* Click on the northernmost section of the map.

Your screen should look like the one in Figure 14.37.

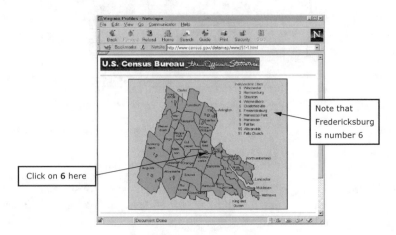

Figure 14.37—U.S. Census Map of Northern Virginia

Note that Fredericksburg is an independent city surrounded by two counties: Stafford and Spotsylvania. If we want to find marketing information for the entire area, we'll have to look at statistics for these counties as well as the city of Fredericksburg, as it appears to be so small. In this project we're going to show what we found for the city of Fredericksburg only, but if this were an actual research project, you'd be wise to look in the counties as well.

❀*Do It!* Click on **6**, as shown in Figure 14.37.

The screen that appears includes some hyperlinks that you can explore, as shown in Figure 14.38. We could look at a map of Fredericksburg. We could open a general statistical file about the city, a business and economic profile, and statistical tables. *STF* stands for *Summary Tape File.* Let's look at STF3A.

❀*Do It!* Click on **STF3A**.

Figure 14.38—Data Hyperlinks for Fredericksburg, Virginia

Now you should see a long list of data elements, or tables, as shown in Figure 14.39. Each one represents a different census statistic. For example, P1 is the total number of people in Fredericksburg. If we wanted to know this amount, we'd have to check the box next to P1. For this example, let's find out how many people are in Fredericksburg. Remembering how the American Booksellers Association's Web page mentioned that single people buy more books, let's also see how many single-person households there are.

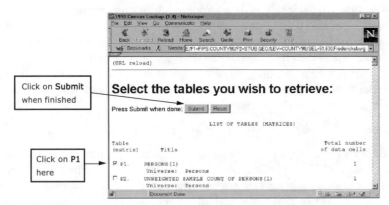

Figure 14.39—Selecting Data from Census Files

❃Do It! Click on **P1**, which represents the total number of people in Fredericksburg, as shown in Figure 14.39.

❃Do It! Scroll down until you come to **P16**, which represents the number of people in each household.

❃Do It! Click on **Submit**.

The next screen will ask you how you want your data to be retrieved. The default is **HTML format**. Leave it on that option.

❃Do It! Click on **Submit**, as shown in Figure 14.40.

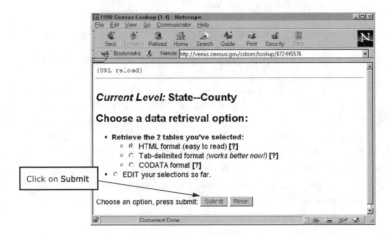

Figure 14.40—Data Retrieval Options in Census Data Search

The data search results appear in Figure 14.41.

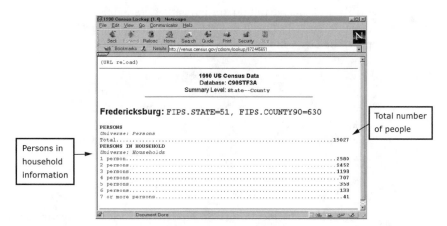

Figure 14.41—Results of the Statistical Data Search

4   Bookmark the demographic information.

You'll want to bookmark this information for later use. If you book-mark this page, however, your data won't be saved. Instead, you'll have to go back to the table selection screen pictured in Figure 14.39 and bookmark that screen.

❋*Do It!* Click **Back** on the toolbar until you are at the screen pictured in Figure 14.39.

❋*Do It!* Point to the location toolbar and click on **Bookmarks**.

❋*Do It!* Point to **Add Bookmark** and click.

Evidently, we can find a great deal of marketing data for the Fredericksburg, Virginia, area by exploring the U.S. Census Bureau Web site. There will be questions, however, that census data won't answer. You may need to search a state, city, or county government Web page to find other types of information. For example, counties and other juris-dictions often have commissions or councils who research development concerns in a particular area and then publish demographic and other types of results. To find local information such as this, you'll probably do best to use a search engine and search by keyword.

Activity 2-C   **Perform a Search in a Search Engine**

Overview

At the beginning of this project, we had a list of questions that we wanted to answer. Thus far, we have found an association Web page with infor-mation about the bookstore industry. We have also found census data about demographics, such as the number of households, the population's education level, and other types of population-related questions. We still haven't found a population projection for the Fredericksburg area, how-

Chapter 14

ever. To find this particular statistic and detailed information about the area's business climate, it might be smart to use a search engine. We can type in the city's name and see what happens. We'll try that next. We'll follow these steps:

1. Go to the location for WebCrawler.
2. Search for Web pages about Fredericksburg, Virginia.
3. Open StarWeb and follow some hyperlinks.
4. Bookmark a useful Web page.
5. Try to relocate the information by browsing in a search engine.

Details

1 Go to the location for WebCrawler.

✹*Do It!* Click on the location field, type **http://www.webcrawler.com**, and press **Enter**.

We chose WebCrawler because it is a fast, full-text search engine that supports all the major search features: phrase searching, Boolean searching, and nested Boolean searching. We may need to use all of them.

2 Search for Web pages about Fredericksburg, Virginia.

✹*Do It!* Type **"Fredericksburg Virginia"** in the search form. We know that WebCrawler supports phrase searching by reading the help screen.

✹*Do It!* Click on **Search**, as shown in Figure 14.42.

Figure 14.42—WebCrawler Search Form

3 Open StarWeb and follow some hyperlinks.

Figure 14.43 shows a partial list of results. Notice that several hyperlinks on the first page are for real estate agents.

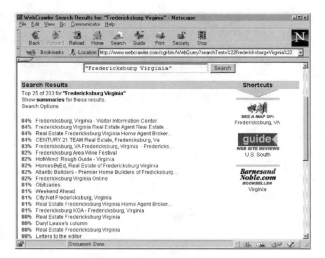

Figure 14.43—Results of WebCrawler Search

Let's try the first Web page that appears.

✿*Do It!* Click on **Fredericksburg, Virginia - Visitor Information Center**.

This Web page has several links to information about Fredericksburg. The Fredericksburg newspaper, the *Free Lance-Star,* may be a good place to start. Newspapers themselves can be a great source of information, not to mention all the hyperlinks that can appear there. Many newspapers will have the most current paper on the Web.

✿*Do It!* Click on **Fredericksburg Free Lance-Star**.

In the next few steps, keep in mind that Web research can take a lot of time. Many promising links don't yield good resources, and links that don't appear to be relevant often turn out to be exactly what you want. This project may make it look as if Web research is easy, but this is not always the case.

✿*Do It!* Click on the **Tourism** button, which is on the left side of the page.

Your screen will fill with a list of several tourism and travel hyperlinks. Many of these hyperlinks may help in locating information about doing business and living in the Fredericksburg area. For example, if you clicked on **Welcome to Virginia**, you'd be connected to the State of Virginia home page, which would have several links to state, county, and city government agencies.

✿*Do It!* Click on **Around the state**, as shown in Figure 14.44.

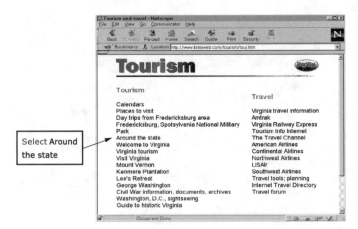

Figure 14.44—Tourism Hyperlinks in StarWeb

Once you're in "Around the State," you'll notice that this is part of the State of Virginia Web site, as shown in Figure 14.45.

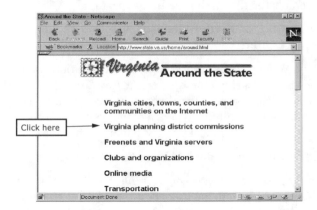

Figure 14.45—Virginia's "Around the State" Web Page

As we're trying to find local information, let's see if there are any planning district commissions in the area that interests us.

✳️*Do It!* Click on **Virginia planning district commissions**.

Several hyperlinks will appear. Each one represents an area planning commission. If we didn't know anything about the area, we'd have to use trial and error to select the right hyperlink. We happen to know, however, that the Rappahannock River runs through the Fredericksburg area, and that the Rappahannock Area Development Commission is located in Fredericksburg.

✳️*Do It!* Click on **Rappahannock Area Development Commission**.

Figure 14.46 shows a portion of the page that appears.

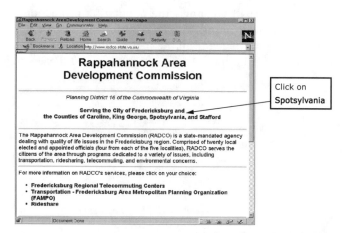

Figure 14.46—"Rappahannock Area Development Commission" Web Page

If we clicked on **City of Fredericksburg**, we'd go back to StarWeb. We can try clicking on several of the hyperlinks. Let's see what **Spotsylvania** has to offer.

❀*Do It!* Click on **Spotsylvania**, as shown in Figure 14.46.

After your screen fills, scroll down until you see **Why you want to do business here**, **Why you want to live here**, and the other hyperlinks shown in Figure 14.47. Each one of these hyperlinks gives you an incredible amount of information about the area. If you clicked on **Why you want to do business here**, you'd find all sorts of labor statistics, including the unemployment rate and tax information. Many of the statistics listed come from the U.S. Bureau of the Census, others are compiled by the state of Virginia, and others are provided by universities, commissions, and other entities.

❀*Do It!* Click on **Why you want to live here**.

Figure 14.47—Portion of Spotsylvania County's Economic Development Page

Your screen will fill with many more choices.

❀*Do It!* Click on **Housing**.

❀*Do It!* Click on **Population Profile**.

❀*Do It!* Click on **Profile**.

Figure 14.48 shows the population projection we've been seeking. If you were doing this investigation as a research project, you would probably want a copy of the report done by the University of Virginia, Center for Public Service, which produced these statistics.

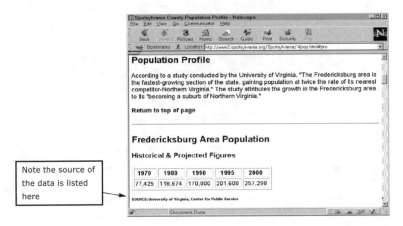

Note the source of the data is listed here

Figure 14.48—Population Profile for Fredericksburg Area

4   Bookmark a useful Web page.

Let's bookmark this page so we don't lose track of it.

Do It! Point to the menu commands at the top of the screen and click on **Bookmarks**.

Do It! Point to **Add Bookmark** and click.

5   Try to relocate the information by browsing in a search engine.

Let's do an experiment. Now that we know where the information is and what words are on the page, let's do a search in WebCrawler using words that appear in the Web page to see if we come upon this page again. First, go to WebCrawler.

Do It! Point to the location field, type **http://www.webcrawler.com**, and press **Enter**. (You could also get to WebCrawler by pressing **Back** in the menu bar several times.)

Do It! In the search query box, type **Fredericksburg and "population profile"** (WebCrawler is case insensitive, so we don't need to capitalize **population** and **profile**, even though they are capitalized on the Web page).

Do It! Click on **Search**.

Figure 14.49 shows the response we receive. This just goes to show you that a search engine isn't always able to find pages with the keywords you request. Sometimes serendipity and plain old persistence are needed to find the most important information on the Web.

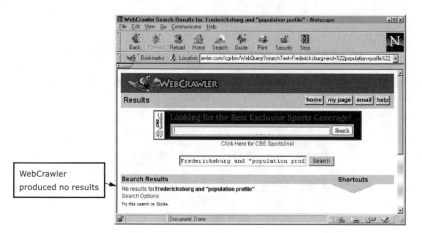

WebCrawler produced no results

Figure 14.49—WebCrawler Results

Activity 2-D   Evaluate the Resources Found

Overview

In this project, we bookmarked three references. We'll evaluate one of these resources, just as we did in the first project, by applying the evaluation guidelines introduced in Chapter 12. We'll follow these steps:

1. Go to your bookmark list and select "BookWeb: Home Page."
2. Evaluate this resource using the evaluation guidelines.

Details

1   Go to your bookmark list and select "BookWeb: Home Page."

✿*Do It!* Point to the menu commands at the top of the screen and click on **Bookmarks**. Drag the mouse down until you come to **BookWeb: Home Page**.

✿*Do It!* Click on **BookWeb: Home Page**.

2   Evaluate this resource using the evaluation guidelines.

You should be at the home page for the American Booksellers Association. We'll go through each of the guidelines for this Web page.

Who Is the Author or Institution?

It's evident when you get BookWeb up on your screen that it's put out by the American Booksellers Association (ABA), because its name appears just before **BookWeb** at the beginning of the Web page. We also know that the ABA is an organizational Web page, because it has **.org** in its URL. But we'd like to know more about it. Scroll down the page until you come to **Contents**.

❉*Do It!* Click on **Find out about**.

❉*Do It!* Click on **The American Booksellers Association**.

Part of the page appears in Figure 14.50. We find out that the association has existed since 1900 and is devoted to promoting the book-retailing industry. If you scroll down to the bottom of the page, you'll find an email address for the association, in addition to a street address.

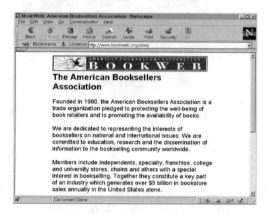

Figure 14.50—American Booksellers Association's Web Page "BookWeb"

How Current Is the Information?

At the beginning of the Web page, there is a date that indicates when it was updated. It appears to be updated every weekday. To find out when it was last updated, you can click **View** in the menu bar and choose **Page Info**. This will tell you the date on which it was last modified. It may match the date on the first page.

Who Is the Audience?

The audience is clearly stated in the mission statement, which is partially shown in Figure 14.50. The audience consists of people who are involved in the book-retailing business. These would be bookstore owners and managers, as well as people in the book-publishing industry. From the looks of some features in the Web page, you could argue that this Web site is for any avid reader who loves books and bookstores.

Is the Content Accurate and Objective?

After looking at several of the statistical pages in the Reference Desk section, noting that all of them are properly cited, and noticing that everything in the site is attributed to a source, we can reasonably conclude that the content is accurate. BookWeb is an advocate of artistic freedom, however, as evidenced by its section on free expression. You can find a list of banned books in the United States, along with articles on censorship legal cases and other issues. This would make BookWeb subjective. The association isn't going to give both sides of the censorship issue, because it's in its best interest to show only one side, which is that expression in its purest form should be supported. This doesn't mean, however, that this resource can't be trusted. It's just something you should keep in mind.

What Is the Purpose of the Information?

The purpose, which is clearly stated in the mission statement and implied throughout the Web page, is to inform booksellers across the country about the state of the industry. Its purpose is to inform people in a timely manner about how the book business is faring and to present related issues.

Activity 2-E   Cite the Resources Found

Overview

We'll look at all of your bookmarks now to determine their bibliographic format, according to the guidelines in Chapter 13. Here are the steps you'll take:

1. Open your bookmarks.
2. Determine how to cite each resource properly.
3. Assemble the citations in a bibliography.

Details

1   Open your bookmarks.

❋*Do It!* While in Netscape, point to **Bookmarks** in the location toolbar and move the pointer to the bookmarks.

❋*Do It!* Select each bookmark one by one, starting with **BookWeb: Home Page**.

2   Determine how to cite each resource properly.

We'll use the guidelines from Chapter 13 to determine the best way to cite these resources.

Resource: BookWeb: Home Page

Type of resource: Web page

- ❋ **Name of author:** American Booksellers Association
- ❋ **Title of the work (in quotes):** "American Booksellers Association BookWeb"
- ❋ **Title of the Web page (in italics):** *BookWeb: Home Page*
- ❋ **Date of last revision:** 23 April 1997

❊ **URL:** http://www.bookweb.org
❊ **Date accessed:** 23 April 1997

Resource: Census Lookup (1.4)

When you open this bookmark, you'll have to look for the data again. Go back to the project and search for the same data elements you searched for earlier, and then cite the information that you need.

Type of resource: Web page

❊ **Name of author:** U.S. Census Bureau
❊ **Title of work (in quotes):** "1990 US Census Data"
❊ **Title of the Web page (in italics):** *Census Lookup (1.4)*
❊ **Date of the last revision:** Not available
❊ **URL:** http://venus.census.gov/cdrom/lookup/861845234
❊ **Date accessed:** 23 April 1997

Resource: Spotsylvania County Population Profile

Type of resource: Web page

❊ **Name of author:** Spotsylvania County Office of Economic Development, Spotsylvania, VA
❊ **Title of the work (in quotes):** "Population Profile"
❊ **Title of the Web page (in italics):** *Spotsylvania County Population Profile*
❊ **Date of the last revision:** 20 December 1996
❊ **URL:** http://www2.spotsylvania.org/spotsylvania/14pop.html#pro
❊ **Date accessed:** 23 April 1997

3 Assemble the citations in a bibliography.

Now that we've determined the elements in each citation, we can see what they'd all look like in a bibliography:

Bibliography
American Booksellers Association. "American Booksellers Association BookWeb." *BookWeb: Home Page.* 23 April 1997. http://www.bookweb.org
23 April 1997.

Spotsylvania County Office of Economic Development, Spotsylvania, VA. "Population Profile." *Spotsylvania County Population Profile.* 20 December 1996. http://www2.spotsylvania.org/spotsylvania/14pop.html#pro
23 April 1997.

U.S. Census Bureau. "1990 US Census Data." *Census Lookup (1.4)*. Date of last revision not available.
http://venus.census.gov/cdrom/lookup/861845234
23 April 1997.

Summary

This chapter focused on two research projects that were very different from each other not only in content but also in approach. The first was a broad, open-ended topic in the sense that we had no clear expectations about the search results. We researched the topic of women and computing with no idea of what we were going to find or how we were going to narrow the topic as we went along. The second research project was also broad but required a different approach. In that project, we knew what we needed to find and looked for it. Our topic—marketing data for the bookstore industry in Fredericksburg, Virginia—was much more focused and required an almost formulaic approach.

The chapter taught us the following lessons:

❋ Research on the World Wide Web doesn't always follow a systematic process. Sometimes you may start with a library catalog, sometimes with a search engine.

❋ Most search engines claim that they index the full text of every Web page, but this is not always the case.

❋ Guidelines for evaluating resources are just that—guidelines. If a particular site doesn't give both sides of an issue, that doesn't mean it is unreliable. It's good for you to know that there may be an underlying bias to the information and that you should make allowances for this.

❋ Sometimes finding information on the World Wide Web requires a great deal of persistence.

The chapter brought together skills on how to find a specialized database, how to search a library catalog, and how to find information in a Usenet archive. You practiced evaluating resources and citing them properly in a bibliography.

15
Chapter

Social Issues, Legal Issues, and Security

It's easy to get excited about using the Internet and the World Wide Web. They're vivacious, interesting, and important places to work, learn, do business, and just have fun. The World Wide Web always seems to have something new. You find not only new resources, but better services and programs, making the WWW and the Internet easier to use and more powerful. There's also a great deal of diversity; different cultures, nations, and outlooks are represented on the WWW. All these things make for an exciting environment, but as the Internet and the World Wide Web become more popular and the number of users increases, it's reasonable to expect rules, regulations, and laws governing their use. You also have to consider the effect the Internet has on our lives, our communities, and society as its use becomes more widespread. In this chapter we'll discuss a few of these issues associated with using the Internet and the World Wide Web. We'll cover these topics:

* Brief History of the Internet
* Privacy and Civil Liberties
* Intellectual Property and Copyright
* Internet Security

Brief History of the Internet

In the late 1960s the United States Department of Defense, through its **Advanced Research Projects Agency (ARPA)**, funded research into the establishment of a decentralized computer network. Some of the researchers saw the advantages of having a network in which computer systems of differing types and operating systems could communicate. They also foresaw the development of a community among the users of this national and international network. The network, named ARPANET, linked researchers at universities and research laboratories.

Throughout the 1970s, ARPANET was developed further and connections were established with networks in other countries. Usenet originated in 1979, and in the early 1980s other networks in the United States and elsewhere were established. The number of sites or hosts on these networks was still relatively small, less than 1,000. In the late 1980s, the National Science Foundation funded the development of a network (using the Internet protocols) that would connect supercomputer centers in the United States. That network, called NSFNET, allowed colleges and universities to become connected. The number of sites or hosts increased rapidly, passing 10,000 in 1987. In 1989 there were over 100,000 hosts on NSFNET. The 1980s also saw the development of Cleveland Free-Net, a community-based network, and the use of NSFNET to relay email from commercial networks.

Governments have heavily subsidized the funding for the development and operation of ARPANET, NSFNET, and several other networks throughout the world. These networks established *acceptable-use policies*, which gave rules for their use, stating what type of activities were allowed on these publicly supported networks. The policies prohibited any purely commercial activities and set the tone for a developing code of network ethics or etiquette. Commercial networks were also being developed, although they could not, under the acceptable-use policies, use the transmission links of the public networks. So for some time commercial activity on the major portion of the Internet in the United States was prohibited. However, in 1988 some of these commercial networks reached an agreement with NSFNET to allow email from commercial networks to be carried on NSFNET. That way a user on CompuServe or MCImail could send a message to someone with an Internet address at a public institution such as a college or university. Likewise, messages could be sent from NSFNET to these private networks, but email from one user on a private service couldn't be transported over NSFNET to another user on a private service.

In 1990 ARPANET ceased to exist as an administrative entity, and the public network in the United States was turned over to NSFNET. The Internet was growing at a remarkable rate and clearly becoming bigger than what the public institutions wanted to manage or support. In fact, they never had planned to support it forever. In the early 1990s commercial networks with their own Internet exchanges or gateways

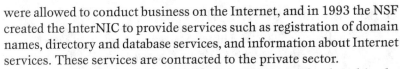

were allowed to conduct business on the Internet, and in 1993 the NSF created the InterNIC to provide services such as registration of domain names, directory and database services, and information about Internet services. These services are contracted to the private sector.

The notions behind the World Wide Web were developed in the early 1990s and Mosaic, the first graphical Web browser, was released to the public in the latter part of 1993. Web browsers and the availability of Internet connections through modems made the Internet much more accessible. These developments have led to an unprecedented growth in the number of individuals, businesses, and organizations that are using the Internet for communication, information, and commerce.

This explosive growth of the World Wide Web and the inclusion of commercial networks and services into the Internet have been accompanied by an astounding increase in the population of Internet users. Many of the new users feel that networks and computers, like a public utility, should be available anywhere, reliable, and easy to use. As the Internet becomes available to a much wider portion of the population, older modes of behavior on the Internet have changed. Commercial activity and advertising are firmly established as common Internet activity. Businesses are determining effective and secure ways of engaging in commerce on the Internet. As the use of the Internet becomes more widespread in the areas of education, research, business, and recreation, issues of security, reliability, ownership, and liability become more important. Many local laws and international agreements are directly applicable to Internet activities. On the other hand, this is a rather new medium using technology that came into existence after many applicable laws were written. New laws and agreements recognizing these changes and differences are being established.

The Internet and the World Wide Web have grown rapidly from a research project into something that involves millions of people worldwide. Much of the Internet's usefulness comes from the fact that users and service providers depend on each other and need to support each other. Hopefully, that sort of sharing and respect will continue. Your behavior, your expectations of others, and your activities will make the difference.

Privacy and Civil Liberties

What's Reasonable to Expect in Terms of Privacy and Civil Liberties as They Relate to Use of the Internet?

Your initial response might be that you expect the same protection of your *privacy* and the same *civil liberties*—such as freedom of expression, safeguards against the arbitrary exercise of authority, and protection from abusive or offensive actions—on the Internet as you have in your other dealings in society. Codes of behavior or rules of etiquette have developed on the Internet over the years.

In some cases laws have been adopted to provide the same level of protection of privacy and guarantees of civil liberties for working with electronic media as with any other media. An important point is that privacy and civil liberties are often defined in terms of their expression or environment. The laws in the United States dealing with privacy and expression in printed form, on paper, needed to be changed to suit electronic communications. Laws need to be modified to take into account new media and new means of transmitting information. Furthermore, the people who develop, act on, and enforce laws need to be informed of the impact of technological changes. We'll cover a few of the important issues related to privacy and civil liberties: email privacy, unwarranted search and seizure, and offensive messages and libel.

Email Privacy

When you send a message by email, the message is broken into packets and the packets are sent out over the Internet. The number of packets depends on the size of the message. Each message has the Internet address of the sender (your address) and the address of the recipient. Packets from a single message may take different routes to the destination, or may take different routes at different times. This works well for the Internet and for you. Since packets are generally sent through the best path, depending on the traffic load on the Internet, the path doesn't depend on certain systems being in operation, and all you have to give is the address of the destination.

The packets making up an email message may pass through several different systems before reaching their destination. This means there may be some places between you and the destination where the packets could be intercepted and examined. Since all the systems have to be able to look at the address of the destination, each system could be able to examine the contents of the message. If you're using a computer system shared by others or if the system at the destination is shared by others, there is usually someone (a system administrator) capable of examining all the messages. So, in the absence of codes of ethics or without the protection of law, email could be very public. Needless to say, you shouldn't be reading someone else's email. Most system administrators adopt a code of ethics under which they will not examine email unless they feel it's important to support the system(s) they administer. The truth of the matter is they are generally too busy to bother reading other people's mail.

Electronic Communications Privacy Act

One example of a law to ensure the privacy of email is the ***Electronic Communications Privacy Act (ECPA)*** passed in 1986 by Congress. It prohibits anyone from intentionally intercepting, using, and/or disclosing email messages without the sender's permission. The ECPA was passed to protect individuals from having their private messages accessed by government officers or others without legal permission. That bill extended the protections that existed for voice communications to nonvoice communications conveyed through wires or over the airwaves. You can, of course, give your permission for someone to access your email. However, law enforcement officials or others cannot access your email in stored form (on a disk or tape) without a warrant, and electronic transmission of your email can't be intercepted or "tapped" without a court order. The ECPA does allow a system administrator to access users' email on a computer system if it's necessary for the operation or security of the system. The ECPA then gives the system administrator the responsibility to allow no access to email passing within or through a system without a court order or warrant. She can and indeed should refuse any requests to examine email unless the proper legal steps are followed.

Encryption

When you send a message by email it's often transmitted in the same form you've typed it. Even though it's unethical and illegal for someone else to read it, the message is in a form that's easy to read. This is similar to sending a message written on a postcard through the postal service. One way to avoid this is to use encryption to put a message into an unreadable form. The characters in the message can be changed by substitution or scrambling, usually based on some secret code. The message can't be read unless the code and method of encryption are known. The code is called a *key*. Many messages are encoded by a method called *public key encryption*. If you encrypt a message and send it on to someone, that person has to know the key to decode your message. If the key is also sent by email, it might be easy to intercept the key and decode the encrypted message.

With public key encryption there are two keys, one public and the other private. The public key needs to be known. To send a message to a friend, you use her or his public key to encrypt the message. Your friend then uses her or his private key to decode the message after receiving it. Suppose you want to send an encrypted message to your friend Milo. He tells you his public key; in fact, there's no harm if he tells everybody. You write the message and then encrypt it using Milo's public key. He receives the message and then uses his private key to decode it. It doesn't matter who sent the message to Milo as long as it was encrypted with his public key. Also, even if the message is intercepted, it can't be read without knowing Milo's private key. It's up to him to keep that secret. Likewise, if he wanted to respond, he would use your public key to encrypt the message. You would use your private key to decode it.

You can obtain a version of public key encryption software called PGP, for Pretty Good Privacy. It's freely available to individuals and may be purchased for commercial use. There are some licensing restrictions on the use of the commercial versions in the United States and Canada. Furthermore, United States State Department regulations prohibit the export of some versions of this program to other countries. In fact, current restrictions in the United States prohibit the export of most encryption methods, while other countries allow the export of encryption methods and algorithms. Some people feel strongly that these policies should be changed for the sake of sharing information and for the sake of allowing common encryption of sensitive and business messages, but others don't agree.

To read more about PGP, take a look at one or more of these:

* "Peter's PGP page"
  http://www.gildea.com/pgp

* "Frequently Asked Questions alt.security.pgp"
  ftp://rtfm.mit.edu/pub/usenet-by-hierarchy/news/answers/pgp-faq

* "Where To Get The Pretty Good Privacy Program (PGP) FAQ"
  http://www.cryptography.org/getpgp.htm

One issue that needs to be resolved is whether it should be possible for law enforcement or other government officials to decode encrypted messages. Some argue that because of the need to detect criminal action or in the interests of national security, the means to decode any messages should be available to the appropriate authorities. Others argue that individuals have the right to privacy in their communications. In the United States, the issue has been decided in favor of government access in the case of digital telephone communications. The issue hasn't been settled yet for email or other forms of electronic communications.

Here's a list of some extensive resources for information about electronic privacy:

* "6.805/STS085: Readings on Encryption and National Security"
  http://www-swiss.ai.mit.edu/6095/readings-crypto.html

* "6.805/STS085: Readings on Privacy Implications of Computer Networks"
  http://www-swiss.ai.mit.edu/6095/readings-privacy.html

* "EPIC Online Guide to Privacy Resources"
  http://www.epic.org/privacy/privacy_resources_faq.html

* "The Privacy Pages"
  http://www.2020tech.com/maildrop/privacy.html

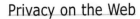

Chapter 15

Privacy on the Web

It's easy to get the impression that we're browsing the Web and using Internet services in an anonymous manner. But that's not the case. Every time you visit a Web site some information about your computer system is transmitted to the server. When you fill out a form the information you provide is passed to a server. Some Web sites track the activities of users through the use of *cookies*, information that's passed from the computer that's using a Web browser to a Web server. You also need to be aware of the risks involved with giving out personal information through email, chat groups, and forms. Since it may be difficult to know with whom you are communicating, you especially need to be careful about disclosing personal information. Children especially need to know about and be informed of the risks and dangers involved in using the Internet.

What Happens When You Go to a Web Site—What the Server Knows

When you go to a Web site, either by clicking on a hyperlink or by typing in a URL in the location field, your browser (the client program) sends a request to a Web server. This request includes the IP address of your computer system, the URL of the file or Web page you've requested, the time the request was made, and whether the request was successful. If you clicked on a hyperlink from a Web page, the URL of the Web page is also passed to the server. All of this information is kept in log files on the server. It's possible to have the log files analyzed and track all access to a Web server.

The Trail Left on Your Computer

We've seen that each server keeps log files to identify requests for Web pages. So in that sense you leave a trail of your activities on each of the Web servers that you contact. There's also a trail of your activities kept on the computer you use to access the Web. Recently accessed Web pages and a list of the URLs accessed are kept in the *cache*—a folder or directory that contains recently viewed Web pages, images, and other resources—and the *history list*. If you're using a computer to access the Web in a public place, such as a lab or library, then it's possible for someone to check on your activities.

Cache

Most Web browsers keep copies of recently accessed Web pages, images, and other files in a folder or directory called the cache. When you return to a Web page you've visited recently, the browser first checks to see if it's available in the cache and retrieves it from your computer rather than retrieving it from a remote site. It's much faster to retrieve a Web page from the cache rather than from a remote site. This is convenient, but it also leaves a record of your activities. It is possible to clear the cache whenever you'd like using the Preferences panel. To do that bring up the Preferences panel by clicking on **Edit** in the menu bar and selecting **Preferences**; next bring up the Cache panel by clicking on **Advanced** and then clicking on **Cache**; and finally clear the disk cache by clicking on **Clear Disk Cache.**

History List

The Web browser keeps a record of the path you've taken to get to the current location. To see the path and select a site from it, click on **Go** in the menu bar. The browser also keeps a list of all the Web pages visited recently in the history list. To bring up the history list, press **Ctrl** + **H** from the keyboard or click on **Communicator** from the menu bar and select **History** from that menu. This list is kept around for a time period specified in days. The number of days an item may be kept on the list is set in the Preferences panel category titled Navigator. To get to the spot where you can set it, click on **Edit** in the menu bar, select **Preferences**, and then click on **Navigator**. You can also clear the history list from this panel by clicking on **Clear History**.

Cookies

A cookie is information that's passed to a Web server by the Web browser program. Netscape developed the terms and methods for working with cookies. The collection of cookies on a computer is kept in a file named **cookies.txt**. A Web server requests and/or writes a cookie to your computer only if you access a Web page that contains the commands to do that. You have the option to not accept any cookies, to accept only cookies that get returned to the server that put them on your computer, or to be warned before accepting a cookie. To do that click on **Edit** in the menu bar, select **Preferences**, and then click on **Advanced**.

Cookies are sometimes viewed as an invasion of privacy, but they are useful to you in some cases. Suppose you want to visit a site frequently that requires you to give a password or a site that you can customize to match your preferences. The protocol HTTP is used when you visit a Web site. When a Web page is requested, a connection is made between the client and the server, the server delivers a Web page, and the connection is terminated. Once the page has been transmitted the connection is terminated. If you visit a site again, the server, through HTTP, has no information about a previous visit. Cookies can be used to keep track of your password or keep track of some preferences you've set for every visit to that site. That way you don't have to enter the information each time you visit.

To get more information about cookies take a look at the Webopaedia entry on cookies at **http://www.webopedia.com/cookie.htm**.

Unwarranted Search and Seizure

Suppose a person is suspected of having illegal items on a computer system, such as pirated software, credit card numbers, telephone access codes, stolen documents, or proprietary information, and law enforcement officials obtain a court order or warrant to search or confiscate the materials. What are reasonable actions?

- Is it reasonable to confiscate all the disks connected to or networked to the suspect's computer system?

- Is it reasonable to confiscate all the suspect's computer equipment including the main computer, printers, modems, and telephones?

- If the items are removed from the premises for searching, how much time should pass before they are returned?

- If the suspect's system is part of a bulletin board or email system with messages for other, presumably innocent persons, should those messages be delivered to the innocent parties?

The answers to these and some related questions depend on the laws governing permissible searches and seizures. The actions taken in cases such as these also depend on how well the technology is understood by the courts and law enforcement officials. For example, the Fourth Amendment to the United States Constitution guards against unreasonable searches and seizures of property. In 1990, all the computer equipment and files of one company, Steve Jackson Games, were confiscated and searched by the United States Secret Service. The warrant application released later showed that the company was not suspected of any crime. However, the law enforcement officials, in their fervor to deal with "computer crime," appeared to disregard accepted civil liberties. Some of this was undoubtedly because they were unfamiliar with the technology at that time. A printer or modem, for example, can't store anything once the power is turned off, so there is no need to confiscate those items if one is searching for what might be illegal information. These actions and the related court cases point out the need to keep the officers of the legal system informed and educated regarding the uses and capabilities of technology.

The Electronic Frontier Foundation (EFF) was formed in 1990 to, among other things, bring issues dealing with civil liberties related to computing and telecommunications technology to the attention of the public at large, legislators, and court and law enforcement officials. As a nonprofit public interest organization, EFF maintains collections of files and documents. Use the URL **http://www.eff.org** to access the home page of the EFF and **http://www.eff.org/pub** to view its FTP library. EFF also produces a number of publications and other materials, many of which are available on the Internet. They have also provided legal services and opinions in cases similar to the one described above.

Offensive Material and Libel

Offensive and Abusive Email

Virtually all codes of etiquette, ethics, and policies for acceptable use of networked computer facilities include statements that prohibit sending offensive or abusive messages by email. This is, naturally, similar to the codes of behavior and laws we adhere to in other, everyday communications. One difference between dealing with this sort of behavior on the Internet and other forms of communication, such as the telephone or postal service, is that no one is in charge of the Internet—it is a cooperative organization. If you have a problem with someone at your site, talk with your supervisor, their supervisor, your system administrator, or your Internet service provider about it. If the problem comes from another site, send email to the address **postmaster@*the.other.site***, and talk with the system administrator at your site or your supervisor about it. (You substitute the Internet domain name of the site in question for *the.other.site*.) Individuals have been arrested and prosecuted for making threatening remarks by email. Civil suits and charges have been filed against individuals in cases of harassment, abuse, and stalking.

Sexually Explicit Material and Pornography

Some material available on the Internet may be classified as sexually explicit or pornographic. It's not surprising since there's a large number of people using the World Wide Web and the Internet with varying preferences, interests, and cultural perspectives. Also, as with other media, there is a market for it. In the past most of this material was available through Usenet newsgroups whose names clearly identified the content, for example, alt.binaries.nude.celebrities.

With the increase in popularity of the WWW, many commercial Web sites that traffic in explicit videos, phone sex, and items with sexually explicit themes have been set up. In fact these so-called "XXX rated" sites were among the first successful commercial ventures on the Web. Most of these sites have a home page warning that the related pages contain material some might find offensive or inappropriate. The home page often contains a form where the user states that she/he is at least 18 or 21 years of age. The commercial sites charge a fee for access. The fee is generally charged to a credit card or some other electronic account. It's not difficult to find this material on the Internet, but in almost every case it has to be sought out; people using the Internet aren't coerced or tricked into viewing it.

The focus of the debate about this so-called "cyberporn" has been whether it's appropriate for the material to be readily available to children and whether it's appropriate to pass laws that restrict the content of the Internet. There are a number of programs that can be installed on a computer to restrict the material that can be accessed on the World Wide Web. The programs work with lists of Web pages and ways of describing the content of Web pages to filter material.

> One source of information about these programs and related topics is "PEDINFO Parental Control of Internet Access," **http://www.uab.edu/pedinfo/Control.html**.

The culture of the Internet has fostered personal rights and liberties, so some argue its content should not be restricted or censored. There are laws banning or restricting pornography; some countries have more stringent laws than others, and some laws restrict the distribution of the material. Private networks such as AOL and Prodigy sometimes enact their own rules regarding content. One online service filtered out messages that contained the word "breast," but rescinded that action due to complaints from users who found information and discussions relating to breast cancer very valuable.

It seems that the current debate regarding pornography and civil liberties on the Internet will continue for some time. The President of the United States signed legislation that had been approved by Congress, the Communications Decency Act of 1996, that made it illegal to transmit certain materials on the Internet. The term used in the legislation is "indecent" material. This legislation presents some problems—monitoring the Internet would greatly increase the expense and complexity of maintaining current networks; the term "indecent" is open to many interpretations. The U.S. Supreme Court declared that legislation to be unconstitutional and implied that expression on the Internet is entitled to full First Amendment protection. So the Internet isn't viewed as a broadcast medium, like radio or television, but as a medium in which individuals are guaranteed free speech. Here are a few sites you may want to visit for more information about these topics:

- "The Cyberporn Debate"
  http://www2000.ogsm.vanderbilt.edu/ cyberporn.debate.cgi

- "Internet Censorship"
  http://epic.org/free_speech/censorship

- "Technology and Freedom"
  http://www.freedomforum.org/technology/ welcome.asp

Inappropriate Business Practices
Portions of the Internet throughout the world were started as national or military networks. The government paid much of the startup costs. In that environment, advertising was generally prohibited. It wasn't until the late 1980s that any commercial traffic was allowed on the primary portion of the Internet in the United States. Because of the relatively recent history of little or no advertising and marketing, efforts in this direction have been met with opposition on some services of the Internet and Usenet. However, it has become common to find advertising, marketing, and commercial activities readily available on Web pages.

One particularly offensive means of advertising is called *spamming*. When used in this way, the term means sending a message to many unrelated newsgroups or interest groups. It's not too hard to do, but it almost always is met with great opposition and feelings of hatred. One way to deal with it is to send a copy of the message and a complaint to **postmaster@***the.other.site*. In one case, a company that spammed virtually every Usenet newsgroup eventually lost its Internet access. It wasn't banned from the Internet, but the organization providing Internet access to the company received so many complaints that they withdrew Internet services from the company. One Web site that has a comprehensive collection of information about spamming and ways to stop it is Julian Byrne's site "Get that spammer!" **http://kryten.eng.monash.edu.au/ gspam.html.**

Advertising and commerce is allowed on the Internet, but most users prefer that it be done in clearly identified newsgroups or Internet locations.

Libel

Some libel suits have been filed based on postings to Usenet or some other network. One person or company feels that another has slandered them or falsely attempted to damage their reputation. Once again, you would expect the same laws or rules for libel in the society at large to be applied to network communications. That's generally the case, but an interesting issue comes up, centering around whether the company or organization that maintains a computer telecommunication system is responsible for libelous or even illegal messages posted there. In the United States the courts have generally drawn an analogy between these systems and a bookstore. The owner of a bookstore is not responsible for the contents of all the books in the store, and likewise, the management of commercial networked systems on the Internet have not been held responsible for all messages on their systems. On the other hand, some commercial network systems claim to screen all messages before they're posted. In that case they may be held accountable for libelous messages. Also, consider that telephone companies aren't held responsible for the speech on their equipment since they fall into the category of a "common carrier." However, television and radio stations are responsible for the content of their broadcasts.

Intellectual Property and Copyright

You know there is a wealth of files, documents, images, and other types of items available on the Internet. They can be viewed, copied, printed, downloaded, saved in a file, or passed on to others. Just because we can copy or duplicate information we find on the Internet, is it legal or ethical to do so? Many, if not most, of these items don't exist in a physical form, so perhaps the issues about ownership that depend on something having a physical form don't make sense. The notion of ownership of something, whether it has a physical form, does still make sense as intellectual property. There are a number of laws and agreements throughout the world to protect intellectual property rights.

Only the owners of the information can grant the right to copy or duplicate materials. This is called the *copyright*. Many documents on the Internet contain a statement asserting the document is copyrighted and giving permission for distributing the document in an electronic form, provided it isn't sold or made part of some commercial product. The copyright laws of the United States, the Universal Copyright Convention, or the Berne Union generally protect items that don't contain these statements. Most copyright conventions or statutes include a provision so that individuals may make copies of portions of a document for short-term use. If information is obtainable on the Internet and there is no charge to access the information, it often can be shared in an electronic form. That certainly doesn't mean you can copy images or documents and make them available on the Internet, or make copies and share them in a printed form with others. Quite naturally, many people who create or provide material available on the Internet expect to get credit and be paid for their work.

One issue that may need to be resolved is the physical nature of information on the Internet. In most cases, it exists on one disk and is viewed in an electronic form. It has no tangible, physical form when it's transmitted. The copyright law in the United States states that copyright protection begins once the work is in "fixed form," so the original portion of these works is protected by copyright. The notion of fixed form is much easier to determine with more traditional works that exist in a physical form, such as books, poems, stories, sound recordings, or motion pictures. Naturally, it seems reasonable to say a work is in fixed form when stored on a disk, but can we say the same about material being transmitted through several networks? If the work only existed on a disk, if that was the only way to obtain the work, then it's clear when the work is being copied and who may be copying the disk. On the other hand, if the information can be accessed through the Internet, one may not know if it is being copied and stored. Current laws and conventions were written for works that exist in some definite physical form, and the nature of that form may make it difficult or time consuming to make unauthorized copies. But information transmitted on the Internet or other networks is very easy to copy. When you copy something in digital form, you make an exact duplicate. Each copy is as good as the original. The ease with which works can be copied and distributed may require a law different from current copyright statutes.

Not all cultures have the same attitudes about ownership of information. Some cultures have a long tradition of sharing information and works created by individuals. Other groups feel all information should be free, and so they think it's appropriate to make works available only if there is no charge for the use of the works. The worldwide nature of the Internet and other networks requires addressing these cultural differences. When the United States deals with some countries, it may withhold a certain level of trading status if they don't abide by international copyright conventions.

These resources give more information about copyright and intellectual property rights:

* "Copyright Basics"
  http://lcweb.loc.gov/copyright/circs/circ1.html
* "INFORMATION POLICY: Copyright and Intellectual Property"
  http://www.nlc-bnc.ca/ifla/II/cpyright.htm

Internet Security

When you use a computer system connected to the Internet, you're able to reach a rich variety of sites and information. By the same token, any system connected to the Internet can be reached in some manner by any of the other computer systems connected to the Internet. Partaking of the material on the Internet also means that you have to be concerned about the security of your computer system and other systems. The reason for the concern about your system is obvious—you don't want unauthorized persons accessing your information or information belonging to others who share your system. You want to protect your system from malicious or unintentional actions that could destroy stored information or halt your system. You don't want others masquerading as you. You need to be concerned about the security of other systems so you can have some faith in the information you retrieve from those systems, and so you can conduct some business transactions. A lack of security results in damage, theft, and what may be worse in some cases, a lack of confidence or trust.

Maintaining security becomes more important as we use the Internet for commercial transactions or transmitting sensitive data. There is always the chance that new services introduced to the Internet won't be completely tested for security flaws or that security problems will be discovered. While it's exciting to be at the cutting edge, there's some virtue in not adopting the latest service or the latest version of software until it has been around for a while. This gives the Internet community a chance to discover problems. Several agencies are dedicated to finding, publicizing, and dealing with security problems. One site that does this is maintained by the National Institute of Standards and Technology (NIST), United States Department of Commerce.

     Use your Web browser to access the NIST Computer Security Resource Clearing House by using the URL **http://first.org**.

In the section "Privacy and Civil Liberties" we mentioned some of the security or privacy problems associated with email. Since information is passed from system to system on the Internet, not always by the same path or through designated secure systems, it can be monitored. Furthermore, you can't always be sure that the address on email hasn't been forged. It appears that an important way to keep transactions secure is to use encryption techniques. These are similar to the ones discussed in that same section on privacy and civil liberties.

If you access the Internet by logging into a computer system, your primary defense against intrusion is your password. You need to choose a password that will be difficult to guess. This means choosing a password that's at least six characters long. You'll also want to use a password that contains upper- and lowercase letters and some nonalphabetic characters. Additionally, the password shouldn't represent a word, and it shouldn't be something that's easy to identify with you such as a phone number, room number, birthdate, or license number. Some bad choices are **Skippy**, **3451234a**, or **gloria4me**. Better choices might be **All452on**, **jmr!pmQ7**, or **sHo$7otg**. Naturally, you have to choose something you'll remember. Never write down your password; doing that makes it easy to find.

Persons who try to gain unauthorized access to a system are called *crackers*. A cracker will, by some means, get a copy of the password file for a system containing the names of all the users along with their passwords. (In some cases the permissions on a password file are set so anyone can read it. This is necessary for certain programs to run. Fortunately, the passwords are encrypted.) Once a cracker gets a copy of a password file, she will run a program that attempts to guess the encrypted passwords. If a password is an encrypted version of a word, a word in reverse order, or a word with one numeral or punctuation mark, it is not too difficult for the program to decipher it. If a cracker has one password on a system, she can gain access to that login name and from there possibly go to other portions of the system. So, in addition to creating a good password, you also need to change it regularly.

Because connecting a network to the Internet allows access to that network, system administrators and other persons concerned with network security are very concerned about making that connection. One device or part of a network that can help enhance security is called a *firewall*. A firewall can be a separate computer, a router, or some other network device that allows certain packets into a network. (Remember that all information is passed throughout the Internet as packets.) By using a firewall and configuring it correctly, only certain types of Internet services can be allowed through to the network. Organizations with firewalls often place their WWW, FTP, and other servers on one part of their network and put a firewall system between those servers and the rest of the network. The firewall restricts access to the protected internal network by letting through only packets associated with certain protocols. Email can still be delivered and sometimes Telnet to the internal network is allowed. If you are on the protected portion of the network, behind the firewall, then you can access Internet and WWW sites on the Internet, but they may not be able to gain direct access to you. Firewalls also perform logging and auditing functions so that if security is breached, the source of the problem may be determined.

> ❊ To find out more about firewalls, read "Internet Firewalls Frequently Asked Questions," **http://www.v-one.com/ documents/fw-faq.htm**.

You don't need to be paranoid about security, but you do need to be aware of anything that seems suspicious. Report any suspicious activity or changes to your directory or files to your system administrator. The system administrator can often take actions to track down a possible break in security. Be suspicious if you're asked for your password at unusual times. You should be asked for it only when you log in. Never give your password to anyone. If a program changes its behavior in terms of requiring more information from you than it did before, it could be an unauthorized user replaced the original program with another. This is called a ***trojan horse***, because of the similarity of the program to the classic Greek tale. What appears to be benign could hide some malicious actions or threats.

One type of program that causes problems for Internet users is called a ***virus***. A virus doesn't necessarily copy your data or attempt to use your system. However, it can make it difficult or impossible to use your system. A virus is a piece of code or instructions that attaches itself to existing programs. Just like a biological virus, a computer virus can't run or exist on its own, but must be part of an executing program. When these programs are run, the added instructions are also executed. Sometimes the virus does nothing more than announce its presence; in other cases the virus erases files from your disk. A virus moves from system to system by being part of an executable program. Be careful where you get programs. You can obtain a program that scans your system for viruses and also checks programs you load onto your system for known viruses. Use these virus scanning programs to check new programs you load on your system. Also be sure to have a backup copy of your files so they can be restored if they're inadvertently or maliciously erased.

Getting documents and images from other sites on the Internet won't bring a virus to your system. It comes only from running programs on your system. Viruses can exist in executable programs and also have been found in word processing documents that contain portions of code called *macros*.

> For more information on viruses, check the hyperlinks at "Other sources of virus information," **http://www.datafellows.fi/vir-info/virother.htm**.

Internet security is very important to many users, as well it should be. We need to make sure that messages are private and that monetary transactions and data sources are secure. Some of these concerns are enforced by laws and acceptable codes of conduct.

> A good document to read about security and privacy is "Identity, Privacy, and Anonymity on the Internet" by L. Detweiler. It's available in three parts through the URL **http://www.eff.org/pub/Privacy/Anonymity/ privacy_anonymity.faq**.

Giving Out Information About Yourself and Your Family

There are a number of situations in which you may be asked or tempted to give out personal information. These can range from being asked to fill out a form to download some software or sign up for a service on the Web to being asked for your address or phone number through email or a chat group. Any information you put into a form will be passed to a Web server and find its way into a database. Disclosing your street address to a business sometimes results in your receiving junk mail, and disclosing your email address may result in your getting unsolicited junk email, or *spam* as it's called. You can't be sure how the information will be used or marketed unless the organization gathering the data makes some explicit guarantees. We hear about and come across situations of fraudulent practices and schemes that swindle money from unsuspecting individuals in our daily lives, and we're just as likely to come across those types of situations when were using the Internet. It's relatively easy to create an Internet or Web presence that makes an individual, a company, or an organization appear to be legitimate and trustworthy. Because of this we need to be all the more skeptical and cautious when conducting personal or commercial dealings on the Internet.

More dangerous situations can arise when we develop a relationship with someone through email or a chat group. These can arise because when we're communicating with someone on the Internet most of the communication is through text. We don't get to hear the person's voice or see them. We may see a picture, they may tell us about themselves, but we may never know with whom we are communicating. For example, I may be involved in a long series of email messages or have several conversations in a chat room with a person who claims to be my age and gender. The person may even send me a photograph. It could be that the person is totally misrepresenting their true self. So we need to be very careful about giving out any personal information, and we certainly wouldn't make arrangements to meet the person without having the meeting take place in a public location and without taking other precautions.

Children particularly need to discuss these issues with their parents, and they need to understand clearly stated rules about not giving out any personal information or telling someone where they go to school or play.

❄ The Web page "Staying Street Smart on the Web!", **http://www.yahooligans.com/docs/safety**, is a good place to find information about Internet safety issues for children and parents.

Common sense tells us not to give out personal information, home phone numbers, or home addresses to people we don't know. We're likely not to do that in our daily lives when we don't know the person who is asking for the information, and it is just as important to apply the same rules when we're using the Internet or the World Wide Web. The Internet and the World Wide Web give us lots of opportunities for learning, recreation, and communication. We don't need to be rude or unfriendly, but we do need to be careful, safe, and secure.

Summary

The Internet has had a tradition of sharing. This includes sharing data, sharing services, exchanging email, having free and generally open discussions, and bringing together ideas and opinions from a diverse population. The rules for behavior, policies for acceptable use, and laws pertaining to activities on the Internet have developed over time. In some cases policies and laws have been adopted from other media, and in other cases the unique qualities of the Internet and electronic communications have been taken into account in establishing laws and policies.

During the transmission of information on the Internet, the information or communication is divided into packets of bytes (characters) that are sent from one system to another. The packets may pass through several different systems, may take different routes to arrive at a destination, and transmissions from one site to another may take different routes at different times. This opens the possibility for intercepting and examining email or other transmissions. Be careful about what you say in email, and think about using encryption techniques so only the recipient can read the email. Laws such as the Electronic Communications Privacy Act (ECPA) have been adopted in some countries to ensure the privacy of electronic communications. The ECPA makes it illegal to intercept or read other people's email and requires government officials to obtain a warrant or court order before searching, seizing, or intercepting electronic communications. Laws regulating slander, libel, threats, and harassment deal with electronic communications as well.

The Internet has grown very rapidly, with a sharp increase in the number of users and a change in the makeup of that population. It continues to become more inclusive, representing users from different countries, cultures, and work groups. This causes some strains between some groups of users and others whose actions seem contrary to past acceptable modes of behavior. For example, in the past the Internet was almost free of commercial transactions, and now commercial uses are condoned and encouraged.

In most cases, the information available on the Internet is the intellectual property of someone or some organization and is protected by copyright laws. Check to see if there are any copyright notices on information. Much of it can be shared in an electronic form, provided the author is given credit and it's not modified. Problems arise because it's so easy to make copies of information available in electronic form. There are very few, if any, ways to know whether a copy has been made. This issue needs to be resolved. Some suggest using methods of encryption to protect against unauthorized copying or dissemination.

Internet security is an important issue for a variety of reasons, including an individual's desire for privacy, the increased use of the Internet for commercial transactions, and the need to maintain the integrity of data. If you access the Internet by logging into a computer system, you need to take care to choose a password that will be difficult to guess. Furthermore, you should notice and report any unusual circumstances or modifications.

The Internet is an important place to learn, work, and enjoy yourself. Some of its strengths have come from the diversity in the user population because there is no central control and because there is two-way access. If you can receive information, you can produce information! The Internet has been relatively free of regulation, but it has codes of ethics and acceptable-use policies to make it a reasonable and safe place for a variety of activities. As the Internet grows and changes, it needs to maintain its sources of strength and vitality. Whether it will maintain its character will depend on the concerns and actions of its users.

Selected Terms Used in This Chapter

acceptable-use policy

ARPA (Advanced Research
    Projects Agency)

cache

civil liberties

cookie

cracker

ECPA (Electronic Communications
    Privacy Act)

firewall

history list

privacy

spam

trojan horse

virus

Appendix

Annotated List of
Selected Search Tools

In this appendix, we'll discuss various search engines and search tools in detail. We'll cover both general-purpose search engines and meta-search tools.

For each search engine or search tool, we will list the URLs of its home page, help page, and FAQ page, along with its output features. For search engines, we'll also identify the types of searches available, the sources to search, and the type of indexing used. For meta-search tools, we'll specify any special features. If the search tool allows for searching several sites concurrently (the parallel search tools), we'll also name the search engines contacted.

Major Search Engines

This section will list some of the major search engines.

AltaVista

Created by Digital Equipment Corporation, AltaVista is one of the most popular and well-regarded search services on the Web. Two types of searching, simple and advanced, are available. AltaVista's home page begins in simple search mode. A hyperlink on each search or results page lets you switch from one type of searching to the other. Information about either type of searching is available if you click on the hyperlink **Help**.

In a simple search, only the implied Boolean operators + and – may be used. In an advanced search, you *must* use the Boolean operators AND, OR, or NOT to form search expressions. The term NEAR may also be used for proximity searching.

In either the simple or advanced mode, you can do phrase searching in which you enclose words in quotes. Furthermore, you can use * as a wildcard character. Finally, you can use capitalization to form a search phrase.

Both modes let you restrict the search to certain fields or portions of a Web page. AltaVista calls this *special functions*. A complete list of fields is available at either help page.

Search results are ranked by relevance in either mode. In the advanced mode, you can specify the ranking by requiring pages that contain certain words to be listed first. This doesn't include or exclude a page from the result; it only affects the ranking. You can specify that you only want links to pages that were indexed or modified during a specified time period. You may specify to see only a count of the results.

You can choose to have the results displayed in compact or standard format. In compact format, only a hyperlink to the title and a few words from the text of the Web page are displayed. In standard format, each result contains the title and URL as hyperlinks, the size (in bytes) of the item, the date it was last visited by the search engine robot, and the first few lines of text from the Web page.

AltaVista offers a *refine* feature, which helps to form search expressions and make the results more precise. Click on **refine** from any page of results. A graphical view (using Java) is available as well. The next Web page lists your expression along with synonyms for terms in the search phrase. By selecting terms you can require that the results include or exclude certain topics.

AltaVista also offers a *translate* service. Web pages can be translated automatically from one language to another. The hyperlink **Translate** appears with each item in the list of results. Then select the language to which the text of the Web page will be translated. A computer program does the translation so that much of the translation is literal.

Home page:	**http://altavista.digital.com**
Help with simple searches:	**http://altavista.digital.com/av/ content/help.htm**
Help with advanced searches:	**http://altavista.digital.com/av/ content/help_advanced.htm**
FAQ:	**http://altavista.digital.com/av/ content/about.htm**
Types of searches:	Keyword or phrase. Implied Boolean expressions in simple search, and full Boolean expressions in advanced search. Proximity, truncation, wildcards, case sensitivity, and field searching supported.
Sources to search:	Web or Usenet. Links to "Zones," specialized search areas titled Careers, Entertainment, Finance, Health, News, and Travel.
Indexing:	Full text.
Output features:	Standard: hyperlink, URL, and text from the Web page. Link to translation service. Compact: hyperlink only. Ranked only by relevancy in simple search. User can supply ranking criteria in advanced search.

Excite

From Excite's home page, you can search the Web, Excite Channels, and Usenet. The home page also contains a link to City.Net; links to business information and maps; Instant Info, an online reference center; links to stock quotes, travel sites, and horoscopes; and ways to find email addresses, street addresses, and phone numbers. The channels are collections of information and ways to retrieve information based on a topic. Here are some examples: *News* is a search service and directory dedicated to magazines and newspapers that are available on the Web. *My Channel* is a personalized list of hyperlinks to news, weather, or entertainment information. *People* and *Chat* are collections of bulletin boards and chat rooms for online discussions, as well as access to search services for finding home pages, email addresses, and street addresses.

Search results are displayed 10 per page and ranked by a relevancy score. Links may also be arranged by site, so all the links from each Web site appear together. When results are displayed, you have the opportunity to select from a list of suggested words to add to the search phrase, but this performs a new search. Each result includes a hyperlink **Click here to perform a search for documents like this one**. These perform a new search for documents similar to the one selected. A list of news articles from a variety of newpapers and periodicals is displayed on the first Web page after the initial 10 results. You can also select the **Power Search** hyperlink. The associated Web page contains several forms to help you create a search phrase by requiring some words, excluding others, and so forth.

You search Excite's index using keywords or phrases. The search tool is one of the few that uses concept searching. For instance, a term such as *young people* may result in links with terms such as *adolescents, juveniles,* or *children.* Excite also offers the implied Boolean operators + and – and the Boolean operators AND, OR, and AND NOT. These Boolean operators *must* be typed in uppercase. Although Excite is case sensitive, it lacks some of the capabilities of other search tools for forming search expressions; it doesn't have truncation, wildcards, or proximity operators, and it doesn't support field searching.

Home page:	**http://www.excite.com**
Help:	**http://www.excite.com/Info/searching.html**
FAQ:	**http://www.excite.com/Info/features.html**
Types of searches:	Keyword (concept search) and phrase. Boolean expressions allowed.
Sources to search:	Web pages (full text), Excite Web Guide, Usenet articles, selected news sources, or City.Net travel guide.
Indexing:	Full text.
Output features:	Title (hyperlink), URL, summary, and a link to similar sites. Ranked by relevancy or site. Links

to sites in Excite Web Guide (Channels), and news stories also displayed.

HotBot

HotBot has become one of the most highly regarded search engines on the Internet. Its home page lets you search the Web. Enter one or more keywords and select from a menu the way the keywords will be used in obtaining results: match all the words or any of the words; use the keywords as a phrase, name, or Boolean expression; or return results with the keywords in the title. A URL can be entered in the search form, and HotBot will return a list of Web pages that contain links to the URL, provided you select **link to this URL** from the menu. You could restrict the date by asking for documents that were added to or updated in the index within a specific time period (click on **Date**). You can specify domains or geographical locations (click on **Continent**). Alternatively, you can specify that results contain certain media types, such as image, audio, video, and Shockwave. Click on **More Search Options** to see other categories and for help in building a search expression.

Results may be displayed from 10 to 100 at a time in brief or detailed format or as URLs. When results are displayed, you have the opportunity to revise the search words or phrase.

Hyperlinks on HotBot's home page take you to forms to use for searching Usenet archives, news sites, classifieds, domain names, stocks, lists of discussion groups, and collections of shareware. You can also follow links to pages you use to find businesses, people, and email addresses.

The home page also contains links to a subject oriented directory, LookSmart. To obtain help in using HotBot and answers to frequently asked questions, click on the button labeled **Help** on the home page. Several selections are available. Follow the link **Search Tips** for an introduction to searching using HotBot. Follow **Advanced Search Features** for a detailed explanation of HotBot's features and operation.

Home page:	**http://www.hotbot.com**
Help:	**http://www.hotbot.com/help/tips**
FAQ:	**http://www.hotbot.com/help**
Types of searches:	Keyword or phrase. Boolean expressions allowed.
Sources to search:	Web, Usenet, news sites, classifieds, domain names, stocks, discussion groups, and shareware.
Indexing:	Full text.
Output features:	Full description: title (hyperlink), excerpt, URL, size, and date indexed. Brief: title (hyperlink) and one-line excerpt.

Infoseek

From Infoseek's home page, you can search the Web, Usenet, news services, and company profiles. It also contains links to Infoseek channels, a collection of Internet and Web resources based on a topic. The Entertainment channel, for example, contains a collection of Web sites; links to movie, TV, music, and book reviews; news about the entertainment industry; and links to tickets and events. The home page also has links to a page you use to find street and world maps (provided by MapQuest) and to Big Yellow, a Web site that is primarily a listing of businesses on the Web (like the yellow pages in a phone book) but that also allows you to find people, look up email addresses, and search country-specific directories from around the world. There's also a link to a reference section that includes a forms-based interface to a dictionary and thesaurus.

You search Infoseek's index using keywords or phrases. You can search for a phrase by enclosing it in quotes. Only the implied Boolean operators + and – are available. Field searching is also available on the title of a Web page, the domain name of a site, or a full or partial URL. Infoseek also has an advanced search page. Here you can construct phrases using keywords and indicating whether a result "should," "must," or "must not" contain a keyword.

Search results are displayed 10 per page and ranked by a relevancy score. You can hide the summaries. You can also arrange the links by site so that all the links from each Web site appear together. When results are displayed, you can begin a new search, but Infoseek makes it rather easy to restrict a search and increase its precision. You can modify the search phrase so that you search either through the current results or on the Web (the part in the Infoseek index).

Home page:	**http://www.infoseek.com**
Help:	**http://www.infoseek.com/** **Help?pg = HomeHelp.html**
FAQ:	None available.
Types of searches:	Keyword or phrase. Implied Boolean expressions allowed.
Sources to search:	Web, Usenet, news services, email addresses, and company profiles.
Indexing:	Full text and keyword.
Output features:	Title (hyperlink), summary, URL, and size. Can hide summary.

Lycos

From Lycos's home page, you can search the Web; search for pictures (image files), sounds (audio files), personal home pages, books, and stocks; and search the annotated listings in the Lycos directory by subject. There are also links to a number of directories and services available through Lycos, including Yellow Pages, a listing of companies on the Web; listings of news stories; Companies Online, a listing of Dun and Bradstreet's information about companies; Road Maps, a search tool that obtains maps and driving directions to street addresses in the United States; a site to get weather information; a site that has links to several chat groups; and Lycos TOP 5 %, a directory of the most popular Web sites. The home page also has links to Lycos Web Guides—a collection of Web and Internet resources arranged into categories. A hyperlink to help is available on each page.

You can perform a simple search from the home page by typing in one or more keywords. The simple search finds sites that match any of the words. The results (10 per page) are ranked by relevancy; pages that match more of the terms rank higher. Lycos takes the words you give plus similar words to find Web pages. When results are displayed, you can modify the search terms, select related sites, or obtain a list of pictures (images, video) or sounds (audio) matching the search terms.

More sophisticated searches are available only if you select Lycos Pro by clicking on the hyperlink **Advanced Search**. In Lycos Pro, you can set search options to allow a match of any word (OR) or all words (AND). That also allows you to set some search parameters, and you may construct Boolean expressions for searching using AND, OR, and NOT, and proximity operators ADJ, NEAR, and FAR. See the "Lycos Help" page for full details.

Display options can also be set from the advanced search page. You select the number of items, from 10 to 40, to be displayed per Web page. The results can be listed in summary form (hyperlinks only, along with a relative score), standard form (hyperlink, score, URL, and an excerpt from the Web page pertinent to your search phrase), or detailed form (standard, along with detailed information about the Web page, including the number of links it has to other Web pages, an outline, and an abstract or excerpt of the page).

Home page:	**http://www.lycos.com**
Help:	**http://www.lycos.com/help**
FAQ:	**http://www.lycos.com/info**
Types of searches:	Keyword. Implied Boolean expressions allowed. Can match all words (AND) or any words (OR). Boolean expressions allowed only with Lycos Pro—similar to advanced search options in other search services. See the "Lycos Help" page for details.
Sources to search:	Web, pictures, sounds, Lycos TOP 5 %, personal home pages, stocks.
Indexing:	Full text.
Output features:	Summary: links only. Standard: title (hyperlink), excerpt, URL, size, and number of terms matched. Detailed: standard format plus outline, abstract, and number of links to external Web pages.

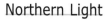
Northern Light

Northern Light is a search engine that indexes the full text of freely available Web resources and items in what it calls its Special Collection. The collection consists of information from over 4,500 (at the time of this writing) periodicals, news items, and databases. Items from the Web are available at no charge, but items from the special collection are only available to account holders. Current charges are $4.95 per month for accounts for individuals. For that fee an individual is allowed to retrieve up to 50 documents from a portion of the special collection; some items require an additional fee.

Results from any search are arranged into custom search folders—a unique feature of searching with Northern Light. The folders are based on your search and arranged by subject, type of resource, and source—such as Web sites, educational institutions, magazines, and so on. Entering the search terms *searching researching* in the search form on the home page, for example, gives a list of results along with the custom folders with various titles that included Search Current News, Special Collection documents, Commercial sites, Personal pages, Web search engines & directories, Public libraries, Human resource development, Ethics, Information literacy, and Technical writing. Clicking on any of these displays the results that Northern Light has grouped in the category represented by the title of the folder, as well as a list of subfolders within the category. In this way Northern Light helps the researcher organize results.

The common search features are supported: nested Boolean search expressions, phrase searching by including terms in quotes, implied Boolean expressions through the use of + and –, the use of * as a wildcard or truncation symbol, and field searching for URL, title, company, and others. It's also possible to limit a search by date and certain types of documents. Selecting Power Search, Publication Search, or Industry Search from the home page does this.

Northern Light doesn't include a subject-oriented directory or searching for specific types of resources such as maps, sounds, or images. It concentrates on searching and arranging results into categories or folders, and it does that task rather well.

Home page:	**http://www.northernlight.com**
Help:	**http://www.northernlight.com/docs/ prod_help.htm**
FAQ:	**http://www.northernlight.com/docs/ annafaq.htm**
Types of searches:	Keyword, phrase, Boolean, and fields.
Sources to search:	Web and Special Collection.
Indexing:	Full text.
Output features:	Title (hyperlink), excerpt, and URL. Items arranged in folders determined for each search.

WebCrawler

WebCrawler was one of the first search engines available on the Web. It was started by Brian Pinkerton as a research project at the University of Washington and has since become part of Excite, Inc. WebCrawler works quickly, and it gives useful results. It also contains a good description of how it and other search engines work, and a very well organized help facility. The home page has a simple search form that can be filled in for simple keyword searching, for phrase searching (enclose the words in quotes), or with expressions using Boolean (AND, OR, NOT) and proximity (NEAR, ADJ) operators. The home page also contains a collection of channels, each of which includes a directory of reviewed Web sites. There are also links to search services for yellow pages (GTE), people finder (WhoWhere), maps, weather, classifieds, horoscopes, and stock quotes. The home page also contains links to a subject-oriented directory, called Channels.

Results are displayed 25 per page, ranked by relevance, and presented in brief format by default, with the title as a hyperlink. Clicking on the hyperlink to show summaries gives an excerpt from each page, the URL for the page, and a link to similar pages.

WebCrawler has a very easy-to-use and effective interface.

Home page:	**http://www.webcrawler.com**
Help:	**http://www.webcrawler.com/Help/Help.html**
FAQ:	**http://www.webcrawler.com/Help/AboutWC/AboutWC.html**
Types of searches:	Keyword, phrase, Boolean.
Sources to search:	Web.
Indexing:	Full text.
Output features:	Title (hyperlink), excerpt, and URL. Can hide excerpt.

Other Resources

Here are some Web sites that have lists of hyperlinks to several general-purpose search engines, including the ones above. Take a look at some of these if you want to try some search engines in addition to the ones mentioned above.

Title of Web Page	URL
Beaucoup Search Engines—Category Page: General Engines	**http://www.beaucoup.com/1geneng.html**
Internet Search Tools (Library of Congress Explore the Internet)	**http://lcweb.loc.gov/global/search.html**
Needle in a Cyberstack - the InfoFinder: Search Engines	**http://home.revealed.net/~albee/pages/search.html**

Search Engine Watch	**http://searchenginewatch.com**
Search Results for: Search Bots	**http://botspot.com/search/s-search.htm**
Yahoo! Computers and Internet: Internet: World Wide Web: Searching the Web: Search Engines	**http://www.yahoo.com/Computers_and_internet/internet/world_wide_web/searching_the_web/search_engines**

Meta-search Tools

Meta-search tools allow you to use several search engines. Some sites merely list World Wide Web search tools with their search forms so you can search one at a time. These are called all-in-one search tools. If a meta-search tool allows you to search several search engines or directories simultaneously, it's called a parallel search tool. Many meta-search tools take your query, search several databases or search engines simultaneously, and then integrate the results. Some meta-search tools are good places to find lists of specialized databases. This section is an annotated list of meta-search tools. Some are all-in-one tools, and most are parallel search tools.

All-in-One Search Page

The All-in-One Search Page is a large collection of forms-based search tools arranged by categories, including World Wide Web, General Internet, Specialized Interest, Software, People, News/Weather, Publications/Literature, Technical Reports, Documentation, Desk Reference, and Other Interesting Searches/Services. After you select a category, you see a list of hyperlinks for the search services in that category, along with a simple frame for submitting a phrase for each tool. This easy-to-use interface was developed and is supported by William D. Cross. The goal is to provide a consistent interface to search for tools from one location on the Web. That goal is met, but there is no search facility that locates resources within All-in-One. The only way to find a specific service is to browse the directory. For example, the search form for the Getty Information Institute is found under Publications/Literature.

Home page:	**http://www.albany.net/allinone**
Help:	None available.
FAQ:	None available.
Output features:	Either displays search result or search page for selected service.
Special features:	Forms-based search services arranged by categories.

Internet Sleuth

Internet Sleuth lists close to 2,000 general-purpose and specialized searchable databases available on the Web. The databases are arranged by subject; the major headings are Arts & Humanities, Business, Computers, Education, Employment, Environment, Government, Health, Internet, News, Recreation, Reference, Regional, Sciences, Shopping, Social Sciences, Society, Sports, Travel, and Veterinary/Zoology. The home page, as well as the other pages, has a search form you can use to find databases or search tools listed by the Internet Sleuth.

A search form that lets you search several databases at once is included on the home page and in several of the sections. Internet Sleuth lists the most popular and useful search engines, including AltaVista, Excite, Infoseek, Lycos, and WebCrawler. Other categories on the home page that allow for parallel searching are News, Business and Finance, Software, and Usenet. For each search, you may specify a maximum search time. The selected search engines or databases are contacted, and the results are presented as if the searching were conducted at the search engine's home site.

Each search tool or database is represented by a hyperlink to the search page for the database, a brief description of the type of information it provides, and a search form that lets you initiate a search from the Internet Sleuth. In many cases, you'll also be able to set options or select types of resources using the form there. The entry for ArtsEdge, for example, allows you to search using phrases or Boolean expressions and to select one or more categories. Internet Sleuth is a good tool to use to find both general-purpose and specialized databases and search tools.

Home page:	**http://www.isleuth.com**
Help:	**http://www.isleuth.com/about.html**
FAQ:	None available.
Output features:	Each service or tool represented by a hyperlink and a form (usually with options) for submitting a query to the service.
Special features:	Search form on home page allows user to search for services available through the Internet Sleuth. Also allows for parallel search of several services.

Dogpile

Dogpile bills itself as a "friendly multi-engine search tool." It has a well-designed and easy-to-use interface. You type keywords in a search form on its home page, select whether to search the Web, Usenet, FTP archives, or news services, and then click on a button labeled **Fetch**. Dogpile then submits the keywords, assuming the words are connected by AND, to three search engines. It then displays the results. If it doesn't come up with 10 documents, then another three search engines are contacted. This continues until at least 10 results are obtained. You can request that other search engines be contacted even if 10 results are found.

You can use Boolean and proximity operators (AND, OR, NOT, and NEAR) in the keyword expression. If you use NEAR, then search engines that allow its use are contacted first. You can also use quotes and parentheses. If a search engine doesn't support these then they're removed before the search expression is passed to one of those.

The search engines and directories contacted for Web resources include AltaVista, Excite, Magellan, Lycos, WebCrawler, Infoseek, HotBot, and Yahoo! For Usenet searches, Dogpile contacts Deja News, Reference.COM, and AltaVista. Filez and FTP searches are contacted when you indicate you want to search FTP archives. When searching news services, Dogpile contacts Yahoo!, News Headlines, Excite News, and Infoseek News Wires.

The search options on the home page let you pick one category of resources to use to start the search and then to go to another category. For example you can choose to have Dogpile first contact Web search engines and then go to Usenet archives. You can set the order in which search engines and other resources are contacted by selecting **Custom Search** from any Dogpile Web page.

Dogpile works well, is well designed, and is easy to use. It's definitely worth considering if you want to use a parallel search tool.

Home page:	**http://www.dogpile.com**
Help:	**http://www.dogpile.com/notes.html**
FAQ:	None available.
Search engines contacted:	Twenty-five search engines, directories, and other resources.
Output features:	Results arranged by relevance according to each search engine or resource contacted.
Special features:	Keywords connected by AND is the default. Searching by phrase, Boolean expressions, or proximity operators.

MetaCrawler

MetaCrawler takes the keywords entered in a search form on its home page and simultaneously conducts a search using several popular search engines and directories. Those include AltaVista, Excite, Lycos, WebCrawler, and Yahoo! Keywords can be passed to the search engines as a phrase. They can be connected by AND (all the words) or by OR (match any of the words). MetaCrawler supports implied Boolean expressions using + and −, as well as phrase searching when the search string is enclosed in quotes. The top 10 results are taken from each search engine, and duplicates are eliminated. MetaCrawler displays results according to relevance. To do so, it computes a score based on the search engines' scores or according to location. It determines location from the domain names in results, including U.S. commercial, U.S. educational, North American, European, and other sites. MetaCrawler has the option Power Search; select it from the home page. The page that appears lets you set the location for searches, the number of results per page, the number of seconds to wait for the search to complete, and the number of results to get from each source. MetaCrawler gives relatively quick access to the most relevant results from several search engines. Read the MetaCrawler FAQ for details and updates.

Home page:	**http://www.metacrawler.com**
Help:	None available.
FAQ:	**http://www.metacrawler.com/help/faq.html**
Search engines contacted:	Six of the most popular search engines.
Output features:	Results arranged by location (domain name) or relevance. Duplicates eliminated.
Special features:	Searching by phrase, as well as AND and OR. Implied Boolean operators may be used. User may select Power Search. Metaspy, **http://www.metaspy.com**, lets you see what search terms other people are using.

SavvySearch

SavvySearch takes keywords entered in the search form on its search page and ranks the suitability of each of the possible search engines. The ranking, done by the software that controls SavvySearch, depends on which search engines will perform best based on the request, as well as the current load and availability of search engines. In ranking the search engines, SavvySearch puts them into groups, each called a *search plan*. SavvySearch performs the search with the first search plan and gives you the option of selecting another plan for a subsequent search.

You may select from a collection of sources and types of information, such as Web Resources, People, News, Software, and Images. When you search for documents that contain the query keywords, you can choose to use all the terms (AND), to use any of the terms (OR), or to do phrase searching. You can also specify how many results you want from each search engine; whether to display results in brief, normal, or verbose format; and whether to integrate the results. The results displayed include the title as a hyperlink, the URL, and the search engine used. Using normal or verbose format gives more information, including an abstract or description of each result. Choosing to display the results in integrated form eliminates duplicates and preserves relative rankings. Otherwise, results are arranged according to search engine. A final choice that SavvySearch presents is one of language; the search form is available in approximately 20 languages.

Home page:	**http://guaraldi.cs.colostate.edu:2000**
Search form:	**http://guaraldi.cs.colostate.edu:2000/form**
Help:	**http://guaraldi.cs.colostate.edu:2000/help**
FAQ:	**http://guaraldi.cs.colostate.edu:2000/faq**
Search engines contacted:	A relatively large number (more than 20) available. Specific ones (three to five) contacted per search, depending on availability and other factors.
Output features:	Title as a hyperlink and search engine name always displayed. More information also available, including author, location, and brief description. Results may be displayed by the search engine used or integrated.
Special features:	User may specify sources and types of information, such as Web resources, people, news, software, and images. SavvySearch uses this, along with availability of search engines, response time, and other factors, to determine a search plan (which search engines and resources to query). User can select another search plan.

SEARCH.COM

SEARCH.COM has put together a collection of more than 100 searchable databases that are available on the Web. These are listed in two ways: by subject (more than 20 categories are listed, from Automotive to Travel) and in alphabetical order (the A–Z list). To find a specific resource, you can use SEARCH.COM's internal search tool by clicking on **Find a Search** or using the URL **http://www.search.com/Find** and browsing the sections. You could also browse the entire list by using the URL **http://www.search.com/Alpha**.

Links are included for other services that search for people (using Snap! White Pages, YellowPages, Stock Quotes, and City Maps. Entries within a category are represented by a one-line description, a hyperlink to a page at SEARCH.COM that contains a hyperlink to the search tool, a form to do the search at SEARCH.COM, a description of the type of information available, and some tips for performing the search. SEARCH.COM gives good coverage about the search tools available on the Web and emphasizes the information you need to use the tools effectively.

Home page: **http://www.search.com**
Help: **http://www.search.com/Help**
FAQ: **http://www.search.com/About**
Output features: Search form, description of search tool, tips for searching, and hyperlink to resource.
Special features: Search services and databases arranged by category and in alphabetical order. Individual services selected with a search form.

Other Resources

Here's a list of collections of Web pages that have links to meta-search tools, including the ones listed above:

Title of Web Page	URL
All-in-One Search Pages	**http://www.voicenet.com/ ~ bertland/searchf/allinone.html**
Meta-Search Engines	**http://www.voicenet.com/ ~ bertland/searchf/ metasearch.html#meta**
Needle in a CyberStack - the InfoFinder: Multi-Search Tools	**http://home.revealed.net/ ~ albee/ #Multi**
Yahoo! Computers and Internet: Internet: World Wide Web: Searching the Web: All-in-One Search Pages	**http://www.yahoo.com/ computers_and_internet/ world_wide_web/ searching_the_web/ all_in_one_search_pages**

B
Appendix

Selected Directories

A directory, or subject catalog, is a collection of Internet and Web resources arranged in categories. There are many general-purpose directories on the Web, as well as lots of specialized ones. Here, we'll discuss some of the more popular and useful ones.

For each tool, we'll give the URLs for its home page, help page, and FAQ page. We'll also indicate whether or how the items in the directory are rated, whether entries are reviewed before being included, and whether it's possible to search the directory. In addition, we'll present the directory's output features and any special features.

Galaxy

From Galaxy's home page, you can search the collection of reviewed and summarized resources that are part of the Galaxy directory. This includes hypertext, Gopher, and Telnet resources. Put together over the past few years by volunteers serving as "guest editors," the Galaxy directory has several thousand entries.

Galaxy also features Professional Directory, the subject guide designed for use by specialists or professionals in a field. It includes the categories Business And Commerce, Engineering And Technology, Government, Humanities, Law, Medicine, Reference, Science, and Social Sciences. The items in each subject area or subtopic are arranged into categories: academic organizations, collections, directories, discussion groups, government organizations, guides, nonprofit organizations, organizations, and periodicals.

When you browse the directory, you will only see the titles of resources listed in the form of hyperlinks. When you use the search form to search the directory, you will also see the following information: an excerpt summary, a list of words that appear frequently in the document, its size, when it was last added to the collection, and where it can be found in the directory.

Home page:	**http://galaxy.einet.net**
Help with searches:	**http://galaxy.einet.net/howto.html**
FAQ:	None available.
Ratings:	None available.

Reviews:	Items reviewed. Excerpts available through search tool. Sections of guide managed by volunteer "guest editors."
Searching:	Yes.
Output features:	Items listed with title (hyperlink).
Special features:	Resources in a subject area arranged by major subcategories (if any), academic organizations, collections, directories, discussion groups, government organizations, guides, nonprofit organizations, organizations, and periodicals. List of resources accessible through Gopher and Telnet.

Infoseek

The Infoseek directory is a subject catalog produced by the same organization that provides the Infoseek search engine described in Appendix A. The major channels include Automotive, Business, Careers, Computer, Entertainment, The Good Life, and others. These topics are listed along with popular subtopics. Some categories—including Business, Computer, Sports, and Personal Finance—also have a hyperlink to relevant news headlines.

You access the entries by browsing the channels and clicking on a hyperlink for a subject area or topic. Each page of the directory (except for the home page) contains a forms-based search tool that you can use to search for entries within the current subject area. Alternately, you can use Infoseek's search engine to search resources on the Web. Each entry in the directory consists of the title (in the form of a hyperlink to the item on the Web), a description, the URL, and the size (in kilobytes) of the item. Some entries are marked with a check mark to indicate that they are especially recommended. Each page has hyperlinks to relevant entries in both Infoseek's specialized guides to news and business information and its directories to email addresses and other addresses.

Infoseek's home page includes a search form with which to search the Web, Usenet, news services, and companies. The search engine is described in Appendix A. It also contains links to Maps, People, Reference Sources, and Big Yellow (a Web site that, like the yellow pages in a phone book, primarily lists businesses on the Web but also contains ways to find people, look up email addresses, and browse directories from various countries).

Home page:	**http://www.infoseek.com**
Help:	**http://www.infoseek.com/Help?pg = channel.html**
FAQ:	None available.
Ratings:	Entries with one or two check marks are especially recommended.

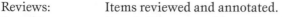

Reviews:	Items reviewed and annotated.
Searching:	Search form on each page lists directory entries and allows user to search current subject area or the Web.
Output features:	Items listed with title (hyperlink), summary, URL, and size.
Special features:	Each page of the directory provides access to specialized directories for news, business information, maps, email and street addresses.

LookSmart

The LookSmart subject guide provides ways to browse the directory that are different from other directories. Instead of using the common practice of replacing a Web page each time a topic or subtopic is selected, LookSmart displays several (up to three) levels of subjects on the screen.

There are relatively few main topics. They include Computers & Internet, Reference & Education, Travel & Vacations, and Home, Family & Auto. The topics and entries appear to provide practical information rather than resources appropriate for a research paper or topic. The directory is constructed so that a reasonable amount of individual entries (usually no more than 30) are displayed in a specific subject area. Individual entries consist of a title (which is a hyperlink to the resource) and a brief description.

In addition to browsing the subject guide, you can select the link Search. This allows you to do keyword searching for items through the LookSmart subject guide or to access the search facilities available through AltaVista. At the time of this writing LookSmart is also featured on the home page for HotBot. This causes some to speculate that HotBot will provide search services in the future. There are also links to search Usenet articles using Deja News, white pages services using BigFoot, and shopping services. You can also select links in the "Personalize" section, which includes links to specialized collections in the following categories: Your Town, News, Magazines, Weather, Live Chat, and Free Email.

Home page:	**http://www.looksmart.com**
Help:	**http://www.looksmart.com/h/info/ helpmain.html**
FAQ:	Links available on help page.
Ratings:	None available.
Reviews:	One-sentence description with each listing.
Searching:	User can search the directory and the Web using search technology licensed from AltaVista.
Output features:	Title (hyperlink) and brief description.
Special features:	Up to three levels of the guide are present on the screen as user moves through a subject area.

Lycos TOP 5% Web Sites

TOP 5% ("Best of the Web") is a subject guide to the best resources on the World Wide Web (according to Lycos). A written review and ratings in the categories of appearance, content, and experience accompany the full entry for each item. According to TOP 5%, the categories may be interpreted as follows:

* Content: The strength, reliability, or uniqueness of the site's content.
* Design: The way in which the site is set up; originality of layout and presentation.
* Overall: Combines content and design factors.

The main subjects range from Autos to Travel, with a good selection of sites in each of the various categories. Entries are arranged by topics, with popular subtopics listed for each category. You access the entries either by browsing the directory or by using the search forms on each directory page to search the directory. On pages listing individual entries, the entries may be viewed in alphabetical order, arranged by date reviewed, or displayed by rating. Each directory entry consists of the title (a hyperlink to the Web item), a description, and a link to related sites. Each title is also a hyperlink to a complete review of the site. The detailed listing includes the title, the score in each of the rating categories, a written review of the site or resource, a hyperlink to the Web site, and a hyperlink to the area or areas of the subject guide that list the item. For some sites, there's also a link to a map giving the geographical location of the site creator. Each page has hyperlinks to the major categories in the directory.

The home page for TOP 5% includes links to the Lycos search engine and a number of directories and services available through Lycos. These include links to news stories, city guides, investing information and services, maps, yellow pages, and shopping.

Home page: **http://point.lycos.com/categories**
Help: **http://www.lycos.com/help/top5-help.html**
FAQ: None available.
Ratings: Entries rated using a scale of 0 to 100 on content, presentation, and experience.
Reviews: Detailed review of each site.
Searching: User can do a forms-based search of the directory (TOP 5%).
Output features: Title (hyperlink), detailed review of the site (which contains a hyperlink to the site itself), and list of ratings. Items may be listed by date reviewed; in alphabetical order; or by ratings of content, presentation, and experience.
Special features: Can search the whole Lycos index for sounds or pictures.

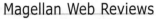

Magellan Web Reviews

The Magellan subject guide includes, for most entries, a description, a rating, and contact information for each site. Magellan used to include more information regarding sites in the directory, but as the result of an acquisition by Excite, Inc., the Magellan directory has been replaced by what was Excite Reviews. In addition to browsing the reviewed sites, it's also possible to search the "old" Magellan directory for sites with a "green light"; these sites are suitable for anyone, not just adult audiences.

The subject guide's major categories are listed on the home page, and you can access subtopics by browsing the directory. Major topics in the directory range from Arts to Sports and include topics such as Business, Entertainment, and Regional. Web sites within a subject area are displayed according to ratings (1 through 4), and then alphabetically within a rating category. Each entry has a rating, a title (which is a hyperlink to the Web site), and a brief review of the Web site. The home page for Magellan has a link to Search Voyuer, a Web page that lists 12 real-time search expressions used by others on the Internet.

Home page:	**http://www.mckinley.com**
Help:	**http://www.mckinley.com/magellan/Info/ advancedtips.html**
FAQ:	None available.
Ratings:	Most sites rated on a scale of 1 to 4. Sites also rated with the "Magellan green light" system regarding content intended for a mature audience.
Reviews:	Summaries and reviews included with many of the entries.
Searching:	Search tool with several options for searching rated and reviewed sites, "green light" sites only, or entire Web.
Output features:	Rating (most but not all sites are rated), title (hyperlink), and brief review. Within a category, sites are alphabetized by ratings.
Special features:	Search Voyeur—a changing list of 12 randomly selected real-time searches and specialized guides, including a guide to cities, email and street addresses, horoscopes, maps, sports scores, stocks, and weather.

NetGuide: Your Guide to the Net

NetGuide's stated aim is to provide a comprehensive daily directory of what's available on the Web. To that end, the home page, **http://www. netguide.com**, offers links to a variety of services including a form to search the reviewed Web sites (all the entries are reviewed and rated before being included in the guide) and links to a set of comprehensive guides to information, tips, and events in a particular subject area.

The home page for the subject guide, **http://www.netguide.com/ Browse**, includes links to the major categories, as well as popular sub-categories of the guide. Major categories include Art & Culture, General Reference & News, **Living, Science & Nature**, and Sports. The listings of Web sites within a subject area are displayed according to ratings (one to five stars), and then alphabetically within a rating category. A listing of entries shows the rating, the title of a site as a hyperlink to the site, an excerpt from the review, and a hyperlink (Site Details) to a detailed review of the site. This detailed review contains the site's overall ratings along with scores for content, design, and personality. Other items noted are parental control (the possibilities include none, nudity, violence, and obscenity) and fees/registration (which applies to access to the site). The site details also contain the title of the Web site as a hyperlink to the site, the name of the information provider, and a detailed review.

The NetGuide site also supports some other guides, including Today's Top Happenings (links to daily top net/media events), How to (a collection of well-developed articles dedicated to using technology or accomplishing a general task on the Web, such as renting an apartment), and a reference section.

A relatively small number of guides or subject areas (10, to be exact) are available on the home page, **http://www.netguide.com**. These topics range from Computing to Travel. Each guide is written and maintained by an individual and contains links to sites arranged in subcategories of the main topics of the guide. The home page for a guide also includes a featured site of the day, other featured sites, and new items in the category. This format presents a comfortable, relatively easy-to-use interface.

Home page:	**http://www.netguide.com**
Help:	**http://www.netguide.com/AboutUs**
FAQ:	None available.
Ratings:	One to five stars based on content, design, and personality.
Reviews:	One-paragraph review with each listing. See **http://www.netguide.com/Browse**.
Searching:	Search form available on each page, giving the option to search this subject guide or to use Lycos to search for resources elsewhere on the Web.
Output features:	Items within a category displayed alphabetically by rating, title (hyperlink), link to a detailed listing, and one-sentence description or review. Each site includes detailed rating, information about cost and parental control, title (hyperlink), name of provider, and one-paragraph review.
Special features:	Links to other portions of NetGuide include Today's Top Happenings (links to daily top net/

media events), How to (a collection of well-developed articles dedicated to using technology or accomplishing a general task on the Web), and a reference section.

WebCrawler Channels

WebCrawler is a search tool that incorporates channels in its organization. Part of WebCrawler's channels is a highly discriminatory collection of Web sites and other resources arranged in a subject directory called the Channels. This is the directory section of WebCrawler. The channels range from Arts to Travel and include Computers & Internet, Health & Fitness, Relationships, and Sports. Some items are reviewed and selected before being added to the collection. The aim is to provide a comprehensive collection of high-quality Web sites and other resources. The help for WebCrawler is very well written, and the site is easy to navigate. Each category entry has a link that allows you to search the Web for related resources using WebCrawler.

The listings within a subject area are arranged into subcategories. Entries in a subcategory are arranged into types of sites and have an accompanying list of Usenet newsgroups related to each topic. There is also a link that begins a search of WebCrawler's database of sites. The entry for an individual listing includes a hyperlink to the entry, a review of the site, a hyperlink that searches WebCrawler for similar sites, and links to take you to other entries in the category. This Web site is very well done and is highly recommended.

Home page:	**http://www.webcrawler.com**
Help:	**http://www.webcrawler.com/Help/Guide.html**
FAQ:	None available.
Ratings:	None available.
Reviews:	Some items reviewed.
Searching:	Searching is not possible in the WebCrawler Guide.
Output features:	Subject guide arranged by category; each item reviewed, annotated, and represented as a hyperlink.
Special features:	Links from each category to related Web sites and related Usenet newsgroups. Links from each listing to related Web sites.

Yahoo!

Yahoo! was one of the first subject guides or directories on the World Wide Web and is undoubtedly the most popular and talked-about subject guide. Thousands of entries are submitted to Yahoo! by information providers or others and are included in the subject guide by the Yahoo! staff. Each item is put into an appropriate category and listed as a title, which is a hyperlink to the site, along with a brief description (provided by the person recommending the site).

Yahoo!'s strengths are the number of sites listed and the organization of the site itself. There are several major categories, including Arts and Humanities, Education, Health, News and Media, Science, and Society and Culture. Each is divided into subcategories, and listings include individual sites and links to other categories. There are no extensive reviews for sites, and Yahoo! does not rate sites, but it does manage the entries by selectively including them in the directory.

You can search for sites throughout Yahoo! or within the currently selected category. All the categories include keyword searching, which supports matching all words (AND), any word (OR), phrase searching, wildcards (use * after a prefix), and limiting a search by date. After performing a search, you can continue the search by using AltaVista, using indexes titled Headlines and Net Events, or selecting another major search engine from a list. Yahoo! also offers other services for finding information, such as directories or subject guides with options to search. These include Yellow Pages, People Search, Maps, News, Stock Quotes, and Sports.

Yahoo! provides subject guides specific to Canada, France, Germany, Japan, the United Kingdom, and Ireland, with listings in each country's language. There are regional guides for some cities in the United States, including Austin, Boston, Los Angeles, New York, San Francisco, Seattle, and Washington D.C. Other subject guides include "Yahooligans! for Kids," "Yahoo! Internet Life," "Yahoo! Store," "Classifieds," "Today's Web Events," "Chat," "Yahoo! Mail," "Yahoo! Pager," and weather forecasts.

Yahoo! began early in the history of the World Wide Web (1994). It is relatively easy to use, provides much useful information, continues to be very popular, and has provided a model and high standards for other subject directories to emulate.

Home page:	**http://www.yahoo.com**
Help (general):	**http://www.yahoo.com/docs/info/help.html**
Help (searching):	**http://search.yahoo.com/search/help**
FAQ:	**http://www.yahoo.com/docs/info/faq.html**
Ratings:	None available.
Reviews:	No written reviews. Items included only after approval by Yahoo!
Searching:	Search form available on each page, giving the option to search within current category, all categories, Headlines, Net Events, AltaVista, or another search engine.
Output features:	Title (hyperlink) and brief annotation.
Special features:	There are several regional or national editions of the guide and other special subject guides, including Shopping, Yellow Pages, People Search, Maps, Classifieds, Personals, Message Boards, Chat, Email, Pager, My Yahoo!, Today's News, Sports, Weather, TV, and Stock Quotes.

Other Resources

Here are some Web pages that contain hyperlinks to directories, including the ones we've discussed above:

Title of Resource	URL
Internet Search Tools (Library of Congress Explore the Internet)	**http://lcweb.loc.gov/global/ search.html#www**
Needle in a CyberStack - the InfoFinder: Directories and Guides	**http://home.revealed.net/ ~ albee/pages/guides.html**
Yahoo! Computers and Internet: Internet: World Wide Web: Searching the Web: Web Directories	**http://www.yahoo.com/ computers_and_internet/ internet/world_wide_web/ searching_the_web/ web_directories**

C
Appendix

Virtual Libraries

Virtual libraries are directories that contain collections of Internet or Web resources that have been reviewed and evaluated before they're included. For this reason, the resources tend to be useful, accurate, and authentic. Most of them are, in fact, selective subject guides. In many cases, you'll find that professional librarians staff and manage these virtual libraries.

For each item, we'll list the URLs for the home page, help page, and FAQ page. We'll also state the output features and any special features.

The Argus Clearinghouse

The Argus Clearinghouse bills itself as "The Internet's Premier Research Library." It is a collection of reviewed and rated Web guides to information about specific topics. The guides are not about a specific site; instead, they are about a certain topic.

The major Argus Clearinghouse categories range from Arts & Humanities to Social Sciences & Social Issues. The guides are arranged in a hierarchical subject arrangement, so you can browse the collection. It's also possible to search the collection using a form that permits two terms. These would be connected by AND or OR; truncation (use * after a prefix) is also an option. For assistance with searching The Argus Clearinghouse, see the help page, **http://www.clearinghouse.net/ searchtips.html**.

Guides in the collection have been reviewed and rated by professional librarians. The rating system, a range of one to five check marks in each category, is based on the following criteria:

- Level of resource description
- Level of resource evaluation
- Guide design
- Guide organizational schemes
- Guide meta-information

The listing for a specific guide includes its title, a separate hyperlink to the Web resource, a list of keywords, the name of the guide's author or producer, the date it was last checked, the overall rating, and a rating in each category. You'll want to check The Argus Clearinghouse when you're looking for guides to resources on the Web and the Internet.

Home page:	**http://www.clearinghouse.net**
Help:	**http://www.clearinghouse.net/ searchtips.html**
FAQ:	**http://www.clearinghouse.net/faq.html**
Output features:	Topics arranged by category, each with a list of resources. Each item represented by title, hyperlink to resource, keywords, author's name and affiliation, date The Argus Clearinghouse last checked resource, overall rating, and rating in each category.
Special features:	Searches full text of information pages, including titles, names of authors, institutions, and key-words.

Infomine: Scholarly Internet Resource Collections

Infomine is a collection of reviewed Internet and Web resources. Its stated aim is to present a collection of resources useful to faculty, students, and researchers at the university level. The site has been developed by people from the Library of the University of California, Riverside.

Information is categorized into several subject-oriented "infomines." These include Biological, Agricultural, and Medical Sciences, Government Information, Internet Enabling Tools, Maps & GIS, Physical Sciences, Engineering, Computing & Math, Social Sciences & Humanities, Visual & Performing Arts, and Regional & General Interest. The home page also has links to the areas General Reference, News Resources, E-Journal Guides, and Search/Finding Tools.

Each of the areas of the collection, each infomine, can be examined either by browsing or by searching using keywords or search expressions. An area can be browsed through a table of contents, a list of subject categories, a list of keywords, or a list of titles. All of these are arranged in alphabetic order using Library of Congress terminology. Additionally, a user can access new items in a category and links to library, education, and featured sites. Items in the collection are reviewed with a brief review and a hyperlink accompanying each listing.

Home page:	**http://lib-www.ucr.edu**
Help:	**http://lib-www.ucr.edu/infomine/ howtouse.html**
FAQ:	**http://lib-www.ucr.edu/infomine/intro.html**
Output features:	List of items in the collection, each as a hyperlink and a brief review.
Special features:	Thousands of items in the collection of reviewed resources. Each area of the collection is called an

infomine. Areas can be browsed or searched. Easy-to-use interface.

Internet Public Library

The Internet Public Library (IPL) was created to give the Internet library services, including the accumulation, evaluation, selection, and classification of materials. IPL is staffed and managed by professional librarians; the project is hosted by the University of Michigan's School of Information. This virtual site is analogous to a real library in terms of its structure or architecture, its collection, and the services it provides.

The IPL home page, called the IPL Lobby, has hyperlinks to the Web site's primary sections, or divisions. These links are both embedded in images and visible as text. Lots of different resources and several types of activities and services are available through the IPL. Many of the guides can be searched, and most divisions have hyperlinks on their pages that encourage and help a patron—someone browsing the Web page—to ask questions of the IPL staff or the reference librarian. This is indeed a very useful and rich resource. The reference collection alone matches in quality (if not quantity) the resources available through other, commercial subject guides.

The major topics are the usual ones you'd expect to see in a library, such as Reference, Arts & Humanities, Education, Health & Medical Sciences, and Social Sciences. The listing for an individual entry includes a review and descriptive annotation, the title as a hyperlink to the resources, the author's name, and the subjects under which it is classified.

To help you find the information you need the information is arranged into collections: Reference, Exhibits, Especially For Librarians, Magazines and Serials, Newspapers, Online Texts, Web Searching, Teen, and Youth. The IPL is the home for some special Internet collections such as Associations on the Net (a guide to professional and scholarly organizations on the Web) and POTUS (a guide to the elections, presidencies, and lives of U.S. presidents).

Home page:	**http://www.ipl.org**
Help:	**http://www.ipl.org/about**
FAQ:	**http://www.ipl.org/about/iplfaq.html**
Output features:	Image-based and text-based interface to the main sections of the library.
Special features:	Thousands of items in the collection of reviewed resources. The IPL is presented as Divisions: Reference (annotated subject guides), Youth, and Teen; Rooms: Exhibit Hall and Reading Room (a collection of online texts, serial publications, and newspapers); and Services: For Librarians, Directory & Tour, and Web Searching.

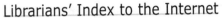
Librarians' Index to the Internet

The Librarians' Index to the Internet is a directory to Web and Internet resources. Each entry is reviewed before being included in the collection. Entries are arranged by subject area, and individual entries are alphabetized within a subject area. These entries are well organized. An entry consists of the title as a hyperlink to the site, an annotation or summary of the site, and hyperlinks to the subject area or areas for an individual resource.

The subjects cover a wide range of topics. At one time called the Index to the Internet for the Berkeley, California, Public Library, the index has an understandable emphasis on a few topics of particular interest to residents of that region. The Librarians' Index to the Internet gives good coverage to a variety of resources on the Web.

You can locate entries by browsing the guide or by using a forms-based search tool. The tool allows you to search in the titles, subjects, annotations, or all fields of the entries. You may choose to search for a match to all or any of the search terms—in other words, a Boolean AND or OR, respectively. It's also possible to truncate words by including an asterisk (*) after a prefix.

Home page:	**http://sunsite.berkeley.edu/ internetindex**
Help:	**http://sunsite.berkeley.edu/ internetindex/tips.html**
FAQ:	None available.
Output features:	Subject guides arranged by category. Items reviewed, annotated, and represented as hyperlinks.
Special features:	Can search by title, subject, annotation, or fields.

World Wide Web Virtual Library

The World Wide Web Virtual Library (WWWVL) was started in 1991 by Tim Berners-Lee, the person credited with the concept of the World Wide Web. It is staffed entirely by volunteers—experts, organizations, or other interested people who take responsibility either to create an entry for the library or to maintain a topic or subject area.

There are more than 100 individual subjects ranging alphabetically from Aboriginal Studies to Zoos. The subject guides reside on several different computer systems throughout the world; the WWWVL is a distributed library. For that reason, and because the work is shared among many people, there's little uniformity in the format for the subject areas.

The URL **http://vlib.stanford.edu/Overview.html** takes you to the home page or Subject Catalogue for the WWWVL—information is arranged by subject. Another view of the collection is Alphabetical Listing, **http://vlib.stanford.edu/AlphaVL.html**.

The WWWVL is a good resource for guides to a variety of subject areas. It's been around since the early days of the World Wide Web, and it has a good reputation for the high quality of its resources and the demonstrated benefits of cooperative, voluntary work.

Home page: **http://vlib.stanford.edu/Overview.html**
Help: None available.
FAQ: **http://vlib.stanford.edu/AboutVL.html**
Output features: Items arranged as a subject catalog or alphabetically, depending on which URL is used to access the Library. No uniformity, because each category or topic is maintained by a volunteer, but each is meant to be a guide to all the major resources related to a specific topic.
Special features: Alphabetical arrangement and category subtree (subject guide).

Other Resources

Here's a list of collections of Web pages that have links to virtual libraries and to other Web resources:

Title of Resource	URL
Internet Search Tools (Library of Congress Explore the Internet)	**http://lcweb.loc.gov/global/ search.html#www**
MWSC Library Links to Virtual Libraries	**http://www.mwsc.edu/ ~libwww/ref2.html**
Needle in a CyberStack - the InfoFinder: Needle Navigator	**http://home.revealed.net/ ~albee**
Yahoo! Computers and Internet: Internet: World Wide Web: Searching the Web: Indices to Web Documents	**http://www.yahoo.com/ computers_and_internet/ internet/world_wide_web/ searching_the_web/ indices_to_web_documents**

D
Appendix

Ways to Stay Current

The content of the World Wide Web is always changing, because tools, resources, and documents are added daily. Many of the tools and resources available for searching and conducting research are very good, but none of them is perfect. You'll want to keep informed of new and improved services. We'll list some ways to do that here. You can regularly visit the Web sites we'll name and read the articles in Usenet newsgroups that carry announcements. You'll also want to keep checking the Web sites that list search tools, directories, and virtual libraries since they sometimes mention new tools; we've mentioned these sites in previous appendices.

Web Sites Listing New Resources

This section contains an annotated list of resources to use to keep track of new Web sites.

The Scout Report

The Scout Report lists new and newly discovered resources of interest to researchers and educators. It is a publication of The Internet Scout Project, which is part of the computer science department at the University of Wisconsin. This project is also supported by InterNIC, the agency that registers Internet domain names.

Weekly issues of The Scout Report contain listings in three categories:

* Research and education
* General interest
* Network tools

Each listing contains the name of the resource, the URL as a hyperlink, and a written description. Instructions for getting weekly issues through a free email subscription service appear at the end of each issue. Instructions to access the weekly reports as Web pages, through Gopher, and FTP are also included.

The URL for The Scout Report is **http://www.cs.wisc.edu/scout/ report**. To receive the weekly issues by email, send email to **listserv@cs.wisc.edu**, and type

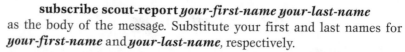

subscribe scout-report *your-first-name your-last-name*
as the body of the message. Substitute your first and last names for
your-first-name and *your-last-name*, respectively.

What's New Web Sites

Several sites on the Web list new Web sites. Most of these are associated
with directories or subject guides and list items that have recently been
added. There's a category in the Yahoo! directory for sites that are dedicated to listing new Web sites. The name of the section, starting from
the top of the Yahoo! directory, is Computers and Internet:
Internet: World Wide Web: Searching the Web: Indices to Web Documents: What's New. The URL is **http://www.yahoo.com/computers_
and_internet/internet/world_wide_web/searching_the_web/
indices_to_web_documents/what_s_new**. More than 40 sites are
listed.

Here's a short list of "What's New" sites that you may want to check
occasionally. You could add them to your bookmark or favorites list.

* **Librarians' Index to the Internet: What's New This
  Week**

  A listing of sites added to the index, it's available as the
  hyperlink **New This Week** on the home page. The URL for
  the home page is **http://sunsite.berkeley.edu/
  internetindex**.

* **Internet Scout Net-Happenings**

  Archives of the articles posted to the Usenet newsgroup
  comp.internet.net-happenings and the corresponding email
  discussion group net-happenings. Each item lists a resource
  that's been submitted to the newsgroup or discussion
  group. Labeled with a category, announcements contain
  URLs and some descriptive information. Net-happenings is
  a service of InterNIC, the Net Scout project, and the list
  moderator, Gleason Sackman. The URL is **http://scout.cs.
  wisc.edu/scout/net-hap/index.html**.

* **What's New Too!**

  A daily listing of new sites. Hundreds of items appear each
  day. Anyone may post an announcement, and all announcements are listed. It is possible, however, to customize the
  listings so you only see announcements in specific categories. The URL is **http://nu2.com**.

* **Yahoo! - What's New**

  A listing of new sites added to Yahoo!'s directory. This Web
  page has links to a list of new sites for each of the past
  seven days, a list of Yahoo!'s daily picks, and a link to
  Yahoo!'s weekly picks. The URL is
  http://www.yahoo.com/new.

Email Discussion Groups Listing
New Web Sites and Resources

Email Discussion Groups for Announcements of New or Changed Web Sites

The primary email discussion group or mailing list for announcing new or changed Web sites and other resources is net-happenings. Messages are submitted to the moderator, who then passes them on to the group. The messages are labeled with a category, such as BOOK, COMP, K12, or SOFT. This discussion group is also available as the Usenet newsgroup comp.internet.net-happenings. Archives are available and may be searched at the Web site *Internet Scout: Net Happenings,* **http://scout.cs.wisc.edu/scout/net-hap/index.html**. Net-happenings is a service of Internet Scout Project in the computer science department at the University of Wisconsin, Madison, and the list moderator, Gleason Sackman. To join the list, send email to **listserv@cs.wisc.edu** and type

subscribe net-happenings *your-first-name your-last-name*

as the body of the message.

Email Discussion Groups for Announcements of New Discussion Groups

The email group NEW-LIST carries announcements of new lists. To join the list, send email to **listserv@cw.wisc.edu** with the message

subscribe new-list *your-first-name your-last-name*

Usenet Newsgroups Listing
New Web Sites and Resources

Newsgroups for Announcements of New or Changed Web Sites

Two primary Usenet newsgroups announce new Web sites and resources. When people with access to Usenet submit announcements to the groups, the moderators post appropriate announcements. A description of each group follows.

comp.infosystems.www.announce
Each announcement is tagged with a keyword indicating the type of resource, such as ART, EDUCATION, RELIGION, or SPORTS. The moderator does not permit announcements of any commercial Web site or Web sites with only local interest. A FAQ for the newsgroup is regularly posted to the newsgroup and is available as a Web page with the URL **http://vader.boutell.com/ ~ grant/charter.html**.

comp.internet.net-happenings

Each announcement is tagged with a keyword indicating the type of resource, such as BOOK, COMP, K12, or SOFT. This newsgroup has an associated Web site that includes archives and searching at **http://scout.cs.wisc.edu/scout/net-hap/index.html**, and the articles in the newsgroup are also available through the email discussion group net-happenings. Net-happenings is a service of Internet Scout Project in the computer science department at the University of Wisconsin, Madison, and the list moderator, Gleason Sackman.

news.announce.newgroups

This is the primary Usenet newsgroup used for announcing new newsgroups. This group also carries discussions related to creating a specific newsgroup. These include requests for discussions (RFD) about new newsgroups and a call for votes (CFV) to determine whether a newsgroup be established.

Glossary

administrative address   The address to use to join an email discussion group or interest group and to send requests for services.

all-in-one search tool   A tool that provides search forms for several search engines and directories all in one site. The tool also provides hyperlinks, which allow you to go to the services directly.

annotated directories   Often referred to as virtual libraries, these directories have brief summaries, descriptions, ratings, or reviews attached to Web pages and subject guides.

annotation   A brief summary or description of a Web page or of any work listed in a database.

anonymous FTP   A means of using FTP to make files readily available to the public. If you start an FTP session with a remote host, you give the login or user name *anonymous,* and enter your email address as a password. When you use a URL starting with **ftp://** and a domain name with a Web browser, an anonymous FTP session begins, and you don't have to enter a user name or password.

article   A message or file that is part of a Usenet newsgroup.

attachment   A file that is sent as part of an email message but that is not part of the main message. Usually images, programs, or word processor files are sent as attachments, because most email programs allow only plain text in the body of a message.

bibliographic database   An online database that includes citations that describe and identify titles, dates, authors, and other parts of written works. It doesn't contain the full text of the information itself. Some bibliographic databases are annotated, which means there is a brief summary of each work listed.

bookmark   A hyperlink that is saved in the bookmark list, a file in your browser. You can use bookmarks to keep track of favorite or important sites and to return there whenever you are on the World Wide Web.

bookmark list   A list of hyperlinks to items on the World Wide Web.

Boolean searching   Searching that uses Boolean operators (AND, OR, and NOT) in the search expression. Especially helpful in multifaceted or specific topics, Boolean operators help expand or narrow the scope of your search. A search for *rivers OR lakes* returns all documents with both words or either word in them. A search for *rivers AND lakes* returns documents with both words in them. A search for *rivers AND lakes NOT swamps* returns only documents that mention both *rivers* and *lakes* but omits those that also mention *swamps*.

browsing The process of going from one hyperlink to another on the World Wide Web. You can browse indiscriminately, or you can do structured browsing, using a hierarchical subject list in a directory.

case sensitivity The ability of a search tool to distinguish between uppercase and lowercase letters. Some search tools aren't case sensitive; no matter what you type, the tool only picks up lowercase matches. Search engines that are case sensitive will strictly follow the search request; they'll return documents containing the words in the case in which they were entered in the search expression.

client/server The interaction between a system that requests information (the client) and another system that provides it (the server). The browser is the client, and a computer at the site that provides the information is the server.

commercial database A database that requires you to pay a subscription cost before accessing it. See also proprietary database.

concept searching A feature enabling a search engine to find synonyms in its database. When you type in a word or phrase, the engine automatically searches for the word or phrase you want, plus words or phrases that may mean the same thing. For example, if the word *teenage* is in your search expression, the search engine would also look for the word *adolescent*.

content area The part of a Web browser window that contains the current Web page, including images, text, or hyperlinks.

cross-posting Posting an article to more than one Usenet newsgroup.

default setting The configuration a search engine uses unless you override the setting by specifying another configuration. For example, in most search engines, the Boolean operator OR is the assumed relationship between two words unless you type AND between the words.

Dewey decimal classification system Originated by Melvil Dewey in the late 19th century, this classification system for library materials divides all knowledge into 10 different classes, which are then subdivided into several sets of subclasses. Within these subclasses, decimals reflect still smaller subdivisions. The Dewey decimal classification system is most prevalent today in public libraries, whereas most other types of libraries, including academic ones, use the Library of Congress classification system.

directory Topical lists of Internet resources, arranged hierarchically. Directories are meant to be browsed, but they can also be searched.

Directories differ from search engines in one major way—the human element involved in collecting and updating the information.

discussion group A group that discusses a single topic via email messages. An individual subscribes to or joins a discussion group electronically, and all messages sent to the group are distributed to the members by email.

domain name The Internet name for a network or computer system. The name consists of a sequence of characters separated by periods, such as **www.mwc.edu**. The domain name is often the first part of a URL that follows **://**. For example, the domain name in the URL **http://sunsite.unc.edu/herbmed/culiherb.html** is **sunsite.unc.edu**.

downloading Transferring or copying a file from another computer (the remote computer) to the computer you're using (the local computer). This term is often applied to the process of retrieving a file from a software library or FTP archive.

duplicate detection An output feature of some search engines and meta-search tools that automatically filters out of your search results any URLs that are duplicated elsewhere in the results.

FAQ (frequently asked questions) A list of commonly asked questions and answers on a specific topic. A FAQ is often associated with Usenet newsgroups, but several search tools also include a FAQ file. This, and online help, is usually the first place you should look to find answers.

field Part of a Web page or bibliographic record that is designated for a particular kind of data or text.

field searching A strategy in which you limit a search to a particular field. In a search engine, you might search only the URL field. In a library catalog, you could search for items by author, title, subject, call number, or any other data element that was designated as a field. By narrowing the scope of searchable items, field searching helps to eliminate the chance of retrieving irrelevant information.

frames A browser feature that displays several Web pages in the browser's content area. Each frame has its own URL and controls.

freeware A software program that's available for use without any charge. This doesn't mean the program isn't copyrighted. Usually, the originator retains the copyright. Anyone can use it, but the program can't be legally sold or distributed without permission.

FTP (File Transfer Protocol) A means of transferring or sharing files across the Internet from one computer system to another.

FTP archive A collection of files available through anonymous FTP.

full-text database A database that contains the full text of the information it describes.

full-text indexing   A search engine feature in which every word, significant or insignificant, is indexed and retrievable through a search.

Gopher   A menu-oriented system that gives access to documents, files, and other Internet services, regardless of where they are on the Internet. The software for Gopher was created and developed at the University of Minnesota to allow users to browse and retrieve documents in a campus environment.

group address   The address to use to send email to each member of a discussion group, interest group, listserv list, or mailing list.

GUI (graphical user interface)   An interface that uses icons and images in addition to text to represent information, input, and output.

helper applications   Programs used with a Web browser to display, view, or work with files that the browser cannot display. For example, Netscape Navigator can display graphic or image files in GIF or JPEG format. If you accessed an image of another type through a hyperlink, then your browser would need a helper application to display it. As another example, some Web browsers can work with several protocols but not with Telnet. If you activate a hyperlink that begins a Telnet session, a Telnet client that is separate from the Web browser must be used. The Web browser can recognize when it's necessary to use specific helper applications.

hierarchy   A list of subjects in a directory. The subjects are organized in successive ranks with the broadest listed first and with more specific aspects or subdivisions listed below.

high precision/high recall   A phenomenon that occurs during a search when you retrieve all the relevant documents in the database and retrieve no unwanted ones.

high precision/low recall   A phenomenon that occurs when a search yields a small set of hits. Although each one may be very relevant to the search topic, some relevant documents will be missed.

history list   A list of Internet sites, services, and resources that have been accessed through a Web browser during recent sessions.

hit list   A list of results obtained from an online search.

home page   The first screen or page of a site accessible through a Web browser.

HTML (Hypertext Markup Language)   The format used for writing documents to be viewed with a Web browser. Items in the document can be text, images, sounds, or links to other HTML documents, sites, services, and resources on the Web.

HTTP (Hypertext Transfer Protocol)   The standard protocol that World Wide Web servers and clients use to communicate.

hyperlink   Words, phrases, images, or regions of an image that are often highlighted or colored differently and that can be selected as part

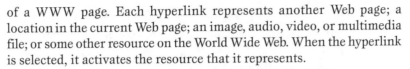

of a WWW page. Each hyperlink represents another Web page; a location in the current Web page; an image, audio, video, or multimedia file; or some other resource on the World Wide Web. When the hyperlink is selected, it activates the resource that it represents.

hypermedia An extension to hypertext that includes graphics and audio.

hypertext A way of viewing or working with a document in text format that allows you to follow cross-references to other Web resources. By clicking on an embedded hyperlink, the user can choose her own path through the hypertext material.

implied Boolean operators Using the characters + and – to require or prohibit a word or phrase as part of a search expression. The + acts somewhat as AND, and the – acts as NOT would in a Boolean expression. For example, the Boolean expression *rivers AND lakes NOT swamps* may be expressed as *+ rivers + lakes –swamps.*

interest group Group discussion and sharing of information about a single topic carried out via email.

Internet The collection of networks throughout the world that agree to communicate using specific telecommunication protocols, the most basic being Internet protocol (IP) and transmission control protocol (TCP), and the services supplied by those networks.

keyword indexing A feature in which each significant word in the entire document or record is indexed and retrievable by the search engine or computer program being used.

keyword searching A feature in which the search engine or computer program searches for every occurrence of a particular word in the database, regardless of where it may appear.

LCSH (Library of Congress subject headings) A list of standardized subject headings that are used to index materials by the Library of Congress. The subject headings are arranged in alphabetical order by the broadest headings, with more precise headings listed under them. Most academic library catalogs are searchable by subject heading as well as by keyword.

Library of Congress classification system Designed originally for the Library of Congress in the late 19th century, this classification system is used by most academic and special libraries throughout the United States and in many parts of the world. It consists of 21 classes, each designated by a letter of the alphabet. Subdivisions are created by the use of other letters and numbers.

limiting by date A search tool feature that allows you to limit search results to pages that were indexed after, before, or between certain dates.

list address See group address.

Listserv The type of software used to manage a listserv list.

listserv list A type of discussion group, interest group, or mailing list.

location field The pane on the browser window that holds the current document's URL.

low precision/high recall A phenomenon that occurs during a search when you retrieve a large set of results, including many unwanted documents.

lurking Reading the email or articles in a discussion group or newsgroup without contributing or posting messages.

mailing list See discussion group.

menu bar The sequence of pulldown menus across the top of the Web browser window. All browser commands are embedded in the menu bar.

meta-search tools Tools that allow you to search either more than one search engine or directory simultaneously or a list of search tools that can be accessed from that site. These two major types of meta-search tools are called parallel search tools and all-in-one search tools.

meta-tags Keywords inserted in the meta-tag portion of the HTML source document by the Web page author. If Web pages don't have much text, meta-tags help them come up in a keyword search.

moderator A person who manages or administers a discussion group, interest group, listserv list, mailing list, or Usenet newsgroup. In most cases, the moderator is a volunteer. Messages sent to the group are first read by the moderator, who then passes appropriate messages to the group.

modifying search results Changing an initial search expression to obtain more relevant results. This can involve narrowing the results by field, limiting by date, adding keywords, subtracting keywords, and so forth.

nested Boolean logic The use of parentheses in Boolean search expressions. For example, the nested expression *((rivers OR lakes) AND canoeing) NOT camping* will first find resources that contain either the words *rivers* or *lakes* and the term *canoeing*, but not resources that contain the term *camping*.

newsgroup A collection of Usenet articles arranged by topic. Some are specialized or technical groups (such as comp.protocols.tcp-ip.domains—topics related to Internet domain style names), some deal with recreational activities (such as rec.outdoors.fishing.saltwater—topics related to saltwater fishing), and one, news.newusers.questions, is dedicated to questions from new Usenet users.

newsreader The software you use to read, reply to, and manage Usenet news.

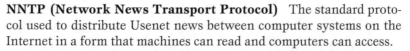

NNTP (Network News Transport Protocol) The standard protocol used to distribute Usenet news between computer systems on the Internet in a form that machines can read and computers can access.

OPAC (Online Public Access Catalog) An electronic catalog of a library's holdings, usually searchable by author, title, subject, keyword, and call number. Thousands of OPACs from libraries all over the world are available on the World Wide Web.

parallel search tools A search tool or service that takes one search expression, submits it to several search services, and returns selected results from each. This is an example of a meta-search tool.

phrase searching A search feature supported by most search engines that allows you to search for words that usually appear next to each other. It is possibly the most important search feature.

plug-in An application software that's used along with a Web browser to view or display certain types of files as part of a Web page. Shockwave from MacroMedia is a plug-in that allows the browser to display interactive multimedia.

PPP (Point-to-Point Protocol) A standard protocol that allows a computer with a modem to communicate using TCP/IP.

proprietary database A privately owned database that isn't available to the public and that is usually password protected. Universities, businesses, and research institutes are the institutions most likely to subscribe to this kind of database and make it available to their employees and students.

protocol A set of rules for exchanging information between networks or computer systems. The rules specify the format and the content of the information, and the procedures to follow during the exchange.

proximity searching A search feature that makes it possible to search for words that are near each other in a document.

reference work A resource used to find quick answers to questions. Traditionally thought of as being in the form of books (such as dictionaries, encyclopedias, quotation directories, manuals, guides, atlases, bibliographies, and indexes), a reference source on the World Wide Web closely resembles its print counterpart. A reference work doesn't necessarily contain hyperlinks to other resources, although it will often have hyperlinks within the document itself.

relevance A measure of how closely a database entry matches a search request. Most search tools on the Web return results based on relevance. The specific algorithm for computing relevance varies from one service to another, but it's often based on the number of times terms in the search expression appear in the document and whether they appear in the appropriate fields.

relevancy ranking A ranking of items retrieved from a database. The ranking is based on the relevancy score that a search engine has assigned.

results per page A feature of some search engines that allows you to designate the number of results listed per page. Search engines usually list 10 results per page.

robot See spider.

scroll bar The rectangular area on the right side of the window that allows you to move up or down in the open document. You move by clicking and dragging it or clicking on the arrow at the bottom of the bar.

search engine A collection of programs that gather information from the Web (see spider), index it, and put it in a database so it can be searched. The search engine takes the keywords or phrases you enter, searches the database for words that match the search expression, and returns them to you. The results are hyperlinks to sources that have descriptions, titles, or contents matching the search expression.

search expression The keywords and syntax that you enter in a search form. With this expression, you ask a search tool to seek relevant documents in a particular way.

search form The rectangular pane or oblong box that appears on the home pages of most search engines and directories. In this space, you enter a search expression.

shareware Software that you are allowed to download and try for a specified period free of charge. If you continue to use the program after that time, you are expected to pay a usually modest fee to continue using the product legally.

SLIP (Serial Line Internet Protocol) Software allowing the use of Internet protocol (IP) over a serial line or through a serial port. Commonly used with a modem connection to a service providing Internet services.

sorting An option in some search engines that allows you to determine how you'd like your search results listed—by URL, relevance, domain or location, date, and so on.

spam Unwanted and unsolicited email. The electronic equivalent of paper junk mail.

special collection A collection of material, usually a separate collection of a large library, that focuses on a particular topic and covers it in great depth.

special library A library that focuses on the interests inherent in the institution it serves. Libraries in hospitals, corporations, associations, museums, and other types of institutions are all special libraries. In many cases, they are not open to the public. A special library's collection may be narrow in scope, but it will have depth within the specialty it covers.

specialized database A self-contained index that is searchable and available on the Web. Items in specialized databases are often not accessible through a keyword search in a search engine.

spider A computer program that travels the Internet to locate such resources as Web documents, FTP archives, and Gopher documents. It indexes the documents in a database, which is then searched using a search engine (such as AltaVista or Excite). A spider can also be referred to as a robot or wanderer. Each search engine uses a spider to build its database.

status bar The bar or rectangular region at the bottom of the browser window that displays information regarding the transfer of a Web document to the browser. When the mouse moves over a hyperlink, the status bar shows the hyperlink's URL. When a Web page is requested, the status bar gives information about contacting and receiving information from a server. During transmission, the status bar displays a percentage that reflects how much of the document has been transferred. The status bar also indicates whether transmissions are occurring in a secure manner.

stop words Words that an indexing program doesn't index. Stop words usually include articles (a, an, the) and other common words.

structured browsing The process of moving through a hierarchically arranged Web directory, from a broad subject heading to a more specific one, until you find the desired information.

subcategory A subject category that is more narrowly focused than the broader subject category above it in a hierarchy.

subject catalog See directory.

subject category A division in a hierarchical subject classification system in a Web directory. You click on the subject category that is likely to contain either the Web pages you want or other subject categories that are more specific.

subject guide A collection of URLs on a particular topic. Most easily found listed in virtual libraries, they are also referred to as meta-pages.

subscribe To join a discussion group, interest group, listserv list, or mailing list. You use this term when writing commands to join such a group and to list a Usenet newsgroup on your newsreader.

syntax The rules governing the construction of search expressions in search engines and directories.

TCP/IP (Transmission Control Protocol/Internet Protocol) A collection of protocols used to provide the basis for Internet and World Wide Web services.

Telnet Allows for remote login capabilities on the Internet. One of the three basic Internet services, Telnet allows you to be on one computer and to access and log in to another.

thread A collection of articles that all deal with a single posting or email message.

toolbar The sequence of icons below the menu bar. Clicking on a toolbar icon executes a command or causes an action.

top-level category One of several main subjects in the top of a hierarchy in a directory's list of subjects.

truncation The phenomenon in which you cut off the end of a word when creating a search expression. When given such a request, a search engine will look for all possible endings to the word, in addition to the root word itself.

unified search interfaces Meta-search tools that allow you to use several search engines simultaneously.

unsubscribe To leave, sign off from, or quit a discussion group, interest group, listserv list, or mailing list. You use the term when writing commands to end a relationship with a discussion group or to remove a Usenet newsgroup from the list of those you would regularly read.

uploading Transferring a file from a local computer (the one you're using) to another, remote computer.

URL (Uniform Resource Locator) A way of describing the location of an item (document, service, or resource) on the Internet and specifying the means by which to access that item.

Usenet news A system for exchanging messages called articles arranged according to specific categories called newsgroups. The articles are passed from one system to another, not as email between individuals.

vendor A company that markets online catalog systems to libraries.

virtual libraries Directories that contain collections of resources that librarians or cybrarians have carefully chosen and organized in a logical way.

Web browser A program used to access the Internet services and resources available through the World Wide Web.

white pages service A search service available on the World Wide Web that finds the email or street address of an individual, business, or government agency.

wildcard A character that stands in for another character or group of characters. Most search tools use an asterisk for this function. Although the wildcard is most often used in truncation, it can also be used in the middle of words (for example, *wom*n*).

WWW (World Wide Web) A collection of different services and resources available on the Internet.

Index

403 Forbidden, 14
404 errors, 13–14
404 Not Found, 13, 315

A

Adobe Acrobat, 15
advertising on the Internet, 385
    spam, 255, 385, 391
All-in-One Search Page, 403
all-in-one search tools, 89–90
    All-in-One Search Page, 403
AltaVista, 134–39, 162–68,
    395–96
    advanced search mode,
      134–39, 337–40
    Boolean searching, 337–38
    field searching, 166–67
    implied Boolean operators,
      45, 164–65
    phrase searching, 45, 164–65
    Refine feature, 45
    search strategy, 164–68,
      337–40
    simple search mode, 42–49,
      162–68
    Usenet archives, 280
annotated directories, 115
annotations, 131
anonymous FTP, 224
    downloading a file, 226
    retrieving a file, 228–30
antivirus software, 234–35
APA style, 315
Archie, 225, 231–32
Argus Clearinghouse, 116–19, 291,
    418–19
ARPANET, 375
.asc, 15

Associations on the Net, 353–54
.au, 16
audio files, 16–17
    .au, 17
    .ra, 17
    .wav, 17

B

basic search strategy, 132–33, 135,
    154, 336
Berners-Lee, Tim, 3
bibliographies
    creating, 350–51, 372–73
bookmark list, 14, 24, 37, 39
bookmarks, 14, 32, 47, 53–58,
    67–68, 88, 94, 346–51
    deleting, 54
Boolean operators, 78–79, 80–84,
    127–28, 337–38
Boolean searching, 337–38
    HotBot, 158–59
    nested, 82, 337–38
Brandeis University library
    catalog, 213–16
breaking a connection, 37
browser help, 40
browsing, 62–68
bulletin board system (BBS), 274
business addresses
    finding, 256–60

C

cache, 380
case sensitivity, 130
    HotBot, 158
CataList, 269
census information, 359–63
children and Internet safety, 391

citing Web and Internet resources,
    349–51, 371–72
    email resources, 321–23
    FTP resources, 320–21
    Gopher resources, 321
    page information, 317
    styles, 315
    Usenet articles, 323
    Web guides, 324–25
    Web pages, 318–20
client/server, 11
.com, 292
Communications Decency Act of
    1996, 385
Companies Online, 188–90
company research, 186–95
    finding business addresses,
        256–60
component bar, 34
compressed files, 15, 233
    PKZIP, 15, 233–34
    WinZip, 15, 233–34
    .zip, 15
concept searching, 130
content area, 33
cookies, 380–82
copy and paste, 29
copyright, 17, 386–87
crackers, 389
cyberporn, 384–85

D

default settings, 126
Deja News, 20, 279–85, 344–46
    author profile, 295, 306–7
digital collections, 203
directories, 409–17
    browsing, 62–68, 101–3
    Galaxy, 409–10
    hierarchy, 63
    LookSmart, 111–15, 411
    Lycos TOP 5%, 412
    Magellan Web Reviews, 413
    searching, 103–4
    strengths, 99
    structured browsing, 62–68

subject categories, 63
weaknesses, 100
WebCrawler Channels, 415
Yahoo!, 8–10, 104–11, 178,
    327–32, 415–16
discussion groups (email), 264
    administrative address,
        265–67
    digest, 265
    etiquette, 285–87
    finding, 269–72
    list address, 265–66
    Listproc, 266–67, 269
    Listserv, 266, 269
    Liszt, 269–73, 279
    lurking, 265
    Majordomo, 266, 269
    moderator, 265, 268
    Reference.COM, 269, 279–80
    retrieving files from archives,
        268–69
    search services, 269
    searching archives, 268
    subscribing, 264, 267, 272
    unsubscribing, 265, 267
.doc, 15
Dogpile, 404–5
domain name endings, 292
domain names, 161, 226, 292
downloading files, 50
    software from software
        archives, 237–43
    using anonymous FTP, 226
driving directions
    finding, 259
duplicate detection, 131

E

.edu, 292
Electronic Frontier Foundation
    (EFF), 383
electronic journals
    citing, 323
email
    citing, 321–23
    libel, 383–84

offensive, 383–84
   privacy, 255–56, 377–78
email addresses
   finding, 251–55
email and telephone directories,
   248–61
      Four11, 251–55
      InfoSpace, 256–60
      reverse searches, 255
      white pages services, 249, 261
emailing Web pages, 51
encryption, 378–79
error messages, 13–14, 315
evaluating Web and Internet
   resources, 346–48, 369–71
      guidelines, 292
evaluating Web pages, 304–8
   accuracy or objectivity, 303–4
   audience, 302–3
   bibliographies, 310
   currency, 302
   guides, 309–10
   purpose, 304
   who is the author?, 293–95
Excite, 168–74, 396–97
   nested Boolean operators, 171
   search features, 170–71
   search strategy, 170–71
extracting files, 243

F

FAQ (frequently asked questions),
   40
      discussion groups, 264
field searching, 130, 249
fields, 130
file formats, 14–17
File Transfer Protocol, *See* FTP
file types, 14–17, 233–34
Find feature, 29, 160, 173–74
finding words in a document, 29,
   36, 160, 173–74
FindLaw: Supreme Court
   Opinions, 196–99
firewall, 389
Four11, 251–55

F-PROT, 234–35
frames, 24, 33
freeware, 232
FTP (File Transfer Protocol), 12
   anonymous, 224
   archives, 224–25, 231
   citing, 320–21
   client programs, 243–46
   search services, 231–32
   URL formats, 225–26
full-text indexing, 126

G–H

Galaxy, 409–10
.gif, 15, 230
Go menu, 29
Gopher, 77
   citing, 321
.gov, 292
graphical user interface (GUI),
   202
helper applications, 24–25, 52,
   227
hierarchy, 63
high precision/high recall, 127
high precision/low recall, 127
history list, 24, 37–39, 380
history of the Internet, 375–76
   ARPANET, 375
   NSFNET, 375
hit list, 103
home page, 4, 36
HotBot, 155–62, 298–300, 398
   Boolean searching, 158–59
   case insensitivity, 158
   limiting by date, 158
   modifying search results, 161
   nested Boolean operations,
      158–59
   search features, 158
   search strategy, 155
   searching for people, 298–99
   Usenet archives, 280
HTTP (Hypertext Transfer
   Protocol), 4, 11
hyperlinks, 3

hypermedia, 5
hypertext, 5
Hypertext Markup Language
   (HTML), 4, 11

I–K

image files, 15
implied Boolean operators, 45,
   128, 145–48
      AltaVista, 164–65
industry research, 186, 351–69
Infomine, 419–20
Infoseek, 84–88, 144–48, 399,
   410–11
      modifying search results, 147
      phrase searching, 145–47
      Usenet archives, 280
InfoSpace, 256–60
install, 242–43
intellectual property, 386–87
Internet, 2
      history, 375–76
Internet Public Library, 71–76,
   177, 291, 353–54, 420
      searching, 75–76
Internet safety for children, 391
Internet Sleuth, 177, 187–88, 190,
   332–34, 404
ISP (Internet service provider), 25
.jpeg or .jpg (Joint Photographic
   Expert Group), 15
junk email, 255
keyboard shortcuts, 28
keyword indexing, 125

L

legal information
      searching for, 195–99
LIBCAT, 204, 210–13
libel, 386
Librarians' Index to the Internet,
   120–22, 177, 179–80, 192, 291,
   352–53, 358–59, 421
Library of Congress
      catalog searching, 205–10
      classification system, 202

home page, 4, 12
      subject headings, 208
library online catalogs, 202,
   340–44
      field searching, 203
      finding, 204
      LIBCAT, 204, 210–13
      Libweb, 204–5
      search strategy, 342
      webCATS, 204, 216–18,
         340–41
library special collections, 202–3,
   210–16
LibrarySpot, 178
Libweb, 204–5
limiting by date, 130
      HotBot, 158
Listproc, 266–67, 269
Listserv, 266, 269
Liszt, 269–73, 279
location field, 32
location toolbar, 32
LookSmart, 111–15, 411
      browsing, 111–13
      searching, 113–14
low precision/high recall, 127
lurking, 265
Lview Pro, 16
Lycos, 399–400
Lycos TOP 5%, 412

M

Magellan, 64–68
Magellan Web Reviews, 413
mailing addresses
      finding, 251–55
Majordomo, 266, 269
map services, 261
maps
      finding, 256–60
market research, 351–69
MEDLINE, 176, 179–86
      search features, 182
      search strategy, 182
menu bar, 27–28
MetaCrawler, 148–52, 405–6

implied Boolean operators, 149–52
modifying search results, 151–52
meta-search tools, 148, 403–8
  All-in-One Search Page, 403
  Dogpile, 404–5
  Internet Sleuth, 177, 187–88, 190, 332–34, 404
  MetaCrawler, 148–52, 405–6
  parallel search tools, 89
  SavvySearch, 91–94, 406–7
  SEARCH.COM, 407–8
  unified search interfaces, 89
meta-tags, 126
Microsoft Internet Explorer
  citing resources, 317
MLA style, 315
modem, 25
modifying search results, 132, 147
.mov, 16
.mpg or .mpeg, 16
multifaceted searches, 136
multimedia files, 17

N–O

navigation toolbar, 30–32
nested Boolean operators, 82, 128, 138, 142, 337–38
  Excite, 171
  HotBot, 158–59
Net Happenings, 424–26
NetGuide, 413–14
Netscape Communicator, 25, 29–30
  Collabra, 275–77
  newsreader, 276–77
Netscape Navigator
  cache, 381
  clear disk, 381
  guide, 249
  history list, 381
  icon, 26
  newsreader, 264
  page information, 302, 317
  preferences, 381

properties, 302
view, 302, 317
Network News Transport Protocol (NNTP), 277
Newspaper Archives on the Web, 192–94
newsreader, 264, 276–77
No Viewer Configured for File Type message, 227
Northern Light, 140–44
Norton AntiVirus, 235
NSFNET, 375
offline mode, 28
OPAC (online public access catalog), 202
opening a Web page, 37–38
output features, 131

P

page information, 29
page source, 29
Paint Shop Pro, 16
parallel search tools, 89
people finders, 249
  privacy and ethical issues, 255–56
personal home page, 4
personal toolbar, 33
phrase searching, 45, 79, 86, 129, 138
  AltaVista, 164–65
PKZIP, 15, 233–34
plug-ins, 24–25
poetry
  finding, 168–74
pornography, 384–85
Portable Document Format (PDF), 15
  Adobe Acrobat, 15
PPP (Point-to-Point Protocol), 25
preferences, 29
printing Web pages, 28, 51
privacy, 34, 376–83, 388
progress bar, 34
proximity searching, 129

PubMed, 180–86
    search features, 182
    search strategy, 182

Q–R

QuickTime, 16
quotations, 168–74
.qt, 16
Readme, 242
RealAudio format, 16
reference works, 70
Reference.COM, 269, 279–80
relevancy ranking, 131
reverse searches, 255
right mouse button, 34–35
robots, 77

S

Save As, 28, 227
Save Link As, 50, 227
saving
    audio files, 50
    files from the Internet, 227
    hyperlinks, 50
    image files, 50, 228–29
    Web pages, 28, 49–50
SavvySearch, 91–94, 406–7
Scout Report, 178, 423–24
scroll bars, 33, 36
search engines, 41–49, 77–80,
    395–403
    basic search strategy, 132–33,
        135, 154, 336
    Boolean operators, 78–79,
        80–84, 127–28, 337–38
    case sensitivity, 130
    default settings, 126
    duplicate detection, 131
    field searching, 130, 249
    full-text indexing, 126
    high precision/high recall, 127
    high precision/low recall, 127
    HotBot, 155–62, 298–300,
        398
    Infoseek, 84–88, 144–48, 399,
        410–11

keyword indexing, 125
limiting by date, 130
low precision/high recall, 127
Lycos, 399–400
Magellan, 64–68
meta-tags, 126
modifying search results, 132,
    147
multifaceted searches, 136
nested Boolean searching, 82,
    337–38
output features, 131
relevancy ranking, 131
robots, 77
spiders, 77, 125–26
stop words, 126
search features, 126–31
    phrase searching, 45, 79, 86,
        129, 138
    proximity searching, 129
    syntax, 127
    truncation, 129, 136, 337–38
search strategy
    basic search strategy, 132–33,
        135, 154, 336
    formulation of, 135–36
search tips, 134
SEARCH.COM, 407–8
searching directories, 68
SEC EDGAR Archives, 191–92
security icon, 34
security information, 30, 34,
    388–89
setup, 243
sexually explicit material,
    384–85
shareware, 225
    antivirus programs, 234–35
    archives, 232–34
    compression programs,
        233–34
    Norton AntiVirus, 235
    PKZIP, 233–34
    self-extracting, 233–34
    VirusScan for Windows 95,
        234

WinZip, 233–34
SLIP (Serial Line Internet Protocol), 25
SMTP gateway, 25
software archives, 232
  downloading software from, 237–43
  searching, 238
  TUCOWS, 235–36
  ZDNet Software Library, 235–36
sorting, 131
spam, 255, 385, 391
special library, 202–3
  World Bank and IMF libraries, 218–22
special library catalogs, 216–22
specialized databases, 71, 333–35
  bibliographic, 176
  commercial, 176
  fee-based, 176
  finding, 177
  FindLaw: Supreme Court Opinions, 196–99
  full-text, 176
  MEDLINE, 179–86
  Newspaper Archives on the Web, 192–94
  proprietary, 176
  SEC EDGAR Archives, 191–92
  U.S. Bureau of the Census, 358–63
  U.S. Supreme Court opinions, 196–99
specific information
  finding, 168–74
spiders, 77, 125–26
status line, 33
stop words, 126
stopping a Web page, 37
streaming technology, 16
structured browsing, 62–68
subject catalog, 63

subject guides, 69–70, 175
syntax, 127

T

telephone numbers
  finding, 251–55
Telnet, 202
ten-step basic search strategy, 135
text files, 15
thread, 276
tile.net, 270
tile.net/news, 279
toolbars, 30–34
truncation, 129, 136, 337–38
TUCOWS, 235–36

U

unified search interfaces, 89
uploading, 225
URL (Uniform Resource Locator), 4, 12–13
URL evaluation, 292
URL formats, 313–14
U.S. Bureau of the Census, 358–63
U.S. Supreme Court opinions, 196–99
Usenet archives
  searching, 280, 344–46
Usenet news, 274–75
  categories, 276
  citing, 323
  cross-posting, 276
  Deja News, 20, 279–85, 344–46
  etiquette, 285–87
  FAQ, 274, 278
  newsreader, 264, 276–77
  posting, 275, 278
  setting news preferences, 277
  thread, 276
  user profile, 25
Usenet newsgroups
  finding, 278–85

V

viewing local files, 51–52
virtual libraries, 69–76, 115, 352–54, 418–22
  annotated directories, 115
  Argus Clearinghouse, 116–19, 291, 418–19
  Infomine, 419–20
  Internet Public Library, 71–76, 177, 291, 353–54, 420
  LibrarySpot, 178
  World Wide Web Virtual Library, 421–22
viruses, 234, 390

W

ways to stay current, 423–26
Web browser, 6–10, 30
Web page, 5
  citing, 318
  major components of, 27
Web privacy, 380
Web-based guides to the Internet and the World Wide Web, 17
webCATS, 204, 216–18, 340–41
WebCrawler, 80–84, 300–301, 364, 368, 402

WebCrawler Channels, 415
What's New Web sites, 424
  Scout Report, 91–94
white pages services, 249, 261
  advantages, 249–50
  disadvantages, 249–50
  privacy and ethical issues, 255–56
wildcards, 129
WinZip, 15, 233–34
World Bank and IMF libraries, 218–22
World Wide Web, 2–3
World Wide Web Virtual Library, 421–22
WS_FTP, 244–46

Y–Z

Yahoo!, 8–10, 104–11, 178, 327–32, 415–16
  browsing, 105–7
  category matches, 103–4
  keyword searching, 108–10
  site matches, 104
  What's New, 424
ZDNet Software Library, 237–43
  searching, 238